Design and Development of
Efficient Energy Systems

Scrivener Publishing
100 Cummings Center, Suite 541J
Beverly, MA 01915-6106

Publishers at Scrivener
Martin Scrivener (martin@scrivenerpublishing.com)
Phillip Carmical (pcarmical@scrivenerpublishing.com)

Design and Development of Efficient Energy Systems

Edited by
**Suman Lata Tripathi,
Dushyant Kumar Singh,
Sanjeevikumar Padmanaban,
and
P. Raja**

Scrivener
Publishing

WILEY

Wiley Global Headquarters
111 River Street, Hoboken, NJ 07030, USA

For details of our global editorial offices, customer services, and more information about Wiley prod-ucts visit us at www.wiley.com.

Limit of Liability/Disclaimer of Warranty
While the publisher and authors have used their best efforts in preparing this work, they make no representations or warranties with respect to the accuracy or completeness of the contents of this work and specifically disclaim all warranties, including without limitation any implied warranties of merchant-ability or fitness for a particular purpose. No warranty may be created or extended by sales representatives, written sales materials, or promotional statements for this work. The fact that an organization, website, or product is referred to in this work as a citation and/or potential source of further information does not mean that the publisher and authors endorse the information or services the organization, website, or product may provide or recommendations it may make. This work is sold with the understanding that the publisher is not engaged in rendering professional services. The advice and strategies contained herein may not be suitable for your situation. You should consult with a specialist where appropriate. Neither the publisher nor authors shall be liable for any loss of profit or any other commercial damages, including but not limited to special, incidental, consequential, or other damages. Further, readers should be aware that websites listed in this work may have changed or disappeared between when this work was written and when it is read.

Library of Congress Cataloging-in-Publication Data

ISBN 9781119761631

Cover images: Electrical Systems - Suman Kumar Singh | Dreamstime.com
           Solar Panels - Adisak Rungjaruchai | Dreamstime.com
Cover design by Kris Hackerott

Set in size of 11pt and Minion Pro by Manila Typesetting Company, Makati, Philippines

Printed in the USA

10 9 8 7 6 5 4 3 2 1

Contents

Preface

The objective of this edition is to provide a broad view of the fundamental concepts of green energy technology and applications in a concise way for fast and easy understanding. This book provides information regarding almost all the aspects to make it highly beneficial for all students, researchers and teachers of this field. Fundamental principles of green energy technology with the latest developments are discussed in a clear and detailed manner with explanatory diagrams wherever necessary. The book focuses on the basic concepts of Internet of Things (IoT) in power conversion, IoT in renewable energy, and adoption of machine learning, low-power device and circuit design including the latest research available depending upon the technological changes based upon their application.

Chapter Organization

Chapter 1 deals with prefabrication low-power device design and analysis on Visual TCAD device simulator with graphical and programming interfaces. Also, the chapter discusses the design of device-based low-power memory and biomedical applications.

Chapter 2 mainly describes Vedic multiplication based on the compressor block that is focused on the reduction of interconnect wire. The multiplier is implemented using Verilog HDL with cadence NC SIM and the constrain areas, power and delay optimize using underlying block.

Chapter 3 deals with gas leakage detection from drainage to offer safety for sanitary workers from gases such as Carbon monoxide (CO), Hydrogen sulphide (H2S), and Methane (CH4), which are some of the hazardous gases present in underground drainage systems.

Chapter 4 presents a smart healthcare system development with machine learning, which is energy efficient, with reduced network latency and minimum bandwidth.

Chapter 5 This chapter presents some of the solutions in literature for implementing security. The chapter also covers different types of attacks such as goal-oriented attack, performer-oriented attack and layer-oriented attack.

Chapter 6 addresses the energy-saving component and the application of digital technology and Internet of Things (IoT) in large-scale process industries.

Chapter 7 discuss the method deployed relay node in such a way that the network will behave like a sensor network with the help of K-Means clustering approach.

Chapter 8 analyzes an MLI fed Induction Motor Drive by considering Solar Energy as a source. The effects of employing various types of MLI for a PV source-based drive, and methods of deriving maximum drive efficiency are elaborated in this chapter with sufficient simulation results.

Chapter 9 describes energy storage systems using a universal controller that can work for a wide range of voltage to both DC and AC loads with high power rating and low power loss.

Chapter 10 explores energy arrangement producers, energy financial analysts, and directors with a review of the job of IoT in enhancement of energy frameworks.

Chapter 11 focuses on integration of photovoltaic cell, wind energy and other forms of renewable energy. It also covers microgrid systems with high reliability, less transmission losses and improved power system efficiency.

Chapter 12 describes state-of-the-art renewable energy systems and highlights the global efforts being made to increase their efficiency.

Chapter 13 is dedicated to Internet of Things (IoT) technologies with best solutions, ease of the task of monitoring and analysis that opens up a wide range of prospects for making better future decisions.

Chapter 14 examines new security challenges in the Internet of Things (IoT) using machine learning algorithm and the system of interrelated computing devices for its quick development and distribution that are essential for internet and smart device users.

Chapter 15 presents a working and solution process, an illustrative fuzzily defined mathematical framework for optimizing food quality. Here, the emphasis is not only on ensuring fruit safety but also avoiding foodborne diseases.

Chapter 16 is an overview of the various requirements for Internet of Things (IoT) systems and architectures, highlighting different research challenges and security issues connected with IoT.

Chapter 17 presents a state-of-the-art of FinFET technology with low power consumption and their application in a low-power VLSI circuit.

Chapter 18 proposes a single-source high step-up switched-capacitor-based 19-level inverter topology with enhanced power quality that can be extended by addition of switched-capacitor units. The extended topology can produce larger gain and voltage steps.

Design of Low Power Junction-Less Double-Gate MOSFET

Namrata Mendiratta and Suman Lata Tripathi*

VLSI Design Laboratory, Lovely Professional University, Phagwara, Punjab, India

Abstract

The requirement of low power consumption and higher IC packing density leads the designer to explore new MOSFET architectures with low leakage current and operating voltages. Multi-gate MOSFET architectures are a promising candidate with increased gate-control over the channel region. Double-gate MOSFET is one of the advanced MOSFETs with a thin-channel region sandwiched into the top and bottom gate. The changes in the position of the top and bottom gate overlap and also have a significant effect on the electrical characteristics of transistors. The higher number of gates increases the drive current capability of the transistor with enhanced gate control that is desired for low-power and high-speed operations of digital circuit and bulk memories. The junction-less feature future improves switching characteristics of multi-gate MOSFETs with more drive current and high I_{ON}/I_{OFF} current ratio. These prefabrication low-power design and analysis can be done on a Visual TCAD device simulator with graphical and programming interfaces that reduce fabrication cost and improve overall throughput.

Keywords: Low power, junction-less, DGMOSFET, TCAD, leakage current, etc.

1.1 Introduction

The size of semiconductor devices is being continuously reduced and has entered into the nanoscale range. Every two years the number of transistors doubles because the size of the MOSFET is reduced. Reducing the size of the MOSFET reduces the size of the channel, which causes short-channel effects and it increases the leakage current. Reduction in the size of semiconductor devices has given rise to short-channel effects (SCEs). The various SCEs are parasitic capacitances, drain field effect on channel field, degraded subthreshold region of operation, mobility degradation, hot carrier effects, etc. To overcome these effects the devices need to be engineered using different techniques like gate or channel engineering. The cause of the SCEs is when the width of the drain barrier extends into the drain and source region barrier lowering. Many MOSFET structures like DG-MOSFET, GAA (Gate-all-around) MOSFET, TG (Triple-gate) MOSFET, SOI (Silicon-on-insulator)

---

*Corresponding author: tri.suman78@gmail.com

Suman Lata Tripathi, Dushyant Kumar Singh, Sanjeevikumar Padmanaban, and P. Raja (eds.) Design and Development of Efficient Energy Systems, (1–12) © 2021 Scrivener Publishing LLC

MOSFET, double-step buried-oxide including junction-less properties have been designed to overcome SCEs [1–6].

MOSFETs are used for analog and RF applications to handle the radio frequency signals that are high in power from devices like televisions, radio transmitters, and amplifiers. MOSFETs are used for biomedical applications [7]. It is used as a biosensor to detect biomolecules. It is useful in detecting molecules like enzymes, nucleotide, protein and antibodies. Using MOSFETs as a biosensor has benefits over other methods as it has more sensitivity, compatibility, mass production and miniaturization. MOSFET is also used to store memory. It is used in the construction of SRAM cells for storing data. MOSFETs were also adopted by NASA to detect interplanetary magnetic fields and interplanetary plasma. MOSFETs are used in digital applications for switching which prevents DC to flow supply and ground that lead to reduced power consumption and providing high input impedance.

1.2   MOSFET Performance Parameters

The MOSFET performance mainly depends on ON and OFF state conditions depending on the different applied bias voltage. The performance analysis is categorized as:

a) *DC Analysis*

In DC analysis, subthreshold parameters are mainly calculated such as I_{OFF}, DIBL, SS, and threshold voltage (V_{th}). These parameters can be defined as:

i) I_{OFF}: It is OFF-state current when the applied gate voltage (V_{gs}) is less than the threshold voltage (V_{th}).

ii) V_{th}: It the required minimum value of the gate voltage to establish channel inversion.

iii) Subthreshold Slope (SS): It is one of SCE that can be derived from the equation:

$$SS = \frac{dV_{gs}}{d(logI_d)} \, mV/decade \tag{1.1}$$

iv) Drain induced barrier lowering (DIBL): DIBL is another important parameter of SCE which is a measure of threshold voltage variations with the variation in drain voltage for constant drain current. It can be derived from the equation:

$$DIBL = \frac{dV_{gs}}{dV_{ds}} (mV/V) \tag{1.2}$$

b) *AC analysis*

AC analysis is dependent on frequency of applied bias voltages. The important ac parameters are:

i)   Transistor Capacitance (Cg): There are several inherent capacitances such as gate to source, the gate to drain and gate to body capacitances.

Transistor capacitances are important for desired switching behavior from OFF to ON state.

ii) Transconductance (g_m): It is a measure of drain current with the variation in gate voltage for constant drain current. It plays an important role to achieve high value of transistor amplifier gain. It can be derived from the equation:

$$g_m = \frac{di_d}{dv_{gs}}$$

(1.3)

c) *Electrostatic Characteristics*

There are a few other important parameters that also have significant importance of MOSFET behavior during ON/OFF state. Energy band diagram, channel potential, electric field distribution and electron-hole density are important electrostatic properties that need to be analysed while designing any MOSFET architecture.

1.3   Comparison of Existing MOSFET Architectures

Table 1.1 shows a comparison of existing MOSFET structures based on their performance and suitable applications.

1.4   Proposed Heavily Doped Junction-Less Double Gate MOSFET (AJ-DGMOSFET)

An AJ-DGMOSFET shown in Figure 1.1 has top and bottom gates arranged asymmetrically with an overlap region of 10nm. An n+ pocket region is added to the source side with heavy doping of donor atoms. p+ polysilicon is used as gate contact material with Hfas an oxide region of high-k dielectric constant. The body thickness is kept very low (6nm). The gate (L_{gate}) is 20 nm, with overlap region ($L_{overlap}$) of 10 nm. The body thickness ($T_{silicon}$) is 6 nm source /drain length ($L_{source} = L_{drain}$) of 8 nm. The oxide thickness (T_{oxide}) is 1 nm. A thin pocket region (n+ doping) is doped with 1×10^{22} cm^{-3} with channel region II doping (n+ doping) of 1×10^{19} cm^{-3}. Including channel region I + and channel region II, the overall channel length becomes 30 nm.

The high doping concentration of the source drain region with heavy doping of n+ pocket region improves the ON-state current transistor. The drain region doping is slightly less than the source to achieve a low value of leakage current, therefore enhanced current ratio (I_{ON}/I_{OFF}). Here channel length is also dependent on bias condition. In ON-state the effective channel length is equal to the length of overlap region of top and bottom gates. In OFF-state, the effective channel length is the length excluding overlap region between top and bottom gate.

Figure 1.2 shows a comparison between ON-state and OFF-state of the transistor. Different characteristics have been drawn with and without pocket region. The proposed AJ-DGMOSFET with heavily doped pocket region shows better ratio in comparison to AJ-DGMOSFET without a doped pocket region.

Table 1.1 Comparison of existing MOSFET structures.

Ref.	Existing MOSFET structure and methodology	Electrical performance and applications
[2]	Ge pockets are inserted in SOI JLT	Reduces the lattice temperature. The channel length is 20 nm.
[3]	Gate all around junctionless MOSFET with source and drain extension	The highly doped regions have also led to an increase in I-ON current magnitude by 70%.
[4]	Gate engineering using double-gate MOSFET	The sub-threshold slope is decreased by 1.61% and ON/OFF current ratio is increased by 17.08% and DIBL is decreased by 4.52%. The channel length is 20 nm.
[5]	Gate material engineering and drain/source Extensions	Improves the RF and analog performance. The figure of merit is also increased compared to the conventional double-gate junctionless MOSFET. The channel length is 100 nm.
[6]	Inducing source and drain extensions electrically	Suppresses short-channel effects for the channel length less than 50 nm and also suppresses hot electron effects.
[7]	Nanogap cavity is formed by the process of etching gate oxide in the channel from both the sides of source and drain	Detecting biomolecules such as DNA, enzymes, cells etc using dielectric modulation technique. The channel length is 100 nm.
[8]	Graded channel dual material gate junctionless (GC-DMGJL) MOSFET	The GC-DMGJL MOSFET gives high drain current and transconductance and also reduces short-channel effects. The channel length is 30 nm.
[9]	Black phosphorus is integrated with the junctionless recessed MOSFET	Structure drain current increases up to 0.3 mA. The off current reduces, improvement in subthreshold slope. The channel length is 44 nm.
[10]	Fully depleted tri material double-gate MOSFET is used	Improvement in the RF performance, linearity and analog performance compared to the DM-DG MOSFET and single material DG MOSFET. The channel length is 35 nm.
[11]	Pocket region is constructed near the source and drain region and is heavily doped	Good immunity from short-channel effects and can meet the specifications of OFF-state current and ON-state current. The channel length is 100 nm.

(Continued)

Table 1.1 Comparison of existing MOSFET structures. (*Continued*)

Ref.	Existing MOSFET structure and methodology	Electrical performance and applications
[12]	A transparent gate recessed channel is used	Enhancement of cut-off frequency by 42% and oscillator frequency is increased by 32%. The channel length is 30nm.
[13]	MOSFET with asymmetrical gate to improve the functioning of the device	Decrease in subthreshold slope (68 mV/dec) and drain induced barrier lowering (65 mV/V). The channel length is 20 nm.
[14]	6-T SRAM cell using silicon on insulator	The area of the junctionless transistor-based 6-T SRAM cell using silicon on inductor is 6.9 μm-cube and that of the conventional structure is 11.3 μm -cube.
[15]	Short-channel dual metal gate with recessed source and drain SOI MOSFET	This device provides high on current, low DIBL value. The channel length is 30 nm -300nm.
[16]	Dual Material Surrounding Gate MOSFET to suppress short-channel effects	DMSG MOSFET (SCEs) more efficient as compared to a conventional SMSG MOSFET
[17]	Misalignment effect introduced by the asymmetrical source and drain	The region which is non-overlapped produces extra series resistance and weak control over the channel, while the additional overlapped region produces extra overlap capacitance and supply to ground leakage current through gate
[18]	Optimized the design of the gate all around MOSFET and compared it with the double gate MOSFET	GAA structure reduced the DIBL value to 81.44 mV/V when compared to the double-gate MOSFET. The ON-state current is increased and OFF-state current is reduced.
[19]	The deviation in the oxide thickness between the two gates is considered small. A surface potential solution is used for symmetric double-gate MOSFET for initial trial approximation for approaching surface potential solution for asymmetric double-gate MOSFET.	Different parameters of MOSFET like drain current, 5channel current, transconductance, gate capacitances and the effect of oxide thickness on these parameters are determined.
[20]	Performance analysis of junctionless double-gate MOSFET based 6T SRAM with gate stack configuration	The use of high k dielectric material in the junctionless DG-MOSFET shows improvement in static noise margin. Scaling down of gate length degrades the stability.

(*Continued*)

Table 1.1 Comparison of existing MOSFET structures. (*Continued*)

Ref.	Existing MOSFET structure and methodology	Electrical performance and applications
[21]	Simulation of junctionless double-gate MOSFET with symmetrical side gates. With the presence of side gates the channel present under the front gate, is electrically insulated from the drain voltage resulting to electron shielding.	The DIBL and SS values improved using the side gates. The drain voltage effect on the channel is reduced so it becomes easy for the gate to have more control over the channel.
[22]	A structure of double-gate MOSFET with symmetrical insulator packets for improving the SCEs. In this, insulator packets were inserted between the channel junction and source/drain ends	Hot electron reliability improves. There is an improvement in the DIBL value and ON/OFF-state current ratio.

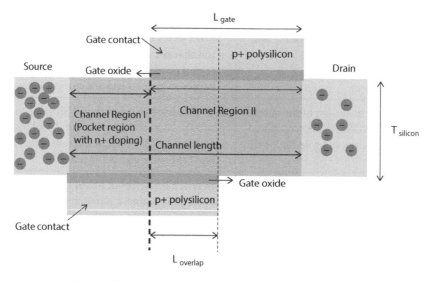

Figure 1.1 2D view of AJ-DGMOSFET.

Figure 1.4 shows the performance of MOSFET when different gate contacts are used like aluminium, polysilicon and copper. MOSFET shows better performance when polysilicon is used as a gate contact. Metal gates like Aluminium and copper operate at voltages 3V to 5V. The lowering of operating voltages leads to the use of polysilicon gate contact. From the graph we can observe at lower operating voltages polysilicon gate contact gives better performance because the OFF-state current is low.

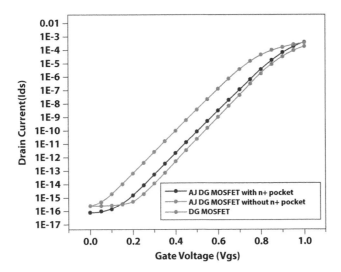

Figure 1.2 I_d versus V_{gs} plot of AJ-DGMOSFET.

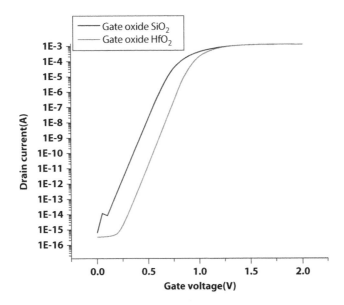

Figure 1.3 Id Versus Vgs plot with different oxide region material.

The proposed JL-DG MOSFET has ratio of 10^{13} which is higher than other existing structures. The calculation of SCE parameters like SS and DIBL is also a deciding factor for device performance. The proposed device show SS value of 59 mV/ decade and DIBL of 13.4 mV/V. Both SS and DIBL values are less than other existing transistors. Therefore, heavily doped AJ-DG MOSFET has superior ON/OFF performances.

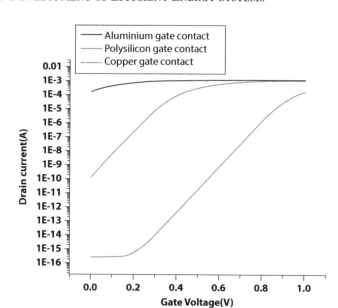

Figure 1.4 I_d versus V_{gs} Plot of different gate contact material.

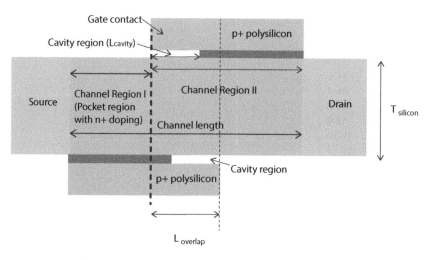

Figure 1.5 JL-DG MOSFET with cavity region.

1.5   Heavily Doped JL-DG MOSFET for Biomedical Application

DG MOSFETs were designed with a nanogap cavity region as bio-sensor that can sense the bio-molecule present in the nanogap cavity [23, 24]. These bio-sensors work on the principle of dielectric modulation with the variation in bio-species present in the air (nanogap cavity) that further varies the electrical parameters of the device.

Figure 1.5 shows the 2-D view of JL-DG MOSFET with a cavity region. Here the cavity plays an important role to sense the bio-species present in air. The presence of bio-species and their concentration affect the dielectric constant of the cavity region that further affects the electrical parameters of transistor. The cavity region with different length (L_{cavity}) and height (H_{cavity}) shows varied device sensitivity towards the presences of biomolecules. This effect has been studied through varying dielectric constant with different materials such as air, SiO_2, HfO_2 and S_3N_4.

Figure 1.5 shows AJ-DG MOSFET with the nanogap cavity region. A thin SiO_2 layer used for binding the molecules entering the cavity region by restricting the movements of bio-molecules. For the presented device the cavity region height (H_{cavity}) is 2.7 nm and SiO_2 layer thickness is 0.3 nm. Another way to analyze device sensitivity is by introducing different types of charged particles in the cavity region.

In Figure 1.6 a sharp change is observed in the threshold voltages with the different dielectric constant of the material added in the cavity region. The longer cavity region length shows more variations in threshold voltage that results in the shifting of channel inversion threshold level. Therefore with a higher value of dielectric constant, the threshold voltage lowers. This shows that the device is highly sensitive towards the change in dielectric material constant depending on biomolecule presence resulting in electrical parameter variations.

A significant variation in threshold voltage is observed with a change in oxide thickness. The changing oxide thickness results in a change in the cavity region thickness that also affects the electrical parameter variations.

1.6 Conclusion

The AJ-DG MOSFET is a suitable choice for low-power applications such as bulk memories that are integral parts of many IoT-enabled systems. The performance of AJ-DG MOSFET can also be varied by adjusting the position of the top and bottom gate overlapping regions. High ON/OFF current ratio and low leakage current are the key features of the AJ-DG MOSFET with low static power consumption and enhanced speed of circuit operation. Another application of JL-DG MOSFET is as biosensor by introducing cavity region

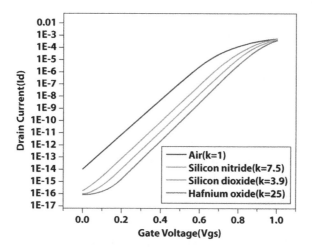

Figure 1.6 I_d Versus V_{gs} of AJ-DG MOSFET with varying dielectric constant (L_{cavity} = 7nm).

between gate and channel. These cavity regions are sensitive to the bio species present in the environment. The variation in biomolecule changes the dielectric constant of the medium that results in the variation in electrical parameters of a device that can be easily measured to detect the presence of bio-species.

References

1. S L Tripathi, Ramanuj Mishra, R A Mishra, "Characteristic comparison of connected DG FINFET, TG FINFET and Independent Gate FINFET on 32 nm technology" *IEEE ICPCES*, pp. 1-7, December, 2012.
2. Ammina, V.P., Vankudothu, S.P., Shaik, R.R. *et al.* An Optimized Ge Pocket SOI JLT with Efforts to Improve the Self-Heating Effect: Doping & Materials Perspective. *Silicon,* 2019. https://doi. org/10.1007/s12633-019-00319-x
3. F. Djeffal, H.Ferhat, T.Bentrcia Improved analog and RF performances of gate-all-around junctionless MOSFET with drain and source extensions, *Superlattices and Microstructures,* 90, 132-140, 2016.
4. Nirmal Ch. Roy, Abhinav Gupta, Sanjeev Rai. Analytical surface potential modeling and simulation of junction-less double gate (JLDG) MOSFET for ultra low-power analog/RF circuits, *Microelectronics Journal,* 46 (10), 916-922, 2015.
5. E. Chebaki, F.Djeffal· H.Ferhati, T.Bentrcia. Improved analog/RF performance of double gate junctionless MOSFET using both gate material engineering and drain/source extensions, *Superlattices and Microstructures,* 92, 80-91, 2016.
6. Ali A. Orouji, M. Jagdeesh. Nanoscale SOI MOSFETs with electrically induced source/drain extension: Novel attributes and design considerations for suppressed short-channel effects, *Superlattices and Microstructures,* 39(5), 395-405, 2006.
7. Ajay, Rakhi Narang· Manoj Saxena· Mridula Gupta. Investigation of dielectric modulated (DM) double gate (DG) junctionless MOSFETs for application as a biosensors, *Superlattices and Microstructures,* 85, 557-572, 2015.
8. Varsha Pathak, Gaurav Saini. A Graded Channel Dual-Material Gate Junctionless MOSFET for Analog Applications, *Procedia Computer Science,* Vol. 125, 825-831, 2018.
9. Ajay Kumar, M.M.Tripathi, Rishu Chaujar. Analysis of sub-20 nm black phosphorus based junctionless-recessed channel MOSFET for analog/RF applications, *Superlattices and Microstructures,* 116, April 171-180, 2018.
10. Angsuman Sarkar, Aloke Kumar Das· Swapnadip De, Chandan Kumar Sarkar. Effect of gate engineering in double-gate MOSFETs for analog/RF applications, *Microelectronics Journal,* 43(11), 873-882, 2012.
11. Yon-Sup Pang, John R Brews. Design of 0.1-lm pocket n-MOSFETs for low-voltage applications, *Solid-State Electronics,* 46(12), 2315-2322, 2002.
12. Ajay Kumar, Neha Gupta, Rishu Chaujar. TCAD RF performance investigation of Transparent Gate Recessed Channel MOSFET, *Microelectronics Journal,* 49, 36-42, 2016.
13. Ying Wang, Yan Tang, Ling-ling Sun, Fei Cao. High performance of junctionless MOSFET with asymmetric gate, *Superlattices and Microstructures,* 97, 8-14, 2016.
14. Vimal Kumar Mishra, R. K. Chauhan. Efficient Layout Design of Junctionless Transistor Based 6-T SRAM Cell Using SOI Technology, *ECS Journal of Solid State Science and Technology,* 7(9)2018.
15. G.K. Saramekala Abirmoya Santra, Sarvesh Dubey, Satyabrata Jit, Pramod Kumar Tiwari. An analytical threshold voltage model for a short-channel dual-metal-gate (DMG) recessed-source/drain (Re-S/D) SOI MOSFET, *Superlattices and Microstructures,* 60, 580-595, 2013.

16. Arobinda Pal, Angsuman Sarkar, Analytical study of Dual Material Surrounding Gate MOSFET to suppress short-channel effects (SCEs), *Engineering Science and Technology,* 17 (4), December 2014, pp. 205-212, 2014.

17. Chunshan, P.C.H. Chan. Investigation of the Source/Drain Asymmetric Effects Due to Gate Misalignment in Planar Double-Gate MOSFETs, *IEEE Transactions on Electron Devices*, 52(1), 85-90, 2005.

18. Jae Young Song, Woo Young Choi, Ju Hee Park, Jong Duk Lee, Byung-Gook Park. Design Optimization of Gate-All-Around (GAA) MOSFETs, *IEEE Transaction on Nanotechnology,* 5(3), 186-191, 2006.

19. Sheng Chang, Gaofeng Wang, Qijun Huang, Hao Wang. Analytic Model for Undoped Symmetric Double-Gate MOSFETs With Small Gate-Oxide-Thickness Asymmetry, *IEEE Transactions on Electron Devices,* 56(10), 2297-230, 2009.

20. Shubham Tayal, Ashutosh Nandi. Performance analysis of junctionless DG-MOSFET-based 6T-SRAM with gate-stack configuration, *Micro & Nano Letters, IET Journal,* 13(6), 838-84, 2018.

21. Bavir, M., Abbasi, A. & Orouji, A.A. A Simulation Study of Junctionless Double-Gate Metal-Oxide-Semiconductor Field-Effect Transistor with Symmetrical Side Gates. *Silicon* (2019). https://doi.org/10.1007/s12633-019-00258-7

22. Zeinab Ramezani, Ali A. Orouji. A Novel Double Gate MOSFET by Symmetrical Insulator Packets with Improved Short Channel Effects, *International Journal of Electronics,* 105(3), 361-374, 2018.

23. Tripathi S. L., Patel R., Agrawal V. K. Low Leakage Pocket Junction-less DGTFET with Bio-Sensing Cavity Region. *Turkish Journal of Electrical Engineering and Computer Sciences* 27(4), 2466-2474, 2019.

24. Mendiratta N., Tripathi S. L., Padmanaban S. and Hossain E. Design and Analysis of Heavily Doped n+ Pocket Asymmetrical Junction-Less Double Gate MOSFET for Biomedical Applications. *Appl. Sci.* 10, 2499, 2020.

VLSI Implementation of Vedic Multiplier

Abhishek Kumar

School of Electronics and Electrical Engineering, Lovely Professional University, Phagwara, India

Abstract

Vedic arithmetic is an old Indian science, discovered from ancient Indian sculptures (Vedas). High-speed more multiple is the primary block in processor architecture. Vedic mathematics developed from a special method of calculations of 16 sutras. This chapter presents VLSI architecture implementation of an 8-bit multiplier with compressors, which shows significant improvement over conventional add shift multiplier. Vedic mathematics developed from 16 principles known as sutras. The technique of Vedic more multiple is Urdhva-Triyakbhyam (Vertically and Crosswise) sutra. This sutra was customarily used in the ancient history of Indian culture to multiply two decimal numbers with minimum time. The hardware architecture of Vedic multiplier is similar to array multiplier. In the performance of digital signal processors which frequently perform multiplication, much depends on the calculation speed of the multiplier block. The existing method of multiplication shift-add, booth multiplication requires hardware resources, which leads to high power consumption. The present method of Vedic multiplication based on the compressor block is focused on the reduction of interconnect wire. The multiplier is implemented using Verilog HDL with cadence NC SIM and the constrain areas, power and delay optimize using underlying block.

Keywords: Vedic multiplier, urdhva-tiryakbhyam, adder, compressor, Hdl, power

2.1 Introduction

High-speed power and low-power multiplication are the fundamental blocks for high-speed processor architecture. It is hard to realize both high-speed and low-power architecture (VLSI tradeoff). There is various multiplier architecture available in the literature. Basically, the multiplier is complete by repeated addition; a full adder is a basic unit of the multiplier, cell area increases proportionally with the number of input increases. Switching power increases with interconnection among the cells. The present work of the Vedic multiplier is focused on reducing the cell count by utilizing a compressor block into the design. The compressor is a combination of multiple adder block. It accepts multiple inputs to perform addition and map the result into a lower number of the output signal.

Vedic arithmetic is derived from Vedas (books of shrewdness) [1]. It is a chunk of Sthapatya-Veda (book on structural building and design), which is an Upaveda (supplement) of Atharva

Email: abhishek.15393@lpu.co.in

Suman Lata Tripathi, Dushyant Kumar Singh, Sanjeevikumar Padmanaban, and P. Raja (eds.) Design and Development of Efficient Energy Systems, (13–30) © 2021 Scrivener Publishing LLC

Table 2.1 Sutra in Vedic mathematics [2–5].

Sutras	Properties
Anurupye Shunyamanyat	One is in proportion, other is zero
ChalanaKalanabyham	Closeness and distinction
EkadhikinaPurven	By one more than the past one
kanyunenaPurvena	By one is greater than previous one
Gunakasamuchyah	Elements of the whole are equivalent to the quantity of components
Gunitasamuchyah	The product of sum (POS) is equivalent to sum of product (SOP)
NikhilamNavatashcaramamDashatah	All from 9 and previous from 10
ParaavartyaYojayet	Interchange and modify
Puranapuranabyham	Completion of the non-completion
Sankalana	Addition and subtraction
ShesanyankenaCharamena	Remainders
ShunyamSaamyasamuccaye	Sum is zero
Sopaantyadvayamantyam	Twice and ultimate
Urdhva-tiryakbhyam	Vertical - crosswise
Vyashtisamanstih	Part – entire
Yaavadunam	Extent of deficiency

Veda. It incorporated the hypothesis of standard numerical terms having a place in number belonging, geometry (plane, co-ordinate), trigonometry, quadratic conditions, factorization, and even math. His Holiness Jagadguru Shankaracharya Bharati Krishna Teerthaji Maharaja (1884-1960) consolidated his work and introduced it as a scientific clarification. Swamiji consolidated 16 sutras (formulae) and 16 Upa sutras (sub-formulae) from Atharva Veda as shown in Table 2.1. Vedic mathematics consists of the special technique of computations based on natural principles. Mathematical problems in trigonometric, algebra, and geometry can be solved simply. The Vedic method contains 16 sutras, describing natural ways of computing. The beauty of Vedic mathematics is that it simplifies complex calculations. The Vedic method shows effective methods of implementation of multiplication with higher bits for the science and engineering field.

2.2 8x8 Vedic Multiplier

Vedic mathematics is one of ancient Indian mathematics computes mathematical operations and is actively based on formulas for fast computations "Urdhva-Tiryakbhyam". Sutra is more generic and appropriate for multiplication. The meaning of Urdhva-Tiryakbhyam is "vertically and crosswise". The significant advantage of the Urdhva-Tiryakbhyam multiplication method is that it requires at most logical "AND" operations, arrangements of half adder (HA) and full adder (FA) to accomplish multiplication [6, 7]. Partial products require in multiplication generated in Parallel, minimizes computation time. In Figure 2.1, darkened circles present the bits of "multiplier and multiplicand"; arrows present bits to multiplied compute each bits of product.

A Vedic sutra is a multiplication algorithm employed into the Vedic multiplier. These sutras were used to multiply decimal numbers traditionally; however, these sutras find application into multiplying binary and hexadecimal numbers equally. Urdhva Tiryakbhyam, Nikhimal sutram and Anurupyena sutras are the most preferred technique among the Vedic algorithm for reduction of delay, power and cell resources with a higher number of inputs [8–10]. Vedic multiplication is a fast method of calculation that provides unique techniques of calculation with half of simple rule and principle.

Here we have implemented multiplication of 8-bit number X[7:0] and Y[7:0]. Here X[0] presents the least significant bits (LSB), X[7] is the most significant bits (MSB), generate product P[15:0]. Each partial product P[0] to P[15] is calculated from equation given below. Equation (2.1) to (2.15) present the partial product P[0] to P[15], which is calculated in the internal multiplication algorithm. Which in turn produces the final product shown in equation (2.16). Internal carry bit created during computation given in as c[1] to c[30]. Carry bits made for P[14] and P[15] are neglected, because of the superfluous. Multiplication implemented with the addition of internal signals on each stage. Partial product P1-P15

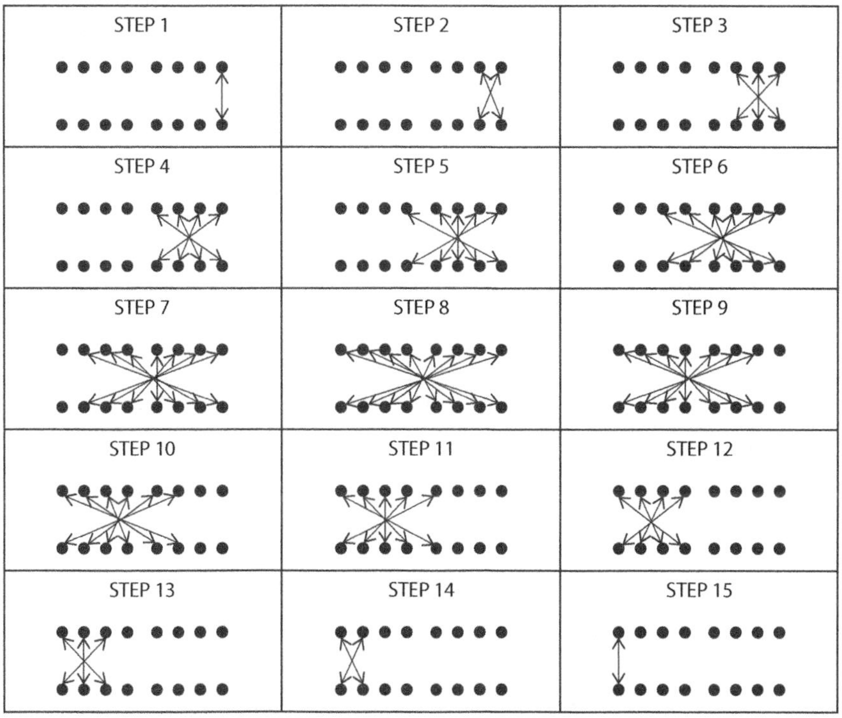

Figure 2.1 Multiplication of two 8-bit number with Urdhwa-Tiryakbhyam Sutra [28].

shown the internal carry generation, which propagated to the next steps. Product P2-P15 requires additional hardware to add 4 bits since full adders can add only 3 bits. The addition of higher input performed using compressors with compressor architectural addition of more than three inputs implemented with reduced architecture and improved speed [11].

2.3 The Architecture of 8x8 Vedic Multiplier (VM)

The hardware architecture of 8x8 multiplier explained below is dependent on Urdhva-Tiryagbhyam. The advantages of VM algorithms found as generation of partial product and performed synchronously. It enhanced the parallel processing and preferred for the implementation of the binary multiplier. An 8x8 Vedic multiplication block diagram, presented in Figure 2.2 implemented as a binary equation is given below. Each stage generates partial product, term as carrying. This carry input added with the next step of a partial product. Here requires adder can accept multiple data together. A full adder is a basic unit that can provide three data together. A compressor derived from the adder used to implement numerous inputs [12–16]. A 4:3 compressor accepts four inputs and maps the result into three output signals. 8x8 VM hardware architecture requires adding 20 input bits together, which is implemented with 20:5 compressor.

$$P[0] = x[0]y[0] \tag{2.1}$$

$$P[1] = x[1]y[0] + x[0]y[1] \; (carry \; c[1]) \tag{2.2}$$

$$P[2] = x[2]y[0] + x[1]y[1] + x[0]y[2] + c[1] \; (carry \; c[2], c[3]) \tag{2.3}$$

$$P[3] = x[3]y[0] + x[2]y[1] + x[1]y[2] + x[0]y[3] + c[2] \; (carry \; c[4], c[5]) \tag{2.4}$$

$$P[4] = x[4]y[0] + x[3]y[1] + x[2]y[2] + x[1]y[3] + x[0]y[4] \\ + c[3] + c[4] \; (Carry \; c[6], c[7]) \tag{2.5}$$

$$P[5] = x[5]y[0] + x[4]y[1] + x[3]y[2] + x[2]y[3] + x[1]y[4] + x[0]y[5] \\ + c[5] + c[6] \; (carry \; c[8], c[9], c[10]) \tag{2.6}$$

$$P[6] = x[6]y[0] + x[5]y[1] + x[4]y[2] + x[3]y[3] + x[2]y[4] \\ + x[1]y[5] + x[0]y[6] + c[7] + c[8] \; (carry \; c[11], c[12], c[13]) \tag{2.7}$$

Figure 2.2 Block diagram of 8*8 multiplier.

$$P[7] = x[7]y[0] + x[6]y[1] + x[5]y[2] + x[4]y[3] + x[3]y[4] + x[2]y[5]$$
$$+ x[1]y[6] + x[0]y[7] + c[9] + c[11] \; (carry \; c[14], c[15], c[16]) \qquad (2.8)$$

$$P[8] = x[7]y[1] + x[6]y[2] + x[5]y[3] + x[4]y[4] + x[3]y[5] + x[2]y[6]$$
$$+ x[1]y[7] + c[10] + c[12] + c[14] \; (carry \; c[17], c[18], c[19]) \qquad (2.9)$$

$$P[9] = x[7]y[2] + x[6]y[3] + x[5]y[4] + x[4]y[5] + x[3]y[6] + x[2]y[7]$$
$$+ c[13] + c[15] + c[17] \; (carry \; c[20], c[21], c[22]) \qquad (2.10)$$

$$P[10] = x[7]y[3] + x[6]y[4] + x[5]y[5] + x[4]y[6] + x[3]y[7] + c[16]$$
$$+ c[18] + c[20] \; (carry \; c[23], c[24], c[25]) \qquad (2.11)$$

$$P[11] = x[7]y[4] + x[6]y[5] + x[5]y[6] + x[4]y[7] + c[19] + c[21]$$
$$+ c[23] \; (carry \; c[26], c[27]) \qquad (2.12)$$

$$P[12] = x[7]y[5] + x[6]y[6] + x[5]y[7] + c[22] + c[24] + c[26]$$
$$(carry \; c[28], c[29]) \qquad (2.13)$$

$$P[13] = x[7]y[6] + x[6]y[7] + c[25] + c[27] + c[28] \; (carry \; c[30]) \qquad (2.14)$$

$$P[14] = x[7]y[7] + c[29] + c[30] \qquad (2.15)$$

$$P[15] = x[7]y[7] \qquad (2.16)$$

2.3.1 Compressor Architecture

The combinational block requires to implement the more multiple are logical AND, OR, XOR. To perform addition half adder and full adder are preferred. The compressor can perform the addition of the higher number of inputs; the compressor focused. The compressor is made up of an adder block. The compressor maps a piece of higher information to lower the number of outputs with summation operation. A full adder is basic 3:2 compressor units of 3:2. It accepts three numbers of input and map as a sum and carries at the output terminal.

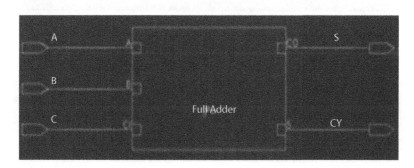

Figure 2.3 Compressor 3:2.

2.3.1.1   3:2 Compressor

In Figure 2.3, the compressor is made of two XOR gates and a MUX Gate and by which we obtain the outputs as the sum and carry. The working principle of 3:2 compressor is similar to full adder, but delay, power, and time of 3:2 compressor is much lower than that of a full adder.

2.3.1.2   4:3 Compressor

In Figure 2.4 the compressor is made of three half adders and one full adder by which we obtain the outputs as the sum and two carries. The working principle of 4:3 compressor is to understand as two of the inputs applied to the half adder (H1), and the other two inputs are applied half adder (H2). The sum of two half adders given to (H3) half adder and the sum which obtained from (H3) is the sum of the compressor, and the carry which derived from all the half adders inputted to full adder. Sum and carry output of this full adder is named as SUM2 and carry is SUM3.

2.3.1.3   5:3 Compressor

In Figure 2.5 5:3 a compressor is shown which is composed of two full adder (F1 & F2) and one-half adder. The working principle of this 5:3 compressor understood as, out of five three are the input to the full adder (F1). Sum output obtained from this full adder and the other two inputs applied to another full adder (F2).

The sum which derived from this full adder is the sum of the compressor, and the carry which obtained from those two full adders given to half adder, the sum of this half adder is taken as SUM2 and carry as SUM3.

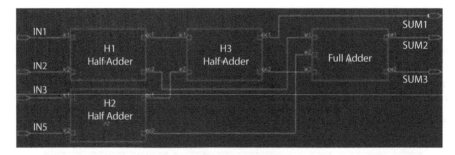

Figure 2.4 Compressor 4:3.

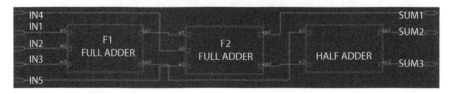

Figure 2.5 Compressor 5:3.

2.3.1.4   8:4 Compressor

In Figure 2.6, an 8:4 compressor is composed of four full adders (F1-F4) and three half adders (H1-H3). The working principle of this compressor is analyzed as three inputs applied to the full adder (F1), and another three contributions given to another full adder (F2) and the last two inputs given to the half adder (H1). The sum obtained from this F1, F2, and H1 propagated to the full adder (F3). The carry which obtained from the F1, F2, and H1 given to another full adder (F4). The sum obtained from the F4 and the carry obtained from F3 provided to (H2) half adder. The sum output from full adder (F4) is the sum of the compressor Y1, the carry which obtained from the half adder (H2) and the carry obtained from full adder (F4) given to the (H2) half adder. The sum output from this half adder (H2) is compressor output Y2. Half adder (H3) output is the final output as Y3 and Y4.

2.3.1.5   10:4 Compressor

In Figure 2.7, a 10:4 compressor is made of five full adders, five half adders, and one OR gate. The working principle of this compressor is three inputs given to the full adder (F1), another three inputs given to another full adder (F2), and another three inputs given to the full adder (F3). The sum of these three full adders (F1), (F2) and (F3) is given to full adder (F5) and carry given to the full adder (F4). The last input and the sum of the full adder (F5)

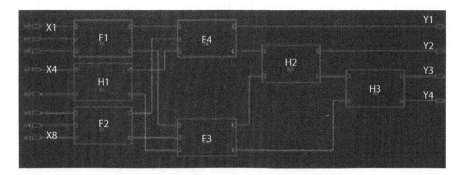

Figure 2.6 Compressor 8 to 4.

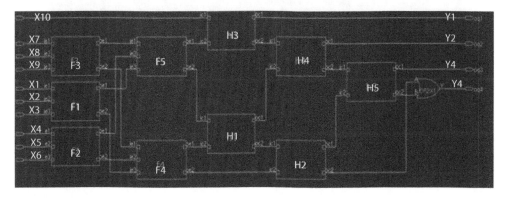

Figure 2.7 Compressor 10 to 4.

is given to (H3) half adder. Carry signal of (FG5) full adder and the output sum of the (F4) full adder acts as input to half adder (H1).

The sum obtained from the half adder (H3) is the Y1 output of the compressor. The carry output of the (H3) half adder and sum of (H1) half adder (H1) acts as input to (H4) half adder. The sum obtained from half adder (H4) taken as output Y2. The carry of the full adder (F4) and half adder (H1) given to half adder (H2). The carry output of (H4) half adder and the sum output of (H2) half adder acts as input to half adder (H5). The sum obtained for half adder (H5) is taken as output Y3. The carry of half adder (H5) and half adder (H2) is given to the OR gate. The result obtained in this OR gate is taken as output Y4.

2.3.1.6   12:5 Compressor

In Figure 2.8, a 12:5 compressor is made of five full adders, two half adders, and two 4:3 compressors. The working principle of this compressor is three inputs given to the full adder (FF1), another three contributions given to the full adder (FF2), another three contributions given to the full adder (FF3) and the last three inputs given to the full adder (FF4). The sum obtained from these full adders (FF1), (FF2), (FF3), and (FF4) is given to 4:3 compressor (CV1), and carry is given to another 4:3 compressor (CV2). The sum obtained from 4:3 compressor (CV1) is the Y1 output of the compressors. The carry1 of the 4:3 compressor (CV1) and the sum of the 4:3 compressor (CV2) acts as input to the (H1) half adder. Output sum of half adder (H1) is taken as output Y2. The carry2 of 4:3 compressor (CV1), carry of (H1) half adder and carry1 of the 4:3 compressor (CV2) is given to the full adder (FF5). The sum which is obtained from this full adder (FF5) is taken as output Y3. The carry of this full adder (FF5) and carry2 of the 4:3 compressor is given to half adder (H2). The sum obtained for half adder (H2) is taken as output Y4 and carry is taken as output Y5. In this compressor, we will provide 12 inputs, and 5 outputs will be obtained.

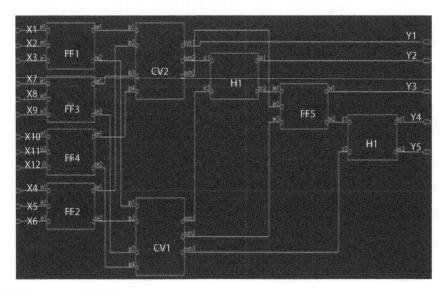

Figure 2.8 Compressor 12 to 5.

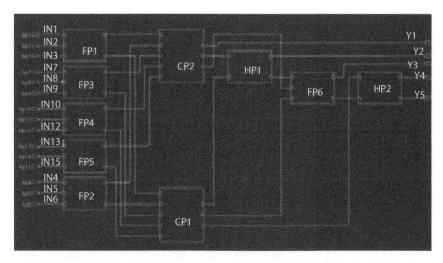

Figure 2.9 Compressor 15 to 5.

2.3.1.7   15:5 Compressor

In Figure 2.9, 15:5 compressor architecture requires six full adder (FP1-FP6), two half adders (HP1-Hp2), and two 5:3 compressors (CP1-CP2). Working principle of 15:5 compressor is (IN1-IN3) inputs given to the full adder (FP1), (IN4-IN6) inputs given to the full adder (FP2), (IN7-IN9) inputs given to the full adder (FP3), inputs (IN10-IN12) are inputted to the FP4 and input (IN13-IN15) are inputted to the FP5. Output signal sum obtained from all these full adders (FP1), (FP2), (FP3), (FP4), and (FP5) is given to the 5:3 compressor (CP2) and carry is given to the 5:3 compressor (CP1). The sum obtained from the 5:3 compressor (CP2) is the output Y1 of the compressor. The carry1 of 5:3 compressor (CP2) and the sum of 5:3 compressor (C1) given to half adder (HP1). The sum obtained from half adder (HP1) taken as output Y2. The carry of this half adder (HP1), carry2 of 5:3 compressor (CP2) and carry1 of 5:3 compressor (CP1) given to full adder (FP6). The sum obtained from full adder (FP6) taken as output Y3. The carry of this full adder (FP6) and carry2 of 5:3 compressor (CP1) given to half adder (HP2). The sum which is obtained from half adder (HP2) is taken as output Y4 and carry is taken as output Y5.

2.3.1.8   20:5 Compressor

In Figure 2.10, 15;5 compressor made of seven full adders, three half adders, and two 7:3 compressors. The working principle of this compressor is understood as input (X1-X3) inputs applied to the full adder (FP11). (X4-X6) inputs are provided to full adder (FP2), (X7-X9) inputs are given to full adder (FP3), (X10-X12) inputs are given to full adder (FP4), (X13-X15) inputs are given to full adder (FP5), (X16-X18) inputs are given to full adder (FP6) and the last two inputs (X19-X20) are given to half adder (HP1). The sum obtained from this (FP1), (FP2), (FP3), (FP4), (FP5), (FP6), and (HP1) is given to 7:3 compressor (CP1) and carry is given to another 7:3 compressor (CP2). The sum obtained from 7:3 compressor (CP1) is the output Y1of the compressor.

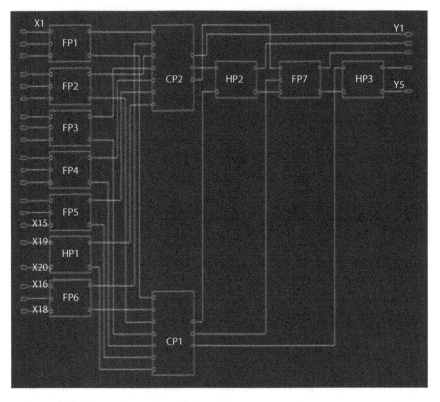

Figure 2.10 Compressor 20 to 5.

The output carry1 of 7:3 compressor (CP1) and the sum obtained from 7:3 compressor (CP2) is given to half adder (HP2). The sum which is obtained from half adder (HP2) is taken as output Y2. The carry of half adder (HP2), carry2 of 7:3 compressor (CP1), and carry1 of 7:3 compressor (CP2) given to full adder (FP7). The sum obtained from full adder (FP7) taken as output Y3. The carry of this full adder (FP7) and carry2 of 7:3 compressor (CP2) given to half adder (HP2). The sum obtained from half adder (HP3) is taken as output Y4 and carry is taken as output Y5. Different compressor blocks are integrated to develop the architecture using the Boolean equation.

Figure 2.11 presents the simulated waveform of which obtained while we implemented the 8x8 Vedic Multiplier. We have given input for a specific time, and it goes to the end till

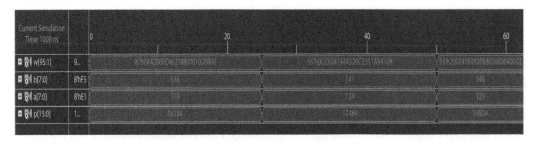

Figure 2.11 Behavioral simulation of 8x8 VM.

Table 2.2 FPGA utilization summary report.

Device utilization summary			
Logic utilizations	**Used**	**Available**	**Utilization**
Slices	418	1672	4%
4 input LUTs	729	17344	4%
Bounded IOBs	67	250	26%

which we have mentioned stop in the test bench. Here a is 8-bit input and b is 8-bit input, and we are getting 16 bit as output, and it is represented in p. The multiplier is implemented with Verilog HDL using the Xilinx ISE tool. The synthesis result obtained from vertex-4 FPGA. An 8-bit VM requires 418 slices, 729 LUT and 67 IOB shown in Table 2.2. A similar effect is verified with cadence NCSIM and the implementation result confirmed with RTL compiler at gpdk 180nm technology. The simulation result shows that

The case I Input A=8'd136 and B=8'd119 result in multiplier values p=16'h16184.
Case II Input A=8'd141 and B=8'd124 result in multiplier values p=16'h17484.
Case III Input A=8'd145 and B=8'd129 result in multiplier values p=16'h18834.

2.4 Results and Discussion

The performance parameter of 8-bit VM is judged by power consumption, delay, and area report obtained by the cadence RTL compiler. Completed implementation of an 8-bit Vedic multiplier is through the combinatorial block. The usage of the compressor reduces the requirement of resources. As the number of the logic gate but increases the interconnecting wires. Similarly, area requirements to interface multiple compressors significantly enhance the area and delay. In this section area, power and delay are presented due to logical resources and wires.

2.4.1 Instance Power

This pie chart in Figure 2.12 presents the instance power used in the 8x8 Vedic Multiplier. In this chart, g1 and g2 determine compressor 10to4 and its usage of instance power is 15.79%. z1 and z2 define compressor 8to4, and its usage of instance power is 12.93%. d1 and d2 limit compressor 9to4 and its usage of instance power is 14.29%. N1 and N2 is a compressor of 7to3 whose power consumption is 8.19% of total power. M1 represents compressor 6to3, and its usage of instance power is 4.02%. V2 defines compressor 5to3, and its usage of instance power is 2.33%. Remaining all other compressors like t1 represents compressor 4to3, v1 represents compressor 5to3 and h1 defines about compressor 3to2 usage of instance power is 40.48%. An 8-bit Vedic more multiple logical blocks consume only 59.52% of total power. 40.48% of total power is consumed by another factor. The similar power distribution of the 16-bit multiplier is presented in Figure 2.13. Compressor block requires 37.78% of total power which 62.22% of total power consumed by other factors like wire.

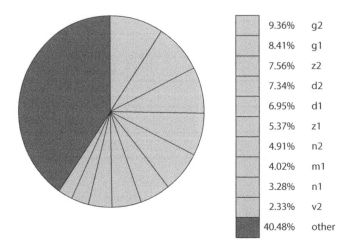

9.36%	g2
8.41%	g1
7.56%	z2
7.34%	d2
6.95%	d1
5.37%	z1
4.91%	n2
4.02%	m1
3.28%	n1
2.33%	v2
40.48%	other

Figure 2.12 Instance power usage of 8X8 vedic multiplier.

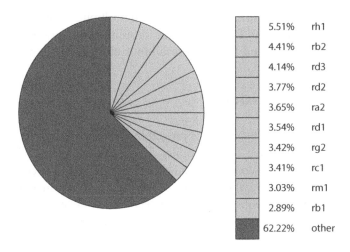

5.51%	rh1
4.41%	rb2
4.14%	rd3
3.77%	rd2
3.65%	ra2
3.54%	rd1
3.42%	rg2
3.41%	rc1
3.03%	rm1
2.89%	rb1
62.22%	other

Figure 2.13 Instance power usage of 16X16 VM.

2.4.2   Net Power

This pie chart in Figure 2.14 defines the Net power used in the 8x8 Vedic Multiplier. The identification of the power-hungry block is identified from this chart. In this chart, g1 and g2 determine compressor 10to4; consumes 5.64% of the total net power. z1 and z2 define compressor 8to4, and its usage of net power is 3.72%. d1 and d2 define compressor 9to4, and its usage of net power is 4.27%. n1 and n2 define compressor 7to3, and its usage of net power is 2.29%. m1 defines compressor 6to3, and its usage of net power is 1.23%. v2 defines compressor 5to3, and its usage of net power is 0.60%. Remaining all other compressors like t1 denotes about compressor 4to3, v1 represents compressor 5to3 and h1defines about compressor 3to2 usage of net power is 82.24%. This pie chart in Figure 2.15 defines the Net power distribution in the 16-bit multiplier.

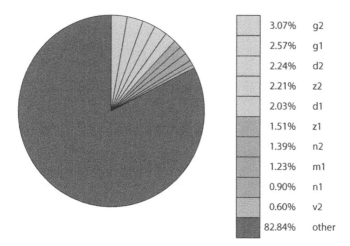

3.07%	g2
2.57%	g1
2.24%	d2
2.21%	z2
2.03%	d1
1.51%	z1
1.39%	n2
1.23%	m1
0.90%	n1
0.60%	v2
82.84%	other

Figure 2.14 Net power usage of 8X8 VM.

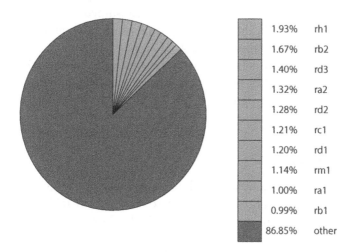

1.93%	rh1
1.67%	rb2
1.40%	rd3
1.32%	ra2
1.28%	rd2
1.21%	rc1
1.20%	rd1
1.14%	rm1
1.00%	ra1
0.99%	rb1
86.85%	other

Figure 2.15 Net power usage of 16X16 VM.

2.4.3   8-Bit Multiplier

Table 2.3 presents the cell area requirement of the 8x8 Vedic Multiplier. Cell area report models the number of the basic cell requires to the design. To implement this project 139 cells are required, and the area which is obtained by cells is 1517, and the net area is "zero". The total area which is accomplished is 1517, and there is no Wire Load for this Vedic Multiplier.

Table 2.3 Cell area of 8x8 vedic multiplier.

Instance	Cells	Cell area	Net area	Total area	Wire load
Vedic Multiplier	139	1517	0	1517	<none> (D)

Table 2.4 Power constraints of 8x8 vedic multiplier.

Instance	Cells	Leakage power(nW)	Dynamic power(nW)	Total power(nW)
vedicmultiplier	139	13442.07	86424.01	99866.08

Table 2.5 Time constraint of 8x8 vedic multiplier.

Pins	Type	Fan out	Load (fF)	Slew (ps)	Delay (ps)	Arrival (ps)
p[14]	out port				0	2637 R

An instance of an 8-bit VM named Vedic multiplier requires 139 cells in this project; there is an unwanted sub-threshold current which is leakage of power in 13422.07nW (Nano Watt). Dynamic power, a part of power that consumed while the inputs are active, obtained value is 86424.01 nW and the total power which is obtained for this 8x8 Vedic Multiplier is 99866.08 nW shown in Table 2.4.

Here pin p[14] defines that it is the last output pin of 8x8 Vedic Multiplier and type defines whether it is input port or output port. The longest path arrival time (AT) of signal is calculated as the latency for a signal to arrive at point of consideration, for this project is 2637 ps shown in Table 2.5.

2.4.4　16-Bit Multiplier

The 16x16 Vedic Multiplier requires 666 cells to implement this project, and the area which is obtained by cells is 5967, and the net area is "zero" as shown in Table 2.6. The total area in which it is accomplished is 5967, and there is no wire load for this Vedic Multiplier.

16-bit multiplier needs 666 cells to implement. Here unwanted sub-threshold current which is leakage of power in 60576.57 nW. The dynamic power of 16-bit multiplier to complete product are 444556.31 nW and the total power obtained to 505132.87 nW as shown in Table 2.7.

Table 2.6 Cell area of 16x16 vedic multiplier.

Instance	Cells	Cell area	Net area	Total area	Wire load
16-bit VM	666	5967	0	5967	<none> (D)

Table 2.7 Power constraints of 16x16 vedic multiplier.

Instance	Cells	Leakage power (nW)	Dynamic power (nW)	Total power (nW)
16-bit VM	666	60576.57	444556.31	505132.87

Table 2.8 Time constraint of 16x16 vedic multiplier.

Pin	Type	Fanout	Load (fF)	Slew (ps)	Delay (ps)	Arrival (ps)
p[30]	out port				0	5476 R

Table 2.9 Comparison of multiplier architecture.

8-bit Multiplier	Leakage power (μW)	Dynamic power (micro μW)	Total power (μW)	Delay (ns)	Cell count	Cell area
Vedic Multiplier	13.44	86.42	99.86	2.637	139	1517
Booth Multiplier [21]	5.69	324.53	330.22	3.75	214	5115
Wallace Tree Multiplier [21]	5.6263	655.55	661.17	3.02	248	1470
Dadda Multiplier [21]	5.62	655.807	2661.47	2.56	266	1330

Here pin p[30] defines that it is the last output pin of 16x16 Vedic Multiplier and type defines whether it is input port or output port. The longest path arrival time form input to pin p[30] is 5476 ps shown in Table 2.8.

The present work of 8-bit Vedic multiplier is compared with the existing different architecture of multiplier, shown in Table 2.9 in terms of power, delay and cell area. It is observed that the Dadda multiplier needs a large number of nets that require a lower area than the Wallace tree multiplier. Booth requires a lower number of cells but the total area increases to approximately three- to four-fold compare to the Wallace tree and Dadda multiplier [17–19]. Since the booth multiplication algorithm requires multiple time shifting-adding greater number of wire resources.

Vedic multiplier replaces the underlying cell by compressors logic, made up of adder block. Utilization of compressor greatly reduces the wiring resource save area. The leakage power of the Vedic multiplier is larger than other compare multipliers but shows very low dynamic power consumption. Dadda multiplier requires maximum power to reduce the delay 2.56ns. A Vedic multiplier attains significant reduction in dynamic power requirement and delay of multiplication architecture. Cell count of VM is 139 which is much smaller than other multipliers.

2.4.5 Applications of Multiplier

The present work Vedic multiplier finds application to implement the architecture of the following [21–25]

1) High-speed signal processing
2) DSP based application
3) DWT and DCT transformation
4) FIT and IIR filter

5) Multirate signal processing
6) Up-Down converters
7) Multiply - Accumulate unit

2.5   Conclusion

An efficient productive strategy for multiplication based on Urdhva Tiryakbhyam Sutra (Algorithm) in view of Vedic mathematics is implemented in this paper with Verilog HDL. Here a fast 8-bit multiplier is implemented that incorporates architecture of compressor. Compressor is a derived structure of full adder and half adder, map multiple input to lesser number of output signals. Hierarchical multiplier structure and shows the computational speed by offered by Vedic methods. Essential inspiration of this work is to decrease the delay in complex multiplication achieve 2.637 ns. We can deduce that the compressor-based architecture of Vedic math's multiplier is more favorable than conventional multipliers and preferred in complex algorithm implementation. Hence, we have concluded that Instance Power usage of 8x8 Vedic Multiplier is 40.48% and 16x16 Vedic Multiplier is 62.22%. The Net Power usage of 8x8 Vedic Multiplier is 82.24%, and the 16x16 Vedic Multiplier is 86.85%.

References

1. Thapliyal, H., & Arabnia, H. R. (2004, June). A Time-Area-Power Efficient Multiplier and Square Architecture Based on Ancient Indian Vedic Mathematics. In *ESA/VLS*, 2004I (pp. 434-439).
2. Ciminiera, L., & Valenzano, A. (1988). Low-cost serial multipliers for high-speed specialized processors. *The Proceedings IEEE (Computers and Digital Techniques)*, 135(5), 259-265.
3. Hsiao, S. F., Jiang, M. R., & Yeh, J. S. (1998). Design of high-speed low-power 3-2 counter and 4-2 compressor for fast multipliers. *Electronics Letters*, 34(4), 341-343.
4.. Ramalatha, M., Dayalan, K. D., Dharani, P., & Priya, S. D. (2009, July). High-speed energy efficient ALU design using Vedic multiplication techniques. In *International Conference on Advances in Computational Tools for Engineering Applications*, 2009, IEEE (pp. 600-603).
5. Tiwari, H. D., Gankhuyag, G., Kim, C. M., & Cho, Y. B. (2008, November). Multiplier design based on ancient Indian Vedic Mathematics. In *International SoC Design Conference, 2008*, IEEE (Vol. 2, pp. II-65).
6. Ma, W., & Li, S. (2008, October). A new high compression compressor for large multiplier. In *9th International Conference on Solid-State and Integrated-Circuit Technology. 2008*, IEEE (pp. 1877-1880).
7. Chandrakasan, A. P., Bowhill, W. J., & Fox, F. (2000). *Design of high-performance microprocessor circuits*. Wiley-IEEE Press.
8. Radhakrishnan, D., & Preethy, A. P. (2000, August). Low power CMOS pass logic 4-2 compressor for high-speed multiplication. In *Proceedings of the 43rd IEEE Midwest Symposium on Circuits and Systems (Cat. No. CH37144). 2000*, IEEE (Vol. 3, pp. 1296-1298).
9. Mutoh, S. I., Douseki, T., Matsuya, Y., Aoki, T., Shigematsu, S., & Yamada, J. (1995). 1-V power supply high-speed digital circuit technology with multithreshold-voltage CMOS. *IEEE Journal of Solid-state Circuits*, 30(8), 847-854.

10. Sriraman, L., & Prabakar, T. N. (2012, March). Design and implementation of two variable multiplier using KCM and Vedic mathematics. In *1st International Conference on Recent Advances in Information Technology (RAIT). 2012*, IEEEE (pp. 782-787).

11. Tiwari, H. D., Gankhuyag, G., Kim, C. M., & Cho, Y. B. (2008, November). Multiplier design based on ancient Indian Vedic Mathematics. In *International SoC Design Conference. 2008*, IEEE (Vol. 2, pp. II-65).

12. Dandapat, A., Ghosal, S., Sarkar, P., & Mukhopadhyay, D. (2010). A 1.2-ns16× 16-bit binary multiplier using high speed compressors. *International Journal of Electrical and Electronics Engineering*, 4(3), 234-239.

13. Swee, K. L. S., & Hiung, L. H. (2012, June). Performance comparison review of 32-bit multiplier designs. In *4th International Conference on Intelligent and Advanced Systems (ICIAS2012). 2012*, IEEE (Vol. 2, pp. 836-841).

14. Radhakrishnan, D., & Preethy, A. P. (2000, August). Low power CMOS pass logic 4-2 compressor for high-speed multiplication. *In Proceedings of the 43rd IEEE Midwest Symposium on Circuits and Systems (Cat. No. CH37144). 2000*, IEEE (Vol. 3, pp. 1296-1298).

15. Ram, G. C., Lakshmanna, Y. R., Rani, D. S., & Sindhuri, K. B. (2016, March). Area efficient modified vedic multiplier. In *International Conference on Circuit, Power and Computing Technologies (ICCPCT). 2006*, IEEE (pp. 1-5).

16. Prabhu, E., Mangalam, H., & Gokul, P. R. (2019). A delay efficient vedic multiplier. *Proceedings of the National Academy of Sciences, India Section A: Physical Sciences*, 89(2), 257-268.

17. Dutta, K., Chattopadhyay, S., Biswas, V., & Ghatak, S. R. (2019, November). Design of Power Efficient Vedic Multiplier using Adiabatic Logic. In *International Conference on Electrical, Electronics and Computer Engineering (UPCON)*, 2019, IEEE (pp. 1-6).\

18. Shukla, V., Singh, O. P., Mishra, G. R., & Tiwari, R. K. (2020). A Novel Approach for Reversible Realization of 4× 4 Bit Vedic Multiplier Circuit. In *Advances in VLSI, Communication, and Signal Processing*, 2020, Springer, Singapore, (pp. 733-745).

19. Karthikeyan, S., & Jagadeeswari, M. (2020). Performance improvement of elliptic curve cryptography system using low power, high speed 16× 16 Vedic multiplier based on reversible logic. *Journal of Ambient Intelligence and Humanized Computing*, 1-10.

20. Koul, R., Yadav, M., & Suneja, K. (2020). Novel FPGA-Based Hardware Design of Canonical Signed Digit Matrix Multiplier and Its Comparative Analysis with Other Multipliers. In *International Conference on Artificial Intelligence: Advances and Applications 2019*, Springer, Singapore (pp. 65-75).

21. Kyaw, K. Y., Goh, W. L., & Yeo, K. S. (2010, December). Low-power high-speed multiplier for error-tolerant application. In *International Conference of Electron Devices and Solid-State Circuits (EDSSC)*, 2010, IEEE (pp. 1-4).

22. Raju, B. R., & Satish, D. V. (2013). A high speed 16* 16 multiplier based on Urdhva Tiryakbhyam Sutra. *International Journal of Science Engineering and Advance Technology, IJSEAT*, 1(5), 126-132.

23. Panda, S. K., Das, R., & Sahoo, T. R. (2015). VLSI implementation of vedic multiplier using Urdhva–Tiryakbhyam sutra in VHDL environment: A novelty. *IOSR Journal of VLSI and Signal Processing (IOSR-JVSP)*, 5(1), 17-24.

24. Kerur, S. S., Prakash Narchi, J. C., Kittur, H. M., & Girish, V. A. (2011). Implementation of Vedic multiplier for digital signal processing. In *International Conference on VLSI, Communication & Instrumentation* (ICVCI), 2011 (pp. 1-6).

25. Mehta, P., & Gawali, D. (2009, December). Conventional versus Vedic mathematical method for Hardware implementation of a multiplier. In *International Conference on Advances in Computing, Control, and Telecommunication Technologies*, 2009, IEEE (pp. 640-642).

26. Bansal, Y., Madhu, C., & Kaur, P. (2014, March). High speed vedic multiplier designs-A review. In *Recent Advances in Engineering and Computational Sciences*, 2014, IEEE (RAECS) (pp. 1-6).
27. Huddar, S.R., Rupanagudi, S.R., Kalpana, M., & Mohan, S. (2013). Novel high speed vedic mathematics multiplier using compressors. 2013 International Mutli-Conference on Automation, Computing, Communication, Control and Compressed Sensing (iMac4s), 2013 (465-469).

Gas Leakage Detection from Drainage to Offer Safety for Sanitary Workers

Dr. D. Jeyabharathi[1]*, Dr. D. Kesavaraja[2] and D. Sasireka[3]

[1]Assistant professor, Department of Information Technology, Sri Krishna College of Technology, Coimbatore
[2]Associate professor, Dept. of CSE, Dr Sivanthi Aditanar College of Engineering, Tiruchendur, India
[3]Research Scholar, VV College of Engineering, Tisaiyanvillai, India

Abstract

A drainage system is an arrangement to move liquids away from where they are not required for disposal in appropriate locations. A drainage system can include anything from gutters and drains in houses to remove rain water, storm water systems to drain rainwater from roads into roadside drains and drainage systems to remove sewage from houses into municipal sewers for disposal. Within the medical industry, drainage systems can mean methods to drain unwanted fluids from the body, such as pus from wounds, and colostomy bags to remove body wastes and fluids from internal abscesses and ulcers. Within engineering it can mean systems for removing spent oil, coolant liquids and by-products from industry referred to as industrial waste.

Gas leaks are a serious hazard that can cause harm to workers, buildings and the environment. Detecting leaked gas can help to reduce these risks. Gases such as Carbon monoxide (CO), Hydrogen sulphide (H2S), Methane (CH4) are some of the hazardous gases present in underground drainage systems. These gases are very harmful to human beings and may lead to death. To avoid those problems, we have proposed a gas leakage detection system.

Keywords: Sewer gas detection, crack detection

3.1 Introduction

3.1.1 IOT-Based Sewer Gas Detection

A drainage system is a system that forms wastewater from various patterns such as streams, rivers, and lakes. The function of a drainage system goes beyond the removal of wastewater. During this time many deaths will occur due to sewer gases leakage from wastage.

Drainage systems must also be designed to prevent backflow, while keeping sewer gases away from indoor spaces. The expression "sewer gas" is utilized to portray the blend of gases discharged by sewage, and singular gases can be poisonous or non-harmful.

**Corresponding author*: bharathi.durai@gmail.com

Suman Lata Tripathi, Dushyant Kumar Singh, Sanjeevikumar Padmanaban, and P. Raja (eds.) Design and Development of Efficient Energy Systems, (31–42) © 2021 Scrivener Publishing LLC

Many sewer gases are scentless, and the trademark smell when they break can be credited to hydrogen sulfide. This gas is likewise poisonous and combustible, which makes it risky in higher fixations. Once sewer gases can be smelled in a structure conditions could be hazardous or unsanitary. Since sewer gas contains methane gas (CH4) there is a danger of a blast peril or even deadly suffocation.

In addition, some writers opine that there are possible health hazards from sewer gas exposure, such as a bacterial infection of the sinuses (which can occur due to any sinus irritation). Contingent upon the sewer gas source and different factors, for example, mugginess and building and climate conditions, spores may form and may likewise be present in sewer gases.

In a little over a year, more than 20 workers have died in sewers. It affects human life and such workers put their lives at risk. This is because of the lack of adequate emergency facilities available in our country.

To improve this, there is a need to alert the emergency services to investigate the sewer gas leakage as soon as possible when the risk factor is high. That is, to find the risk level in the sewer gas leakage based on thresholding and give the alert once it exceeds it. With the help of IoT sensors, when the situation is abnormal, people's lives can be saved. So, IoT-based sewer gas leakage detection and prevention is essential.

The Internet of Things (IoT) is an arrangement of interrelated computing gadgets, mechanical and digital machines, objects, animals or individuals that are given one kind of a identifier and the capacity to exchange information over a system without requiring human to human intervention. Using IoT technique, an automatic sewer gas leakage detection and prevention system can be built [10–23].

3.1.1.1   IoT Sensors

Compared to hardware equipment, sensors are getting simpler to collect data and less expensive. Whether using sounds, vibrations, images, electrical signals or accelerometer or other kinds of sensor data, richer analytics can be built by teaching a machine to detect and classify events happening in real time, at the edge, using an inexpensive microcontroller for processing—even with noisy, high variation data.

Sensor datas such as sounds, vibrations, images, electrical signals or accelerometer or other kinds of sensor datas are collected and trained by various classifiers. The classifier Support Vector Machine (SVM), Neural Networks (NN) and Convolution Neural Network (CNN) can be used to train the data.

The proposed system estimates the risk factor in sewer gas leakage. Hence it provides a cheaper solution than other existing mechanisms and is well suited for real-time applications.

3.1.2   Objective

The main objective of this project is to monitor the level of toxic gases present in the drainage.

- To increase safety for sanitary workers.
- To prevent the damage at initial stage. The system is very useful to create awareness among the public.

3.1.3   Contribution of this Chapter

The following are the contribution of this chapter:

- Carbon Monoxide sensor, Hydrogen sulphide sensor and Methane gas sensors can be used to detect sewer gas.
- Ultrasonic sensor can be used to detect the crack [1–3].
- Consequent Tristate Pattern classifier is proposed to train the sensor data. Based on thresholding sewer gas leakage risk factor is detected.
- Proposed Consequent Tristate pattern can be used to give an accurate detection process.

3.1.4   Outline of the Chapter

The rest of this thesis is organized as follows.

Section 3.2 discusses the previous works related to crack and sewer gas leakage level detection. Section 3.3 discusses the working process of the proposed system. Also, it gives details about the proposed feature descriptors constituting the Tristate Pattern. Section 3.4 presents the implementation of the proposed approach and the experimental results. Section 3.5 presents conclusions and also future directions for research.

3.2   Related Works

A detailed survey of previous works on sewer gas and crack detection is made in this chapter, and the problems associated with these approaches are highlighted.

3.2.1   Sewer Gas Leakage Detection

Mahyar *et al.* have proposed the system for sewer gas detection. The authors present another sensor and supporting stage for aggravation sewer gas identification and checking. The sensor is manufactured utilizing a profoundly specific microfluidic gas channel combined with a delicate metaloxide semiconductor (MOS) sensor. The supporting stage comprises an exceptionally manufactured syringe siphon, robotized test conveyance, and vaporization chamber. To exhibit the sensor's affectability to H2S (a significant segment in sewer gas blends), various convergences of H2S in a fluid stage are distinguished utilizing exceptional element extraction strategies and adjusted utilizing gas chromatography. Also, another arrangement for checking and identification of gaseous H2S tests is created and analyzed against the aftereffects of the aqueous examples. This correlation shows that in spite of the fact that the highlights of the gaseous and aqueous examples share a few likenesses, the moistness in the last hoses the reaction of the sensor. At long last, the capacity and capability of the proposed detecting stage is additionally shown by recognizing H2S from different gases present in the sewer.

In review [9] a plan is recommended that gets Wireless Sensor Networks (WSN) for air contamination checking framework, called Wireless Sensor Network Air Pollution Monitoring Framework (WAPMS). This uses Air Quality Index (AQI) as the primary parameter and utilizes information conglomeration calculation to blend information to expel copies and channel out invalid readings. Proposition [5], the creators have planned an astute private security alert and remote-control framework based on single chip PC to beware of dangerous gas spillage in homes. The Internet of Things (IoT) [6–9] is extensively being seen by investigators as a standout among most present-day developments with the capability to fundamentally change prosperity, security and security and address genuine impacts inside the overall population.

3.2.2   Crack Detection

Crack is one of the most widely recognized deformities happening in the metal parts, with specific results in liquid vehicle pipes. The reason for the cracks is the presentation of the metal to mechanical and warm pressure, bringing about an imperfection in the partition of the inner precious stones, because of weakness. For pipes, this demonstrates there is a tempestuous weight inside, during activity, which prompts a slight change in their shape, bringing about steady shortcoming and the presence of cracks, which can become bigger over time. The most significant techniques used to identify the channels' cracks, which can fit to a portable robot for outer funnel examination are: PC vision frameworks (camera), attractive field estimations and acoustic identification (receiver). Picture examination methods were likewise used to recognize welding absconds in pipelines [24], recently a warm picture examination framework has been proposed for non-ruinous tests (NDT), during warm pressure tests [25]. The utilization of a profoundly delicate framework to identify little cracks (around 500 μm) [26] demonstrated that the location of cracks was dependent on warm imaging in excitation techniques relying upon whirlpool flows [27]. Beat stage thermography [4] and subsidiary systems for crack recognition were likewise evolved [26], while a laser innovation for "dynamic warm imaging of the spot plane" was utilized [27]. This one depends on the nearby fervor of where the laser shaft from the camera falls on the assessed pipe, like the examination strategy utilized in the task ThermoBot [8].

This project targets giving keen answers for screening toxic sewage gases and takes a shot at an arrangement of live sewage level discovery and observation. At whatever point a specific edge is crossed, an alarm is sent to whoever is inspecting the conditions from a remote area.

3.3   Methodology

The proposed system can be used to detect the sewer gas level as well as cracks in the drainage pipe system. The overall architecture of the proposed system is shown in Figure 3.1.

The system has three tasks: 1. Sewer gas detection using proposed consequent Tristate pattern, 2. Crack detection, 3. Alert is given when the level exceeds the threshold.

3.3.1   Sewer Gas Detection

A sewer system is an underground system of pipes commonly used to transport wastewater from homes and businesses either to a treatment facility, where the water is treated and released into natural water bodies like lakes and streams or in a river to permanently drain

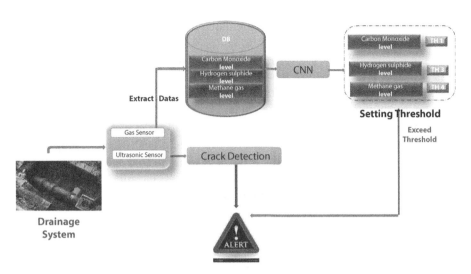

Figure 3.1 Architecture of the proposed system.

out from the area. The sewer manhole is one of the most important parts of the sewer system. A sewer manhole is a structure through which a person can gain access to the underground wastewater collection system. Manholes are not designed for someone to work in regularly, but workers may need to enter the manhole to complete their jobs such as cleaning, repair, inspection, etc. The neglect of sewage systems is responsible for the deaths of thousands of sewage cleaners throughout the year from accidents and various diseases such as hepatitis and typhoid due to sudden or sustained exposure to hazardous gases like carbon monoxide, hydrogen sulphide, and methane. A better knowledge of hazards in the surroundings is necessary for the prevention of poisonous gases. These gases have to be kept on track so that an enormous rise in the normal level of effluents should be known and corrective measures taken.

The first step of the proposed system is to detect sewer gas level. A gas sensor can be used to detect the level of the gas. The level of Carbon Monoxide, Hydrogen sulphide and Methane has been measured using a gas sensor. The sensor data is fed to the proposed Tristate pattern. This pattern trains the data based on continues 3 ones and predicts the threshold for each gas. If the level exceeds the threshold value then it gives the alert.

3.3.1.1 Proposed Tristate Pattern

The gas sensor data is given to the input of the proposed system. The proposed system provides 1 for 3 consequent ones and .5 for 2 consequent ones and .25 for one. The Table 3.1 below shows the structure of the Tristate pattern.

Table 3.1 Tristate pattern.

Patterns	Score
Consequent 3 ones	3
Consequent 2 ones	2
Single one	1

Finally, the sum of the values has been calculated using the formula below:

$$TH1 = C = 1nH = 1mM = 1pC + H + M$$

Where C,H,M denotes Carbon Monoxide, Hydrogen sulphide and Methane sensor datas and n,m, p denotes the range of the datas.

All these major components are connected in the arduino board with connecting wires and fitted in the required places (underground drainage pipes) where damaged occurred. It will easily detect the gases and also the leakage of pipes in that specific area. It also gives a notification to the authorities about the leakage by a message and it is able to identify the location by GSM module and fix the problem as soon as possible.

3.3.2   Crack Detection

A semi-automated battery-operated (Figure 3.2) cart is designed with ultrasonic sensors attached to the front. This ultrasonic sensor sends high-frequency sound waves through the transmitter head, which then goes and reflects back on hitting the surface of the track, and comes back to the receiver head. This is then converted to distance.

A threshold distance is set, by measuring the distance between the sensor and the surface of the track. At the time of inspection, if the distance exceeds or is less than the threshold distance, it indicates that a crack is present on the track. When a crack as such is detected, the cart stops there. This is the first level of testing.

As a second level of testing, once the cart stops, a camera attached to the front of the cart is triggered on. This camera then takes a picture of the track where the crack is present. This picture is then sent to the Amazon S3 bucket and image processing is performed on the captured image. This is done so as to detect if it is a major or a minor crack.

In case of a major crack, the cart will store the GPS location and return to the previous checkpoint. In case of a minor crack, the cart will continue with its inspection. In either

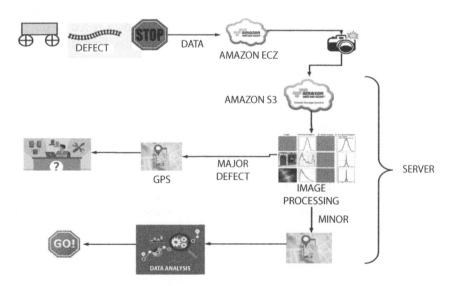

Figure 3.2 Flow diagram of the automated system.

case, the GPS location and the details of the crack and the status are stored in Amazon EC2 and are sent immediately to the concerned authorities to be rectified as soon as possible.

Cart development and sensor:
For the development of the cart, 12V DC motors can be used. Motor controller L298N is used to control the movement of the cart. Ultrasonic sensor HC-SR04 sends high-frequency sound waves and calculates the distance of the reflected wave. This sensor detects the minute defects with high accuracy. This is a non-destructive testing method.

Raspberry Pi 3:
RPi is a low-cost, small credit-card-sized computer. RPi3 is faster than Arduino.

Cloud server and Image processing:
Host server is AWS EC2. Date, time, message status, ID, sensor value, latitude and longitude are stored in the EC2 database. A picture of the defect is taken and stored in AWS S3 bucket. Gaussian Mixture Model can be used for image processing which comes under supervised learning.

3.3.3   Experimental Setup

Gas Sensor
A gas sensor (Figure 3.3) is utilized to identify the nearness of a hazardous LPG spill in a vehicle or in a work station, stockpiling tank condition. This unit is frequently effectively fused into a caution unit, to sound an alert or give a visual sign of the LPG fixation. The sensor has excellent affectability joined with a quick repsonse time. The sensor likewise can detect iso-butane, propane, LNG and tobacco smoke.

Ultrasonic Sensor
Ultrasonic robots for break location contain transducers arranged at an alternate point to the channel divider. This guarantees ultrasonic shear waves spread along a 45° way through the divider. Both inward and outside splits mirror the vitality.

GPS
The GPS module L10 brings the superior of the MTK situating motor to the monetary norm. The L10 bolsters 210 PRN channels. This adaptable, independent recipient consol-idates a careful exhibit of highlights with adaptable availability choices. Their straightfor-ward combination prompts quick time-to-advertise during a wide determination of car, customer and modern applications.

Figure 3.3 Gas sensor.

Raspberry Pi

Raspberry Pi board (Figure 3.4) is a small wonder, pressing extensive registering power into an impression no bigger than a Mastercard. It's prepared to do some stunning things; however, there are a couple of things that the user needs to know before using it. The processor at the core of the Raspberry Pi framework is a Broadcom BCM2835 framework on-chip (SoC) interactive media processor. This implies most by far of the framework's segments, including its focal and illustrations handling units alongside the sound and interchanges equipment, are fabricated onto that solitary segment covered up underneath the 256 MB memory chip at the focal point of the board It's not simply this SoC plan that makes the BCM2835 distinctive to the processor found in a work area or PC, notwithstanding. It likewise utilizes an alternate guidance set engineering (ISA), known as ARM.

GSM Module (Global System for Mobile Communications):

GSM is an open and computerized cell innovation utilized for transmitting portable voice and information administrations works at the 850MHz, 900MHz, 1800MHz and 1900MHz recurrence groups. GSM framework was created as a computerized framework utilizing

Figure 3.4 Raspberry pi.

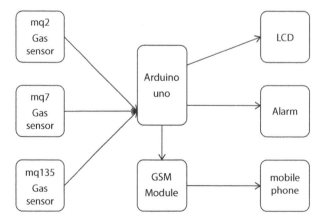

Figure 3.5 Flow diagram of the leakage detection.

time division different access (TDMA) strategy for correspondence reason. Figure 3.5 presents a flow diagram of the leakage detection.

Mobile Application:
A portable application, usually alluded to as an application, is a sort of use programming intended to run on a cell phone, for example, or tablet PC. Portable applications as often as possible serve to give clients comparative administrations to those found on PCs. Applications are commonly little, singular programming units with constrained capacity. This utilization of application programming was initially promoted by Apple Inc. Its App Store offers a large number of utilizations for the iPhone, iPad and iPod Touch.

A versatile application likewise might be known as an application, web application, online application, iPhone application or cell phone application.

3.4 Experimental Results

The trial investigation of both article recognition and following as far as subjective and quantitative is given below.

Despite the ban on manual scavenging in India, over 300 deaths due to manual scavenging were reported across the country in 2017 alone, according to a reply given by the Ministry of Social Justice and Empowerment to the Lok Sabha in December last year.

Compared with other existing methods, the proposed work is suitable for real-time applications as shown in Figure 3.6 and Figure 3.7 for complete experimental design. The proposed system observes the data second by second and immediately gives the alert when the condition is abnormal. Additionally, this framework gives an answer for the progressively changing sewer condition. This occurs since the stream of sewage water differs greatly over time also, relies upon various components, similar to water siphon condition, gas maintenance and harm to office. This framework takes account of these elements as minute-by-minute examination is open from remote areas, on account of the web checking.

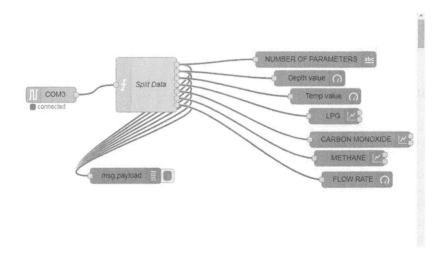

Figure 3.6 Experimental design.

Figure 3.7 Experimental design.

This empowers exact comprehension of CH4, CO and other sewer gases and their emanation from sewers and helps in measuring and powerfully changing city arranging, a component that was absent in past recommendations.

3.5 Conclusion

Many cities across the world are facing drainage system problems. Implementing this proposed system can put an end to manual scavenging and the deaths of many manual scavengers. Such a system can enhance cleanliness and reduce the number of people who get sick from sewage exposure.

The proposed system is used to detect gas leakage and cracks with the help of IOT sensors such as Arduino Uno sensor, Raspberry Pi3. Sewer gas is detected with the help of a gas sensor. An alert is given to the control room when the normal threshold level is exceeded. The proposed Tristate pattern can be used to train the sensor datas and find the risk level of the gas. A vibration sensor attached to Raspberry Pi3 can be used to detect crack and take immediate remedies.

References

1. Okolo, C. and Meydan, T., (2018). Pulsed magnetic flux leakage method for hairline crack detection and characterization. *AIP Advances*, 8(4), p. 047207.
2. Ghidoni, S., Antonello, M., Nanni, L. and Menegatti, E., (2015). A thermographic visual inspection system for crack detection in metal parts exploiting a robotic workcell. *Robotics and Autonomous Systems*, 74, pp. 351-359.
3. Maffren, T., Juncar, P., Lepoutre, F. and Deban, G., (2012). Crack detection in high-pressure turbine blades with flying spot active thermography in the SWIR range.
4. Maldague, X., Galmiche, F. and Ziadi, A., (2002). Advances in pulsed phase thermography. *Infrared Physics & Technology*, 43(3-5), pp. 175-181.

5. Kostson, E., Weekes, B., Almond, D., Wilson, J., Tian, G., Thompson, D. and Chimenti, D., (2011). Crack Detection Using Pulsed Eddy Current Stimulated Thermography. *AIP Conference Proceedings* 1335, 415 (2011); https://doi.org/10.1063/1.3591882

6. Ghidoni, S., Antonello, M., Nanni, L. and Menegatti, E., (2015). A thermographic visual inspection system for crack detection in metal parts exploiting a robotic workcell. *Robotics and Autonomous Systems*, 74, pp. 351-359.

7. Kersey, R., Staroselsky, A., Dudzinski, D. and Genest, M., (2013). Thermomechanical fatigue crack growth from laser drilled holes in single crystal nickel based superalloy. *International Journal of Fatigue*, 55, pp. 183-193.

8. Shafeek, H., Gadelmawla, E., Abdel-Shafy, A. and Elewa, I., (2004). Assessment of welding defects for gas pipeline radiographs using computer vision. *NDT & E International*, 37(4), pp. 291-299.

9. Mehrabi, P., Hui, J., Janfaza, S., O'Brien, A., Tasnim, N., Najjaran, H. and Hoorfar, M., (2020). Fabrication of SnO2 Composite Nanofiber-Based Gas Sensor Using the Electrospinning Method for Tetrahydrocannabinol (THC) Detection. *Micromachines*, 11(2), p. 190.

10. Bandyopadhyay, D. and Sen, J., (2011). Internet of Things: Applications and Challenges in Technology and Standardization. *Wireless Personal Communications*, 58(1), pp .49-69.

11. Hu, Z., Bai, Z., Bian, K., Wang, T. and Song, L., (2019). Real-Time Fine-Grained Air Quality Sensing Networks in Smart City: Design, Implementation, and Optimization. *IEEE Internet of Things Journal*, 6(5), pp. 7526-7542.

12. Lihui Lv, L., Wenqing Liu, W., Guangqiang Fan, G., Tianshu Zhang, T., Yunsheng Dong, Y., Zhenyi Chen, Z., Yang Liu, Y., Haoyun Huang, H. and and Yang Zhou, a., (2016). Application of mobile vehicle lidar for urban air pollution monitoring. *Chinese Optics Letters*, 14(6), pp. 060101-60106.

13. Kersey, R., Staroselsky, A., Dudzinski, D. and Genest, M., (2013). Thermomechanical fatigue crack growth from laser drilled holes in single crystal nickel based superalloy. *International Journal of Fatigue*, 55, pp. 183-193.

14. Li, X., Lu, R., Liang, X., Shen, X., Chen, J. and Lin, X., (2011). Smart community: an internet of things application. *IEEE Communications Magazine*, 49(11), pp. 68-75.

15. Ramos, P., Pereira, J., Ramos, H. and Ribeiro, A., (2008). A Four-Terminal Water-Quality-Monitoring Conductivity Sensor. *IEEE Transactions on Instrumentation and Measurement*, 57(3), pp. 577-583.

16. Sinha, N. and Alex, J., (2015). IoT Based iPower Saver Meter. *Indian Journal of Science and Technology*, 8(19).

17. Mukherjee, S., Pramanik, S. and Mukherjee, S., (2014). A Comprehensive Review of Recent Advances in Magnesia Carbon Refractories. Interceram - *International Ceramic Review*, 63(3), pp.90-98.

18. HU, M. and WU, G., (2008). Multiple model control algorithm based on immune system. *Journal of Computer Applications*, 28(2), pp. 297-301.

19. Fioccola, G., Donadio, P., Canonico, R. and Ventre, G., (2016). A PCE-based architecture for green management of virtual infrastructures. *Computer Communications*, 91-92, pp.62-75.

20. http://www.thehindu.com/todays-paper/tp-national/tp-tamilnadu/Their-life-clogged-with-dangers/article15322576.ece

21. http://www.thehindu.com/opinion/op-ed/deaths-in-the-drains/article5868090.ece

22. https://www.arduino.cc/reference/en/

23. http://howtomechatronics.com/tutorials/arduino/ultrasonic-sensor-hc-sr04/

24. http://www.learningaboutelectronics.com/Articles/LM35-temperature-sensor-circuit.php

25. http://www.instructables.com/id/How-to-use-MQ2-Gas-Sensor-Arduino-Tutorial/

26. https://circuits4you.com/2016/05/13/water-flow-sensor-arduino/
27. Naperalsky, M.E., Anderson, J.-H., An Upper Extremity Active Dynamic Warm-Up for Sport Participation, *Strength Cond. J.*, 34(1), 51-54, 2012. doi: 10.1519/SSC.0b013e318231f53d

4

Machine Learning for Smart Healthcare Energy-Efficient System

S. Porkodi* and Dr. D. Kesavaraja†

Department of Computer Science and Engineering, Dr. Sivanthi Aditanar College of Engineering, Tiruchendur, Tamil Nadu, India

Abstract

IoT devices have gained global interest over the last decade and are advancing in many industries in today's digital world. In the healthcare sector, a real-time remote health monitoring system has been developed with wearable IoT devices and machine learning to provide early intimation of risk and preventive measures during a time of emergency. The main problem is that if the data are stored in cloud and processed, huge network latency is required. Thus edge-cloud computing is used to reduce the network latency and the complex computations at the user end is processed by the machine learning techniques to obtain better performance. Usage of the edge computing also gives a better response in real-time computing, minimized bandwidth cost and efficient power consumption. In this chapter, smart healthcare energy-efficient systems with a machine learning framework is proposed. The healthcare system makes use of IoT devices for data acquisition and relevant information is extracted from the huge set of collected data. Front-end machine learning is used to make decisions intelligently based on the extracted information within the sensor framework. In back end, the machine learning automatically learns from the training data set samples and guidelines, which are already fed into the system, for intelligent decision-making capabilities. Thus a smart healthcare system is developed with machine learning, which is energy efficient, with reduced network latency and minimized bandwidth.

Keywords: Smart healthcare, internet of things, machine learning, energy-efficient system, edge computing

4.1 Introduction

4.1.1 IoT in the Digital Age

The Internet of Things (IoT) is basically the collection of sensors, actuators, wearables and similar things which have connectivity to the internet [29, 35]. These things are connected with each other to form a network and can communicate with each other. IoT devices have

---

**Corresponding author*: ishwaryaporkodi6296@gmail.com

†*Corresponding author*: dkesavraj@gmail.com

Suman Lata Tripathi, Dushyant Kumar Singh, Sanjeevikumar Padmanaban, and P. Raja (eds.) Design and Development of Efficient Energy Systems, (43–56) © 2021 Scrivener Publishing LLC

the capability to sense the surrounding environment and collect the data which can be processed by small computations within the IoT framework, which can lead to the development of real-time solutions. The real-time entities have their corresponding virtual entities. There also exists a communication between the virtual objects which is used to inform the real-life entities of the thing's state. This control mechanism is also present within the IoT framework.

4.1.2   Using IoT to Enhance Healthcare Services

The IoT sensors and wearables are used vastly in the world today for various healthcare applications and services. IoT devices minimize the overall cost and save the lives of patients. IoT devices can be used to monitor real-time healthcare of patients, track patient activities, and collect patients' data to provide an effective and mature solution [2]. The communication and interaction between patient and the healthcare provider becomes easier. In real-time monitoring of a patient, the wearable and sensor acquire data and sends it to the healthcare providers or doctors for monitoring health, which leads to the improvement of the treatment process [33]. IoT devices are connected with smartphones for self-monitoring of health, and also support chronic diseases management, track patient, staff and equipment, and can be used to monitor aged patients [25]. Some of the challenges in IoT devices are, IoT devices are used in telehealth and telemedicine services. For example, the wireless glucometer, which is an IoT device, collects data from the patient and monitors the level of glucose on a real time-basis and sends notification to the patient's mobile when there is a fall in the glucose level, indicating the need to take insulin. The advantages of IoT devices are monitoring remote patients, preventing unwanted hospitalization, minimizing cost, faster response time during an emergency, and effective treatment.

4.1.3   Edge Computing

Edge computing [26] brings data storage and computation closer; that is, these tasks are done within the IoT framework in the location that is nearer for the user end. It is a distributed computing, mainly designed to minimize the response time and to eliminate network latency, saving bandwidth. As the storage and computation is done in the edge nodes, data can be protected efficiently. When edge computing is coupled with machine learning technology, real-time solutions with high efficiency can be developed easily [4, 15, 39].

4.1.4   Machine Learning

Machine learning is basically the study of statistical models and algorithms with which the computer can automatically perform the specific tasks without any explicitly given human instruction. The computer relays on inference and patterns to perform the task. The training data is used to make the system learn to make decisions or predictions, thus eliminating the instructions that are programmed for performing tasks. Machine learning is currently used in a variety of industries to automate the process of decision making. For example, in the healthcare industry, machine learning is used in chronic disease management. It can, for example, predict seizures from electroencephalography data and notify the patient and healthcare provider before anything wrong occurs or it can perform a decision-making operation when an emergency situation arises [28, 38, 42].

4.1.5   Application in Healthcare

As population growth increases rapidly, the challenges to maintain patient health records and to analyze a huge amount of patient information also increase. Thus IoT and machine learning is used to automatically collect and process the huge set of data and thereby make healthcare systems more robust and dynamic. There are various applications of machine learning in the field of healthcare. These include identifying the diseases and diagnosing, smart health record systems, drug discovering and manufacturing, developing personalized medicines, emergency care, medical image diagnosis, clinical research and trails, disease outbreak prediction, etc. [16]. Some of the real-time applications are:

- Determine sudden fluctuations in blood pressure. The observed fluctuations are analyzed and checked to see if they are normal or not and the emergency alert service is activated accordingly. Real-time monitoring is necessary to find such critical data and act accordingly. The data patterns of the patients are studied with the machine learning technique.
- Closest healthcare center can be located and an ambulance can be guided there. The body sensors collect patient data which can be used to check up on the patient's health.
- Patient's body posture and movement can be deducted and used to check if a patient is in need of help. Solutions on assisted living can be developed based on these types of services.

4.2   Related Works

In 2014, Sourav, *et al.* [8] proposed a healthcare monitoring system that can be used to monitor all the sensors that could function together; the interference within the sensors are removed. Each sensor's delay in monitoring equipment and sample rate maintenance are mandatory for monitoring the healthcare system. As there are only limited resources, this system provides maintenance of best possible sampling rate and better healthcare quality. A variety of sensors are maintained simultaneously and with better quality of the data transfer, network bandwidth is used effectively.

In 2016, Vippalapalli, *et al.* [43] proposed an IoT-based smart healthcare system that collects data through wearable sensors. It is a low-cost system; the sensors are used to collect a patient's real-time healthcare data, and that data is shared among themselves, analyzed and stored. It eliminates all the inefficiencies in the manual process. The data acquisition process is carried out by a wearable device based on Audrino with Body Sensor Network. This framework is integrated to Labview for providing remote monitoring of patients. In 2016, Dinesh, *et al.* [9] proposed a hadoop framework for monitoring the healthcare of the patient based on IoT, in which big data is used for analyzing the healthcare data and generating an emergency alert when necessary. Body Sensor network (BSN) is used for extracting the critical information. A summary of the observed critical data is sent to the healthcare provider on a real-time basis, thus improving the standards of the healthcare.

In 2017, Kinthada, *et al.* [19] proposed a framework which is used for monitoring patients' medicine intake. It is used to monitor the dispensing of prescribed medicine and tracking the history of medication, including any dosage that has been missed. With the help of alarms, it sends an alert notification to the patients to take their medications. If the patient misses the dosage then a notification is sent to the healthcare provider and in times of emergency, medical staff are alerted. In 2017, Pinto, *et al.* [31] proposed an IoT-based living assistance for aged people that has the capability to monitor and store all the vital information regarding the patients' if an emergency situation arises an alarm will be triggered. This work comprises a wrist band which is connected to a cloud server for monitoring and assisting the old-aged people. It is a low-cost solution working on low power with devices that have wireless communication. In 2017, Kirttana, *et al.* [20] proposed Heart Rate Variability (HRV) monitoring systems for remote hypertensive patients based on IoT. It is designed as a user friendly and low-cost system. HRV is used for measuring the variation of the time interval that is observed between consecutive sequences of heartbeats. The analysis of HRV can be used for the deduction of diabetics, cardiovascular diseases, chronic conditions and hypertension-related diseases. HRV data are monitored to deduct these type of diseases. In the proposed work, the data acquisition is carried out by a sensor based on wireless zigbee. The collected data are used to calculate the parameters of HRV system. The collected data from the patient are transmitted by a system based on arduino to the backend server that is using an IoT protocol called MQTT. The HRV data at the server is plotted as a graph.

In 2015, Madakam, *et al.* [23] proposed an overview about the IoT, its architecture and different technologies and its usage in day-to-day life. One of the major observations in the document is that IoT has no standard definition. These technologies vary from vendor to vendor and so interoperability is needed. The architectural level requires universal standardization. No standard protocols are created for global management betterment.

In 2017, Taleb, *et al.* [37] published a survey on Mobile Edge Computing (MEC) that explores the enabling technologies. The MEC deployment considers the MEC network platform with the mobility support and individual service perspectives. The mobile edge computing reference architecture, which offers third-party, content provider and multitenncy support to the developers' application, is analyzed. In 2017, Mao, *et al.* [24] proposed a survey based on the mobile edge computing start of art technology. This proposal mainly focused on optimizing the computational resources and radio network. In 2017, Dolui, *et al.* [10] explored various edge computing types, such as Mobile Edge Computing, Cloudlet and fog computing along with the feature sets. To achieve real-time responses, edge computing becomes the research area for many researchers.

Observations from related works, in the solutions based on IoT, show the importance of context aware computing. The sensors, connectivity and computing technologies have been experiencing a bigger advancement in the past decade, thus now the focus is on developing low-cost wearables that could sense human health condition. Most of the applications in healthcare are now IoT-based systems. Many applications in real-time healthcare systems use cloud computing for computation and storage, but this has unpredictable or high network latency. Thus edge computing is preferred; it brings the data computation nearer to the user device. The usage of edge computing generates energy-efficient systems [7].

4.3 Edge Computing

4.3.1 Architecture

An extension or supplement of cloud computing is edge computing, in which the computation process is carried out nearer to the source of data, thus reducing network latency and improving the overall efficiency of the network [21]. The computation is placed on the network's edge to minimize the bandwidth that is required compared to the bandwidth that are used for cloud computing. Thus applications such as healthcare monitoring, which require critical time solution are based on edge computing since that is a computing platform that is aware of network latency. The edge computing architecture is shown in Figure 4.1. The network that is used for processing the acquired data could be Radio Access Network [13] or Local Area Network or IoT network [3]. Then processing is carried out locally in the device edge. To perform tasks with high computation, the data processed in the edge device is transmitted to the cloud and data storage takes place in the cloud [18, 22, 36].

4.3.2 Advantages of Edge Computing over Cloud Computing

When compared to cloud computing, edge computing possesses many advantages [41] including:

Spontaneous Response: Some services can be handled by edge devices at the time of the emergency, thus eliminating the delay in the transmission of data from the cloud. So the response speed is spontaneous.

Efficient Data Management: The data collected from the IoT devices can be processed at the edge device by reducing the tasks of cloud computing. Latency could be reduced and computation can be performed faster due to the low dependency on cloud computing.

Bandwidth Utilized Efficiently: Any large amount of tasks in computation can be handled by distributed nodes of edge computing, eliminating the process of data transmission to the

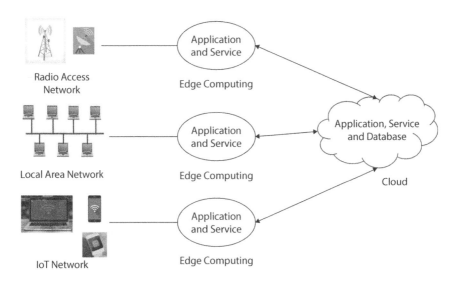

Figure 4.1 Edge computing architecture.

cloud. Thus the pressure of additional transmission in the network is eliminated and the bandwidth is utilized efficiently.

Powerful Data Storage: Backup of the data for edge devices that consist of an enormous storage area and high processing capabilities of huge data can be obtained from the cloud.

4.3.3   Applications of Edge Computing in Healthcare

The service providers are facilitated by edge computing to reach the deepest data, analytics are performed, knowledge is gathered and better decisions can be made [44]. Edge computing solves challenges (such as, security, latency, monitor and governance) extensively that are faced in various application services. The healthcare sector relies deeply on services that are fast-paced. Even a minimum latency would not be acceptable since it could stop access to vital services by patients. It has been proved that one of the pervasive challenges in the world is to ensure responsive healthcare. Edge computing can be used to achieve this as in the edge computing process the data is nearer to the source of data, thus eliminating unwanted latency. Some of the applications of edge computing [12] in healthcare applications are shown in Figure 4.2.

Self-Care by Patients: Wearable sensors, heartbeat monitoring, glucose monitoring in blood and various healthcare applications have grown common over the last decade. These sensors collect a huge amount of patient data which can be used by healthcare providers to diagnose the problem better. Also, the health of the patient can be monitored for a long time, creating an improved outcome. The problem here is to secure and handle such a huge amount of unstructured data. If these data are sent to the cloud, where it is sorted and analyzed, it would be highly difficult at the time of an emergency to provide an instant response to the patient. Thus edge computing is preferred to solve such problems [14, 40].

Rural Medicine: In rural and isolated areas it is difficult to provide quality healthcare even after the innovation of telemedicine. Since rural regions have poor internet connectivity or limited access to the internet, it is highly difficult to provide quality healthcare, and quick delivery of medicines is not possible. This can be made easier by the IoT devices combined with edge computing. IoT healthcare devices, which are small and portable, can be used to

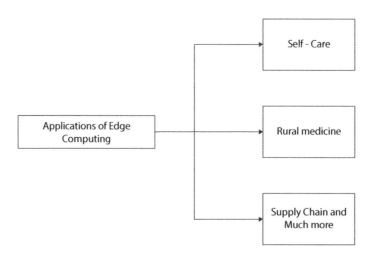

Figure 4.2 Some of the applications of edge computing.

acquire data, process, and store and analyze a patient's critical data, eliminating the need of internet connectivity. The patients using an IoT wearable can be quickly diagnosed and required measures can be taken immediately at the time of an emergency, and later the feedback or report is sent to the healthcare provider [11].

Supply Chain: There are lots of medical equipment and medical components, from the smallest bandage to expensive surgery tools assisted by robots to save lives. They are maintained properly in the supply chain; if any disruption arises then significant risk is created in patient health outcomes. Thus edge devices are equipped with sensors for managing their inventories in a potential way. The data acquired from the equipment are analyzed to predict when the hardware will fail and RFID smart tags are used for efficient inventory management. This eliminates lots of paperwork, saves time and eliminates manual ordering [17].

4.3.4   Edge Computing Advantages

Edge computing consists of a decentralized architecture of the cloud [5, 27, 34], enabling it to process the data in the network edge nearer to the source of the data. The edge computing characters that make edge computing more appropriate for applications in the healthcare sector is shown in Figure 4.3.

Spontaneous Response: As the processing of data is done on the edge devices, instant responses are produced in the services. In the healthcare industry, this is one of the lifesaving features.

Bandwidth Utilized Efficiently: as the data is processed in the edge devices, the process of data transmission to the cloud is eliminated, thus improving efficiency of the system and reducing network traffic.

Reliability: The data processing that happens nearer to the end user improves the reliability of edge computing, which is invulnerable to network outage and security threats.

Energy Efficient System: A limited amount of power supply is consumed by end devices, thus those devices are energy constrained. Edge computing brings the data computation

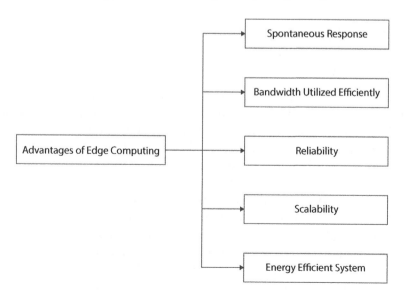

Figure 4.3 Advantages of edge computing.

nearer to the user end device. Thus usage of edge computing generates energy-efficient systems.

Scalability: Scalability in edge computing can be achieved in an uncomplicated way, which helps in increasing the count of monitoring patients with a healthcare monitoring system. The capacity of the computing can be expanded by combining the Internet of Things devices with data centers in edge to achieve scalability. If there is a new addition in the end user, no demand of substantial bandwidth is imposed on the network core since the devices of edge computing are capable for processing. The scalability feature makes the edge computing more versatile for applications in the healthcare industry.

4.3.5 Challenges

There are some challenges in edge computing [30] when the services are offered. These include: *Deployment of Edge Computing*: Physical environment and space are shortage in edge devices. So, the design is made more suitable for the environment of the application. In the edge, computing capability can be brought until the space is available.

Power Supply: Only a limited amount of power supply is consumed by end devices, thus those devices are energy constrained. The edge devices must have the capability to process at any instant of time without outages. Thus it is mandatory for edge devices to utilize the power proficiently, which improves the efficiency of the system operations.

Data Backup: All the data are acquired from the sources and the processing of data is done in edge computing. It is crucial to give protection to all the collected data by the service provider. Data access and data storage reliability are critical for adding application security.

Maintenance: As the architecture is distributive in nature, proper maintenance is necessary for a system to work better. Device failures must be sorted to prevent any disturbance in the services offered by the system.

4.4 Smart Healthcare System

4.4.1 Methodology

In the IoT framework, the network resources are prioritized and intelligently used over a trustworthy and secure transmission channel that is used for applications of the healthcare sector. The inputs are acquired from the sensors of the leaf devices in the IoT framework. The acquired inputs are preprocessed efficiently. If there is any high computation process involved, then the leaf device takes assistance from cloud servers at the backend. A large quantity of processes can be performed by backend cloud server and end devices can be advised by the backend cloud server on the preprocessing steps to give priority to the incoming data from the sensor. Data mining and machine language concepts are used at the backend for extracting the signatures from the sensor data. The healthcare interpretations are provided respectively to the captured sensor data. These steps are used by frontend devices for providing healthcare assessment of the patient.

This system can further be extended where a physician can be included at the back end to analyze the patient's healthcare data for prominent fluctuations. Thus remote diagnosis can

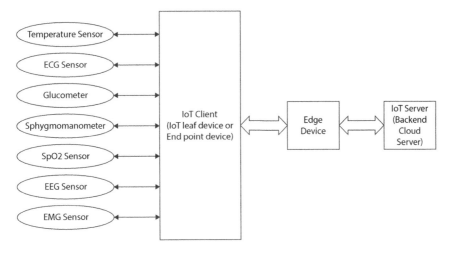

Figure 4.4 Methodology of Smart Healthcare System.

be improved and rural medication can also be provided as well, even with the healthcare provider far from the patient. The methodology of the smart healthcare system is shown in Figure 4.4.

In healthcare, low network latency, real-time responses are required. So cloud computing is not suitable in such situations because of its high network latency. Thus edge computing is proposed as a new distributive computing architecture that can perform most of the computations within the IoT edge devices instead of the cloud. In this chapter, the major focus is on combining the concepts of IoT and edge computing and improving the techniques of edge computing in the field of healthcare.

4.4.2   Data Acquisition and IoT End Device

IoT sensors and devices are used to collect the patient's healthcare data. Sensors such as temperature sensor, ECG sensor, glucometer, sphygmomanometer, SpO2 sensor, EEG sensor, EMG sensor, and body position sensor are used in the system. Glucometer is used to measure the glucose content in the patient's blood. Sphygmomanometer is mainly used for checking the blood pressure of the patient. SpO2 sensor is used to measure oxygen amounts present in the blood. EEG sensor is used to record the brain activities. EMG sensor is used to deduct the movements in the body. All these multiple sensors are connected to the leaf device or end point device, which is connected to the server at the backend via wireless network. IoT leaf device communicates with the backend server over a wireless communication medium by using IoT protocols such as Message Queuing Telemetry Transport (MQTT), Constrained Application Protocol (CoAP).

4.4.3   IoT End Device and Backend Server

Further, control messages and acquired healthcare data are exchanged between the leaf device and edge data server. The end devices send the patient's condition data collected from various sensors to the edge data server and gets instructions to perform from the backend server. The computation tasks are carried out by using various techniques like machine learning. The severs at the back end can compute any number of heavy data and uses intensive algorithms computation for processing all the data acquired from the end devices; the instructions are sent as a notification to the end device.

Data analytics are performed in real time and for achieving optimized solution with low latency edge computing is used. The computation can be done by the end IoT devices that are based on the instruction and guidelines from the edge device which is provided by the cloud server. The MQTT client runs on IoT end device while the MQTT server runs on the edge server that can also further request various services from the cloud. MQTT can also be replaced by CoAP IoT protocol as an alternative. Tensor Flow can be used for machine learning [1, 6, 32]. It is an open-source free library that consists of tools with a flexible ecosystem, community resources and libraries for building and deploying machine learning applications.

4.5 Conclusion and Future Directions

The smart healthcare system consists of IoT wearables and sensors to collect patients' healthcare data. Edge computing technology is used to extract the relevant information from the huge set of data. It is mainly used to minimize the response time, to eliminate network latency, saving bandwidth, and to provide an energy-efficient system. As the storage and computation is done in the edge nodes, data can be protected efficiently. The edge computing is coupled with machine learning technology to obtain real-time solutions with high efficiency. The machine learning is used to predict and make correct decisions in an emergency situation based on the patient's health condition and to provide early intimation of risk so that preventive measures can be taken. The usage of IoT devices and smartphones improves patient interaction and is highly useful for remote monitoring systems, caring for aged persons, managing people with chronic diseases, etc. Various self-caring applications can be developed, so that patients can monitor their own health, and the application would notify the healthcare provider or even an ambulance in the case of an emergency. The smart healthcare system adopts IoT and machine learning technologies to provide better decision making, real-time monitoring, personalized healthcare, long term care, low hospital expenses, improved hospital service, and better treatment.

In future, any emergency situation in the field of healthcare can be easily handled by smart healthcare systems. These systems are highly used to cure diabetics, many heart diseases can be predicted and prevented, home care for aged persons can be provided, the healthcare provider can be contacted anytime and anywhere for the consultation via virtual care, etc. Basically, patient-centric healthcare systems will be developed and used efficiently, which has benefits both for the healthcare providers in the hospitals and patients.

References

1. M. Abadi, P. Barham, J. Chen, Z. Chen, A. Davis, J. Dean, M. Devin, S. Ghemawat, G. Irving, M. Isard, M. Kudlur, J. Levenberg, R. Monga, S. Moore, D.G. Murray, B. Steiner, P.A. Tucker, V. Vasudevan, P. Warden, M. Wicke, Y. Yu, and X. Zhang, Tensor Flow: A system for large-scale machine learning, OSDI, 2016.

2. Aniket, The Role of IoT in Healthcare: Applications and Implementation, finoIT, https://www.finoit.com/blog/the-role-of-iot-in-healthcare-space/, 2020.

3. Y. Ai, M. Peng and K, Zhang, Edge computing technologies for Internet of Things: a primer, *Digital Communications and Networks*, Vol. 4(2), P. 77-86, 2018.

4. I. Azimi, J. Takalo-Mattila, A. Anzanpour, A.M. Rahmani, J.P. Soininen and P. Liljeberg, Empowering healthcare IoT systems with hierarchical edge-based deep learning, In IEEE/ACM International *Conference on Connected Health: Applications, Systems and Engineering Technologies (CHASE)*, IEEE, P. 63–68, 2018.

5. Z. Becvar and P. Mach Mobile Edge Computing: A Survey on Architecture and Computation Offloading, *IEEE Communications Surveys and Tutorials*, Vol. 19(3) p. 1628 - 1656, 2017.

6. L. Bote-Curiel, S. Muñoz-Romero, A. Gerrero-Curieses and J.L. Rojo-Álvarez, Deep Learning and Big Data in Healthcare: A Double Review for Critical Beginners, *Applied Science*, Vol. 9(2331), 2019.

7. L. Chen, S. Zhou and J. Xu, Energy Efficient Mobile Edge Computing in Dense Cellular Networks, *IEEE ICC Green Communications Systems and Networks Symposium*, 2017.

8. S.K. Dhar, S.S. Bhunia and N. Mukherjee, Interference Aware Scheduling of Sensors in IoT Enabled Health-Care Monitoring Systems, *Fourth International Conference of Emerging Applications of Information Technology*, P. 152 – 157, 2014.

9. P. Dineshkumar, R. SenthilKumar, K. Sujatha, R.S. Ponmagal, V.N. Rajavarman, Big data Analytics of IoT based Health Care Monitoring System, *IEEE Uttar Pradesh Section International Conference on Electrical, Computer and Electronics Engineering (UPCON)*, Indian Institute of Technology (Banaras Hindu University) Varanasi, India, P. 55 – 60, 2016.

10. K. Dolui and S.K. Datta, Comparison of edge computing implementations: Fog computing, cloudlet and mobile edge computing, *Conference on Global Internet of Things Summit (GIoTS)* P. 1-6 2017.

11. E.O. Dowd, How Edge Computing Enhances Health IT Infrastructure, HIT Infrastructure, https://hitinfrastructure.com/news/how-edge-computing-enhances-health-it-infrastructure, 2018.

12. B. Felter, 5 Use Cases You Need to Know for Edge Computing and Healthcare, Vxchnge, https://www.vxchnge.com/blog/edge-computing-use-cases-healthcare, 2019.

13. A. Garcia-Saavedra, G. Iosifidis, X. Costa-Pérez, and D.J. Leith, Joint Optimization of Edge Computing Architectures and Radio Access Networks, *IEEE Journal on Selected Areas in Communications*, P. 99, 2018.

14. T. N. Gia, I.B. Dhaou, M. Ali, A.M. Rahmani, T. Westerlund, P. Liljeberg, and H. Tenhunen, Energy efficient fog-assisted IoT system for monitoring diabetic patients with cardiovascular disease, *Future Generation Computer Systems*, Vol. 93, P. 198-211, 2019.

15. Y. Hao, Y. Jiang, M.S. Hossain, M.F. Alhamid and S.U. Amin, Learning for smart edge: cognitive learning-based computation offloading, In *Mobile Networks and Applications*, Springer, P. 1–7, 2018.

16. M. Hasan, Top 10 Potential Applications of Machine Learning in Healthcare, UbuntuPIT, https://www.ubuntupit.com/top-10-potential-applications-of-machine-learning-in-healthcare/, 2019.

17. IoT & Edge Technology: Transforming the Global Supply Chain, ACSIS, https://acsisinc.com/blog/iot-edge-technology-transforming-the-global-supply-chain/, 2020.

18. F. Jalali, S. Khodadustan, C. Gray, K. Hinton and F. Suits, Greening IoT with fog: a survey. In *2017 IEEE International Conference on Edge Computing (EDGE)*, P. 25–31, 2017.

19. M.R. Kinthada, S, Bodda, and S.B.K. Mande, eMedicare: mHealth solution for Patient Medication Guidance and Assistance, *International conference on Signal Processing, Communication, Power and Embedded System (SCOPES)*, P. 657-661, 2016.

20. R.N. Kirtana and Y.V. Lokeswari, An IoT Based Remote HRV Monitoring System for Hypertensive Patients, *IEEE International Conference on Computer, Communication, and Signal Processing*, 2017.

21. J.H. Ko, T. Na, M.F. Amir and S. Mukhopadhyay, Edge-host partitioning of deep neural networks with feature space encoding for resource-constrained internet-of-things platforms, 15th *IEEE International Conference on Advanced Video and Signal Based Surveillance (AVSS)*, IEEE, P. 1–6, 2018.

22. T. Leppänen and J. Riekki, Energy Efficient Opportunistic Edge Computing for the Internet of Things. *Web Intelligence and Agent Systems*. Vol. 17(3). 2018.

23. S. Madakam, R. Ramaswamy and Tripathi, Internet of Things (IoT): A Literature Review, *Journal of Computer and Communications*, Vol. 3, P. 164-173, 2015.

24. Y. Mao. C. You, J. Zhang, K. Huang and K.B. Letaief, A Survey on Mobile Edge Computing: The Communication Perspective. *IEEE Communications Surveys & Tutorials*, P. 9, 2017.

25. K. Matthews, 6 Exciting IoT Use Cases in Healthcare, IoTforall, https://www.iotforall.com/exciting-iot-use-cases-in-healthcare/, 2020.

26. P. Miller, What is edge computing?, The Verge, https://www.theverge.com/circuit-breaker/2018/5/7/17327584/edge-computing-cloud-google-microsoft-apple-amazon, 2018.

27. J. Mocnej, M. Miškuf, P. Papcun, I. Zolotová, Impact of Edge Computing Paradigm on Energy Consumption in IoT, *IFAC-PapersOnLine*, Elsevier, Vol. 51(6), P. 162-167, 2018.

28. N. Moghim and D.W. Corne, Predicting epileptic seizures in advance, *PLoS ONE*, Vol. 9(6), Article ID e99334, 2014.

29. J. Ocampos, The Future of IoT in 2020, Ingeniumweb, https://www.ingeniumweb.com/blog/post/the-future-of-iot-in-2020/4924/, 2020.

30. R. Parikh and V. Chemitiganti, Edge Computing: Challenges and Opportunities, Platform 9, https://platform9.com/blog/edge-computing-challenges-and-opportunities/, 2019.

31. S. Pinto, J. Cabral, T. Gomes, We-Care: An IoT-based Health Care System for Elderly People, *IEEE*, P 1378 – 1383, 2017.

32. A. Qayyum, J. Qadir, M. Bilal, and A. Al-Fuqaha, Secure and Robust Machine Learning for Healthcare: A Survey, *arXiv*: 2001.08103v1 [cs.LG], 2020.

33. J.P. Queralta, T.N. Gia, H. Tenhunen, T. Westerlund, Edge-AI in LoRa-based health monitoring: fall detection system with fog computing and LSTM recurrent neural networks. *42nd International Conference on Telecommunications and Signal Processing (TSP)*. IEEE, P. 601–604, 2019.

34. P. Raj and, J. Pushpa, Expounding the edge/fog computing infrastructures for data science, In *Handbook of Research on Cloud and Fog Computing Infrastructures for Data Science*, IGI Global, P. 1–32, 2018.

35. A. Shrimali, Influence of IoT Maturity Model in New Digital Era, DZone, https://dzone.com/articles/influence-of-iot-maturity-model-in-new-digital-wor, 2019.

36. I. Sittón-Candanedo, R.S. Alonso, Ó. García, A.B. Gil, and S. Rodríguez-González, A Review on Edge Computing in Smart Energy by means of a Systematic Mapping Study, *Electronics* 2020, Vol. 9(1), P. 48, 2019.

37. T. Taleb, K. Samdanis, B. Mada, H. Flinck, S. Dutta and D. Sabella, On Multi-Access Edge Computing: A Survey of the Emerging 5G Network Edge Cloud Architecture and Orchestration, *IEEE Communications Surveys and Tutorials*, Vol. 19(3), P. 1657 - 1681, 2017.

38. S. Tofiq and M. Mohammadi, Epileptic Seizure Detection using Deep Learning Approach, *UHD Journal of Science and Technology*, Vol. 3(41), P. 41-50, 2019.

39. A. Toor, S. ul Islam, G. Ahmed, S. Jabbar, S. Khalid and A.M. Sharif, Energy efficient edge-of things, *EURASIP Journal of Wireless Communication Network*, Vol. 2019(1), P. 82, 2019.

40. S. Taherizadeh, A.C. Jones, I. Taylor, Z. Zhao and V. Stankovski, Monitoring self-adaptive applications within edge computing frameworks: A state-of-the-art review, *Journal of Systems and Software*, Vol. 136, P. 19-38, 2018.

41. The Benefits of Edge Computing vs. Cloud Computing, https://www.rcn.com/business/insights-and-news/insights-articles/edge-computing-vs-cloud-computing/, 2020.
42. S.M. Usman, M. Usman and S. Fong, Epileptic Seizures Prediction Using Machine Learning Methods, *Comput. Math Methods Med.* 2017, doi: https://doi.org/10.1155/2017/9074759.
43. V. Vippalapalli and S. Ananthula, Internet of things (IoT) based Smart Health Care System, *International Conference on Signal Processing, Communication, Power and Embedded System (SCOPES)*, P. 1229 – 1233, 2016.
44. H. Zhangi, F. Guo and H. Ji, Combinational Auction-Based Service Provider Selection in Mobile Edge Computing Networks, Special Section on Emerging Trends, Issues and Challenges in Energy-Efficient Cloud Computing, *IEEE Access*, Vol. 5. P. 13455-13464, 2017.

5

Review of Machine Learning Techniques Used for Intrusion and Malware Detection in WSNs and IoT Devices

Dr. Jeyabharathi[1]*, **Dr. A. Sherly Alphonse[2]**, **Ms. E.L. Dhivya Priya[1] and Dr. M. Kowsigan[3]**

[1]Assistant Professor/IT, Sri Krishna College of Technology, Coimbatore, India
[2]Associate Professor/CSE, Ponjesly Engineering College, Nagercoil, India
[3]Assistant Professor/Computer Science & Engineering, SRM IST, Kattankulathur, India

Abstract

The Internet of Things (IoT) connects various devices into a network for providing smart and intelligent services. But this paves the way for hackers and security breaches. There are different security solutions based on machine learning techniques. The machine learning techniques are categorized as supervised and unsupervised techniques. Because of the heterogenous structure and the mobility of the devices used in IoT-based services, the security solutions are very difficult to implement. The resource constraints and computational capacities of the IoT-enabled applications limit the usage of various security algorithms. Intrusion is a common security breach in the IoT Services as they use Wireless Sensor Networks. Domain name system security extensions (DNSSEC) is a security solution used for device identification using Domain Name Service (DNS). But it cannot be used in IoT services because of its high computational complexity. The public key cryptography technique is a right cryptosystem, but due to its computational overhead it cannot be used in the sensor nodes used in IoT services. Thus, computational overhead is a serious challenge in implementing security solutions, and as a result, the method of implementing security approaches is an ongoing research.

Keywords: IoT devices, WSN, neural network, SVM etc.

5.1 Introduction

This chapter presents some of the solutions presented in literature for implementing security. There are different types of attacks such as goal-oriented attack, performer-oriented attack and layer-oriented attack. The layered architecture of IoT services results in attacks at different layers. Machine learning techniques are often used to analyse data. The usage of machine learning techniques for security solutions is still at an early stage. IoT services have different types of communication and different configurations of systems. The machine learning algorithms are capable of handling complex and Big data. Thus, they have the ability to provide good security

*Corresponding author: bharathi.durai@gmail.com

Suman Lata Tripathi, Dushyant Kumar Singh, Sanjeevikumar Padmanaban, and P. Raja (eds.) Design and Development of Efficient Energy Systems, (57–66) © 2021 Scrivener Publishing LLC

solutions to IoT services. This chapter presents the machine learning techniques commonly used to provide security solutions for IoT devices in literature. Also, the issues that occur while providing machine learning-based security solutions are presented in this chapter. The chapter provides the detailed procedure of implementing machine learning technique-based security solutions presented in literature. The various lightweight machine learning techniques used for intrusion detection, malware detection, anomaly detection, etc., are presented in this chapter. An analysis of the machine learning algorithms is also provided. Support Vector Machine (SVM) is the most common machine learning algorithm used in literature. SVM performs well in providing authentication, but performs poorly in detecting intrusions. Various other machine learning algorithms like Neural Networks (NN), K-Nearest Neighbor (K-NN) and Bayes Network are also used in literature. This chapter presents a detailed survey of all such machine algorithms and concludes the best algorithm for IoT services based on their performance.

5.2   Types of Attacks

The IoT is enabling devices across the whole world to interact with each other [1]. The interacting entities are from different environments. They belong to different families, countries and working environments. This leads the way to different types of attacks. In Wireless Sensor networks, there is a layered classification of the attacks. The attacks found on the physical layer are addressed as Jammers; Relay attacks, Sybil, Selective forwarding and synchronization attacks. The attacks found on the network layer are addressed as Sinkhole, unfairness, False routing, Hello and session flooding and Eaves dropping. The attacks found on the application layer are Injection and Buffer overflows. Side channel attacks, replay attacks, Traffic analysis and crypto attacks are the multi-layered attacks.

The layered classification attacks on the RFID are passive interference, Sybil attack, disabling attacks and destruction of RFID attacks. The attacks present in the network layer are Tag attacks, reader attacks and network protocol attack. The attacks present in the application layer are injection, buffer overflows, unauthorized tag reading and tag modification. The security attacks on IoT are classified as i) Physical attacks, ii) Side channel attacks, iii) Cryptanalysis attacks, iv) Software attacks, and v) Network Attacks.

Physical attacks: These types of attacks are directly performed on the hardware components. Some examples are chip destruction, reforming the layout, micro-probing, etc.

Side channel attacks: These attacks are done on the encryption devices by obtaining side channel information that is neither obtained from an information to be encrypted nor from the decrypted information. The different information like timing details and other power consuming details can be easily obtained from the encryption devices. This information can be retrieved by the attackers during side channel attacks that can be easily used to identify the key. The logic actions depend upon certain physical characteristics.

Cryptanalysis attacks: These types of attacks are performed on the cipher-text to get the plain attacks. Different types of such attacks are plaintext attack, cipher attack and man-in-the-middle attack.

Software attacks: The jamming, Trojan horses, viruses and worms cause the software attacks.

Network Attacks: The network attacks frequently attack the Wireless Sensor Networks. These attacks are known as active and passive attacks. Examples are eavesdropping and Traffic analysis. The active attacks are denial of service and node malfunction [2].

5.3   Some Countermeasures for the Attacks

Jamming: Regulated power supply and Direct Sequence Spread Spectrum are the counter-measures for jamming.

Worms and Viruses: Continuous monitoring of the network using source routing can prevent these types of worms and viruses.

Replay attacks: Time stamps and One-time passwords are the countermeasures for preventing replay attacks.

Eaves dropping: Session keys prevent eavesdropping.

Sybil: Resource testing and privilege attenuations are countermeasures.

5.4   Machine Learning Solutions

The different security components needed at different levels in an IoT-based application are given in Figure 5.1. The IoT applications are resource-constrained and this makes the way for the cyber attacks. The privacy and security risks are prevented by using the cryptographic techniques. Because of the real-time data used in the applications, machine learning techniques and deep learning techniques can provide solutions with artificial intelligence.

5.5   Machine Learning Algorithms

The fundamental algorithms in machine learning can be classified into four types mainly: supervised, semi-supervised, unsupervised and reinforcement learning algorithms [3].

Supervised Learning: There are some labelled data in the supervised learning algorithms. These labelled data are known as the training data. Certain rules are formed from the available datasets and various classes are defined. From this definition the predictions of the elements are done.

Unsupervised Learning: There is no requirement of labelled data or training set. Based upon the similarity among the data, they are classified into different groups. The supervised and unsupervised algorithms are used for data analysis problems. The reinforcement

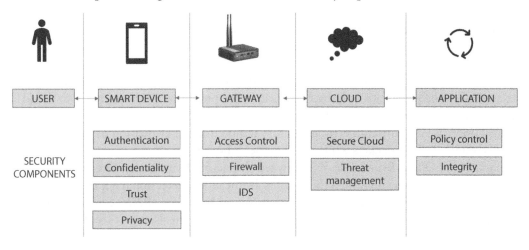

Figure 5.1 Security components.

algorithms are for the decision-making problems. Classification and regression are examples of the supervised machine learning algorithms.

The Support Vector Machine (SVM) and K-Nearest Neighbour (KNN) are the most common classification algorithms. There are also various regression algorithms like linear regression, polynomial regression and Support Vector Regression techniques.

Semi-supervised Learning: When there is no label specification for some data the best option is to use Semi-supervised learning.

Reinforcement Learning: In case of reinforcement learning the feedback obtained from the environment is used by the agent to train the system. Each action has a reward and decisions are made based on the reward. This system is based on the learning characteristics of humans. This type of learning is very useful for robotic applications. Deep learning and Deep Reinforcement learning are based upon these techniques.

Deep Learning: Deep learning is based upon Artificial Neural Networks. The neural networks are composed of neurons connected through weights. The learning is performed in the neural networks through either supervised or unsupervised learning. There are more layers in the case of deep learning. This is very helpful in distributed computing and also in the analysis of semi-supervised or unsupervised data. Deep learning is based upon the learning process of the human brain. Deep learning is very helpful in the classification or prediction applications. They are also helpful in compression of data in spatial and time domains because they are very effective in extracting patterns and features from raw data and images [1].

5.6   Authentication Process Based on Machine Learning

Conventional techniques are not able to provide authentication in case of identification attacks like Sybil attacks [2]. In physical layer authentication attacks the MAC addresses cannot provide enough security because of the computation complexities and leakage of private information.

Certain methods like physical layer authentication techniques use the hypothesis test to check the genuineness of the transmitted message using the records of the transmitter. The accuracies depend upon the test threshold. But it is difficult to set threshold for the IoT devices. These authentication techniques are based upon the Markov Decision Process. The test threshold is decided using the Reinforcement Learning Techniques.

Frank-Wolfe (dFW) and incremental aggregated gradient (IAG) [3] are the supervised learning techniques used for identifying spoofing attacks. They depend upon the RSSI and can reduce the communication overhead. Unsupervised learning techniques like IGMM are applied in the proximity-based authentication for providing Authentication to the IoT devices without the leakage of information. These authentication techniques that are based upon IGMM use a non-parametric Bayesian method, for the evaluation of the RSSIs and the Arrival time of the packets while sending the radio signals [4].

The authors Oliver Brun *et al.* [5] analyzed the network attacks in Internet of Things (IoT) gateways, and also identified the metrics for the attack detection from the packet captures. They used deep learning using Random Neural Networks (RNN) for the identification of the attacks. The empirical validation of the attack is done. Using a threshold detector, the accuracies are compared.

The concept of dense structured ganglia was used in creating dense RNN. The Dense RNN has a dense structure of a number of identical cells. The architecture used in DRNN is as follows. The first layer is made up of RNN cells. The further layers are hidden layers having dense clusters that receive the output from the previous layer. The last layer is known as RNN-ELM (Random Neural Networks-Extreme Learning Machine) (RNN-ELM).

If there is a dataset then the weights are determined using both supervised and unsupervised learning. The software installed on the gateway captured the data packets and analyzed. There is a tool called 'Scapy' which is used for packet manipulations. It can capture and decode the packets. It can scan, trace-route the packets.

Secure signal authentication [6] is one of the vital problems of security due to its man-in-the-middle attacks and the large scalability. Aidin Ferdowsi *et al.* proposed a novel algorithm based upon watermarking for the detection of cyber attacks. This is based upon deep learning long short-term memory (LSTM) architecture. The stochastic features are created from the signal and then later watermarked into signal. Thus, the signals are authenticated in IoT devices. The mixed-strategy Nash equilibrium (MSNE) is needed to be derived. Deep Reinforcement Learning (DRL) takes the decision and authenticates the IoT devices. The messages transmitted using this approach have good reliability.

A DRL algorithm is used in a deep network and reinforcement learning to decide the best action. In order to perform an action that has maximum utility, Q-learning algorithm, which is a special form of RL, is used. A state value functions has the expected return calculated from gateway when performing an action from a particular state.

There are also evolutionary techniques-based Intrusion Detection Systems in literature [7]. In most of the classification algorithms, the training and the testing data must be in the same feature space and have the same distribution. But in most real-world applications, this may not happen as the training and the testing data may belong to a different feature space and have different distributions. Therefore, in such applications the concept of knowledge transfer [8, 9] will be able to achieve the objective. The transfer learning can be used for classification, clustering and regression problems.

Botnet attacks in IoT applications are a major threat to security [10]. Botnet attacks pave the way for other attacks like Distributed Denial of Service attacks (DDoS), spying of organization and identity theft. In the case of the prevention of botnet attacks the neural networks perform well when compared to other methods. But there is a need of large amounts of data that is not possible in the case of real-time applications. The unsupervised method like clustering does not require a larger training data, but has a low accuracy when compared to the supervised algorithms. In case of RNN methods there is no need of manual feature extraction but it needs a large amount of training data.

The Distributed Denial of Service attacks cause the website and the server to be unavailable to users. It is very much different from the other security threats. It creates a temporary shutdown of the server. It is different from other cyber threats that breach security parameters; the features should be carefully chosen in order to avoid the security threats. If a larger number of irrelevant features is selected it will create computational overhead. The ensemble feature selection algorithm provides good results in such cases. The ensemble algorithm along with the threshold provides good performance. The features that are selected used as input for a classification algorithm provide good results in less amount of time. A multi-layer perceptron provides good results when used as the classifier in the final stage.

5.7   Internet of Things (IoT)

Internet of things (IoT) is to improve the speed of the process. It connects all the computing devices digitally. These devices are embedded with internet connectivity, sensors and other hardware that allow communication and control via the web. IoT-based applications are worked under the network strategy. So commonly, all the attacks under network are also affected by IoT.

5.8   IoT-Based Attacks

5.8.1   Botnets

A botnet is a system of frameworks consolidated together with the end goal of remotely taking control and disseminating malware. Constrained by botnet administrators by means of Command-and-Control-Servers (C&C Server), they are frequently utilized by criminals for activities such as taking private data, misusing web-based financial information, DDos-assaults or for spam and phishing messages. With the ascent of the IoT, numerous articles and gadgets are at risk for, or are as of now being a piece of, alleged thingbots—botnets that consolidate autonomous associated objects. Botnets, like thingbots, comprise a wide range of gadgets, all associated with one another—from PCs, cell phones and tablets to now additionally those "shrewd" gadgets. For all intents and purposes, these things share two fundamental qualities: they are internet empowered and they can move information consequently by means of a system. Hostile to spam innovation can spot pretty dependably in the event that one machine sends a large number of comparable messages; however, it's significantly harder to spot if those messages are being sent from different gadgets that are a piece of a botnet. They all have one objective: sending a huge number of email solicitations to an objective with the expectation that the stage crashes while battling to adapt to the colossal measure of solicitations.

5.8.2   Man-in-the-Middle

This idea is the place an assailant or programmer is hoping to hinder and rupture inter-changes between two separate frameworks. It very well may be a hazardous assault since it is one where the assailant furtively catches and transmits messages between two gath-erings when they are under the conviction that they are discussing straightforwardly with one another. As the aggressor has the first correspondence, the recipient can be fooled into believing they are getting a genuine message. Numerous cases have just been accounted for inside this risk territory, instances of hacked vehicles and hacked "keen fridges". These assaults can be incredibly risky in the IoT, as a result of the idea of the "things" being hacked. For instance, these gadgets can be anything from mechanical apparatuses, hardware, or vehi-cles to harmless associated "things," for example, savvy TVs or carport entryway openers.

5.9   Information and Identity Theft

While the news is brimming with frightening and capricious programmers getting to infor-mation and cash with a wide range of great hacks, we are often additionally our own greatest security adversary. Thoughtless supervision of internet-associated gadgets (for example, cell phone, iPad, Kindle, smartwatch, and so on) allows entry to the schemes of noxious cheats and artful discoverers. The principle system of wholesale fraud is to gather information—and with a tad of persistence, there is a great deal to discover. General information accessible on the internet, joined with online life data, in addition to information from brilliant watches, wellness trackers and, if accessible, savvy meters, keen ice chests and a lot more give an incredible all-round picture of a person's life. The more subtleties that can be found about a client, the simpler and the more modern can be an assault based on data fraud.

5.10   Social Engineering

Social building is the demonstration of how to control individuals so they surrender classified data. The kinds of data that crooks are looking for can differ, but when people are the target, the criminals are normally attempting to hoodwink the individual into giving them passwords or bank data. Or on the other hand, they could be attempting to get to a PC so as to furtively introduce malevolent software that will at that point give them access to individual data, and give them authority over the PC. Commonly, social designing hacks are done through phishing messages, which try to get people to reveal their data, or sidetrack them to sites like banking or shopping locales that look authentic, luring the individual into entering their personal information.

5.11   Denial of Service

A Denial of Service (DoS) assault happens when a URL that would typically work is inaccessible. There can be numerous purposes behind inaccessibility, yet it as a rule it alludes to foundation that can't adapt because of limit over-burden. In a Distributed Denial of Service (DDoS) assault, countless frameworks malignantly assault one objective. This is often done through a botnet, where numerous gadgets are modified (often unbeknownst to the proprietor) to demand assistance simultaneously.

In contrast with hacking assaults like phishing or savage power assaults, DoS doesn't for the most part attempt to take data or prompt security misfortune; however, the loss for the influenced organization can cost a great deal of time and cash. Often clients likewise choose to change to a competitor, as they dread security issues or basically can't stand to have accessibility issues. Often a DoS assault suits activists and blackmailers.

5.12   Concerns

A significant worry about the IoT is the affirmation of protection. By what method will shopper information be utilized and by whom? A situation where a person's home, office, vehicles, apparatuses, office hardware and numerous different gadgets are associated with the internet raises new worries for purchasers and organizations about where their information will go and how, obviously, it will be utilized. Organizations should assess the approaches for protection and information security and guarantee gathered information is shielded and kept private. Just when organizations begin doing this, there will be confirmations of security.

While businesses are probably going to be confronted with various sorts of assaults over time, the primary objective isn't to get diverted by the endeavor of the week. Instead, businesses should put their time and cash in a strong security structure, center around the most widely recognized assaults, and offer standard preparations to their staff to guarantee they can spot assaults when they occur. When businesses concentrate on the dangers that lurk in IoT, they are well on the way to enhancd security. The responses to security concerns are out there: as expanded security, validation and the executives of information.

5.13 Conclusion

This chapter identifies the different types of attacks and the IoT authentication processes. When the RL techniques are used they evaluate the reward for each action. At the beginning of the learning process there will be more wrong actions. There will be security disaster, if they are used in the IoT devices. A good solution is transfer learning, which analyzes with the help of data mining and therefore avoids random exploration. This avoids the bad actions that happen normally in the beginning of a learning process. Also, most of the existing machine learning algorithms have high computational cost and computation overhead. They also require a large amount of training data to get good accuracy. The deep learning methods normally achieve good accuracy, but they have several layers of neurons. They require a larger training data set and also consume huge amounts of time. Also, if it is a supervised or an unsupervised Machine K-learning algorithm, a high accuracy is not guaranteed all the time. In order to achieve that, some back-up solutions are needed in the case of IoT-based applications.

References

1. Hussain F, Hussain R, Hassan SA, Hossain E. Machine Learning in IoT Security: Current Solutions and Future Challenges. arXiv preprint arXiv:1904.05735. 2019 Mar 14.
2. Xiao L, Wan X, Lu X, Zhang Y, Wu D. IoT security techniques based on machine learning. arXiv preprint arXiv:1801.06275. 2018 Jan 19.
3. Xiao L, Wan X, Han Z. PHY-layer authentication with multiple landmarks with reduced overhead. *IEEE Transactions on Wireless Communications*. 2017 Dec 22;17(3):1676-87.
4. L. Xiao, Q. Yan, W. Lou, G. Chen, and Y. T. Hou, "Proximity-based security techniques for mobile users in wireless networks," *IEEE Trans. Information Forensics and Security*, vol. 8, no. 12, pp. 2089–2100, Oct. 2013.
5. Brun O, Yin Y, Gelenbe E. Deep learning with dense random neural network for detecting attacks against iot-connected home environments. *Procedia Computer Science*. 2018 Jan 1;134:458-63.
6. Ferdowsi A, Saad W. Deep learning for signal authentication and security in massive internet-of-things systems. *IEEE Transactions on Communications*. 2018 Oct 25;67(2):1371-87.
7. E. M. Shakshuki, N. Kang, and T. R. Sheltami, "EAACK — a secure intrusion-detection system for MANETs," *IEEE Transactions on Industrial Electronics*, vol. 60, no. 3, pp. 1089–1098, 2013.

8. Xiao L, Wan X, Lu X, Zhang Y, Wu D. IoT security techniques based on machine learning. arXiv preprint arXiv:1801.06275. 2018 Jan 19.

9. S. J. Pan and Q. Yang, "A survey on transfer learning," *IEEE Trans. Knowledge and Data Engineering*, vol. 22, no. 10, pp. 1345–1359, Oct. 2010.

10. Bansal A, Mahapatra S. A comparative analysis of machine learning techniques for botnet detection. In *Proceedings of the 10th International Conference on Security of Information and Networks* 2017 Oct 13 (pp. 91-98). ACM.

11. Singh KJ, De T. Efficient classification of DDoS attacks using an ensemble feature selection algorithm. *Journal of Intelligent Systems*. 2017.

6

Smart Energy-Efficient Techniques for Large-Scale Process Industries

B Koti Reddy[1]* and N V Raghavaiah[2]

[1]Dept. of Atomic Energy, Govt. of India and Dept. of Electronics and Electrical Engg., Lovely Professional University, Jallandhar, India
[2]Dept. of Atomic Energy, Govt. of India and Dept. of Mechanical Engg., National Institute of Technology, Warangal, India

Abstract

Globally, with an increase in electrical power demands and the need of a variety of process equipment, industries emphasize two important issues, namely Energy conservation and Environment protection in the production process systems in large industries. Keeping these points as key factors, industries adopt various energy-efficient systems like modifying the electrical and mechanical equipment, processes and their sub-systems, introducing smart devices with Internet of Things (IOT) to have better process control and to optimize the industrial operation parameters. The International Energy Agency (IEA) estimated that 50% of the world's electricity is being consumed by only four main equipments, viz., motors, air conditioners, refrigerators, and lighting. It is clear that there is lot of scope for energy conservation in these areas. All of this electrical equipment will be discussed in detail with respect to energy-saving components in each of them and the application of digital technology and IoT in large-scale process industries.

Keywords: Energy efficiency, LED lighting, VFD, heat exchanger, induction motor, BLDC fan motor, IoT, VAR

6.1 Pumps Operation

A centrifugal pump is a purely mechanical device designed to raise the energy level of liquid or to move from one point to another by means of the transfer of rotational energy of its rotating component, called impeller, in a stationary casing. Impeller rotational energy is imparted by its connected prime mover like an electrical motor or diesel engine or steam turbine or wind or tidal power. These pumps were developed about 500 years ago and some have been commercially available for 300 years for industries.

---

*Corresponding author: kotireddy1965@gmail.com

Suman Lata Tripathi, Dushyant Kumar Singh, Sanjeevikumar Padmanaban, and P. Raja (eds.) Design and Development of Efficient Energy Systems, (67–100) © 2021 Scrivener Publishing LLC

6.1.1   Parts in a Centrifugal Pump

Any centrifugal pump has essentially the following main parts, as shown in Figure 6.1.

A centrifugal pump is classified under the roto-dynamic pumps or dynamic pressure pumps category. An impeller is a circular disc with a built-in passage for liquid flow. In these type of pumps, liquid enters the impeller axially at its center and moves out in a radial direction towards the discharge. The importance of the centrifugal pump is its compact and symmetrical design. They are efficient for heads up to 60 m in single stage. The discharge decreases with increase in delivery head. They can develop a definite maximum amount of head for a particular speed. Efficiency may vary from 40% to 90%, but if they are accurately selected as per duty cycle optimum range is over 60% [1].

Pumps may be operated with flooded suction or suction from lower elevation with in-built suction vessel or priming chambers. These vessels may be designed with suitable design code. To avoid breakdowns, proper methodology may be implemented such as preventive maintenance, condition-based maintenance, reliability centered maintenance and complete overhauling [2].

Pump performance can be read from various characteristic curves drawn taking the parameters like head (H), power (P), efficiency (n), net positive suction head (NPSH), net positive suction head required (NPSHR), impeller diameter (D), viscosity (μ), speed (N), specific speed (Ns) against capacity (Q) i.e., discharge rate of pump. Normally manufacturers supply a set of curves for the pump impeller diameter as shown in Figure 6.2.

6.1.2   Pump Efficiency

In most industries, pumps may run inefficiently because of oversized pumps installed to allow for future increase in capacity, other design factors chosen at the expense of pump efficiency when energy cost was low, or conservative design factors used to ensure the pump would meet the required conditions, whereas present operating conditions may be

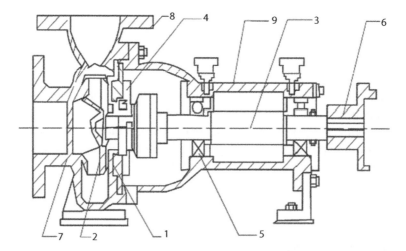

Figure 6.1 Pump cross section (Source: Horizontal centrifugal pump, DMPF) 1. Casing, 2. Impeller, 3. Shaft, 4. Stuffing box, 5. Bearings, 6. Coupling, 7. Suction connection, 8. Discharge connection, 9. Bearing housing.

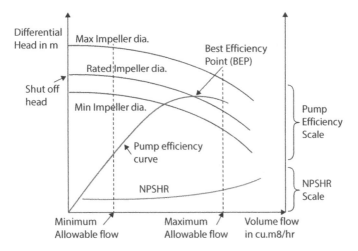

Figure 6.2 Pump impeller diameter characteristic curves (Source: www.enggcyclopedia.com).

different from the design conditions. This change often occurs after an industry has undertaken a water or energy conservation program. Trimming of large-sized centrifugal pump impellers to suit the operating conditions of flow, head and power characteristics and also to eliminate the throttling of valves for reduction in head loss across disc, etc., are helping in achieving energy-efficient industrial processes.

Impeller trimming is to be done to match the operating conditions of the system by reducing its diameter. The circumferential speed at the impeller outlet will get reduced. Trimming of impeller results in a change in outlet angle of the vane, length as well as the width of the impeller at the outlet.

For a given speed of impeller, variation in pump performance due to change in impeller diameter is given by the law of similitude (6.1),

$$\frac{D1}{D2} = \frac{Q1}{Q2} = \frac{\sqrt{H1}}{\sqrt{H2}} = \frac{\sqrt[3]{P1}}{\sqrt[3]{P2}} \qquad (6.1)$$

Where D1, H1, P1, Q1 are diameter, head, power, capacity respectively before trimming and D2, H2, P2, Q2 are corresponding values after trimming the impeller.

Under constant speed condition, simultaneous reduction of head and flow rate by throttling is not possible. Reduction of outside impeller diameter is simple and hydraulically effective for reducing both head and flow rate without changing impeller speed. Impeller trimming is mostly carried on single vane and diagonal type within narrow limits. Realistic data shows that a reduction of impeller diameter greater than 15% of the original diameter should not be allowed and keeping safety margins in mind that the trim cut of 70% of mathematical calculation of what we obtain from law of similitude.

Suppose as an example under constant speed (1480 RPM) of an impeller with in-built original diameter (D1) 400 mm with head developed at 40 m. Now a change in system requirement is required to supply the same quantity of liquid at a head of 36 m. To meet this condition, it is planned to reduce impeller diameter without reducing the speed of impeller.

Table 6.1 Details of Case Studied Pump.

Description	Before trimming	After trimming
Impeller diameter	400 mm	385.3 mm
Head developed	40 m	36 m
Speed	1480 RPM	1480 RPM
Flow rate	System requirement by more throttling discharge valve.	System requirement by less throttling discharge valve.
Power	Wasted across discharge valve.	Got reduced due to trimmingby 11.6%.

Solution:

H1 = 40 m, H2 = 36m, D1 = 0.4m
From laws of similitudes,

$$\frac{H1}{H2} = \left(\frac{D1}{D2}\right)^2 \tag{6.2}$$

D2 = 0.379m
Reduction in diameter = 0.021m
% reduction in diameter = 5.25%
By considering safe margin with 70% of reduction on affinity laws, is 0.0147 m
New diameter is 0.4-0.0147 = 0.3853m or 385.3 mm.

The brief details of results are shown in Table 6.1.

Hence as per system requirement, excess diameter of impeller can be trimmed to a limiting value of 15% of in-built size keeping a safe margin of 70% of reduction on affinity laws. This limitation can be overcome by providing a Variable Frequency Drive (VFD) on motor for getting variable speed drives on pumps. The affinity laws for constant impeller diameter with variable speeds are related by the following equation (6.3).

$$\frac{N1}{N2} = \frac{Q1}{Q2} = \frac{\sqrt{H1}}{\sqrt{H2}} = \frac{\sqrt[3]{P1}}{\sqrt[3]{P2}} \tag{6.3}$$

6.1.3   VFD

A VFD is used to switch a Motor on or off, reduce starting current, and control speed, torque, and change direction of rotation; it saves a huge amount of energy on the order of 10 to 30% during lower load demand. The VFD as shown in Figure 6.3 is basically a converter-inverter device in which the control board, basically either a Microprocessor-based or Digital Signal Processor (DSP), adjusts the firing angle of Power Electronic Devices to get the desired output of voltage and frequency.

With the growing demand for energy-efficient equipment universally, VFDs are gaining momentum, and it is estimated that the global VFD market is to post a Combined Annual Growth Rate (CAGR) of around 5% during 2019-2023 [3]. There are certain apprehensions about control, maintenance, and troubleshooting of complex electronic circuits of VFDs [4]. These problems can be overcome by IoT. However, the VFD population is to be limited to 25% of the total load of any industry to keep harmonics and their security in limits.

The advent of IoT (Internet of Things) will further increase the use of VFDs very conveniently to save energy. As per IEEE, IoT is, "A network of items, each embedded with sensors, which are connected to the internet" [5]. The technique of IoT, having a wide-range of network controls, can be incorporated into VFDs to monitor and control the VFDs with the help of Wi-Fi, Internet, etc. Use of IoT in industries, known as Industrial Internet of Things (IIoT) will make not only for ease of operation, but also maintenance of VFDs. The IIoT technique will remotely monitor the performance of VFDs and correct it in advance as and when required, without allowing it to go for a breakdown. The IIoT also allows for the upgrading of the software, attends to preventive maintenance and maintains the history records of VFD. VFDs, being the globally significant energy-efficient equipment, are now working with IOT, which is in line with the industrial revolution RI 4.0. Now the future industries have to depend on ABCDs of automation and communication, i.e., Artificial Intelligence (AI), Blockchain technology, Cloud computing and Data mining. VFDs are widely used in power generation, oil and gas sector, water treatment plants, pharmaceutical industries, mining, paper and many other manufacturing industries.

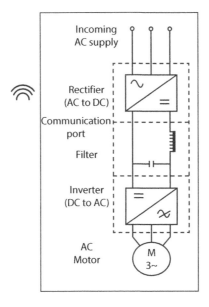

Figure 6.3 Motor with VFD.

6.1.4   VFD and Pump Motor

Induction Motors (IM) are robust equipment in any process industry and do a faithful job of driving their coupled loads of mostly either a pump or compressor. AC Induction Motors consume almost 40% of the world's generated power. The main drawback of an Induction Motor is lower efficiency at reduced loads, which can be offset by lower speed. The speed (N) of a three-phase Induction Motor can be adjusted by changing either number of poles (P) or supply frequency (f) as in (6.4).

$$N \propto \frac{f}{P} \tag{6.4}$$

Since the pole-changing method can give the speed in fixed steps with higher core losses due to large number of poles, the only option left is adjusting frequency. The frequency can be adjusted with the help of power electronics, and the speed controller is known as Variable Frequency Drive (VFD) or Variable Speed Drive (VSD). Electrical motors fed from power electronic drives have great potential not only in energy savings, but for reliable performance. In case of centrifugal pumps, the affinity law specifies the relation between Speed and HP.

$$\text{Horsepower (HP)} = \text{Flow (Q)} \times \text{Head (H)} \tag{6.5}$$

$$\text{where } Q \propto N \tag{6.6}$$

$$\text{and } H \propto N^2 \tag{6.7}$$

$$\therefore \qquad HP \propto N^3 \tag{6.8}$$

Hence it is the best option to adjust the supply frequency (f), in turn speed, to control the flow instead of traditional valve throttling, which saves a huge amount of power, as shown in Figure 6.4.

The pump curve is shown in Figure 6.5.

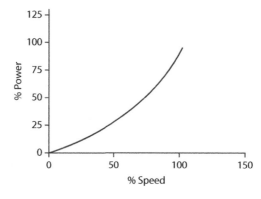

Figure 6.4 Power and speed relationship.

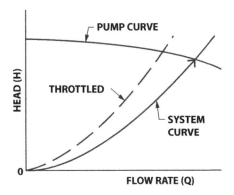

Figure 6.5 Pump curve.

For LV Induction Motors (up to 200 KW and 480V rating), it is preferable to incorporate VFD directly for control and energy savings. In the case of HV Induction Motors (above 200 KW and 6.6 KV), the MV VFD option is very complex, hence it is preferable to convert the same into LV Induction Motor (up to 400KW) and incorporate VFD.

6.1.5   Large HT Motors

In the case of high-powered HV Induction Motors, it can be implemented by adding a Transformer as shown in Figure 6.6.

6.1.6   Smart Pumps

Use of technology reduces errors with a new generation of infusion devices called smart pumps. It reduces medication errors, improves workflow, and provides a new source of data for continuous quality improvement (CQI). One of the benefits of using smart pumps was intercepting errors such as the wrong flow rate, improper dose, and pump setting mistakes. Other advantages include less adverse drug events, system improvements and total cost effectiveness. The basic concept of smart pump operation, with the key benefits, is shown in Figure 6.7.

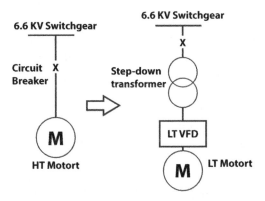

Figure 6.6 Retrofitted HT motor with LT motor and VFD.

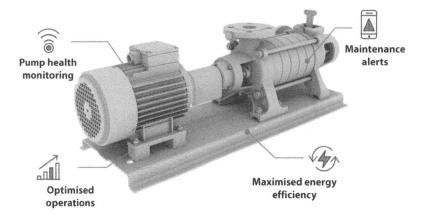

Pump health monitoring

Maintenance alerts

Optimised operations

Maximised energy efficiency

Figure 6.7 Smart Industrial pump concept.

These pumps are being widely used in medical fields, drug manufacturing and hospitals. In future this technology may be adopted for fine tuning of pump parameters in industries.

6.2   Vapour Absorption Refrigeration System

Refrigeration can be defined as a process of cooling and maintaining the temperature of objects or products at a value lower than its surrounding temperature. The history of refrigeration may be traced back 3,000 years when the Greeks and Romans harvested ice from the Alps Mountains for use in ice houses. In the Indian sub-continent, water-soaked mats were hung across windows and doors to provide cooling by evaporation during dry hot weather.

6.2.1   Vapour Compression Refrigeration

In the 1850s, a much advanced vapour compression refrigeration (VCR) system was developed. The basis of Vapour compression refrigeration system is the ability of certain liquid refrigerants to absorb enormous quantities of heat energy as they vaporize. Advantages of this system are that the refrigerating effect can be started or stopped at will, the rate of cooling can be predetermined and the vapourising temperatures can be governed by controlling the pressure at which the liquid vapourises. The vapour can be readily collected and condensed back into liquid state so that same liquid can be recirculated to obtain refrigeration effect. Thus, the vapour compression system employs a liquid refrigerant which evaporates and condenses readily. Basic components of a vapor compression refrigeration system are shown in Figure 6.8.

Compressor (1) normally, is a motor-driven equipment. It sucks vapor refrigerant from the evaporator and compresses to a high pressure. Condenser (2) receives high pressure and high temperature vapor refrigerant and condensed into liquid form using cooling media such as air or water. The high pressure liquid refrigerant is throttled down to evaporator pressure by an expansion valve (3). The metered refrigerant flow from the expansion valve enters evaporator (4), a cooling chamber in which products are placed. After absorbing heat from products, the refrigerant vapors leaves for compressor.

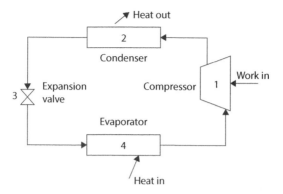

Figure 6.8 Basic componets of VCR.

The refrigerants used in VCR systems of industries up to 1990 are Chlorofluorocarbons (CFC). These refrigerant CFCs, the first generation of refrigerant gases, are capable of depleting the ozone and cause global warming. These CFCs are considered the worst refrigerants for VCR systems in terms of environmental impact. Various international protocols emphasize the phasing out of these CFCs to protect the environment.

6.2.2 Vapour Absorption Refrigeration

Phasing out ozone-depleting substances and using low-grade thermal energy in place of high-grade electrical energy is made possible by implementing Vapour Absorption Refrigeration (VAR), as shown in Figure 6.9.

VAR system uses Lithium Bromide as absorbent and water as refrigerant in place of Vapor Compression (VC) Refrigeration systems which use environment-harming chlorofluorocarbon refrigerant substances. Absorption Chillers have very low Power Consumption and virtually eliminate dependency on electrical power. These systems are environmentally friendly and need relatively low maintenance. This can be applied to process Cooling, air-conditioning, hot water requirements up to 80°C and is also useful with cogeneration applications.

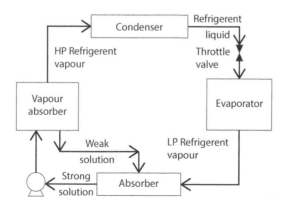

Figure 6.9 VAR system.

In a vapor compression system the motive force that circulates the refrigerant through the system is provided by a compressor, whereas in a vapor absorption system this force is provided by an absorber and generator. The vapour absorption system was invented by Ferdinand Carre, a French engineer. In this system the low-pressure vapour coming out of the evaporator is first absorbed in an appropriate absorbing liquid and is thus converted into liquid form. This process is similar to condensation where refrigerant vapor loses heat. The next step is to elevate the pressure of the liquid out of the pump. Lithium Bromide (Li-Br) vapour absoption system uses water as refrigerent and Li-Br, a highly higroscopic salt is used as an absorbent. The vapour generator and condenser are at relatively high pressure compared to Evaporator and absorber. In the generator, the solution of lithium bromide and water is heated by means of steam or solar energy. Water, the refrigerant leaves to condenser and absorbent returns to absorber unit. Further process is similar to VCR.

Advantages of VAR over VCR:

- Phasing out of CFCs
- Operates on low-grade heat energy
- System is not affected by load variations
- High-capacity units in the order of thousands of tons of refrigeration can be built

Table 6.2 Major differences between VCR and VAR.

Description	Vapour Compression Refrigeration (VCR)	Vapour Absorption Refrigeration (VAR)
Energy input	Takes in high grades as electrical or mechanical energy for its operation	Takes in low-grade energy as waste heat from the furnace, exhaust steam or solar heat for its operations
Working principle	Refrigerant vapor compression	Refrigerant absorbed and heated
Type of the energy supplied	Mechanical work supply to the compressor	Heat energy supply to the generator
Input work required	More compression work is required	Less mechanical energy is required to run pump
COP	High (Approx. 4.2)	Low (Approx. 1.4)
Capacity	Limited up to 1000 tons for single compressor	It may be above 1000 tons
Noise	More	Quiet operation
Leakage	More leakage due to high pressure	Almost no Leakage
Operating cost	High because of compressor consumes more work	Less because of less heat energy is required
Suitable refrigerant	R-12, R-22	Lithium Bromide–water, water-Ammonia

- Uses eco-friendly refrigerant water
- As the total system works on low pressure, there is no danger of bursting of piping and equipment.

The major differences between VCR and VAR are listed in Table 6.2.

6.3   Heat Recovery Equipment

Waste Heat Recovery (WHR) is an energy recovery system that transfers heat from a process outlet which is at high temperature to another part of the process at low temperature for some useful purpose. The aim is to increase overall efficiency by reusing heat that would otherwise be disposed of or simply released into the atmosphere. This acts as a tool involved in the cogeneration process. By recovering this heat, industries can reduce energy costs and greenhouse emissions.

The idea of waste heat recovery is mainly from the sensible heat contained in waste fluids, i.e., gases and liquids generated from various industrial manufacturing processes, as steam blowdowns/hot water/exhaust gases from Diesel Generator (DG) Sets/Turbines/Industrial Process liquids. This recovered heat is used for generation of steam, process heating and power generation as applicable.

6.3.1   Case Study

In one of the industries, process outlet 200 m³/h as drain is going out at a temperature of 75°C. Before discharging out this plant drain to outside, the temperature is brought down to 40°C to meet pollution control norms by mixing with normal water and further by allowing to cool in ponds with cooling towers and mist cooling system. The heat energy going to waste in this system is calculated as (200/(60/60) ×1000×4.2×35) = 8167 kJ/s.

The process feed water of the same industry, at a flow rate of 160 m³/h being heated from 30°C to 70°C using steam. The required heat input for this feed water heating is (160/(60/60) ×1000×4.2×40) = 7467 kJ/s.

The required energy for heating the feed water is catered by the introduction of heat exchanger using process outlet drain. A schematic representation is shown in Figure 6.10.

Installation of heat recovery equipment like heat exchangers recovers thermal energy from the fluids that are being discharged as waste, i.e., waste heat can be recovered from relatively high temperature effluents for heating other process fluids. Waste heat recovery

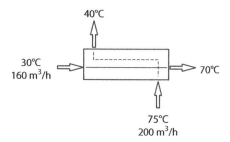

Figure 6.10 WHR scheme.

methods include capturing and transferring the waste heat from a process with a gas or liquid back to the system as an extra energy source. The energy source can be used to create additional heat or to generate electrical and mechanical power. The same can be used for heat source for hot water-based refrigeration and air-conditioning systems in the industry.

6.3.2   Advantages of Heat Recovery

The main advantages of heat recovery system are as follows:

- Waste reduction
- Energy Conservation
- Increased efficiency
- Reduction in plant operating cost
- Pollution control

6.4   Lighting System

6.4.1   Technical Terms

The main technical terms used in this section are briefly summarized here:

i.   Luminous Flux is the perceived power of light.
ii. Illuminance is the luminous flux incident on a surface per unit area ans is measured in lux.

$$1 \text{ lux} = 1 \text{ l/m}^2$$

iii. LE: Luminous efficacy is the Luminous per unit input power, (l/w).
iv. Color Rendering Index (CRI): It is a measure of the degree to which the colours of surfaces illuminated by a given light source conform to those of the same surfaces under a reference illuminent. Day light will have CRI of above 90.
v.   **BEE**: The Bureau of Energy Efficiency is an agency of the Government of India, whose function is to develop programs which will increase the conservation and efficient use of energy in India.
vi. **EEI** = Pcor/Pref = Rated power/Reference power obtained from useful luminous flux.   (6.9)
vii. **Energy Star**: It is a program run by the U.S. Environmental Protection Agency which promotes energy efficiency in the USA.

6.4.2   Introduction

According to an IEA study 2017; lighting, which is essential in human life, consumes 19% of global electricity. In India, the figure is 20% [5]. There is lot of scope for improving its efficiency. It contribute a lot to the peak load of any country. There are various types of lamps in the market and their details are shown in Table 6.3 [6].

Table 6.3 Type of lamps.

S. No.	Type	Average efficacy (l/w)	CRI (%)	Rated average life (hours)
1	Incandescent	14	99	1000
2	Fluorescent	50	49-96	5000
3	Metal Halide	75	65-96	6000
4	HPMV	70	60	5000
5	HPSV	90	21-65	12000
6	LED	102*	92	>50000
7	Halogen	20	99	2000
8	Induction	90	80**	>50000
9	CFL	60	82-96	8000-10000

*Attaining 120 l/w as of date and expected to reach higher values in future.
**Immature technology as well as of date, but offers uniform lighting unlike focused from LEDs, but contains toxic mercury.

6.4.3   LED Lighting

They are the most energy-efficient lights as of date and do not contain any toxic mercury, unlike fluorescent lamps. BEE star ratings w.e.f 1.1.2018 are shown in Table 6.4 [7].

6.4.4   Energy-Efficiency Techniques

Following are some of the techniques that can be followed for energy efficiency:

- Use of natural daylight and optimum use of light during daytime.
- Regular maintenance.
- Power factor improvement.
- Replace the less efficient lamps (like Incandescent).
- Use of latest lighting control system (i.e., intelligent lighting).

Table 6.4 BEE star ratings for LED lamps.

Star rating	Rated luminous efficacy (l/w)
1	$68 \geq LE < 79$
2	$79 \geq LE < 90$
3	$90 \geq LE < 105$
4	$105 \geq LE < 120$
5	$\geq LE120$

- Improved sensors in rooms, ceilings. They can take preprogrammed commands and control lights.
- Motion sensors or movement detector which will give command to controllers.
- Automatic dimmers and Servo stabilised feeders.
- GSM/GRPS-based centralised control.
- Use of electronic chokes in place of conventional electromagnetic chokes (35% savings are possible).
- SCADA algorithm for office, warehose and Laboratory lighting optimization and to regulate traffic lights.
- Exclusive lighting transformers to supply exact voltage to the lights so as to get the required light output with rated power input and life as expected.

6.4.5   Light Control with IoT

LEDs use IoT towards digitalization of lighting. With proper design of control system lot of energy can be saved.

6.4.5.1   Wipro Scheme

A sample scheme proposed by Wipro lighting is shown in Figure 6.11 [8].

6.4.5.2   Tata Scheme

A model control scheme developed by Tata Communications is shown in Figure 6.12 [9].

Figure 6.11 Street light control scheme by Wipro.

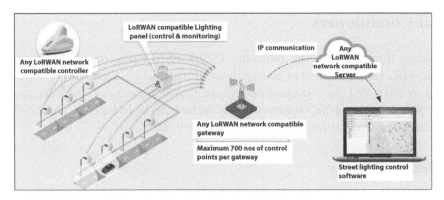

Figure 6.12 Street light control scheme by Tata Communications.

With LOR technology city street lights can be maintained and controlled towards an energy-efficient smart environment. The controller integrates with the LED light through NEMA connection (for dimming) for outdoor use. For improved life of LEDs, the temperature should be kept low by proper design of heat sink to dissipate the generated heat very quickly.

6.4.6   EU Practices

Lighting products shall come with energy labels and the EEI rating system, which ranges from A++, most efficient to G, least efficient, as shown in Table 6.5.

Note   1. Regulation on energy labelling for light sources up to 31.8.2021, this will be repeated and replaced by new energy labelling.
2. New labels w.e.f 1.9.2021: With a scale ranging from A (most efficient) to G (least efficient), as per Commission Regulation (EU) 2019/2020 of October 2019 with this regulation, most halogen lamps and the traditional fluorescent tube lighting will be phased out from September 2023 onwards.

Table 6.5 LED Luminaire Efficiency Labels of EU (EU 2019/2015) w.e.f 1st September 2021 [10].

Energy label	Energy-Efficiency Index (EEI)	
	Non-directional lumoinaire	Directional lumoinaire
A++	EEI≤0.11 or 11%.	EEI≤0.13 or 13%.
A+	0.11≤EEI≤0.17	0.13≤EEI≤0.17
A	0.17≤EEI≤0.24	0.17≤EEI≤0.40
B	0.24≤EEI≤0.60	0.40≤EEI≤0.95
C	0.60≤EEI≤0.80	0.95≤EEI≤1.20
D	0.80≤EEI≤0.95	1.20≤EEI≤1.75
E	EEI≤0.95	EEI≤1.75

6.5   Air Conditioners

As per Indian Bureau of Energy Efficiency (BEE), energy-efficient electrical appliances saved 140.54 BU (Billion Units) of electricity in India from 2011 to 2019, of which 20 BU was saved in 2018-19 [11]. Air conditioners are the most energy-consuming appliances at all places such as domestic, commercial and industrial. In India BEE Star labelling was made mandatory for all air conditioners w.e.f. January 2009.

6.5.1   Technical Terms

    i.   Co-efficient of performance, COP is the declared capacity for heating (watt).

    ii.   SCOP is the Seasonal Coefficient Of Performance, the overall coefficient of performance of the unit, representative for the whole designated heating.

    iii.   EER: It is developed by BEE and is known as Energy Efficient Ratio. The star rating (1to5) describes energy efficiency of appliance.

    iv.   EER = output wattage / input voltage = Amount of heat removed per hour/ Power consumed by air conditioner when providing cooling at started rated conditions.

    v.   ISEER: It can be defined as the ratio of total annual amount of heat the equipment may remove from indoor when operated for cooling in active mode known as Cooling Seasonal Total Load (CSTL) of energy consumed by the equipment during same period known as Cooling Seasonal Energy Consumption (CSEC).

$$ISEER = CSTL/CSEC \qquad (6.10)$$

    vi.   Bin: It means a combination of an outdoor temperature and bin hours per season the outdoor temperature occurs for each bin.

    vii.   Single-duct Air Conditioner: During cooling or heating, the condenser or evaporator intake air is introduced from the space containing the unit and discharged outside the space.

    viii.   Double-duct Air Conditioner: During cooling and heating, the condenser or evaporator intake air is introduced from the outdoor environment to the unit by a duct and ejected to the outside environment by a second duct and which is placed wholly inside the space to be conditioned, near a wall.

6.5.2   Types of Air Conditioners

    i.   Based on type of mounting:
       a. Window mounted
       b. Split type
       c. Ceiling mounted

    ii.   Based on speed:
       a. Fixed speed
       b. Variable speed (Inverter operated)

6.5.3   Star Rating of BEE

The higher the star rating, the higher is the heat removed for same wattage. The star ratings are given by considering a reference ambient conditions of temperatures of 27^{0}C at indoor and 35^{0}C at outdoor at a relative humidity of 50%. This EER rating does not reflect the cooling during off-peak hours and variable speed operated Air Conditioners. To overcome these issues, BEE has introduced the concept of Indian Seasonal Energy Efficiency Ratio (ISEER) to take care of the seasonal variations [12]. It is estimated based on the bin hours of national climatic zone, bin temperature range of 24 to 43^{0}C and 1600 operating hours per year.

As per BEE, ISEEER ratings w.e.f 1.1.2018 are shown in Table 6.6.

From the above it is clear that the energy efficiency of a split air conditioner is higher than that of the window type. Table 6.7 displays bin hours against bin temperature [13].

6.5.4   EU Practices

Energy-efficiency classes for air conditioners are shown in Table 6.8 [14].

Sample star rating labels of BEE [15] and EU are shown in Figure 6.13a and 6.13b, respectively.

6.5.5   Energy-Efficiency Tips

- Choose tight tonnage of air conditioner i.e., neither oversizing (loss of energy) nor undersizing (not getting required cooling)
- Buy higher star rated air conditioner.

Table 6.6 Star ratings.

Star level	Window A/c		Split A/c	
	Minimum ISEER	Maximum ISEEER	Minimum ISEER	Maximum ISEEER
1	2.5	2.69	3.1	3.29
2	2.7	2.89	3.3	3.49
3	2.9	3.09	3.5	3.99
4	3.1	3.29	4.0	4.49
5	3.3	–	4.5	–

Table 6.7 Reference outdoor temperature in distribution.

Temperature in °C	24	25	26	27	30	35	40	43	Total hours
Average annual hours	527	590	639	660	451	165	44	10	5774
Fraction	9.1	10.2	11.1	11.4	7.8	2.9	0.8	0.2	100
Bin hours	146	163	177	183	125	46	12	3	1600

Table 6.8 EU energy efficiency ratings.

Energy-efficiency class	SEER	SCOP
A+++	SEER≥8.5	SCOP≥5.1
A++	6.1≤SEER≤8.5	4.6≤SCOP≤5.1
A+	5.6≤SEER≤6.1	4.0≤SCOP≤4.6
A	5.1≤SEER≤5.6	3.4≤SCOP≤4.0
B	4.6≤SEER≤5.1	3.1≤SCOP≤3.4
C	4.1≤SEER≤4.6	2.8≤SCOP≤3.1
D	3.6≤SEER≤4.1	2.5≤SCOP≤2.8
E	3.1≤SEER≤3.6	2.2≤SCOP≤2.5
F	2.6≤SEER≥3.1	1.9≤SCOP≤2.2
G	SEER≤2.6	≤SCOP≤1.9

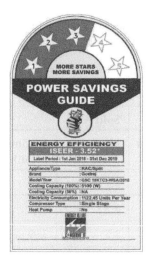

(a) BEE   (b) EU

Figure 6.13 Sample star rating label.

- The lower temperature setting shall be minimum of 24°C.
- The curtains, blinds and drapes to be kept in place to keep sunlight away from room.
- The room shall be well insulated.
- Regular maintenance of air conditioner, especially cleaning of air filters.
- Replace old units with star-rated units.

Note   1. BEE has estimated that the total connected air conditioning by 2030 will be 200GW.
        2. The Indian Power Ministry has instructed all the air-conditioner manufacturing companies to maintain a default temperature setting at 24° C [16]. It is expected that this will save a billion units of electricity in a year.

6.5.6   Inverter Air Conditioners

These are variable speed and tonnage air conditioners in contrast to single-speed compressor and tonnage. Adjusts speed or tonnage based on heat load of room which changes with size and seasons. It is estimated that 3-star-rated inverter-operated air conditioners are 7% more energy efficient than that of the same rated non-inverter air conditioners. Its basic operation in comparison with non-inverter air condioner is shown in Figure 6.14.

When the unit is switched on, it reaches the comfort zone quickly and maintains almost steadily by adjusting speed, whereas a non-inverter air conditioner reaches the comfort zone slowly and goes on and off as shown in above figure.

6.5.7   IoT-Based Air Conditioners

The temperature of a room, office or function hall can be managed remotely with the help of a smartphone-enabled air conditioner. The basic idea of an IoT-enabled air conditioner is shown in Figure 6.15.

The basic idea of Wi-Fi controlled smart air conditioner is shown in Figure 6.16.

Benefits of smart air conditioner:

- Remote control for on/off and all control features like temperature, fan speeds.
- Increased comfortability.
- Scheduling in advance.
- On-line diagnosis by service providers.
- Star rating.
- The more the stars, the more the energy savings, e.g., 2 star = 542 KWh/year and will be 318 KWh/year with a 3-star-rated air conditioner.

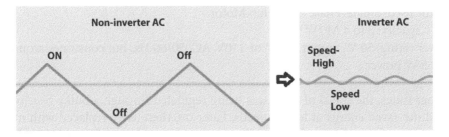

Figure 6.14 Inverter operation.

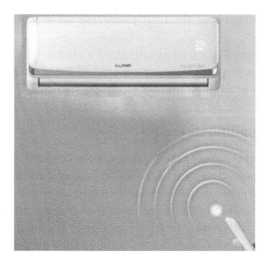

Figure 6.15 IoT-enabled air conditioner.

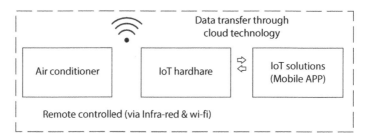

Figure 6.16 Smart air conditioner.

6.6 Fans and Other Smart Appliances

We know that globally, millions of people depend on electrically operated fans (whether ceiling, table-top or wall mounted) for their comfortable living whether in home or office or on a journey. It is estimated that fans use around 10% of the total energy usage of the USA and 9% of Indian energy in 2020 [17]. There is a great potential of energy savings in this field which is now recognized by global energy managers. Brief details of the majority of fans in the world are as follows:

Motor used: Single-Phase Induction Motor
Air Capacity: 3 to 4 M^3/W
Power rating: 50 W output, 220V or 110V AC, 50/60 Hz, but consumes around
65 W power.

In earlier times, the speed of a fan was being regulated through a bulky resistor which consumed the saved energy at lower speeds. Later on, these were replaced with manually operated electronic regulators which saved energy to some extent with manual intervention for speed regulation. Since then a lot of improvements have taken place in Motor front as well as control side.

6.6.1 BLDC Fan Motors

Efficiency of the fan (mostly ceiling fan) can be improved by 50% from existing technology which in turn can save 70 TWh/year and 25 million MT CO_2 [18] equivalent emissions per year. The traditional induction motor can be replaced with a Brushless DC Motor (BLDC) which has a lot of potential to conserve energy. The basic comparison between a traditional induction motor-driven fan and a BLDC-driven fan is shown in Table 6.9.

It is estimated that the BLDC motor saves energy @ 55 Wh/hr which has an attractive payback of less than a year. Energy cost of $1/10 KWh and eight hours run in day. Also these BLDC motors have the controlling facility with a TV-like remote or are Wi-Fi/Bluetooth enabled. Enabled (IOT) app in mobile phone. Models of traditional induction motor-driven fan and BLDC fan are shown in Figure 6.17a and 6.17b, respectively.

6.6.2 Star Ratings

Energy star, USA, has notified (2012) fan efficacy or energy performance of 4.2 M³/Min/W at low speed and 2.1 M³/Min/W at high speed [19]. It has has specified the star rating with labels, as shown in Figure 6.18.

Bureau of Energy Efficiency (BEE), India has introduced the star rating as shown in Table 6.10 [20].

Table 6.9 Induction and BLDC motor fans.

S. No.	Parameter	Induction motor driven Fan	BLDC motor driven Fan
1	Motor Volts	220 or 110 V AC	28 or 48 V DC (derived from AC)
2	Watt Rating (given/actual)	50 (65)	28 (30)
3	Air handling capacity (M³/W)	3-4	6-18
4	Cost ($)	30	40

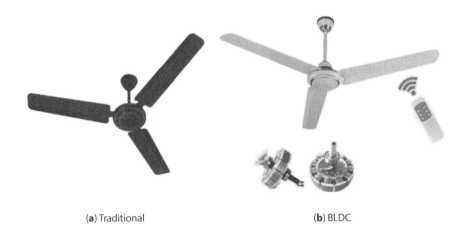

(a) Traditional   **(b)** BLDC

Figure 6.17 Fan models.

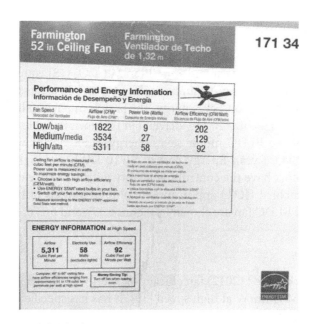

Figure 6.18 USA Star rating label for fan.

Table 6.10 Star Rating of 1200 mm Size Ceiling Fan, 2010.

S. No.	Star rating	Efficacy of Fan (M³/Minute/Watt)
1	1 Star	≥3.2 to <3.4
2	2 Star	≥3.4 to <3.6
3	3 Star	≥3.6 to <3.8
4	4 Star	≥3.8 to <4.0
5	5 star*	≥4.0

*Minimum air delivery of 210 M³/Min/50 Watt fan.

6.6.3   Group Drive of Fans

In case of Seminar Halls, Function Halls, Auditorium, etc., where a large number of fans are to be installed, a group controlled drive VFD (Variable Frequency Drive) can be used for speed control, based on the ambient condition and comfortability requirement. This scheme facilitates a uniform control and huge energy savings. The basic idea is shown in Figure 6.19.

The VFD can have the facility of IoT-based control with sensors.

6.6.4   Other Smart Appliances

On the domestic front, there are so many smart appliances being developed which have the facility of intelligent operation, IoT-based control in addition to energy savings. Some of these Smart Appliances are illustrated here with their features.

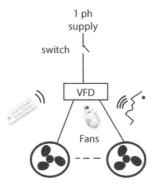

Figure 6.19 Group control of fans.

i.   Samsung's Apple Fridge/Refrigerator allows:

- To keep grocery list
- Search recipes
- Check weather & control Fridge's temperature
- Upload photos

ii. Home energy gadget by Agilewaves:

- Records home energy consumption pattern and adjusts lighting, heating and cooling of all the connected appliances.

iii.   THINQ Smart Washing Machine by LG:

- It can be controlled from a control network. Commands to clean clothes and can choose the most cost-effective time of day i.e., off-peak hours.

iv.   THINQ Fridge by LG:

- Based on the peak and off-peak hours of electrical energy, it adjusts the cooling requirements. It alerts when the door is open via mobile or Wi-Fi.

v.   Smart Oven by LG:

- Can download and use preprogrammed recipes.
- Roasting via mobile phone

vi. Smart Washing Machine by Samsung:

- Bubble Washer
- Saves 70% of energy

vii. Thermostat by Nest:

- Records home energy used over a week which gives scope for thinking of energy savings
- Controls heating and cooling
- Saves 20% energy

viii. Robotic Vacuum Machine by LG:

- Eye-mapping feature
- Two cameras (top & bottom)

- To map the home completely
- For most efficient cleaning paths

ix.   Induction Heater by Electrolux:

- Syncs with a Smart phone app
- Intelligent drying of food

With the advent of smart technology, and the presence of IoT in every part of human life, it is expected that all these smart appliances will account for a huge amount of energy savings.

6.7   Motors

Most industrial equipment is driven by three-phase induction motors and consuming 65 to 80% of total energy consumed by any industry. According to an IEA study in 2017, electrical motors consume 45% of global electricity. It refers to motors in all sectors—residential, commercial and industrial.

6.7.1   Motor Efficiency

The efficiency of an electrical motor is a measure of its ability to convert its electrical input into mechanical output available at its shaft for the driven equipment. Thus, electrical motor efficiency is expressed as the ratio between Mechanical Energy output at shaft and the Electrical Energy input to motor. Therefore, to improve the efficiency of a motor, the losses, i.e., the difference between input and output is to be reduced. The major losses are Conductor losses and Iron losses, which in turn are classified into hysteresis and eddy current losses.

The power flow diagram of a motor is shown in Figure 6.20.

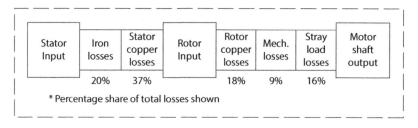

Figure 6.20 Power flow stages in a motor.

Conductor loss: These losses, also known as copper or load losses (= I^2R) depend upon Current and resistance of stator and rotor conductors. These are familiarly known as Copper losses since copper is mostly used as Conductor.

$$\text{Stator Copper loss} = I^2R \tag{6.11}$$

These losses can be reduced by improving power factor and using qualitative material and more copper or both together

$$\text{Rotor Copper loss} = \text{Slip (S)} \times \text{Rotor input} \tag{6.12}$$

The rotor copper losses can be reduced by reducing the slip of motor which in turn is possible only with the help of more amount of conductor material in Rotor.

Iron loss or Core loss: The core losses mainly depend upon the magnetic structure of core. These losses are of two types, namely

$$\text{Hysteresis loss, } W_n \alpha \, B_m{}^{1.6} \times f \tag{6.13}$$

$$\text{Eddy currentloss, } W_e \alpha \, B_m{}^2 \, f^2 \, t^2 \tag{6.14}$$

$$\text{Where } B_m = \text{Maximum Flux density} = \text{Flux (\O)/Area (a)(16)} \tag{6.15}$$

f = supply frequency
t = thickness of laminations

The core losses can be decreased to the extent of 15% to 40% by reducing the area of core and laminations and by increasing the length of magnetic structure.

Mechanical losses: These are mainly due to Friction in the bearings and ventilation of Motor cooling fans and other moving ports. These Friction losses can be reduced by selecting proper size of bearings and timely lubrication. The other part of mechanical losses is windage losses, which can be reduced by proper design of ventilating fan.

Stray load losses: These are unaccounted or residual losses which cannot be measured directly. Various factors like design process, air-gap, slot design, etc. These losses can be reduced by careful design of motor.

6.7.2   Underrated Operation

Motor efficiency reduces drastically with the reduction in load. For a standard motor of 200HP, the efficiency at different loading conditions, as per IS-325 Induction Motors, is shown in Table 6.11.

Table 6.11 Underrated operation of a 200 HP, 4 pole motor.

% Load	100	80	70	50	40	25
Efficiency	90	80	60	50	30	20

From the table, it is concluded that the motor shall run always at its name plate rating for better efficiency.

6.7.3   Energy-Efficient Motors

From the previous sections, it is clear that motor efficiency can be improved by proper design and selection of winding material (copper or aluminum), magnetic circuit and mechanical components [21]. The global electrical industry is putting continuous efforts to increase the efficiency of motors. The loss reduction, as of date was around 40% and various standards are developed on energy-efficient motors; like NEMA-MG1-12.54.2 (National Electrical Manufacturers Association, USA) and IS 12615:2011, by Bureau of Indian Standards.

6.7.3.1   Energy-Efficiency Ratings of BEE

The ratings are shown in Table 6.12 [22].

Bureau of Indian standards has recommended minimum energy performance values in IS 12615-2011, out of which one sample is shown in Table 6.13.

6.7.3.2   Energy-Efficiency Ratings of IEC

IEC has specified various categories of energy-efficiency ratings as per IEC 60034-30-1 classification scheme comprising four levels of motor efficiency ("IE-Code"). The IEC prescribed efficiency of various classes are shown in Table 6.14 and Figure 6.21 [23].

Table 6.12 Energy-efficiency ratings of BEE.

Efficiency class	Description	Definition
IE1	Only for variable frequency drive application.	Motors with ratedfull load efficiency ≥the correspondinglimits listed in tables.
IE2	High	–
IE3	Premium	–
IE4	Super premium	Under consideration

Table 6.13 Minimum energy performance standards of a 250 KW motor.

IS code	Star rating	250 KW, 2980 RPM	250 KW, 1480 RPM
IE 1	Only for VFD application	94%	94%
IE 2	High efficiency	95%	95.1%
IE 3	Premium efficiency	95.8%	96%
IE 4	Super premium efficiency (under consideration)	–	–

SMART ENERGY TECHNIQUES FOR INDUSTRIES 95

Table 6.14 Energy-efficiency ratings of IEC.

Minimum 50 Hz efficiency according to IEC 60034-30-1:2014 (random values given)												
Power (KW)	IE1 (Standard)			IE2 (High)			IE3 (Premium)			IE4 (Super Prem.)		
	2 pole	4 pole	6 pole	2 P	4 P	6 P	2 P	4 P	6 P	2 P	4 P	6 P
90	93	93	92.9	94.1	94.2	94	95	95.2	94.9	95.8	96.1	95.6
110	93.3	93.3	93.3	94.3	94.3	94.3	95.2	95.4	95.1	96	96.3	95.8
160	93.8	93.8	93.8	94.8	94.9	94.8	95.6	95.8	95.6	96.3	96.6	96.2
200	94	94	94	95	95.1	95	95.8	96	95.8	96.5	96.7	96.3
355	94	94	94	95	95.1	95	95.8	96	95.8	96.5	96.7	96.6
400	94	94	94	95	95.1	95	95.8	96	95.8	96.5	96.7	96.6
450	94	94	94	95	95.1	95	95.8	96	95.8	96.5	96.7	96.6

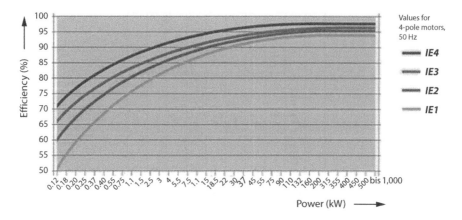

Figure 6.21 Energy-efficiency ratings by EU.

The major advantage of these energy-efficient motors is maintaining good efficiency levels even at reduced loads.

6.7.4 Retrofit of Standard Motors with Energy-Efficient Motors

For energy-efficient operation of industrial process systems, the following actions are to be taken, wherever possible:

- Survey and recording the average load factor of existing standard motors.
- Estimation of annual running hours and efficiency of motors.
- If the average actual load is less than 75% of motor rating, it is preferred to replace the existing motors with energy-efficient motors.
- In case of new purchase also, it is preferred to go for energy-efficient motors, even though their cost is on the high side, which can be offset by its attractive payback period of less than three years.
- In case of rewinding requirement, due to Stator Winding failure, it is preferable to go for a new motor instead of rewinding, since each rewinding reduces the efficiency by 5% approximately.
- Proper preventive maintenance of motors like condition monitoring [24] and reliability centered maintenance.
- Regular lubrication of Motor bearings and their timely replacement, as and when required.
- Use of VFDs as discussed in previous sections.
- Regular energy audit of running loads.
- Use of smart energy meters which alerts in case of running under load or low power factor. In case of low power factor, incorporation of capacitors in auto-mode.
- Improved power quality with unbalance in supply voltage not more than 3%. It is estimated a voltage unbalance of 5.4% leads to increased unbalanced current of 40% and temperature of order of 40°C.

6.7.5   Other Salient Points

- EU and China started using IE 3 from 2017 onwards.
- USA started using IE 3 from 2011 onwards.
- Canada started using IE 3 from 2012 onwards.
- Japan started using IE 3 from 2015 onwards.
- The German Federal Environmental Agency has estimated that increasing motor efficiency can save 135 billion KWh and 63 million ton CO_2 by 2020 in EU alone.
- MEMA estimates that its premium efficiency motor is expected to save 5800 GW of electricity and 80 million tons of CO_2.
- Design features of IE3 Premium efficiency motors:
  - Lower stator and rotor resistances
  - Longer motor length
  - Improved silicon steel and laminations
  - Improvements in design of rotor, bearings and cooling.

6.7.6   Use of Star-Delta Starter Motor

In general, Star-Delta starters are used to control the starting current of induction motors. Medium-sized motors, having significant impact on its Switchgear, due to its higher startup current, are started in star mode and subsequently run in delta mode, after attaining its rated speed. The same can be used in reverse order, i.e., delta to star where the motor is running on light local, i.e., less than 50%. This operation reduces the losses by approximately 50%.

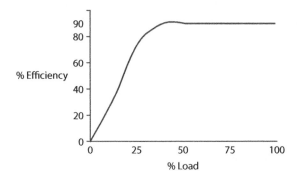

Figure 6.22 Efficiency graph of transformer.

Table 6.15 Transformer population progression.

Description/year	Unit	2020	2030	2040
World's electricity generation	TWh/year	24,222	30,875	37,352
Losses by transformers	TWh/year	1,181	1,462	1,845
World's electricity use	%	4.88	4.73	4.99
Savings with energy efficient transformers	TWh/year	34	400	776

6.8 Energy-Efficient Transformers

Energy-Efficient Transformers will help in reducing the existing transmission and distribution losses of around 30 to 40% and save around 5% of the world's electrical energy. Modern transformers have efficiency levels of 98%. Transformers reach their maximum efficiency point where conductor losses are equal to core loss. Most of the distribution transformers attain this at 40% of load power transformers at 80% load. Unlike motors, transformers have almost constant efficiency at all loads right from 25% to 100% load, shown in Figure 6.22 for a typical transformer.

Conduction losses vary approximately with load current squared,

$$\text{i.e., Conductor loss } \alpha \ I^2R$$

With proper selection of conductor material, mostly copper, this value can be kept under control. Also the temperature of winding shall be kept low so that the resistance of conductor is low, hence this loss is low. This is possible with better cooling.

Transformer losses can be reduced by mostly material management. Core losses can be reduced up to 70% by using thinner laminations [25]. Amorphous core, an alloy with non-crystalline structure and non-Iron as main ingredient, have a reduced core loss of around 80% of conventional CRGO (Cold Rolled Grain Oriented) steel. It is an alloy of Iron, Nickel, Phosphorous and Boron. At present, they are available upto 1000 KVA rating. They are very thin of the order of 0.025mm against the traditional CRGO steel of 0.29mm, hence the reduction in core loss. The number of transformers is expected to double from 2015 to 2040 @ 4% per year. By 2040, annual electricity savings of over 750 TWh are possible by using energy-efficient transformers; which can save more than 450 million tons of greenhouse gas emissions [26], as shown in Table 6.15. Liquid (or oil) filled Transformers will have more efficiency than dry-type transformers due to their better cooling.

6.8.1 IEC Recommendation

The peak efficiency recommended in IEC 60076 – 20 (2017) at 50% load with two levels of losses as in Table 6.16 [27].

Table 6.16 IEC recommendation (in %).

Rated KVA	Level 1 basic energy performance Um≤24 KV	Level 2 high energy performance Um≤24 KV	Level 1 basic energy performance 24 KV≤ 36 KV	Level 2 high energy performance 24 KV≤ 36 KV	Level 1 basic energy performance ≥36 KV	Level 2 high energy performance ≥ 36 KV
500	99.33	99.465	99.247	99.398	–	–
1600	99.488	99.550	99.424	99.494	–	–
10000	–	–	–	–	99.560	99.615
25000	–	–	–	–	99.657	99.700
50000	–	–	–	–	99.698	99.734
≥100000	–	–	–	–	99.737	99.770

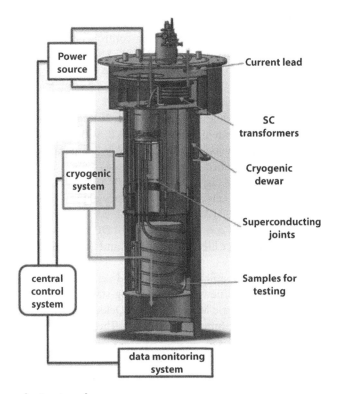

Figure 6.23 Super conducting transformers.

6.8.2 Super Conducting Transformers

High-temperature super conducting (HTS) transformers are under experiment with which the efficiency of TFR will reach almost 100%. A New Zealand firm has developed an 1000KVA HTS Transformer whose efficiency was 99.86% (3.3KV/220V). A sample HTS transformer is shown in Figure 6.23 [28].

References

1. V. K. Jain (2013), *Pump: Theory and Practice*, Galgotia Booksource, New Delhi, ISBN-13: 978-8193296059.
2. N. V. Raghavaiah, Overview of Pressure Vessel Design using ASME Boiler and Pressure Vessel CodeSection VIII Division-1 and Division-2. Available from: https://www.researchgate.net/publication/339874374_BPVC_Sec_VIII_div_1_and_2.
3. Global variable frequency drives (VFD) market 2019-2023, Feb 2019 by Technario.
4. B. Koti. Reddy, and B. SreeBindu, "Recent Challenges in Electrical Engineering and the Solution with IT", *International Journal of Recent Technology and Engineering (IJRTE)*, vol.issue. 2S11, September 2019, pp. 2412-2418.
5. https://www.iea.org/reports/world-energy-outlook-2017
6. https://en.wikipedia.org/wiki/Electric_light
7. Bureau of Energy Efficiency, Third Technical Committee Meeting for Tubular Fluorescent lamps and LED lamps, 16-09-2016.

8. https://www.wiprolighting.com/smart-outdoors

9. https://iot.tatacommunications.com/product/nema-controller-with-dimming

10. Commission Delegated Regulation (EU) 2019/2015 of 11 March 2019 supplementing Regulation (EU) 2017/1369 of the European Parliament and of the C, *Official Journal of the European Union*, L 315/68, 5-12-2019.

11. https://powermin.nic.in/en/content/energy-efficiency

12. Bureau of Energy Efficiency Schedule 19, Date: 29 June, 2015.

13. https://www.beestarlabel.com/Content/Files/Inverter%20AC%20schedule%20final.pdf

14. https://www.energystar.gov/products/heating_cooling/air_conditioning_room

15. https://www.beeindia.in/iseer-eer-bee-cop-star-ratings-ac/

16. https://pib.gov.in/PressReleasePage.aspx?PRID=1598508#

17. Shah, N., Sathaye, N., Phadke, A., Letschert, V., "Efficiency improvement opportunities for ceiling fans. *Energy Efficiency,* 8, 37–50 (2015).

18. A. Saxena, "Performance and cost comparison of PM BLDC motors for ceiling fan," 2014 IEEE International Conference on Power Electronics, Drives and Energy Systems (PEDES), Mumbai, 2014, pp. 1-5.

19. https://www.energystar.gov/most-efficient/me-certified-ceiling-fans

20. https://www.bijlibachao.com/fans/new-beee-star-rating-standards-ceiling-fans.html

21. Ali Emadi, "Energy Efficient Electric Motors", Marcel Dekkr Inc, USA, 2005.

22. IS12615: 2011-: Energy Efficient Induction Motors - Three Phase Squirrel Cage. Bureau of Indian Standards.

23. IEC 60034-30-1 classification scheme comprising four levels of motor efficiency ("IE-Code").

24. B. Koti Reddy, "Condition Monitoring and Life extension of Induction Motor", TEST Engineering & Management, vol. 82, pp. 8645-8651, Jan-Feb 2020.

25. https://metglas.com/distribution-transformer-electrical-steel/

26. UN Environment (2017) Global market model to calculate energy savings potential of power transformer.

27. IEC/TS 60076-20 (2017): *Power Transformers – part-20. Energy efficiency.*

28. https://www.sciencedirect.com/science/article/abs/pii/S0011227517301820.

7

Link Restoration and Relay Node Placement in Partitioned Wireless Sensor Network

Manwinder Singh[1]* and Anudeep Gandam[2]

School of Electronics & Electrical Engineering, LPU, Phagwara, Punjab, India
PhD Research Scholar, IKG-PTU Jal, India

Abstract

The main motive of WSN node is to sense and gather information from a specific domain and then send it to the sink where the application lies. It set up the direct link between a sensor and the sink that may allow nodes to transfer their messages. In this work, an approach for optimum relay node placement is proposed. The objective function is estimated depending on the values of energy, number of packets lost in a node, distance between the source and the base station. The traditional craft-based approach deployed relay node every time when sensor node failed to form a hexagon structure and it will disturb the basis structure of WSN architecture, whereas the proposed method deployed relay node in such a way that the network will behave like a sensor network with the help of K-Means clustering approach.

Keywords: Wireless Sensor Network (WSN), link restoration, relay node placement, K-mean clustering, residual energy, packet loss, end to end delay

7.1 Introduction

In advancement of technology, computing and excessive usage of portable devices have increased the importance of devices like mobile and wireless networks. In a Wireless sensor network (WSN), sensor nodes are required with minimum energy. The primary task of a sensor network is to sense, gather and process the information efficiently regarding the given object from the surroundings and then transfer it to the observer for processing and analysing. These wireless sensor networks are used in various fields such as industrial and consumer applications (precision agriculture, machine health monitoring, etc.), and military applications (aircraft control, marine environment monitoring) etc. The whole network of wireless sensor network must have capability to work in very ruthless environments. In harsh conditions, WSN can't be easily scheduled or efficiently managed. Also, in this type of condition, network was not feasible at all [1]. Moreover, wireless sensors are energy constrained in these ruthless conditions and their batteries generally not recharged.

Corresponding author: manwinder.25231@lpu.co.in

Suman Lata Tripathi, Dushyant Kumar Singh, Sanjeevikumar Padmanaban, and P. Raja (eds.) Design and Development of Efficient Energy Systems, (101–118) © 2021 Scrivener Publishing LLC

Wireless Sensor Network is the most growing industry for research nowadays. With the improvement in technology and growth of industries, many consider WSN as the basic requirement for setting up the industries. The sensors are placed everywhere in the industry to retrieve live data and to take correct decisions [2]. Wireless sensor networks are the sensors arranged in various monitoring environments which are managed by a central receiving unit called Base Station. Base Station is liable for the collection and processing of data collected from various distinct kinds of sensors. These sensors in the network are categorized as the heterogeneous and homogenous sensors. The sensors setup in the network are either the same type of sensors or of different kind relies on the application [3]. In the various applications for military and police investigation, wireless sensor networks can be used. Various developments within the hardware minimize the cost of production or development in wireless communications technologies that have created probably various applications with a high numbers of sensors. In some other cases, the main purpose of the access space must be checked and thus a result to be Set up the sensor to locate then from craft network. When the positions are not located, the only way to contribute enough target coverage by sensors in order to use multiple sensors than the fastened variety [4]. After the placement of the sensors in the network the second and the most important part is clustering. Clustering of the sensors in the network is either fixed and usually depends on the geographical location of the network or it is dynamic, which means the nodes in each cluster are dynamically distributed and there is some algorithm for the selection of the nodes in the cluster. The algorithm must either be energy efficient or bandwidth efficient or both. There is commonly a basic problem in sensing networks which is named network lifespan. To keep the technology, the sensors area units are hopped-up with the battery [5]. The value and size constraints offer energy within the detector to sense the communication and globally have an effect on the lifespan of the node.

Sensor nodes must achieve their own target by transmitting the collected data to BS accurately and rapidly. The functions are the keys to this kind of imperfect environment. Some authors have attempted an approach to Wireless sensor networks with Unequal Cluster based Routing Protocol (UCR) which depends on a different cluster routing protocol. In this type the nodes are grouped into clusters of different sizes [6–8]. Smaller-size clusters stay near to the Base Station (BS) whereas others are at some distance from BS. Therefore, small-size clusters can keep some energy to forward intercluster data. But if the distance of the node is far from BS and energy is relatively more than other nodes, then it is a challenge for Unequal Cluster-based Routing Protocol to determine the cluster head. In this situation, it is not at all easy for Unequal Cluster-based Routing Protocol to select the cluster head and problems such as hot spots exist. So the challenge is to combine UCR with added re-cluster node each level on multi-hop transmission of data to generate a Hybrid Unequal Routing Protocol (HUCR), which is a new algorithm, Wireless Sensor Networks which needs to be addressed too. Furthermore, the nodes which are relatively closer to base station or sink for them the data forwarding task is to be taken on tremendously [9–13]. Another major problem addressed in this dissertation concerns what way the survival time of the network can be increased.

Partitioned Wireless Sensor Networks is one of the most important areas of research in recent years. Partitioning is *"the process of managing the nodes into groups those who are similar in one or the other some ways"*. In the hierarchical network, every cluster is called

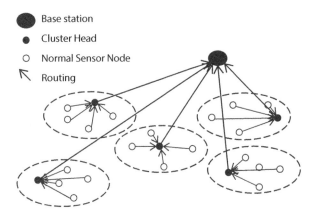

Figure 7.1 Clustered wireless sensor network [32].

the cluster head (CH) and usually it is performing some unique task and several common sensor nodes (SN) as members. In the two-level hierarchy, cluster heads consist from higher layer and other member nodes of cluster consist from lower layers. The sensor nodes periodically transmit their data to the corresponding CH nodes. An example of cluster communication in wireless sensor networks is shown in Figure 7.1.

7.2   Related Work

A. A. Imani [18] presented a mathematical model. This model was used for solving the nonlinear equations depending on the travelling wave algorithm. This wave algorithm may be utilized to resolve several results that need iterative approaches to provide optimum solution [19]. These nonlinear equations depend on the propagation, breaking and refraction properties of the waves. P. Sasikumar and Sibaram Khara [20] proposed both distributed and centralized k-means clustering algorithms. In centralized k-means clustering algorithm a centralized node make decisions for clustering but in distributed k-means clustering each node has information required for clustering. Simulation results show that distributed k-means is more efficient than centralized k-means [21–23]. Wang, Sheng-Shih, and Ze-Ping Chen [24] proposed QELAR (Q-learning-based Routing) in this paper. This approach was dependent on associate degree accommodative, energy-efficient, and lifetime aware routing protocol [25–27]. Lo, Shou-Chih, Jhih-Siao Gao, and Chih-Cheng Tseng [28] presented a water wavebased technique. The proposed approach was used to deliver the messages in VANET. Moreover, Network congestion was used for the delivery of the information and to minimize the loss of packets in the network. Alam Bhuiyan and Md Zakirul [29] presented an energy and frequency efficient algorithm which was used for sensor networks. This work analyzes the use of energy for transferring the information. The proposed approach worked on this problem and found out most favorable location for the placement of Cluster Heads. If these cluster heads are located at suitable location then all the nodes require sufficient amount of energy data transmission efficiently. Owojaiye, Gbenga, and Yichuang Sun [30] proposed the mutual operation of the wireless sensor network to get critical advantages over the earliest communication technologies for oil and gas pipeline monitoring. The current progress of wireless sensor network were being expressed to identify with the inexpensive embedded electrical utility observance and diagnostics system. M. Gholami, N. Cai, and R. W. Brennan [31] presented the scheme which was used to resolve the issue of localization and optimum placement of wireless sensors in the network. In order to locate the optimum location, Neural-based approaches have been used. In these neural approaches, the sensors should be located to provide better results in terms of enhancement in effectiveness and precision. Bencan, Gong, Jiang Tingyao, Xu Shouzhi, and Chen Peng [32] proposed an unequal density-based node deployment clustering (UDNDC). In this method, nodes are deployed in different areas which depend on load for data forwarding; therefore extra energy was given to nodes for data forwarding early energy drain of some nodes. Results of the simulation were that the proposed algorithm increases network lifetime and performs better than LEACH-C and HEED [30–33]. Bahmani-Firouzi, Bahman, and Rasoul Azizipanah-Abarghooee [34], proposed Dynamic Source routing algorithm.

This proposed algorithm was the same as data-based routing. This algorithm uses a formal logic utilization-based system in order to calculate the nodes. These calculated nodes must forward a packet to the neighboring node should maintain the gap and angle between two neighboring detector nodes. The result of the proposed algorithm indicates that the proposed method has an identical packet delivery magnitude with much less energy consumption.

Many problems related to the partitioning of the network have emerged and been dealt with in recent times. A network needs to be partitioned when the number of sensor nodes in the network increases to a certain limit which can no longer be managed by a single base station. In this type of network in which the number of nodes is large, the nodes are categorized into different partition sets which may or may not be of equal size. When the communication cycle in the network starts the nodes involved in the communication either act as a source or destination or the hopping nodes start losing their energy. These nodes work fine until the residual energy of the node decreases below a threshold value; they are then considered as a dead node and no longer take part in the communication process. The data which directs towards the node (which is going to be dead soon) is lost in the network and connection reestablishment phase begins.

The reestablishment of path or the connectivity restoration has been an important task for researches in recent years. Many techniques have been evolved and their merits and demerits have been compared with their counterparts.

The placement of relay nodes close to the base station is very important and challenging in the design of partitioned network. The relay nodes must be placed so that it serves the purpose of communication and works only as the hopping node in the network. Relay nodes itself does not produce any sensor data. The partitions can be equal and unequal depends on the nature of the network and application of the WSN. Restoration in link connectivity is placed in such a manner in case or when there is a fault or delay be minimized. Also, the number of relay nodes placed in the network must also be minimized and the effectiveness of the nodes in terms of connectivity must be increased.

In the cluster-based hierarchical model, data are grouped together in single cluster and then it travels to higher level CH from the lower layer of cluster. It travels over large distances, therefore minimizing the latency and travel time. This type of cluster-based hierarchical model is better than the one-hop or multi-hop model.

7.2.1   Existing Techniques

Connectivity Restoration on Assured Fault Tolerance (CRAFT) algorithm can form a back polygon (BP) around the damaged part taken centre of the damaged area. For the connection of each outer partition relay nodes are placed in the inner damaged area forming two non-overlapping paths.

- The minimum number of relay nodes to be placed in order to establish connectivity with the other partitions in a network. It localizes the problem by setting the recovery process on the failure node area.
- The nodes in the network which are used regularly and frequently for the transfer of data in the network. A backup node is placed with these nodes so in case of failure of the nodes, backup nodes will take charge in case of emergency.

7.3   Proposed K-Means Clustering Algorithm

There are many ways to distinguish the sensor nodes in WSN environment, but they are broadly classified into two types.

7.3.1   Homogenous and Heterogeneous Network Clustering Algorithms

In this type of clustering the functionality and the characteristics of the sensors are considered. In homogenous clustering the clustering is done on the nodes which have almost the same capability to process and sense the data. In this type of network every sensor node has the capability to become the cluster head. The CH has been rotated according to a certain rule or can be randomly assigned to the sensor nodes. In this case better load balancing is achieved in the network, while in the case of heterogeneous networks, a few sensor nodes have the capability to process the data and others simply sense the environment. In this case all the sensor nodes work in unison to transfer the data from source to destination. In our case we consider the homogenous network clustering approach.

7.3.2   Dynamic and Static Clustering

In a dynamic scenario the CH election and organization adjusts its clusters according to the changes in the network organization and topological architecture. In the dynamic approach all the clusters make better use of the sensor nodes and this leads to improved energy consumption by the nodes in the network, while in static clustering the clusters are fixed and are ineffective of all the topological or organizational changes in the network. In our work dynamic clustering is used.

   In the basic technique, every time a relay node is placed in case of any node failure, but by using this practice the system or network will become a relay network instead of a sensor network. If this occurs the network will no longer be a sensor network. Deploying relay node is not fair for the network because the relay only passes on the packet or information as it is; it doesn't generate anything by itself. So, if relay node placed cannot be avoided then its deployment should be such that it should maintain the decorum of the wireless sensor network. In this report the same has been accomplished and better results received by using k-means clustering algorithm.

7.3.2.1   Routing

Reactive routing technique is used in the proposed methodology. In the reactive routing technique the route is determined in real time. RREQ message is generated when a node wants to transfer the information or data which simply defines as the route request message. In reactive routing a single hop or multi-hop route is considered on the basis of RREQ message. In these types of protocol there is a provision of route recovery also and many routing schemes consider the following three route recovery mechanisms:

RREQ - Source node initiates the route request message to the destination node. These requests generally have a time to live (TTL) parameter which is initially set as a predefined value and can be increased when there is a loss of packets in the network.

RREP - It is a unidirectional message targeted towards the source node from the destination node. Route Reply message is used to inform the source node about the route to the destination node.

RERR – An RERR message notifies the other nodes for the loss of the link. Nodes in the network monitor the link status and update the next hop information in the network.

7.3.3   Flow Diagram

The flow chart of proposed algorithm is as shown in Figure 7.2.

7.3.4   Objective Function

An objective function is proposed on the basis of parameters depicted below:

- **Residual Energy:** It computes the time till the node of a network remains in existence. The energy drained by a node during data transmission or reception with other nodes or remain in idle condition. The expression is as given below.

$$Residual\ Energy = Total\ Energy\ available - Energy\ consumed \qquad (7.1)$$

- **Distance:** The distance is a crucial factor, as the amount of energy consumed during transmission of a packet directly relies upon the distance between the nodes. Euclidean Formula is used to compute the distance and is calculated as:

$$Distance = \sqrt{(x_1 - x_2)^2 + (y_1 - y_2)^2} \qquad (7.2)$$

- **Normalized Packet Loss Rate:** The number of packets lost while transmitting them from one node to another plays a vital role in the detection of

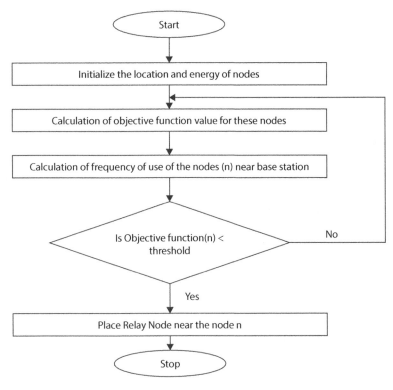

Figure 7.2 Flow diagram.

congestion. There are two major reasons for the packet loss within the network, first, the queue length of the node and second, the collision of packets in the network. There is a need to reduce the rate at which packets are lost to improve the performance of the congestion detection and control algorithm.

$$Objective\ Function = \sqrt{(w_1 * P_L + w_2 * R_E + w_3 * d_{ij})} \tag{7.3}$$

- where w_1, w_2 and w_3 are weights which satisfy the equation

$$w_1 + w_2 + w_3 = 1 \tag{7.4}$$

- and P_L is the packets lost,

R_E is the residual energy and d_{ij} is the distance between nodes

Based on the value of this objective function a decision of placing the relay node is considered. If the value of the objective function for the route is less than threshold (30% of the maximum value) then the relay node is placed in the route.

$$Objective\ Function = \sqrt{(w_1 * P_L + w_2 * R_E + w_3 * d_{ij})}$$

7.4 System Model and Assumption

Wireless Sensor Networks consist of n number of sensor nodes out of which m number of cluster heads and a base station. By using the k-means clustering method, the network is grouped into clusters. This method is approached by taking the mean value of the nodes. It is performed until the same value as node cannot be obtained and then the cluster is formed. Each cluster has its cluster head which is formed on two aspects; one is geographical area of the nodes, the other is on some performance parameter such as energy. Cluster head plays a vital role in communication within or outside the cluster. In this work, the K-means clustering with objective function with relay node position function is implemented; where average of all the distance can be calculated then the nodes in that average will be considered and the clusters are formed. The number of clusters completely depends upon the bandwidth. This method of forming a cluster is also referred to as a dynamic clustering, where cluster head (node with high energy) is decided first, then the cluster is formed.

Message/packet can be sent within or outside the cluster, i.e., inter- and intra-cluster message. Both these are basically performed by the cluster head. Figure 7.3 shows the system model with cluster head and sensor nodes and base station.

7.4.1 Simulation Parameters

In order to design the simulation environment, a 1000*1000 grid is considered in Network Simulator 2.35. The total number of nodes involved in the grid is 50. Wireless parameters required in it, like antenna type, channel type and propagation model are defined for each node. MAC layer is used for the extraction of energy from each node following IEEE 802.11 standard and the radio model used. The various performance parameters are as follows:

7.4.1.1 Residual Energy

Energy left after the communication cycle (forwarding and receiving of packets). The residual energy has a vital role; it is a measure of the performance of the system as more residual energy means the improved energy efficiency of the network.

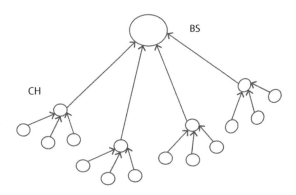

Figure 7.3 System model [34].

$$\text{Residual Energy} = \text{Initial Energy} - \text{Energy consumed} \qquad (7.5)$$

7.4.1.2   End-to-End Delay

It is defined as:

$$\text{Delay} = (\text{Packet received by receiver time} - \text{generated time}) \qquad (7.6)$$

This parameter clearly defines that if the loss of packets in the network reduces, the average end-to-end delay in the network also minimized. It implies that loss of packets and end-to-end delay are directly proportional to each other.

7.4.1.3   Number of Hops or Hop Count in the Network

Number of hops in the network means the number of nodes present in the path from source to destination. The number of hops after placing the relay node at optimized location should be reduced.

7.5   Results and Discussion

Figures 7.4 and 7.5 depict the network design using the network simulator ns 2.35. Nodes (50) are deployed in the network and a base station is located in the middle of the network.

As in Figure 7.4 base stations are shown as yellow color in the middle of the network and the rest of the nodes are deployed randomly in the network.

The simulation results of the proposed system are shown in Figure 7.4. Above network describes the stored information of each node with regard to simulation time. The members of each node are shown in the Figure 7.4.

Figure 7.6 depicts end-to-end delay obtained by proposed method w.r.t. state-of-the-art methods, which clearly shows the correctness of the proposed method. Figure 7.3 depicts the energy remaining at the node in the proposed system is more than the basic or primary system.

Tables 7.1 and 7.2 depict the comparison of various performance parameters of different protocols. Then, the results of the one of them are used with a protocol to obtain the better results. Figure 7.7 shows a comparison among the residual energies for existing network models.

The graph shown above (Figure 7.8) represents the primary method as well as proposed method between residual energy and simulation time of the nodes. Residual energy obtained in the proposed method is more as compared to primary method because the number of retransmissions increased in the proposed method.

The comparison table for the above figure is displayed below:

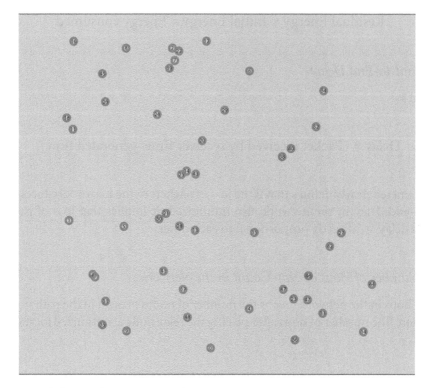

Figure 7.4 Network design of WSN in proposed system.

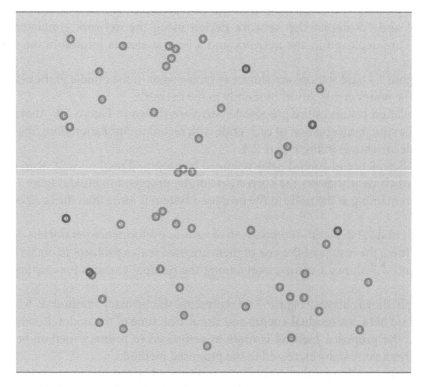

Figure 7.5 Network design with cluster head in the proposed system.

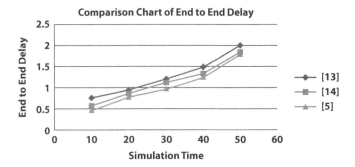

Figure 7.6 Results comparison of Reference paper [5, 13, 14].

Table 7.1 Values (End-to-end Delay) compared of Reference papers [5, 13, 14].

Simulation time	[13]	[14]	[5]
10	0.75	0.55	0.46
20	0.95	0.85	0.77
30	1.21	1.11	0.96
40	1.47	1.33	1.24
50	1.99	1.83	1.78

Table 7.2 Values (Residual energy) compared of Reference papers [5, 13, 14].

Simulation time	[13]	[14]	[5]
0	99	99	100
10	70	75	82.83
20	60	69	74.43
30	49	58	65.51
40	45	50	56.31
50	37	40	47.71

Figure 7.9 shows the graph between end-to-end delay and the simulation time. As the number of packets lost in the network decreases, the end-to-end delay in the network also decreases as numbers of retransmission decreases. Table 7.3 presents the primary and the proposed method comparison of simulation time for residual energy. Table 7.4 give a comparative details of primary and a proposed method of network design with simulation time and end-to-end delay.

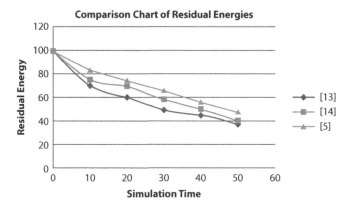

Figure 7.7 Results comparison of various performance parameters.

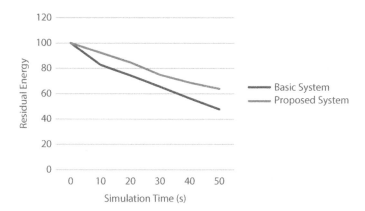

Figure 7.8 Shows the residual energy of the system w.r.t. simulation time.

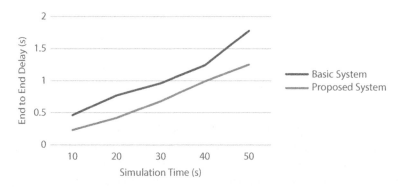

Figure 7.9 End-to-end delay vs. simulation time.

Table 7.3 Table showing the primary and the proposed method comparison of simulation time w.r.t. residual energy.

Simulation time	Residual energy	
	Basic system	Proposed system
0	100	100
10	82.83	92.31
20	74.43	84.63
30	65.51	74.9
40	56.31	68.66
50	47.71	63.78

Table 7.4 Comparison Table of a primary and a proposed method between simulation time and end-to-end delay.

Simulation time	End-to-end delay	
	Basic system	Proposed system
10	0.46	0.23
20	0.77	0.42
30	0.96	0.68
40	1.24	0.99
50	1.78	1.25

Figure 7.10 shows the number of hops in the network. Figure 7.10 depicts the code which represents the creation of the neighbourhood table for the hopping in the network. It is evident from the graph that the number of hops in the network increases whenever the simulation time rises. This is because of the fact that more and more nodes are trying to transmit

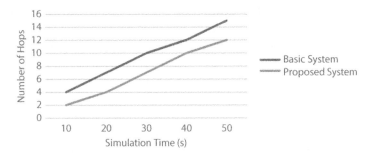

Figure 7.10 Shows the number of hops is less and requires less number of relay nodes w.r.t. increase in simulation time.

Table 7.5 Comparison Table of basic and proposed system between simulation time and number of hops.

Simulation time	Number of hops	
	Basic system	Proposed system
10	4	2
20	7	4
30	10	7
40	12	10
50	15	12

the data and a greater number of new paths are calculated. The relay nodes are placed near the nodes whose energy is more consumed as compared to the rest of the nodes in the network. The graph shows the proposed method uses a smaller number of hops as compared to the primary method and requires a smaller number of relay nodes.

The results shown in Table 7.5 clearly show that the proposed system outperforms the existing system in terms of speed also which gives an opportunity to use this system for real-time application also as it uses a smaller number of relay nodes.

7.6   Conclusions

The development of modern technologies has led to the development of modern devices of various kinds, effectively working in small- and large-scale industries. Wireless sensor network (WSN) play a vital role in them, where residual energy, end-to-end delay and hops count have equally important parameters. Residual energy of each communication cycle must be considered as it gives an important idea about the adjustment of location of the node. The objective function value is calculated for each node in the network and then the relay node is placed accordingly at the most frequently used route in the network. These approaches are implemented and compared with the existing techniques and an analysis is performed on the basis of their merits and demerits. In the present work for placing the relay node in the network firstly the location for the placement is defined. For the location calculation an objective function is designed which is based on the values of the number of packets lost, residual energy of nodes in the network and distance between the nodes by using k-means algorithm. Several other statistical approaches must also be used like Bayesian Filters, Kalman Filters and Extended Kalman Filters to improve the non-linearity of the problem so as to improve the acceptance of results. The results also show that the proposed method outperforms the existing method on the basis of various performance parameters like residual energy, end-to-end delay and the number of hops required in the network from source to destination. K-means clustering algorithm implementation has reduced the number of relay nodes usage whereas CRAFT usually creates the hexagonal network by using frequently relay nodes, which in turn makes network more of the relay network but proposed technique deployed in such a way that network remains the sensor network.

Further recommendation is that further work can be done for enhancing the lifetime of the WSN by minimizing the energy used in the network and enhancing the average energy of the node by considering the residual energy and working towards increasing it. Various other machine learning and Meta heuristic algorithms must be implemented on the objective function to further improve the accuracy of the results.

References

1. Kumar N., Deborah, Ramesh Govindan, John Heidemann, and Satish Kumar. "Next century challenges: Scalable coordination in sensor networks." In *Proceedings of the 5th annual ACM/IEEE International Conference on Mobile Computing and Networking*, pp. 263-270. ACM, 1999.

2. Cardei, Mihaela, and Ding-Zhu Du. "Improving wireless sensor network lifetime through power aware organization." *Wireless Networks* 11.3 (2005): 333-340.

3. Mao, Guoqiang, Barış Fidan, and Brian D.O. Anderson. "Wireless sensor network localization techniques." *IEEE Conference on Computer networks* 51.10 (2007): 2529-2553.

4. Guozhi Liu Wang, Rui, , and Cuie Zheng. "A clustering algorithm based on virtual area partition for heterogeneous wireless sensor networks." In *2007 International Conference on Mechatronics and Automation*, pp. 372-376. IEEE, 2007.

5. Mao, Guoqiang, Barış Fidan, and Brian D.O. Anderson. "Wireless sensor network localization techniques." *Computer Networks* 51.10 (2007): 2529-2553.

6. Ngo Hung Quoc, LeeYoung-Koo, Lee Sungyoung. "MEPA: a new protocol for energy-efficient, distributed clustering in wireless sensor networks" In: *Proceedings of the ISWCS2007;17–19 October 2007*, p. 40-44.

7. Xin, Guan, Wu Hua Yang, and Bi DeGang. "EEHCA: An energy-efficient hierarchical clustering algorithm for wireless sensor networks." *Information Technology Journal 7*, no. 2 (2008): 245-252.

8. Yick, Jennifer, Biswanath Mukherjee, and Dipak Ghosal. "Wireless sensor network survey." *Computer Networks* 52.12 (2008): 2292-2330.

9. Sam Danis Konstantinos, Friderikos Vasilis, A. Hamid Aghvami. "Auto no michier-archical reconfiguration for wireless access networks" *Journal of Network and Computer Applications* 2009; 32(3):630–41.

10. Duan Cuiqin, Sun Jingjing, Zhou Duan, Zhang Jianxian. "An energy efficient regional partitioned clustering routing algorithm for wireless sensor networks". In: *Second International Conference on Intelligent Networks and Intelligent Systems (ICINIS-2009)*. IEEE, 2009, pp. 205–8.

11. Chang-ri, Luo, Zhu Yun, Zhang Xin-hua, and Zhou Zi-bo. "A clustering algorithm based on cell combination for wireless sensor networks." In *Education Technology and Computer Science (ETCS), 2010 Second International Workshop on*, vol. 2, pp. 74-77. IEEE, 2010.

12. Peng Zhiyong, LIXiaojuan. "The improvement and simulation on of leach protocol for WSNs". *Journal of Computer Networks*, pp. 321- 344, IEEE20.

13. A. A. Khan, N. Javaid, U. Qasim, Z. Lu, Z. A. Khan. "HSEP: Heterogeneity-aware Hierarchical Stable Election Protocol for WSNs" COMSATS Institute of Information Technology, Islamabad, Pakistan.University of Alberta, Alberta, Canada. (2012)

14. Garcia, Miguel, *et al.* "Saving energy and improving communications using cooperative group-based wireless sensor networks." *International Journal of Telecommunication Systems* 52.4 (2013): 2489-2502.

15. Salvador Climent, Juan Vicente Capella, Nirvana Meratnia and Juan Jos Serrano, "Underwater sensor networks: A new energy efficient and robust architecture", *Journal of Sensors and Its Applications*, volume 12, pp. 704–731, 2012.

16. Seokhoon Yoon, Abul K. Azad, Hoon Oh and Sunghwan Kim. "Aurp: An auv-aided underwater routing protocol for underwater acoustic sensor networks", *Journal of Sensors and Its Applications*, vol. 12, pp. 1827–1845, 2012.

17. Yang, Xin-She, and Amir Hossein Gandomi. "Bat algorithm: a novel approach for global engineering optimization." *Engineering Computations Conference* 29.5 (2012): 464-483.

18. Imani, A. A., "Approximate travelling wave solution for shallow water wave equation", *Applied Mathematical Modelling, IEEE Journal* 36.4 (2012):1550-1557.

19. Malathi, L., R. K. Gnanamurthy, and A. Thamaraiselvi. "Unequal Clustering with Layer based Data Collection for Prolonging WSNs Lifetime", *Journal of Computer Networks*, 0232-0241, IEEE 2012.

20. Sasikumar, P., and Sibaram Khara. "Performance Comparison of Clustering Algorithms for Wireless Sensor Networks", *Journal of Computer Networks,* pp. 0201-0209, IEEE 2012.

21. Kim, Jeong-Sam, and Tae-Young Byun. "A Density-Based Clustering Scheme for Wireless Sensor Networks." In *Advanced Computer Science and Information Technology*, pp. 267-276. Springer Berlin Heidelberg, 2011.

22. A. A. Khan, N. Javaid, U. Qasim, Z. Lu, Z. A. Khan " HSEP: Heterogeneity-aware Hierarchical Stable Election Protocol for WSNs" COMSATS Institute of Information Technology, Islamabad, Pakistan.University of Alberta, Alberta, Canada. (2012)

23. Ortiz, Antonio M., *et al.* "Fuzzy-logic based routing for dense wireless sensor networks." *Telecommunication Systems* 52.4 (2013): 2687-2697.

24. Wang, Sheng-Shih, and Ze-Ping Chen. "LCM: a link-aware clustering mechanism for energy-efficient routing in wireless sensor networks." *Sensors Journal*, IEEE 13.2 (2013): 728-736.

25. Yilmaz, Selim, and Ecir U. Kucuksille. "Improved bat algorithm (IBA) on continuous optimization problems." *Lecture Notes on Software Engineering* 1.3 (2013): 279-283.

26. Garcia, Miguel, *et al.* "Saving energy and improving communications using cooperative group-based wireless sensor networks." *International Journal of Telecommunication Systems* 52.4 (2013): 2489-2502.

27. Gandomi, Amir Hossein, *et al.* "Bat algorithm for constrained optimization tasks." *IEEE Journal of Neural Computing and Applications* 22.6 (2013): 1239-1255.

28. Lo, Shou-Chih, Jhih-Siao Gao, and Chih-Cheng Tseng, "A water-wave broadcast scheme for emergency messages in VANET" *International Journal of Wireless Personal Communications* 71.1 (2013): 217-241.

29. Alam Bhuiyan, Md Zakirul, "Energy and bandwidth-efficient wireless sensor networks for monitoring high-frequency events", *Sensor, Mesh and Ad Hoc Communications and Networks (SECON), 2013 10th Annual IEEE Communications Society Conference on*. IEEE, 2013.

30. Owojaiye, Gbenga, and Yichuang Sun, "Focal design issues affecting the deployment of wireless sensor networks for pipeline monitoring", *International Journal on Ad Hoc Networks* 11.3 (2013): 1237-1253.

31. Gholami, M., N. Cai, and R. W. Brennan, "An artificial neural network approach to the problem of wireless sensors network localization", *Journal of Robotics and Computer-Integrated Manufacturing* 29.1 (2013): 96-109.

32. Bencan, Gong, Jiang Tingyao, Xu Shouzhi, and Chen Peng. "An energy-heterogeneous clustering scheme to avoid energy holes in wireless sensor networks." *International Journal of Distributed Sensor Networks* 2013 (2013).

33. Mostafa, Baghouri, ChakkorSaad, and HajraouiAbderrahmane. "Fuzzy logic approach to improving Stable Election Protocol for clustered heterogeneous wireless sensor networks.", *Journal of Theoretical and Applied Information Technology* 53.3 (2013).

34. Bahmani-Firouzi, Bahman, and Rasoul Azizipanah-Abarghooee. "Optimal sizing of battery energy storage for micro-grid operation management using a new improved bat algorithm." *International Journal of Electrical Power & Energy Systems* 56 (2014): 42-54.

8

Frequency Modulated PV Powered MLI Fed Induction Motor Drive for Water Pumping Applications

Arunkumar S[1], Mohana Sundaram N[1*] and K. Malarvizhi[2]

[1]*Assistant Professor, EEE Department, Kumaraguru College of Technology, Tamil Nadu, India*
[2]*Professor & Head, EEE Department, Kumaraguru College of Technology, Tamil Nadu, India*

Abstract

In present scenario, almost every parts of the world have realized the importance of switching over to renewable sources rather than depending on the conventional energy suppliers. With this growing awareness, various research activities have been currently carried out on deriving maximum output of the existing setup. Thus, we are now much directed towards improvising the Energy Efficiency. The extensive use of Drives in the field of industries, agriculture have in turn created challenges for maintaining the power quality. This is because, AC Drives require Voltage Source Inverters (VSI), which is the primary source of harmonics generation. In this proposed chapter, the outcomes of employing various levels of PV fed Multi Level Inverter are discussed for a specific Water Pumping Application. These discussions are supported by simulation results and the discussion concludes that the CHB MLI supersedes other types. The idea of replacing the existing machine with a special electrical machine, including other types of renewable energy will also be discussed in the chapter, in detail.

Keywords: PV panel, Diode Clamped Multi-Level Inverter (DCMLI), H Bridge, Amplitude Modulation (AM), Frequency Modulation (FM), water pumping, induction motor

8.1 Introduction

The world has realized the alarming depletion of conventional energy sources like fossil fuels, and thus reliance on renewable energy sources has gained more importance [1]. The developmnt of renewable sources like solar, wind, etc., are not only helpful in satisfying the energy demand, but are also customizable for industrial requirements [2]. Since the output obtained from the renewable sources cannot be used for the loads directly, suitable converting techniques are required before connecting them to the load. Thus for Renewable Energy fed AC Drives, Inverters have become an unavoidable component [3, 4].

Corresponding author: mohanasundaram.n.eee@kct.ac.in

Suman Lata Tripathi, Dushyant Kumar Singh, Sanjeevikumar Padmanaban, and P. Raja (eds.) Design and Development of Efficient Energy Systems, (119–130) © 2021 Scrivener Publishing LLC

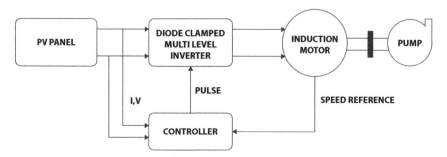

Figure 8.1 Block diagram of PV-based inverter fed drive.

There are various types of Inverter Topologies which have assumed importance in each phase of inverter evolution. The commonly faced problem in inverters is its non-sinusoidal input or in other words, AC output with harmonics. These harmonics are in turn responsible for generation of heat, noise and other associated losses [5–7]. The present challenge lies in increasing the sinusoidal nature of the inverter output by increasing the step size of conversion. This feature is most apparent in Multi-Level Inverter (MLI) [11, 12].

In this work, the analysis of an MLI fed Induction Motor Drive is done, by considering Solar Energy as a source. The effects of employing various types of MLI for a PV source-based Drive, methods of deriving maximum drive efficiency are elaborated in this chapter with sufficient simulation results.

The block diagram of the generalized PV-based Inverter fed Drive is given in Figure 8.1. The application area identified for this work is Pumping Applications, especially in the field of agriculture. In order to account this, Induction Motor-based drive is considered for the analysis. The switching pulse for the inverter is usually generated with the help of the Pulse Width Modulation (PWM) technique, which takes the panel voltage value and current value as references. The actual speed of the motor is also considered for pulse generation, for maintaining constant speed.

8.2   PV Panel as Energy Source

8.2.1   Solar Cell

The Solar Energy is converted into electricity by using Solar/PV Panels. The PV Panels comprise a series and parallel arrangement of Solar Cells, their basic component [8–10]. The electrical model of a single Solar Cell is shown in Figure 8.2. PV Panel is a renewable

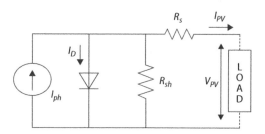

Figure 8.2 Electrical model of Solar cell.

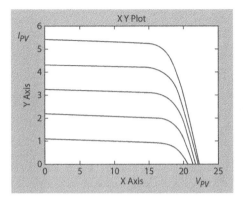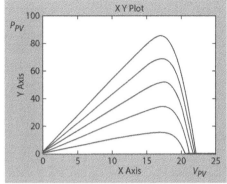

Figure 8.3 I-V and P-V characteristics of PV array.

energy source which provides maximum output power at specified ratings. The Figure 8.3 shows the IV and PV Characteristics of the PV Array. In this work, this model is used as a source that drives the Induction Motor Load.

8.3 Multi-Level Inverter Topologies

8.3.1 Types of Inverters Used for Drives

Inverters, in general, are used to convert DC into AC output. In the case of industrial and agricultural applications, inverters with provisions for variable voltage and frequency are mostly preferred. The H Bridge Inverter is a simple configuration with four switches that converts the fixed DC voltage into AC voltage, by suitable switching schemes.

The common disadvantage faced in these type of Inverters is the non-sinusoidal nature of output and the presence of harmonics, which in turn demands filter requirements. This is overcome by using the concept of Multi-Level Inverters.

8.3.2 Multi-Level Inverters

Multi-Level Inverter (MLI) is a power electronic concept, which yields improvised sinusoidal output from several DC voltage sources. These DC sources can be solar cells, fuel cells, ultra capacitors, etc., thereby paving the way for its adaptability to renewable energy sources. There are about three types of MLIs, namely, Diode Clamped, Flying Capacitor and Cascaded H Bridge (CHB) MLIs. Figure 8.4 and Figure 8.5 displays the Simulation Model of a Single Phase H Bridge Inverter and the square shaped Output Voltage waveform respectively.

Here, a 5-Level Diode Clamped MLI is modelled using MATLAB Simulink as shown in Figure 8.6 and its output is simulated.

It can be seen that the output voltage and current waveforms are nearer to sinusoidal nature. When the number of steps are increased, the output becomes closer to sinusoidal waveform. This is achieved with increased use of power electronic switches and capacitor.

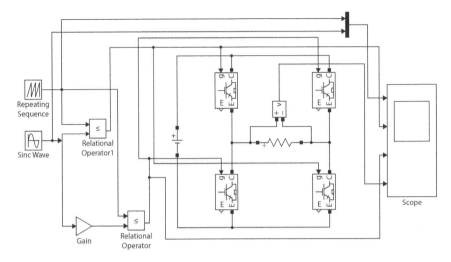

Figure 8.4 MATLAB Simulink Model of Single-Phase H Bridge Inverter.

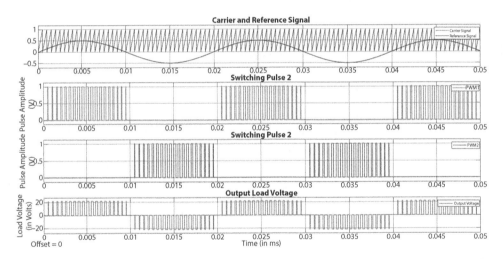

Figure 8.5 Simulation Output of Single-Phase H Bridge Inverter.

The five level Output Line Voltage and Phase Voltage waveforms are provided in Figure 8.7 and Figure 8.8 respectively.

8.4   Experimental Results and Discussion

Based on the discussions in the previous sections, the Induction Motor Drive is considered for analysis, coupled with a PV Source and Inverter. The operation and response of the drive by employing an ordinary H Bridge Inverter and Diode Clamped MLI are tested using MATLAB Simulink.

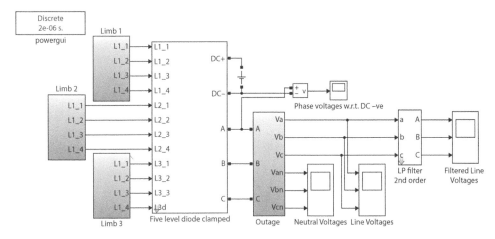

Figure 8.6 MATLAB Simulink Model of Diode Clamped Multi-Level Inverter.

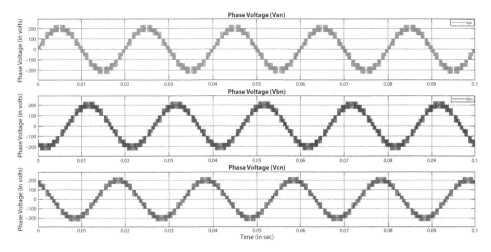

Figure 8.7 Five Level Line Voltage Waveform.

8.4.1   PV Powered H Bridge Inverter-Fed Drive

The five level Voltage referred to DC Terminal side is shown in Figure 8.9, while Figure 8.10 shows the MATLAB Simulink model created for a PV Source powered H Bridge Inverter fed Capacitor Start Capacitor Run Induction Motor Drive.

From the ouput waveforms of PV fed drive shown in Figure 8.11, it can be inferred that, the current flowing through the Main & Auxiliary Winding is quite high, which results vibrations and noise in the motor. And the ripple in electromagnetic torque is also very high.

Figure 8.12 depicts the Simulink Model of a PV Powered DCMLI fed drive. This model is simulated and the behaviour of various parameters are studied with the help of Figure 8.13.

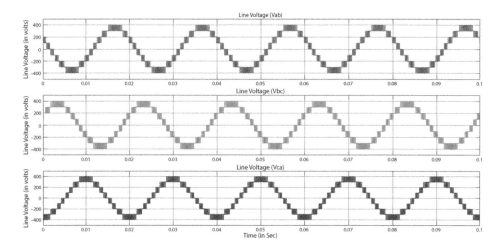

Figure 8.8 Five Level Phase Voltage Waveform.

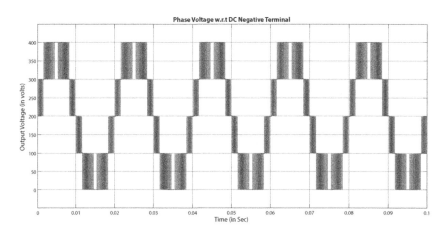

Figure 8.9 Five level voltage w.r.t. to DC terminal.

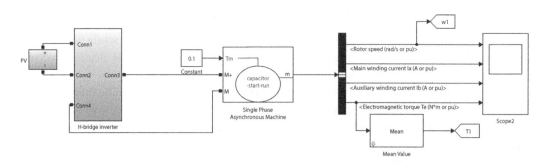

Figure 8.10 MATLAB Simulink Model of PV powered H Bridge Inverter fed Drive.

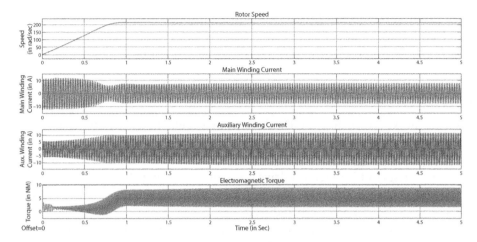

Figure 8.11 Output Waveforms of PV powered H Bridge Inverter fed Drive.

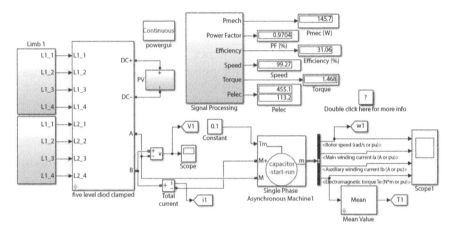

Figure 8.12 MATLAB Simulink Model of PV powered DCMLI fed Drive.

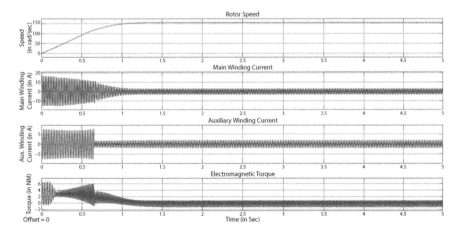

Figure 8.13 Output Waveforms of PV powered DCMLI fed Drive.

From the results, it is clear that the current flowing through main and auxiliary winding is comparatively low and the ripple in electromagnetic torque is also very less. So compare to H-bridge drive, the proposed drive offers less noise and vibrations.

8.4.2   PV Powered DCMLI Fed Drive

Here, the circuit is simulated using Diode Clamped Multi-Level Inverter that uses PWM base switching scheme.

Compared to H-Bridge Inverter fed Induction Motor, the main and auxiliary winding current characteristics of MLI fed IM drive keeps on decreasing after the settling time. This reduces the torque ripple and provides maximum efficiency. The harmonics in the waveform also seems to be comparatively reduced.

Since the MLI requires a higher number of switches in series and parallel connection, the switching angles are to be properly used, because only these determine the harmonic nature of output voltage and current waveform.

Both H Bridge Inverter and Diode Clamped MLI use switching devices, which can work on either Amplitude Modulation (AM) Scheme or Frequency Modulation (FM) Scheme. Hence, in order to analytically find out the best Modulation scheme, both types of Inverter Drives are simulated for both AM and FM Schemes. The performance comparison is done by varying the Modulation Index of the firing pulse and the results obtained for various parameters are tabulated in Table 8.1 and Table 8.2.

The comparative analysis of both the tabulated values helps in arriving at the following conclusions:

i) The MLI fed drive gives better efficiency than H Bridge Inverter configuration, especially for water pumping applications.
ii) Frequency Modulation Technique seems to be more efficient in terms of improved starting and running condition, power factor and speed.

Table 8.1 Performance comparison of H-bridge inverter and MLI fed drives based on Amplitude Modulation.

Mod. Index MI	MLI fed capacitor start capacitor run induction motor					H bridge inverter fed capacitor start capacitor run induction motor				
	P_{mec}	P.F.	η	Speed	Torque	P_{mec}	P.F.	η	Speed	Torque
0.41	785.2	0.84	70	147.9	5.3	254.7	0.68	57.4	152.3	1.914
0.53	830.5	0.691	55.17	156.1	5.412	109.3	0.151	19	146.2	0.821
0.71	795.2	0.674	49.78	152.4	5.614	189.5	0.162	21.11	151.9	1.317
0.8	767.4	0.68	53.33	159.6	5.58	238.7	0.184	22.12	160.3	1.461
0.91	861.3	0.695	52.3	151.7	4.876	312.9	0.192	17.7	161.7	2.01

Table 8.2 Performance comparison of H-bridge inverter and MLI fed drives based on Frequency Modulation.

Mod. Index MI	MLI fed capacitor start capacitor run induction motor					H bridge inverter fedcapacitor start capacitor run induction motor				
	Speed	P_{mech}	Torque	P.F.	η	Speed	P_{Mech}	Torque	PF	Eff
0.62	19.58	19.22	0.1145	0.214	47.88	98.99	463.1	4.651	0.9112	55.15
0.81	137.4	479	3.670	0.399	17.56	128	481.5	3.512	0.3181	28.11
0.83	147.2	619.4	5.418	0.467	19.78	133	739.2	6.117	0.4029	47.09
0.91	151.1	866.3	5.879	0.433	22.61	149	1161	6.969	0.497	59.12
0.92	154.2	890.2	5.549	0.498	24.57	141.79	1281	8.128	0.511	51.57
0.95	156.7	777.2	4.099	0.379	19.078	145.66	1103	7.095	0.61	39.12
1	169.1	598.7	3.593	0.289	19.01	159.01	1099	6.123	0.681	50.12

Hence, it can be decided that MLI with Frequency Modulation will be a better choice for water pumping applications. But the overall efficiency is still comparatively less and there is a scope for improvement. Hence Cascaded H Bridge Multi-Level Inverter (CHBMLI) will be helpful to overcome these deficiencies. Also, with availability of various robust controllers, the Induction Machine can also be replaced using Special Electrical Machines like PM BLDC Motor, for better results. The following CHBMLI Circuit Model shown in Figures 8.14 and 8.15 and its output waveform helps in supporting the above arguments. These can be seen in Figures 8.16 and 8.17.

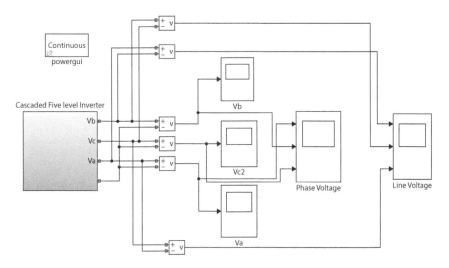

Figure 8.14 MATLAB Simulink Model of PV powered Cascaded H Bridge MLI-fed Drive.

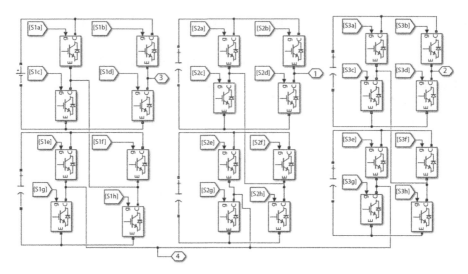

Figure 8.15 Subsystem Block of PV powered Cascaded H Bridge MLI-fed Drive.

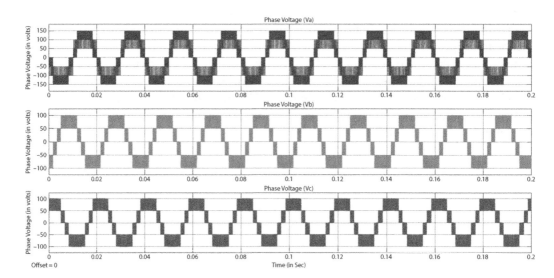

Figure 8.16 Phase voltage waveform.

8.5   Conclusion and Future Scope

This work focuses on devising an efficient renewable energy-based system for Water Pumping Applications in the Agricultural field. Since an Induction Motor is a commonly used AC Drive, the study is carried out on an IM Drive coupled to a PV Source. This arrangement generally requires an Inverter, with suitable controlling schemes for obtaining the desired output. The various Inverter types are discussed individually and the effects of adding them to the Drive Circuit are also illustrated using MATLAB Simulink Model.

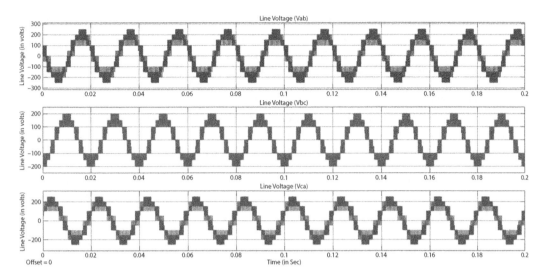

Figure 8.17 Line voltage waveform.

From the results obtained, it is concluded that PWM-Based Multi-Level Inverter will be more suitable for the chosen application, as it helps in overcoming problems like harmonics, motor heating, etc. The further improvement in efficiency can be obtained by using a CHBMLI fed IM Drive.

References

1. Karampuri, R., Jain, S., & Somasekhar, V. T. (2014). A single-stage solar PV power fed open-end winding induction motor pump drive with MPPT. In *IEEE International Conference on Power Electronics, Drives and Energy Systems (PEDES)*, 2014 (pp. 1–6).
2. Eduard Muljadi (1997). PV Water Pumping with a Peak Power Tracker using a Simple Six-Step Square Wave Inverter. *IEEE Industrial Applications*, 33.
3. Saadi & Moussi (2006). Optimisation of Chopping Ratio of Back-Boost Converter by MPPT Technique with a Variable Reference Voltage Applied to the Photovoltaic Water Pumping System. *IEEE Industrial Electronics*, 3.
4. Abdolzadeh, M., & Ameri, M. (2009). Improving the Effectiveness of a Photovoltaic Water Pumping System by Spraying Water over the front of Photovoltaic Cells. *IEEE Power Electronics*, 3.
5. Kurtoglu, M., Eroglu, F., Arslan, A. O., & Vural, A. M. (2019). Recent Contributions and Future Prospects of the Modular Multilevel Converters: A Comprehensive Review. *International Transactions on Electrical Energy Systems*, doi: 10.1002/etep.2763.
6. Mozafari Niapoor, S. A. K. H., Danyali, S., & Sharifian, M. B. B. (2010). PV Power System based MPPT Z-Source Inverter to Supply a sensorless BLDC Motor. *IEEE*, 978-1-4673-0136-7/11.
7. Chandel, S. S., Nagaraju Naik, M., & Chandel, R. (2015). Review of Solar Photovoltaic Water Pumping System Technology for Irrigation and Community Drinking Water Supplies. *Renewable and Sustainable Energy Reviews*, 49, 1084–1099, doi: 10.1016/j.rser.2015.04.083.
8. Jordehi, A. R. (2016). Parameter Estimation of Solar Photovoltaic (PV) Cells: A Review. *Renewable and Sustainable Energy Reviews*, 61, 354–371, doi: 10.1016/j.rser.2016.03.049.

9. Packiam, P., Jain, N. K., & Singh, I. P. (2013). Microcontroller-based Simple Maximum Power Point Tracking Controller for Single-Stage Solar Stand-Alone Water Pumping System, *Progress in Photovoltaics*, 21, 462–471, doi: 10.1002/pip.1207.

10. Poompavai, T., & Kowsalya, M. (2019). Control and Energy Management Strategies applied for Solar Photovoltaic and Wind Energy fed Water Pumping System: A Review. *Renewable and Sustainable Energy Reviews*, 107, 108–122, doi: 10.1016/j.rser.2019.02.023.

11. Poompavai, T., & Vijayapriya, P. (2017). Comparative Analysis of Modified Multilevel DC Link Inverter with Conventional Cascaded Multilevel Inverter fed Induction Motor Drive. *Energy Procedia*, 117, 336–344, doi: 10.1016/j.egypro.2017.05.140.

12. Ramulu, C., Sanjeevikumar, P., Karampuri, R., Jain, S., Ertas, A. H., & Fedak, V. A. (2016). Solar PV Water Pumping Solution using a Three-Level Cascaded Inverter Connected Induction Motor Drive. *International Journal of Engineering Science and Technology*, 19, 1731–1741, doi: 10.1016/j.jestch.2016.08.019.

9

Analysis and Design of Bidirectional Circuits for Energy Storage Application

Suresh K[1]*, Sanjeevikumar Padmanaban[2] and S Vivek[3]

[1]Sree Vidyanikethan Engineering College, Tirupathi, A.P. India
[2]Aalborg University, Denmark
[3]SVEC, A.P. India

Abstract

The central focus of this chapter is to make an energy storage system to store power and also supply adequate energy to the load. Energy conversion process also gives clean, pollution free environment and also eco-friendly, the contribution of renewable energy will be the global effort to meet the challenges from global warming. To eliminate this drawback an energy storage device is used to store the energy, it also supplies smooth and continuous output power to the load. Bidirectional Chopper is a device used to convert fixed DC to variable DC and vice-versa. Embedded chopper (E-chopper) also a type of bidirectional chopper can produce wide range of voltages. The complete system is configured by closed loop and entire operation is based on five modes namely wind sourced battery mode, wind sourced battery-output mode, wind sourced output mode, battery sourced output mode and Grid sourced battery mode. In the simulink platform, circuit design is made through MATLAB for all the five modes are testing by giving inputs. The system involves three phase rectifier, UDC for initial step-up operation followed by BDC for buck-boost operations and rectifier/inverter grid synchronization. PID controller controls the BDC, UDC and Inverter operations in the closed loop.

Keywords: Embedded chopper, Wind Energy Conversion System (WECS), MATLAB Simulink, PID controller, Universal controller, energy storage system, inverter, rectifier etc.

9.1 Introduction

Electrical energy storage is very much required to avoid power failure, in domestic, industrial and commercial power systems. Worldwide, researchers are doing research to create a pollution-free environment. To achieve a clean and green environment, electrical drive-based vehicle is required in the present and future scenarios to save natural resources such as coals and fossil fuels. Power generation from renewable energies like wind, solar

*Corresponding author: sureshk340@gmail.com

Suman Lata Tripathi, Dushyant Kumar Singh, Sanjeevikumar Padmanaban, and P. Raja (eds.) Design and Development of Efficient Energy Systems, (131–150) © 2021 Scrivener Publishing LLC

and hydro, etc., are the precious sources from nature, and distribution of energy from the energy storage system to the appliances with low power loss by using efficient devices are at the research and development level. Large-scale energy storage is impossible on the part of the power supplying authorities because of maintenance problems and fault identification issues. But energy storage is possible in places such as domestic and small-scale commercial power systems by using closed loop configuration of the system. In the energy storage system bidirectional power flows are required for charging and discharging the battery.

Hybrid renewable energy storage with small signal energy stability analysis is also proposed in the simulation platform [1], but the autonomous power generation and storage system required less power loss and a wide range of voltage distribution. Valuation of energy storage in a different storage forms in the application of transmission and distributions was also proposed [2], but different level of voltage from a single energy storage is an effective one. Voltage source converter for transient stability analysis with energy storage also designed in a power system [3] which, but pulse width modulation is required to minimize power loss in an inverter circuit. Optimized energy storage and energy management system has also been introduced for grid scale applications [4–6] but e-chopper is required for bidirectional DC-DC conversion in an energy storage system for two direction of power flow. Multiple stage of hybrid energy storage was proposed about marketing strategy of power distribution [7] and application specific energy storage was also proposed [8] but three-phase conversion required a wide range of voltage.

PWM technique is required to increase power rating and reduce power losses in a DC circuit and inverters. This technique was adopted with Vienna rectifiers [9, 10] but this approach is applicable for unidirectional power flow, whereas energy storage applications required bidirectional power flow. Some comparative analysis also happened with space vector PWM in voltage source inverter and H-bridge inverter [11, 12], but the same unidirectional power flow is repeated. Multi-carrier PWM carrier based and reconstructed control signal for cascaded and multi-phase neutral point connection was also proposed in clamped multilevel inverter [13, 14].

In solar or any other renewable energy applications variable structure and sliding mode control technique is proposed to evaluate the performance of the power system [15, 16]; solar power extraction required boost operation with a control technique. The control technique mostly for maximum power point tracking (MPPT) with Secondary ended primary inductor converter (SEPIC) or Cuk or ZETA converter [17, 18], in the load side DC-AC conversion, pure sinusoidal signal sliding mode control of PWM is required. Embedded converter and controller concepts [19, 20] are also required in the bidirectional power flow of wind-based energy storage techniques with cascaded chopper as shown in Figure 9.1.

The proposed system has wind power as the main source and secondary power is grid; battery is the back-up source which has charging from both the sources. Discharging of battery or direct wind source will produce a wide range of voltage to AC or DC load connected to the system. The number of stage of conversion is single/double stage(s) by means of embedded chopper and Pulse width modulation (PWM) controlled three-phase inverters. So, the advantage of the proposed system is a wide range of voltage to both DC and AC

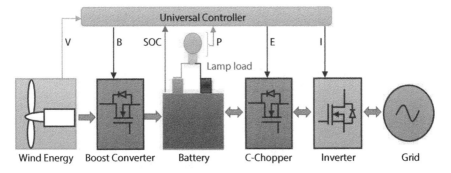

Figure 9.1 Existing energy storage system with universal controller.

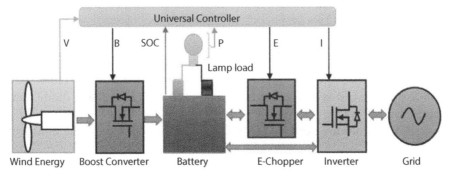

Figure 9.2 Proposed energy storage system with universal controller.

loads with high power rating and low power loss. The block diagram of the proposed system is shown in Figure 9.2.

9.2 Modes of Operation Based on Main Converters

The proposed energy storage system has three converters which are boost converter from wind energy conversion system, e-chopper is connected between battery and inverter and inverter (double-pole type). Inverter consists of twelve transistors (IGBT) and twelve diodes which are connected anti-parallel to the transistors. Six switches with feedback diodes are used to construct normal three-phase bidirectional vertical converter, also called two-stage conversion circuit, and the remaining six swiches are used for horizontal conversion; these six switches are used for single-stage conversion process. This conversion includes both inverter operation and rectifier operation. The overall circuit is shown in Figure 9.3; it includes double-pole 3Ø inverter and e-chopper. E-chopper is a bidirectional DC-DC converter which performs buck operation in one side ($V_L \rightarrow V_H$) and buck operation in another direction ($V_L \leftarrow V_H$). It also consists of two transistors (S_1 & S_2) with two feedback diodes. During boost operation S_1 is duty switch and feedback diode connected with S_2 helps to perform this operation,

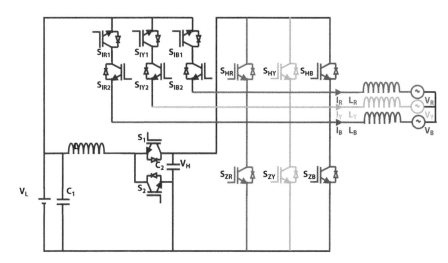

Figure 9.3 Overall proposed converter circuit.

and for buck operation it is vice-versa, S_2 is duty switch and feedback diode connected with S_1 helps to perform this operation.

The overall operations are explained with four modes of operation. The modes of operation are

i)   Single-stage rectification
ii) Single-stage inversion
iii) Two-stage rectification
iv) Two-stage inversion

9.2.1   Single-Stage Rectification

Single-stage rectifier operation includes only three diodes and three transistors. The overall rectifier operation is similar to a three-phase half-wave uncontrolled rectifier. Because all three phases have forward-biased diodes which are connected anti-parallel with S_{IR2}, S_{IY2} and S_{IB2} and duty switches S_{IR1}, S_{IY1} and S_{IB1} are connected series with forward-biased diodes. During this mode of operation e-chopper is excluded from the circuit so switching loss is reduced, which increases overall conversion efficiency input 3Ø voltage is converted DC V_L by means of rectification process as shown in Figure 9.4.

Three power from grid P_{grid} is expressed as

$$P_{grid} = 3VICos\phi \tag{9.1}$$

Phase voltages are expressed as

$$V_{RN} = V_m sin\omega_t$$

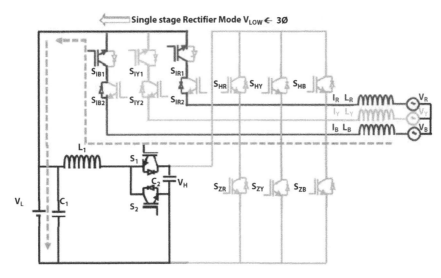

Figure 9.4 Single-stage rectification.

$$V_{YN} = V_m \sin\omega_t - 120° \tag{9.2}$$

$$V_{BN} = V_m \sin\omega_t + 120°$$

Average voltage across battery V_L is derived from phase voltage V_{RN} which is expressed as

$$V_L = \frac{3}{2\pi} \int_0^\pi V_m \sin\omega_t \, d\omega_t \tag{9.3}$$

Final output of average voltage across battery V_L is expressed as

$$V_L = \frac{3V_m}{\pi} \tag{9.4}$$

Output voltage is derived from phase voltages which can be charge battery now battery voltage level is approximately equal to three voltage if converter losses are neglected.

9.2.2   Single-Stage Inversion

Single-stage inverter operation includes three diodes and six transistors (IGBTs). The overall inverter operation is similar to three-phase inverter. DC supply V_{LOW} is splitted to three legs.

Each leg has two switches; the immediate switches of the DC supply are diodes which are connected anti-parallel to the switches S_{IR1}, S_{IY1} and S_{IB1}. These diodes are connected series to the duty switches S_{IR2}, S_{IY2} and S_{IB2} and these three switches are connected in each phase/leg. So duty switches immediate after diodes are called positive group switches (S_{IR2}, S_{IY2} and S_{IB2}).

Output of the negative group switches are connected in the centre part of the vertical inverter. Switches in the vertical inverter: positive group switches (S_{HR}, S_{HY}, S_{HB}), Negative group switches (S_{ZR}, S_{ZY}, S_{ZB}) legs, so the same negative group switches from vertical three-phase inverter S_{ZR}, S_{ZY} and S_{ZB} are used as negative group switches in the horizontal three inverter. So the three legs center part and negative group switches are common to both inverters.

During this mode of operation e-chopper is excluded from the circuit so switching loss is reduced, which increases overall conversion efficiency output 3Ø voltage is extracted from DC V_{LOW} from battery by means of inversion process as shown in Figure 9.5.

Fourier series of output line voltage can be expressed by

$$V_{RY} = \frac{1}{2}a_o + \sum_{n=1,2,3,..}^{\infty}(a_n \cos n\theta + b_n \sin n\theta)$$

(9.5)

$$V_{RY} = \sum_{n=1,2,3,..}^{\infty}\frac{4V_L}{n\pi}\cos\left(n\frac{\pi}{6}\right)\sin n\theta$$

(9.6)

Output line to neutral voltage is expressed as

$$V_{RY} = \frac{4V_L}{\pi}\cos\left(\frac{\pi}{6}\right)$$

(9.7)

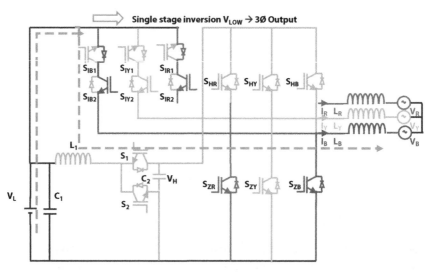

Figure 9.5 Single-stage inversion.

Output line to neutral voltage is expressed as,

$$V_{RY} = \frac{4V_L}{\sqrt{3}\pi}\cos\left(\frac{\pi}{6}\right) = \frac{2V_L}{\pi}$$

(9.8)

9.2.3   Double-Stage Rectification

Double-stage or two-stage rectification process includes two converters, which are 3Ø vertical rectifier and e-chopper. Six feedback diodes from vertical inverter switches are used as three-phase uncontrolled rectifier which converts three-phase AC to DC, which is input to e-chopper again rectifier converter is step down to the required value by means of buck mode from e-chopper. Positive group diodes from vertical inverter which are connected anti-parallel to positive group switches (S_{HR}, S_{HY}, S_{HB}), negative group diodes are from negative group switches (S_{ZR}, S_{ZY}, S_{ZB}) are formed three-leg three-phase bridge; each leg consists of two diodes which convert three-phase AC to DC according to the phase sequences.

E-chopper is as shown in Figure 9.6. Output from three-phase rectifier is DC voltage V_H which is input to E-chopper. This e-chopper is also called bidirection DC-DC converter during $V_H \rightarrow V_L$ i.e., buck mode operation. During this mode of operation already capacitor C_2 connected across V_H, now the transistor S_1 and Diode which is connected anti-parallel to S_2 are the duty switches to do the buck operation. There are two modes of operation: i) duty mode and ii) freewheeling mode.

9.2.3.1   Duty Mode - Interval -I

During duty mode switch S_1 is in ON state so the input voltage V_H is flowing to inductor L and output battery, now inductor L and battery are connected in series so, input voltage is the sum of Voltage inductor V_{Li} and voltage across the battery V_L is as shown in Figure 9.7. Output voltage across the battery is defined as the product of duty cycle δ and input voltage V_H, which is expressed as

$$V_L = V_H \frac{t_{on}}{T} = V_H \delta$$

(9.9)

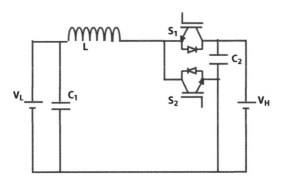

Figure 9.6 e-Chopper.

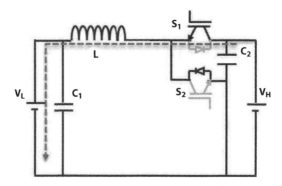

Figure 9.7 Mode-1 duty interval.

9.2.3.2 Freewheeling Mode - Interval -II

During freewheeling mode switch S_1 is turned to OFF state so the input voltage V_H is isolated from the inductor L and output battery, now inductor L and battery are in freewheeling via diode which is connected anti-parallel to S_2 which is as shown in Figure 9.8.

Overall conversion process taking two stage of conversion, this rectication process has an advantage, because two levels of DC voltages are possible. Output voltage of three-phase uncontrolled bridge rectifier V_H and V_H is again step down to V_L. The overall conversion circuit is as shown in Figure 9.9. Current flowing direction is indicated in the dotted line from grid to battery.

Rectifier output voltage V_H is input to the e-chopper. V_H is derived from three-phase rectifier. Three-phase input voltage to the uncontrolled bridge rectifier is already defined in the equation (9.2). Single-stage rectification output/e-chopper input is as shown in Figure 9.10. The output average voltage can be expressed in the equation (9.9) and (9.10).

$$V_H = \frac{3}{2\pi} \int_0^\pi V_m \sin \omega_t d\omega_t \tag{9.10}$$

$$V_H = \frac{3V_m}{\pi} \tag{9.11}$$

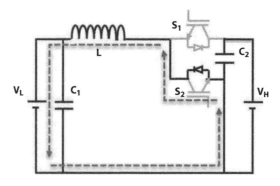

Figure 9.8 Mode-2 free-wheeling interval.

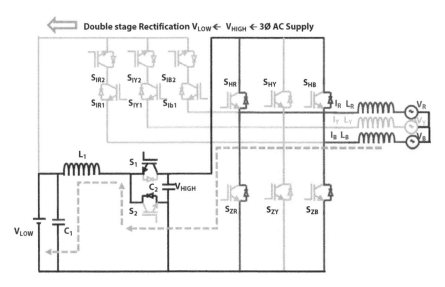

Figure 9.9 Double-stage rectification.

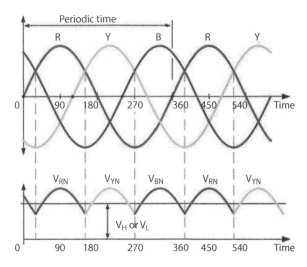

Figure 9.10 Single-stage rectification output/e-chopper input.

9.2.4   Double-Stage Inversion

Double-stage or two-stage inversion process includes two converters, which are e-chopper and 3Ø vertical inverter as shown in Figure 9.11. Six vertical inverter switches are used as three-phase inverter which converts three-phase DC to AC, which is output to e-chopper. E-chopper is a DC-DC converter which is step up to the required value by means of boost mode from battery voltage V_L. Positive group switches from vertical inverter (S_{HR}, S_{HY}, S_{HB}), negative group switches (S_{ZR}, S_{ZY}, S_{ZB}) are formed three-leg three-phase bridge inverter; each leg consists of two transistors which are converts DC to three-phase AC according to the grid frequency.

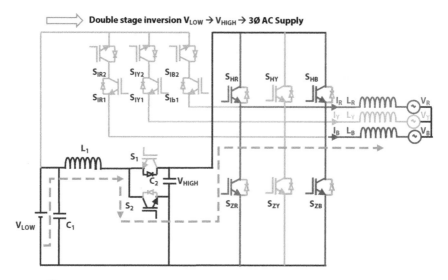

Figure 9.11 Double-stage inversion.

E-chopper is as shown in Figure 9.6. Output from battery is DC voltage V_L which is input to E-chopper; this e-chopper is also called bidirection DC-DC converter during $V_L \rightarrow V_H$ i.e., boost mode operation. During this mode of operation already capacitor C_1 connected across V_L, now the transistor S_2 and Diode which is connected anti-parallel to S_1 are the duty switches to do the boost operation. There are two modes of operation: i) Charging mode and ii) duty mode.

9.2.4.1   Charging Mode - Interval -I

During charging mode switch S_2 is in ON state so the input voltage V_L is flowing to inductor L from battery, now inductor L and battery are connected in series so, input voltage V_L is equal to inductor Voltage V_{Li} as shown in Figure 9.12. Output voltage across the inverter V_H, which is expressed as

$$V_H = V_L \frac{1}{1-\delta} \qquad (9.12)$$

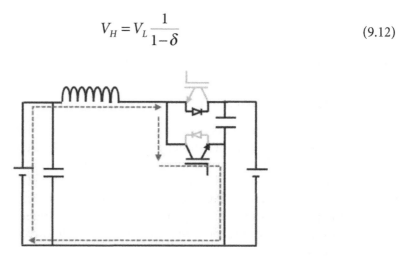

Figure 9.12 Charging mode.

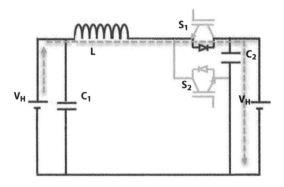

Figure 9.13 Duty mode.

Inductor design equation for all the modes are given by

$$L = \frac{DV_L T_S}{\Delta I_{o\max}}$$ (9.13)

Where V_L are input voltages
Capacitor design equation for all the modes are given by,

$$C_2 = \frac{DI_{o\max} T_s}{\Delta V_L}$$ (9.14)

Where V_H is output voltages, Ts is the total switching time period
D is the duty cycle
$I_{o\max}$ is the maximum current from changing current from I_1 to I_2
ΔV_L is the changing output voltage from minimum to maximum

9.2.4.2 Duty Mode - Interval -II

During duty mode switch S_2 is in OFF state so the input voltage V_{Li} (is equal to V_L) is combined with inductor voltage V_L appeared at the output, now sources discharging inductor L and battery are connected in series so, output voltage is the sum of Voltage inductor V_{Li} and voltage across the battery V_L is as shown in Figure 9.13. Output voltage across the inverter is expressed as.

9.3 Proposed Methodology for Three-Phase System

The proposed system has wind power as the main source and the secondary power is grid; battery is the back-up source which has charging from both the sources. Discharging of battery or direct wind source will produce wide range of voltage to AC or DC load connected to the system. Number of stage of conversion is single/double stage(s) by

Table 9.1 R phase power transfer switching.

Figure	S_{HR}	S_{ZR}	S_{LR1}	S_{LR2}
A	1	0	1	0
B	0	0	1	1
C	0	1	0	1

1 = Duty switches 0 = Switches are in OFF state.

means of embedded chopper and Pulse width modulation (PWM) controlled three-phase inverters.

During Inverter mode of operation power flows from WECS to grid; here two types of voltages are transfer from grid high voltage (V_1) and low voltage (V_2). Voltage from E-chopper is high voltage, Circuit operation of R phase is divided into three modes which are shown in Figure 9.14a, 9.14b and 9.14c. Figure 9.14a shows two-stage conversion (S_{HR} & S_{LR1} are duty switches) power from WECS is transferred to grid, because this power is excess power to the system, i.e., all the loads are in OFF state and battery is also in fully charged condition so this is excess if fed to the grid. Figure 9.14b shows single-stage conversion (S_{LR1} & S_{LR2} are duty switches) with low voltage transfer to grid. Figure 9.14c shows zero power transfer mode, because grid is completely isolated from the circuit (S_{LR2} & S_{ZR} are duty switches).

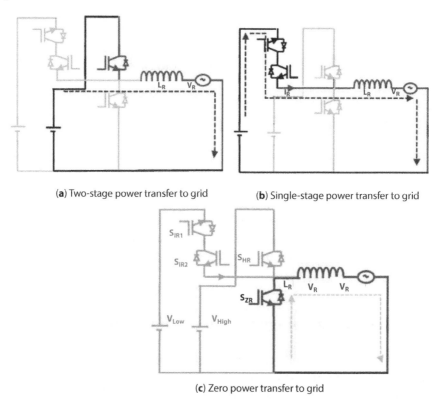

(**a**) Two-stage power transfer to grid   (**b**) Single-stage power transfer to grid

(**c**) Zero power transfer to grid

Figure 9.14 Inverter mode (power flow from WECS to grid).

9.3.1 Control Block of Overall System

E-chopper is a type of bidirectional converter switch S_1 for boost operation and transistor S_2 is for buck operation during both charging (buck) and discharging (boost) operation output voltage is regulated by PI controller. Control block diagram of E-chopper is shown in Figure 9.15; E-chopper is a type of bidirectional converter, switch S1 is for boost operation and transistor S2 is for buck operation during both charging (buck) and discharging (boost) operation output voltage is regulated by PI controller.

Output voltage is controlled to the required value by closed loop configuration of e-chopper which is shown in Figure 9.15. Output voltage is compared with reference signal $V_H{}^*$ or $V_L{}^*$ during boost and buck mode with outout voltages V_H or V_L. Result from comparator is error voltage is multiplied with SG (sine function) which are input to the PI controller, the signal is make as stable and finally given this control signal to Pulse Width Modulation (PWM).

Based on the modes of operations explained in section 2 switching operation is done; these switching operations are according to the requirement from the overall operation. During two-stage conversion this e-chopper and control system are in active state; otherwise e-chopper is in hidden mode. Three-phase inverter control block is explain the grid integration and related operation is as shown in Figure 9.16.

Output voltage V_L taken and compared with $\mathbf{V_H}{}^*$ (reference voltage) Calculated error is multiplied with SG (sign function), which is input to PI controller, stability of the signal is controlled finally fed to PWM. PWM has a carrier signal which is compared with control signal and final pulse is switching pulse to S_1 and S_2. During buck operation V_L is input to the control block. V_H is reference signal to control the operation of three inverter (DC-AC). If wind energy is the input to the system if any excess energy that have to export to grid. During grid integration frequency and phase matching is a very important task. So, PLL and park transformation plays an important role to do this task. Three-phase inverter output voltage is the input to the control block. Two number of (3Ø-2Ø) transformation is used to do this operation. First (3Ø-2Ø) transformation is control the phase by using Phase locked loop (PLL). Second (3Ø-2Ø) transformation output actual parameters are i_d & i_q which are compared with $i_d{}^*$ & $i_q{}^*$, error calculated. Error signal is input to PI controllers

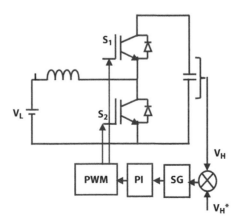

Figure 9.15 E-chopper control.

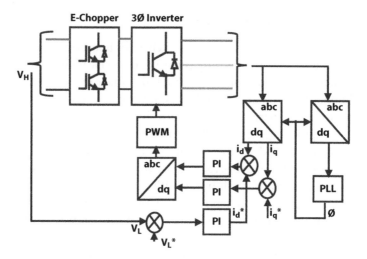

Figure 9.16 3Ø inverter control system.

which making these signals are stable and finally signals are again converted to 3Ø by using (2Ø-3Ø) transformation.

9.3.2 Proposed Carrier-Based PWM Strategy

Bidirectional DC-AC three-phase converter with e-Chopper (embedded chopper) is proposed for an energy storage system. The main purpose of using e-Chopper is to vary the supply voltage into different level to supply load and grid. For power rating and power loss reduction a carrier-based pulse width modulation (CB-PWM) technique with zero sequence injected embedded chopper is proposed. The proposed technique adopts very small power for the circuit process. By using this methodology power loss can be reduced. By using single-stage conversion-based power loss reduction converter overall efficiency

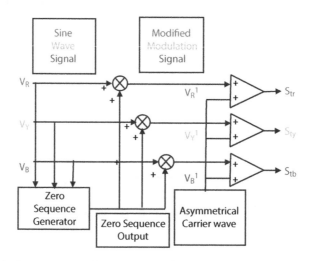

Figure 9.17 Proposed CB-PWM approach representation by zero-sequence injection.

can be improved; this technique is also called quasi-single-stage power conversion. Characteristics, working principle and real-time implementation of the proposed converter and its modulation techniques are to be analysed. The purpose of embedded chopper, effectiveness from the result, feasibility are to be analyzed in detail in the experiment. The novel converter has two positive group switches, one from normal vertical side and next positive group switch is from horizontal side, because battery voltage is V_L or minimum voltage. Load can be connected in the V_{HIGH}, or extra battery can be added with battery when voltage is high.

E-chopper is included in the circuit when different voltage is required; otherwise it can be excluded. The overall three-phase conversion is based on carrier-based pulse width modulation, which is used to integrate the stand-alone system with grid. Vertical positive group switches are used for two-stage inversion and also diodes in those switches are used for two-stage rectification. Horizontal switches are used for single-stage inversion and rectification purpose. Hardware is implemented and overall results are obtained with reduced power loss. This converter can be used for grid-tied renewable energy-based energy storage system where a different range of voltage required. Hardware implemented and the resulting discussion is explained in section 2.

9.3.3   Experiment Results

Output waveforms of the wind system is represented in Figure 9.18 to Figure 9.21. The input source is obtained from solar boost converter and wind PMSG are having variable supply is converted initially into DC voltage from Wind through three-phase uncontrolled bridge Rectifier.

Power loss comparion traditional versus proposed are illustrated in Figure 9.22. It is perceived that when null order signal added to sinusoidal modulation signals, then improved modulation signals clipped at -1, throughout 120 degrees' intermission of major sequence. Thus it can be obtained that equivalent phase could not control in the course of intervals besides the destructive current flows to the Vmin port is censored off.

The output of variable DC voltage and Bridge Rectifier output voltage is converted to fixed DC through boost converter in both the two primary sources. Those boost converters are controlled by PI controller as well as converter voltage is nearly constant through

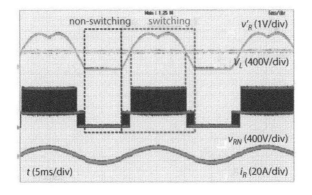

Figure 9.18 Experiment result VL.

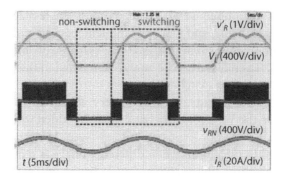

Figure 9.19 Experiment result of line voltage when $V_L = 250V$.

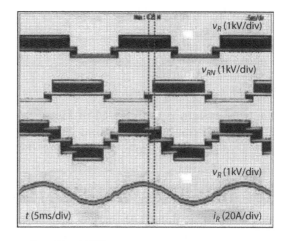

Figure 9.20 Steady state waveform $V_L = 350V$.

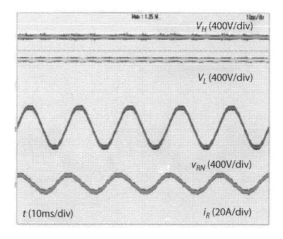

Figure 9.21 Proposed system dynamic waveform.

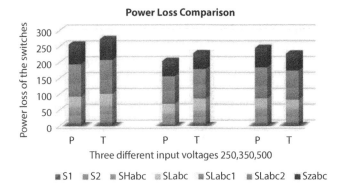

Figure 9.22 Power loss comparion T-Traditional, P-Proposed.

less amount of ripple content. Throughout the intermission of $0 \leq \theta \leq 2\pi/3$, the modulation phase VBI is compressed at -1, later phase B could not change also destructive phase current iB is prohibited for min voltage (Vmin) ports.

As a result, the inserted null-order signals can help to raise the normal significance of Il and consequently upturn the power PLow on behalf of three-phase proposed inverter. Meanwhile

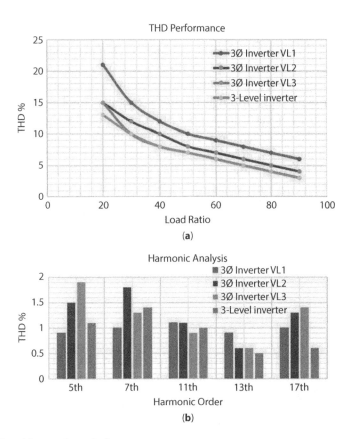

Figure 9.23 THD and harmonic analysis.

alterations SLx1 and SZx of each phase is not accomplished through 120 degrees' intermission of major sequence, the normal switching incidence of these alterations are condensed by 33%, thus defines minor power losses of the alterations ensured through three-phase proposed inverter. That results in extra benefit of suggested CB-Pulse Width Modulation approach. This constant DC is a straight connection and formed a DC bus. DC power is supplied to e-chopper. In the other side, the bidirectional converter operates in boost mode as well as buck mode. Again, the input energy is further converted from DC-AC and to the required level which is supplied to the resitive load. Figure 9.23 (a) and Figure 9.23 (b) are illustrated THD performance and Harmonic analysis.

Bidirectional energy storage interface by using a novel circuit of 3Ø inverter with embedded chopper. Bidirectional Chopper is a device used to convert fixed DC to variable DC and vice-versa. Embedded chopper (E-chopper) also a type of bidirectional chopper can produce wide range of voltages. Some of the application required wide range of voltages, but the problem from E-chopper is power loss and low power rating. To overcome these drawbacks a pulse width modulation technique is added with zero sequence injection. By using this proposed strategy e-chopper consumed very small power and mostly power is processed in the 3Ø inverter with a one-stage conversion. As a result, one-stage power conversion has more efficiency because of less power loss.

9.4   Conclusion

Novel bidirectional three-phase inverter through e-chopper and its CB-Pulse Width Modulation strategy is implemented, we observed that suggested DC-AC conversion through CB-PWM approach has salient features from theoretical approach, i.e., voltage of battery varies in wide range through help of e-chopper. Implementation of suggested CB-PWM approach gives the most active power for processing, through the three-phase proposed inverter by one-stage conversion as well as minimum power ratio needs for processing of e-chopper. Hence power requirement as well as power loss of e-chopper is minimized. In this, the suggested CB-PWM approach of three-phase proposed inverter minimizes the average switching frequency; consequently, minimized power losses are obtained. Because quasi-single-step conversion of power is obtained through suggested DC to AC conversion, hence transformation efficiency of whole DC to AC power is improved. Finally, whole features noticed that, suggested DC to AC conversion through CB-PWM approach is attractive for several maximum efficiency of bidirectional three-phase DC to AC conversion applications, i.e., energy storage systems, microgrids and electric vehicles, etc.

References

1. Lee, D., & Wang, L. (2008). Small-Signal Stability Analysis of an Autonomous Hybrid Renewable Energy Power Generation/Energy Storage System Part I: Time-Domain Simulations. *IEEE Transactions on Energy Conversion*, 23(1), 311-320.
2. Kleinberg, M. (2014) Energy Storage Valuation Under Different Storage Forms and Functions in Transmission and Distribution Applications. *Proceedings of the IEEE*. 102(7), 1073-1083.

3. Ortega, A., & Milano, F. (2016). Generalized Model of VSC-Based Energy Storage Systems for Transient Stability Analysis. *IEEE Transactions on Power Systems*, 31(5), 3369-3380.

4. Lawder, M. T. (2014). Battery Energy Storage System (BESS) and Battery Management System (BMS) for Grid-Scale Applications. *Proceedings of the IEEE*, 102(6), 1014-1030.

5. Byrne, R. H., Nguyen, T. A., Copp, D. A., Chalamala, B. R., & Gyuk, I. (2018). Energy Management and Optimization Methods for Grid Energy Storage Systems. *IEEE Access*, 6(1), 13231-13260.

6. Zhang, Z., Zhang, Y., Huang, Q., & Lee, W. (2018). Market-oriented optimal dispatching strategy for a wind farm with a multiple stage hybrid energy storage system. *CSEE Journal of Power and Energy Systems*, 4(4), 417-424.

7. Nishikawa, N., Nakano, M., & Kitsuregawa. M. (2015). Application Sensitive Energy Management Framework for Storage Systems. *IEEE Transactions on Knowledge and Data Engineering*, 27(9), 2335-2348.

8. Shu, Z., & Jirutitijaroen, P. (2014). Optimal Operation Strategy of Energy Storage System for Grid-Connected Wind Power Plants. *IEEE Transactions on Sustainable Energy*, 5(1), 190-199.

9. Lee, J., & Lee, K. (2015). Carrier-Based Discontinuous PWM Method for Vienna Rectifiers. *IEEE Transactions on Power Electronics*. 30(6), 2896-2900.

10. Al-Hitmi, M. A., Moinoddin, S., Iqbal, A., Rahman, K., & Meraj, M. (2019). Space vector vs. sinusoidal carrier-based pulse width modulation for a seven-phase voltage source inverter. *CPSS Transactions on Power Electronics and Applications*, 4(3), 230-243.

11. Huang, Q., & Huang, A. Q. (2018). Feedforward Proportional Carrier-Based PWM for Cascaded H-Bridge PV Inverter. *IEEE Journal of Emerging and Selected Topics in Power Electronics*, 6(4), 2192-2205.

12. Lee, J. & Lee, K. (2016). Performance Analysis of Carrier-Based Discontinuous PWM Method for Vienna Rectifiers with Neutral-Point Voltage Balance. *IEEE Transactions on Power Electronics*, 31(6), 4075-4084.

13. Ye, M., Chen, L., Kang, L., Li, S., Zhang, J., & Wu, H. (2019). Hybrid Multi-Carrier PWM Technique Based on Carrier Reconstruction for Cascaded H-bridge Inverter. *IEEE Access*, 7(1). 53152-53162.

14. Jiang, W., Huang, X., Wang, J., Wang, J. & Li, J. (2019). A Carrier-Based PWM Strategy Providing Neutral-Point Voltage Oscillation Elimination for Multi-Phase Neutral Point Clamped 3-Level Inverter. *IEEE Access*, 7(1), 124066-124076.

15. Agorreta, J. L., Reinaldos, L., Gonzalez, R., Borrega, M., Balda, J. & Marroyo, L. (2009). Fuzzy Switching Technique Applied to PWM Boost Converter Operating in Mixed Conduction Mode for PV Systems. *IEEE Transactions on Industrial Electronics*, 56(11), 4363-4373.

16. Feshara, H. F., Ibrahim, A. M., El-Amary, N. H. & Sharaf, S. M. (2019). Performance Evaluation of Variable Structure Controller Based on Sliding Mode Technique for a Grid-Connected Solar Network. *IEEE Access*, 7(1) 84349-84359.

17. Chung, H. S., Tse, K. K., Hui, S. Y. R., Mok, C. M. & Ho, M. T. (2003) A novel maximum power point tracking technique for solar panels using a SEPIC or Cuk converter. *IEEE Transactions on Power Electronics*, 18(3), 717-724.

18. Kumar, N. T., Saha, K. & Dey, J. (2016). Sliding-Mode Control of PWM Dual Inverter-Based Grid-Connected PV System: Modeling and Performance Analysis. in *IEEE Journal of Emerging and Selected Topics in Power Electronics*, 4(2), 435-444.

19. Reddy, B. D., A. N. K., Selvan, M. P. & Moorthi, S. (2015). Embedded Control of n-Level DC–DC–AC Inverter. *IEEE Transactions on Power Electronics*, 30(7), 3703-3711.

20. Ledoux, C., Lefranc, P., & Larouci, C. (2013). Pre-sizing methodology of embedded static converters using a virtual prototyping tool based on an optimisation under constraints method: comparaison of two power-sharing topologies. *IET Electrical Systems in Transportation*, 3(1), 1-9.

10

Low-Power IOT-Enabled Energy Systems

Yogini Dilip Borole[1]* and Dr. C. G. Dethe[2]

[1]Department of E&TC (GHRIET, Pune), Assistant Professor, SPPU Pune University Pune, Pune, India
[2]UGC - Academic Staff College, Nagpur, Director, Nagpur, India

Abstract

Synchronization of sustainable power source and streamlining of energy usage remain significant empowering influences of reasonable vitality developments plus relieving environmental modification. Present-day improvements in the field of Internet of Things (IoT) provides a wide-ranging amount of utilizations in the vitality area, i.e., in vitality supply, broadcast in addition with appropriation, plus application. IoT can be utilized for cultivating vitality productivity, expanding the portion of sustainable power source, besides diminishing ecological effects of the vitality use. This chapter surveys the current writing on the utilization of IoT in vitality frameworks, specifically, with regards to intense frames in detail. Moreover, we talk about empowering advancements of IoT, containing distributed work out as well as various stages for information investigation. Besides, we audit difficulties of sending IoT in the vitality partition, as well as protection in addition to security, using certain arrangements with the difficulties, for example, blockchain innovation. This review gives energy arrangement producers, energy financial analysts, and directors a review of the job of IoT in enhancement of energy frameworks. Here we examine and summarize the IoT worldview with an uncommon spotlight on energy utilization and furthermore, techniques for its minimization. Moreover, we examine about unwavering quality with regard to IoT devices. Taking all things together, this paper endeavors to be a beginning stage for users inspired by creating life-skilled IoT devices.

Keywords: Internet of Things, IoT devices, vitality productivity, vitality in structures, smart vitality schemes, smart network, bendable application, vitality storing

10.1 Overview

10.1.1 Conceptions

Machine-driven upheaval can be conveyed in four phases, each marked by fundamental new wellsprings of vitality. First was the mass extraction of coal and the improvement of steam power plants. This was followed by large-scale manufacturing and the power age. This was a time of fast improvement in industry, as shown by huge iron and steel creation.

**Corresponding author*: yogini.borole@raisoni.net

Suman Lata Tripathi, Dushyant Kumar Singh, Sanjeevikumar Padmanaban, and P. Raja (eds.) Design and Development of Efficient Energy Systems, (151–198) © 2021 Scrivener Publishing LLC

During this stage, some enormous scope manufacturing plants with mechanical production systems were built up and shaped new organizations [2]. The third insurgency presented PC and the novel of correspondence advances, e.g., communication framework, which empowered robotization in logostics [2, 3]. A wide-ranging variability of current advances, for example, correspondence frameworks (e.g., 5G), insightful mechanical device, and the Internet of Things (IoT) are relied upon to enable the fourth part, automatic upset [4–6]. IoT interconnects various gadgets, individuals, information, and procedures, by permitting them to interact with one another consistently. Consequently, IoT is able to give advantage for improvement in various procedures to be increasingly quantifiable and what's more, quantifiable, by gathering and handling huge amounts of information [2–7]. IoT can conceivably upgrade the personal satisfaction in various zones including clinical administrations, brilliant urban communities, development industry, agribusiness, water the board, and the vitality part [8]. This is empowered by giving an expanded automatic energetic frequently and encouraging devices for restructuring such choices.

10.1.2   Motivation

A wide series of present-day improvements, for example, correspondence frameworks (e.g., 5G), smart mechanical devices, and the IoT are required to permit the fourth part of the modern upheaval [2–6]. IoT can be linked with various gadgets/tools, individuals, information, as well as procedures, by allowing them to confer. The worldwide energy demand rose by 2.3% in 2018 contrasted with 2017, which is the most noteworthy increment since 2010 [9]. Subsequently, CO_2 outflows from the vitality area hit another peak in 2018 [1]. Compared to the pre-current temperature level, an Earth-wide temperature is pushing toward a rise of 1.5°C [10]. If this pattern should continue, and even surpass the 2°C target, an unnatural weather change will severely affect the world and human society [1]. The ecological distress, such as a worldwide temperature alteration and nearby air contamination, shortage of water assets, the draining of fossil vitality assets, raise a critical requirement for progressively effective utilization of vitality and the utilization of sustainable power causes [2]. Different assessments exhibited that a non-fossil vitality structure is for all intents and purposes impossible without profitable usage of vitality or conceivably abatement of vitality demand; moreover, a critical level of coordination of renewable energy sources, both at a country [11], regional [12], or wide-extending level [13].

In the United Nations Sustainable Development Goals plan [14], vitality capability is an important part of a sensible plan. In addition, vitality adequacy offers money-related points of interest by reducing the cost of fuel imports/supply, vitality stage, and diminishing creations from the vitality division. On behalf of improving vitality profitability in addition to moving toward an inexorably perfect vitality, a fruitful examination of the persistent data in the vitality stock system is a key activity [1–15]. The vitality creation organizes, after resource removal to passing on it in an important structure to the end customers, joins three huge parts: (i) vitality supply with upstream treatment office structures; (ii) vitality change structures including transmission and distribution of vitality bearers; and (iii) vitality demand side, which recollects the use of vitality for structures, transportation division, and the business [16]. Figure 10.1 shows the three portions with their material areas [2]. In this chapter, we discuss the activity of IoT in each and every various area of the vitality

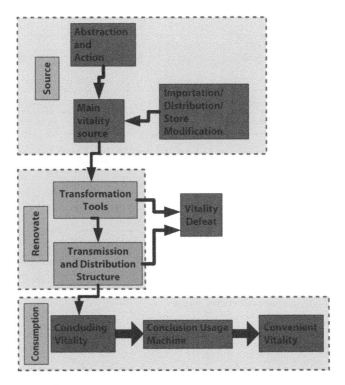

Figure 10.1 Three sections of energy segment.

creation range. Our point is to express the possible ability of IoT to enable usage of vitality, decline of vitality demand and growing the part of renewable energy sources.

IoT utilizes devices and correspondence inventions for detecting as well as communicating ongoing information, which empowers quick calculations plus ideal dynamic [17]. In addition, IoT can support the energy division to change from a brought together to a conveyed, smart, and incorporated vitality framework [1]. This is a significant prerequisite in sending area, spread renewable energy sources, for example, storm as well as sun-oriented vitality [18], also equally transforming some little scope end clients of vitality into prosumers by accumulating their stage and enhancing their interest at whatever point helpful for the framework. IoT-based frameworks mechanize, incorporate, and control forms through sensors and correspondence advances. Huge information collection and utilization of acute calculations for continuous information investigation can assist with checking energy utilization examples of various clients and gadgets in different periods with regulation that utilization all the more productively [1–19]. Figure 10.2 indicates the benefits of IoT in renewable energy sources.

Also the utilizations of IoT in sustainable power source creation include sensors that are joined to age, transmission, and dissemination gear. These gadgets help organizations to screen and control the working of the gear remotely progressively. This prompts diminished operational expenses and brings down our reliance on the effectively constrained petroleum derivatives. The utilization of sustainable power source assets as of now gives an assortment of advantages over regular ones. The usage of IoT will assist us with using these spotless vitality sources to a further degree.

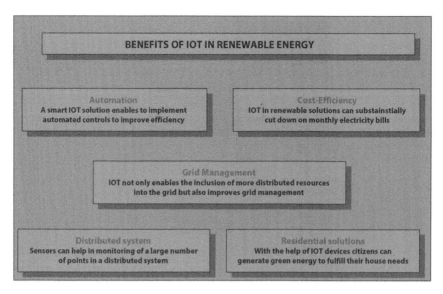

Figure 10.2 Benefits of IOT in renewable energy sources.

10.1.3   Methodology

The use of IoT in various areas and enterprises has been broadly examined in the literature (for instance [20–22]. In addition, difficulties and openings regarding the organization of a unique gathering of Internet of Things advancements have received a lot of specialized evaluation, e.g., devices [1–23] or 5G [1] arrange [24]. As for the vitality area, a large portion of studies have concentrated on unique explicit sections, e.g., structures or the specialized capability of a definite IoT innovation in the [1] vitality area [1]. Stokowski *et al.* [25] audits keen household utilizations of IoT as well as the vision of coordinating those claims interested in an IoT empowered condition. Hui *et al.* [26] examined the strategies, late developments, as well as execution of 5G [1] concentrating on the vitality request sideways. IoT jobs are cultivating vitality effectiveness in [1] structures as well as open vehicle are considered in [27, 28], individually Khatua *et al.* [29] surveys significant difficulties with appropriateness of IoT information change and correspondence conventions for arrangement in smart networks.

Be that as it may, not at all like the examined writing, the spotlight remains generally both in a particular subsector in the energy area or in certain IoT advances [1], this chapter surveys the utilization of IoT in the energy area, from energy stage to transmission and distribution in addition application sideways [1]. In that capacity, the fundamental commitment of this chapter is to broaden the current group of those are writing by giving vitality strategy producers, financial specialists, energy specialists, and others a general diagram of the chances and difficulties of applying IoT [1] in various pieces of the whole energy area. Right now, we will quickly present the IoT structure and its empowering advancements to frame a reason for examining their job in the energy section.

To lead this overview, the ongoing collection of writing about jobs in IoT in the vitality segment was gathered and surveyed [1]. Initially, looking through the expressions "Web of Things" as well as "Energy", the situation was indefinite, with respect to label, theoretical, and sayings of distributions put in different technical research publications. At that point, the restriction is extending towards the exploration of results in the direction of designing, financial aspects with the board divisions somewhere conceivable. Finally, we grouped the significant documents in classifications of vitality age (counting energy sections, auxiliary administrations, also unified sustainable power source), T&D frameworks (counting power, gas and region warming systems, and keen networks), and the interest side (counting vitality use in structures, transportation, and the business segment). We center around the IoT applications that can be for the most part material to the greater part of vitality frameworks without examining explicit circumstances with the limit surroundings [1]. Aimed at instance, the talk about jobs availability in IoT with knowledge structures, short of decreasing intent in the subtleties of structure typology [1], structure substantial, inhabitants' vitality utilization example, nature and amount of household apparatuses, and so forth. The remaining part of this chapter is organized as per surveys. Sections 2 and 3 present IoT with empowering advances, including sensors and correspondence innovations, distributed computing, and information scientific stages. Section 4 surveys the job of IoT in the vitality area. Section 5 discusses the chances and furthermore, the difficulties of sending IoT, while Section 6 depicts future patterns. Section 7 presents the conclusion.

II. Internet of Things

Internet of Things has a rising innovation which utilizes the network to give availability among physical objects or else "things" [1, 30]. Instances of physical objects incorporate household apparatuses as well as modern apparatus. Utilizing fitting devices plus correspondence organizes, this apparatus can give important information plus allow various organizations for individuals. For example, monitoring vitality utilization with structures in an extreme manner empowers the diminishment of energy expenses [1, 31]. IoT has a widespread scope in various applications, for example, trendy assembling, coordination in addition to development engineering [32]. IoT broadly is applied in the field of ecological testing, medicinal services frameworks and administrations, effective administration of energy in arrangements, also in robot built organizations [2, 33–36].

In the initial phase in constructing IoT frameworks, the sections of the IoT must be determined, for example, sensing components, correspondence convention, information storing and calculation should be fitting for the expected use. Designed for instance, an IoT stage calculated for controlling warming, refrigerating with cooling structure, needs significant ecological devices and utilizing reasonable statement innovation [1, 37]. Figure 10.3 indicates the various stages in an IoT [1, 38]. IoT devices such as sensing devices, moving and controlling of machine are the second parts of the IoT platforms, and are used to join the pattern of information mixture, communication, and organizing. Internet of Things elements allow transmitting the information into the IoT [2] framework as well as setting up two-way communication among the gadget to-entryway and entry to-network.

IoT stage is having correspondence conventions as a third part [2] which empowers the various components toward the impart and impart related information to the controlling devices or else the dynamic focuses [2]. As per the applications IoT stages provides flexibility with correspondence advancements (each having explicit highlights). Different wireless technologies with networks LTE-4G and 5G systems [1, 40] can be considered by IoT such as communication between two devices called Wi-Fi, for transferring data Bluetooth module is used, and encryption is done by ZigBee module [1, 39] and cell invention. In the fourth stage of IoT the information is stored. The information is gathered from the sensing elements.

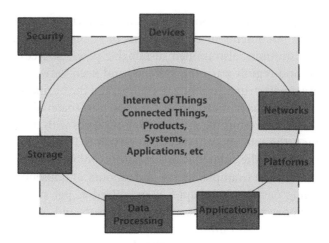

Figure 10.3 Chart representing the parts of an IoT stage.

On a fundamental level, the information gathered from the devices is huge. This requires arranging a proficient information stockpiling that will be available on network servers. In the fifth stage of IoT the acquired information is used for diagnostic commitments [1]. The information examination can be performed disconnected in the wake of putting away the information or it very well may be a type of ongoing investigation. The information diagnostic is necessary for dynamic activity of the [1] claim. As per the usage information examination can be performed disconnected or ongoing. The consume information is first gathered and afterward pictured on premises utilizing representation apparatuses in disconnected examination. If there should arise an occurrence of constant investigation, the network servers are developed for observation, for example stream investigation [41].

10.2 Empowering Tools

Internet of Things shows a worldview in that articles as well as components of a framework that are furnished with devices, machines, and controllers communicate with one another to offer important types of assistance. In IoT frameworks, sensors are utilized to detect and gather information, and through passages course the gathered information to control focuses or the cloud for additional capacity, handling, investigation, and dynamic. Later the choice offers a relating instruction showed back to the machine introduced with framework because of the detected information. As there are a variety of sensing components and moving gadgets, correspondence advances, also information registering drew nearer, right now, clarify the current innovations which empower IoT. At that point, we give models after writing exactly how these advances exist for utilization in the vitality division [1].

10.2.1 Sensing Components

Sensing components are the most significant feature of IoT [42]. These components are used to gather as well as convey information progressively. The utilization of sensors upgrades feasibility, usefulness, and assumes a basic job in the achievement of IoT [1, 43].

Various kinds of sensing devices are available which are formed for different use commitments. Prototypes for claims incorporate farming production, natural observing, and social insurance frameworks as well as administrations, and open wellbeing [44]. By and by, in the vitality segment including vitality creation, transmission and conveyance, and creation, numerous of these sensors are utilized. In the vitality part, sensors are utilized to make reserve funds in both expense and vitality. Sensors empower brilliant energy the executive's framework and give ongoing vitality streamlining and encourage new methodologies for energy load the board. The examination and future patterns of the sensor gadgets are additionally focused on improvement of sensing devices requests to increase capacity forming as well as customers' mindfulness, for example advancement of explicit offices to upgrade creation of sustainable power sources [1, 45]. The utilization of sensing elements inside IoT, with vitality area to a great extent improving diagnostics, dynamic, investigation, streamlining forms and incorporated execution measurements. Because of the enormous number of sensors utilized in the vitality area, in the accompanying we clarify scarcely any instances of usually considered with sensing elements in vitality creation as well as utilization.

Heat sensing devices are available to distinguish the changes between warming and cooling a framework [1, 46]. Heat sensing devices is a significant with normal natural limit. For vitality division, essential standard of intensity age is the way toward converting motorized drive into voltaic vitality, though motorized vitality is accomplished after high temperature vitality, for example warm force undergrowth, blustery weather, liquid stream, and what's more, sun oriented force plants. These energy changes are acquired utilizing warmth, that is heat. At vitality utilization side, the temperature sensors are utilized to amplify the presentation of a framework at the point when temperature changes during ordinary activities. For instance, in local locations the finest period for killing continuously or else the air circulation as well as refrigerating frameworks also observed in heating sensing elements; in this way, vitality is able to be overseen accurately so as to spare energy [42].

Light-sensitive detector is present to use towards gauge brightness (encompassing sunlit glassy) or else the splendor of sunlight. With vitality utilization, light sensing detectors have a few usages in mechanical as well as ordinary shopper claims. Considering primary wellspring of vitality utilization in structures identifies with illumination, represent individually about 15% of all out power utilization [1, 48]. On a worldwide scale, around 20% [1] of power consumed for lighting [1, 49]. In this manner, a light-sensing device can be used toward naturally controlling stages of light inside as well as outside in spinning manner or else darkening the light stages, like electrical signals consequently consider for balancing because of changes in encompassing light. Right now, vitality used for the illumination of the internal situations be able to diminished [19].

Passive Infrared detector (PID) sensing motion device, otherwise called movement detector, is used to estimate the ultraviolet luminous energy produced by effects from the environment. For vitality utilization, sensing elements are used to lessen the vitality utilization in structures [1]. Aimed at instance, by utilizing PID devices, nearness of people intimate solar system can be identified. In the event that not any development recognized by universe, at that point the luminous controller of the universe kills luminous, that is, keen controller of illumination [1]. Right now, power utilization of the structures is diminished [50]. Additionally, this can be applied for cooling frameworks which expend almost 40% of the energy in structures [48].

Closeness sensors are used to recognize the nearness of close by objects with no bodily interaction [51]. With model utilization of vicinity sensing devices is in airstream vitality creation [1]. These sensing devices give life span as well as dependable location detecting execution in windmills. In windmills, utilizations of nearness sensing devices incorporate edge area controller, rotation direction, propeller, and rotation breaking direction; disc brake observing; as well as propeller speediness checking [52].

Non-Contact sensors

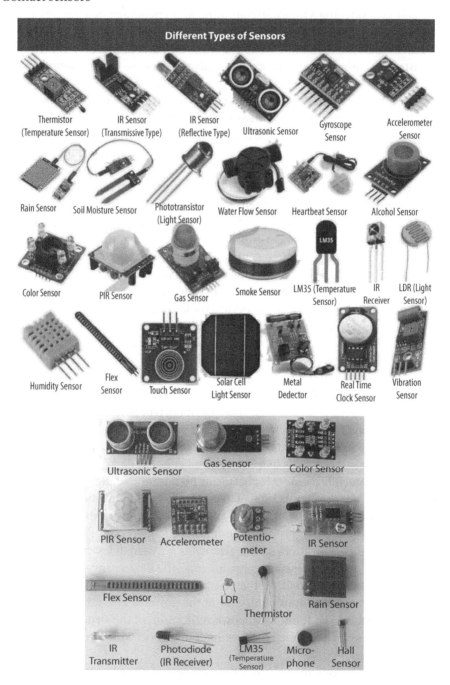

Figure 10.4 Different types of sensors for different applications.   (*Continued*)

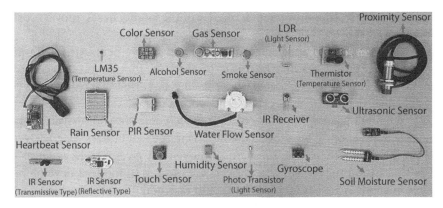

Figure 10.4 (*Continued*) Different types of sensors for different applications.

These sensors are also called as proximity sensors [5]. This device actualized utilizing various procedures such as Visual (Ultra violet), sound waves, voltage levels, charge on conductor, and so on.

Level sensing devices

Level sensing devices are used to work with the wide-ranging waves with repetition more noteworthy as compared to humanoid perceptible series. These devices work by conveying a sound wave at a recurrence over the scope of human hearing. The device decides the separation to an objective by estimating time slips by between the sending and getting of the ultrasonic heartbeat.

This is solid in any illumination condition and can be utilized private or external. These devices can deal with crash evasion for a mechanical device, which show regular motion, extended as it isn't excessively quick. These are so broadly utilized, they can be dependably actualized in grain canister detecting applications, liquid level detecting, ramble applications and detecting vehicles at your nearby drive-through café or bank. It can be ordinarily utilized as gadgets to distinguish a crash.

Various kinds of Sensors in homes, workplaces, vehicles and so on can be discovered. They attempt to make life simpler by recognizing life essence, modifying the temperature of an area, identifying glow or firing, making scrumptious espresso, making an alert when a vehicle is close to a carport entryway and numerous different errands.

Figure 10.4 shows various kinds of sensing components which can be considered for different applications.

10.2.2   Movers

Movers (Actuators) [1] are gadgets that translate more or less, sort of put away vitality, into movement. The put away vitality is as a rule as packed air (air-filled weight), voltage drop, or fluid (water powered) pressure. It is commonly put away inside a fixed chamber made as a rule from metal. It considers potential contribution after mechanization frameworks, can contribute to activity, also follow up on the gadget and equipment inside the Internet of Things frameworks [1, 53]. Movers products distinctive movement examples, for example, direct, oscillatory, or pivoting movements. In view of the vitality bases, movers sorted such as accompanying categories [1, 54].

Air-filled movers utilize compacted gas for producing movement. Air-filled movers are created with cylinder or else a stomach so as to produce the thought process control. These movers are utilized for controlling forms whose need is fast also exact reaction, as per these procedures needn't bother with a lot of thought process power.

Hydraulic actuators use the fluid for creating movement. Pressure-driven actuators are comprised of a chamber or on the other hand liquid engine that utilizes water-driven capacity to give mechanical activity. The mechanical movement gives a yield as far as straight, spinning, or fluctuation movement. The movers are utilized in modern development controller wherever rapid as well as huge powers stand essential.

Warm air movers utilize a warmth hotspot for generating bodily activity. Warm air movers change heat vitality to kinematic vitality, or else movement. By and large, thermoregulatory devices made out of a heat-detecting substance fixed through a stomach which drives in contradiction of an attachment on behalf of touching a cylinder. The heat-detecting substance is of any type of fluid, vapor, slippery substance-similar material, or else somewhat substance that modify capacity dependent on heat.

Electrical drive spread on outer vitality bases, for example cell power unit to produce movement. Electrical drive called machine-driven devices equipped for changing over power into active energy in either a solitary straight or revolving movement. The plans of these actuators depend on the planned assignments inside the procedures.

In the energy area, for instance, in energy station, air-filled movers are generally useful in regulators. Electrical command-taps controller innovation empowers accomplishing vitality proficiency. They are additionally frequently utilized for last controller component for activity in a force unit [1, 55]. Likewise, here assortment of controller created for vitality engineering, for example linear drives provides answers for limiting the vitality squander at entrance of trapdoors as well as securing burst air rotator as well as making movement into sun powered following boards. In the writing there are likewise numerous investigations meant to delineate the uses of the actuators inside Internet of Things. For example, the examination from [1, 56] offers remote based controlling system to give an Internet of Things-build programmed insightful framework. While, by advancing the activity of gadgets and machineries with the use of Internet of Things, the recommended framework accomplishes decrease in general vitality utilization in a specified period.

10.2.3   Telecommunication Technology

Through the rise in the field of the Internet of Things, implanted originators are, similar never before, concentrating and endeavors on framework vitality utilization. A prime model is a remote sensor hub—a moderately basic gadget from a utilitarian perspective that is required to carry out its responsibility for an all-encompassing period (at times, years) while fueled by a battery.

Plan contemplations incorporate significant framework components, for example, the microcontroller (MCU), remote interface, sensor and framework power the board. Figure 10.5 shows an example of wireless sensor node architecture.

The MCU should be amazingly vitality proficient. Computational necessities will probably direct the determination of a 32-piece or 8-piece MCU, yet low vitality prerequisites

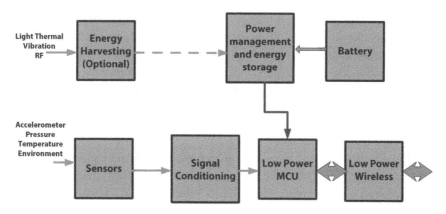

Figure 10.5 Classic wireless sensor node design.

stay paying little mind to the MCU decision. Vitality utilization in low-force and dynamic modes, just as the need to rapidly wake up from low-power modes to max throttle activity, will have a noteworthy effect in monitoring battery power.

> *"Scheme reflections include key system elements such as the microcontroller (MCU), wireless communication, sensor devices and power system management."*

Consider how much the picked MCU can manage without really utilizing the CPU center itself. For instance, huge force reserve funds can be accomplished through independent treatment of sensor interfaces and other fringe capacities. Having the option to create the improvement sign, or force supply, for the sensor from the MCU and read back and decipher the outcomes without waking the MCU until "helpful" information is gotten can go far toward boosting the framework's battery life.

Regarding remote availability. The system topology and the selection of conventions will both affect the force spending plan required to keep up the remote connection. At times, a straightforward point-to-point interface utilizing an exclusive sub-GHz convention may appear to be a suitable decision to yield the most reduced interest on power from the battery. Be that as it may, this design can restrain the extent of where and how the sensor can be conveyed. A star design based on either 2.4 GHz or sub-GHz advances builds the adaptability for different sensor organization, yet this would almost certainly expand the intricacy of the convention, along these lines expanding the measure of RF traffic and framework power.

A third choice to consider is a work setup dependent on a convention, for example, ZigBee. While a work organize forces the greatest channel on the sensor hub battery, it additionally gives the best degree of adaptability. Contingent on the remote stack, a work system can likewise furnish the most dependable organization choice with a self-mending network. In a sensor hub, the measure of information to be sent over the remote connection ought to be moderately little. All things considered, ZigBee gives an ideal work organizing arrangement; Bluetooth Smart is a fantastic decision for norms based, power-touchy point-to-point designs, and exclusive sub-GHz arrangements give greatest adaptability to organize size, transmission capacity and information payloads in star or point-to-point setups.

For wide regions, long-extend advances and stages, for example, LoRa and Sigfox, empower high hub check systems coming up to many kilometers and with low-power frameworks. Information security is getting increasingly significant. On the off chance that the MCU used to run the stack doesn't have encryption equipment, it should consume various cycles to run the calculation in programming affecting the general force utilization. Various sensor decisions are accessible and can extend from discrete to completely coordinated arrangements. Discrete arrangements might be power proficient, yet place extra handling prerequisites on the MCU.

Building signal molding into the sensor gives some noteworthy points of interest. The information that is sent to the MCU will be significant information that can be rapidly and effectively deciphered by the application, which implies the MCU can stay unconscious as far as might be feasible. Having preconditioned information sent over a computerized interface, for example, SPI or I2C, likewise implies the MCU can accumulate the information more proficiently than if it were utilizing its ADC. A last structure thought for low-vitality applications is controlling the framework itself. Contingent on the kind of battery utilized in the application, there is regularly a necessity for help converters or lift exchanging controllers. A cautious decision can bigly affect the framework's general force utilization as arrangements extend from 1 uA – 7 uA utilization.

For progressively complex frameworks, a force the executives incorporated circuit (PMIC) gives increasingly exact power over the entire framework. From a solitary force source, various voltage rails can be created to drive various components of the installed framework, tuning every voltage rail to give simply enough capacity to the application. A PMIC may likewise offer extra usefulness for general framework control, for example, guard dog clocks and reset capacity.

At last, there are a wide range of framework structure viewpoints associated with planning low-vitality, battery-fueled applications. Notwithstanding low-power semiconductor segments, the way to deal with programming, including remote stacks, encryption and information preparing, are significant contemplations. Every one of these plan components can significantly affect the framework's general force spending plan, while empowering designers to make low-vitality IoT gadgets that augment valuable battery life.

So Wireless communication frameworks assume the significant job in initiating IoT. Wireless frameworks interface the sensor gadgets to IoT passages and perform start to finish information interchanges between these components of IoT. Wireless frameworks are created dependent on various remote benchmarks and the utilization of every one relies upon the prerequisite of the application, for example, correspondence go, data transfer capacity, what's more, power utilization prerequisites. For instance, regularly infinite causes of vitality, containing air as well as sunlight based force units remain situated at extremely isolated zones.

In this way, guaranteeing a dependable IoT correspondences in remote spots is testing. Utilizing IoT frameworks on these locales requires determination of reasonable correspondence innovation that can ensure a proceeds with association interface and support current information move in a energy productive way. Because of the significance of correspondence advances in IoT, right now survey a portion of these innovations. We additionally show to not many guides to show their job in the vitality division. At that point, we give a correlation in Table 10.1 to appear distinction of every one of the advancements after functional through Internet of Things.

Table 10.1 Evaluation chart of different wireless technologies [1, 62, 93–98].

Technology	Range	Data rate	Battery usage	Security	System cost	Applications
LoRA	<=50km	0.3–38.4 kbps	8 to 10 yrs	Maximum	Reasonable	Intelligent constructions
Narrow Band	<=50km	<=100kbps	1 to 2 yrs	Maximum	Reasonable	Transmission
LTE-M2	<=200km	0.2–1 Mbps	7 to 8 yrs	Maximum	Average	Intelligent indicator
0G Network	<=50km	100 bps	7 to 8 yrs	Maximum	Average	Electrical paddings
LoRaWPAN	< 5 km	100 kbps	Maximum	Maximum	Reasonable	Intelligent indicator
Blue-tooth	<=50m	1 Mbps	to a small extent	Maximum	Reasonable	Intelligent household usages
Zig Zag Network	<=100m	250 Kbps	5 to 10 yrs	Minimum	Reasonable	Intelligent progression in Solar power
Spacecraft	>=1500km	100 kbps	Maximum	Maximum	Expensive	Lunar & air Energy units

In Blue-tooth private range net small vitality Blue-tooth device is a short series remote correspondence innovation with Internet of Things that empowers trading information utilizing small wireless frequencies. Small vitality Blue-tooth device exists fewer expensive to send, through a common scope of zero meter to thirty meter, that empowers making a moment individual territory organize [1, 64]. Small vitality Blue-tooth device targets little scope Internet of Things requests that expect gadgets towards convey little volumes of information devouring insignificant force. Businesses in the energy segment with an all-around planned IoT procedure can make new types of motor-to-motor as well as motor-to-personage correspondence utilizing such innovation.

Within vitality segment, Small vitality Blue-tooth device is broadly utilized for vitality utilization in private and business structures. As an example, these creators from [1, 65] portray a brilliant workplace vitality the board framework which decreases a vitality utilization in personal computers, screens, as well as illuminations utilizing Small Vitality Blue-tooth device. Other investigation suggests a vitality the board framework used for savvy households which uses Small vitality Blue-tooth device for correspondence among household equipment targeting diminishing the vitality at homes [66]. So also, utilizing Small vitality Blue-tooth device the examination from [67] presents fluffy built answer used for brilliant vitality the board in a household computerization, pointing cultivating household vitality the board conspire.

Zig Zag network (ZigBee) [1] is a correspondence innovation, can be used to make individual zone arrange and targets little scope uses. Zig Zag network is everything but difficult for execution as well as intended toward give minimal effort, small-information rate, and exceptionally dependable systems designed for small energy requests [68, 69].

Zig Zag network as well uses work arrange detail wherever gadgets are associated through numerous interconnectivity. Utilizing work organizing by high point of Zig Zag network, the most extreme correspondence extend, at range of hundred meter is broadened fundamentally. Now the vitality area, the model Internet of Things with Zig Zag network incorporate illumination frameworks (structures as well as road lights), keen networks, for example savvy electrical measurement devices, household robotization frameworks as well as modern computerization. Usage of these types of demands means to give draws near for expending vitality in a productive manner. In writing, expecting to limit the vitality costs of the buyers, the exploration in [70] assesses the exhibition of home vitality the executive's application through building up a remote sensor organize utilizing Zig Zag network.

By inventors of [1, 71] additionally present intelligent household interactions for capability between Zig Zag network, electric hardware, as well as sharp measuring devices for usage of vitality maximum productively. Invention through [1, 72] offerings a Zig Zag network for checking framework can be utilized to gauge as well as move the vitality from household apparatuses next to exits plus the illuminations, targeting lessening vitality utilization. One more examination [1, 73] shows ground investigations utilizing Zig Zag network based which observe solar cell as well as air vitality frameworks. All investigations show capability of Zig Zag networks used for conveyed infinite stage as well as brilliant meter structures.

Low-power wide-area network arrangement with Internet of Things shows the interfacing of sensing elements to the cloud and allows the physical stage message information as well as systematic communication to improve effectiveness and capacity. LoRA is a financially savvy correspondence innovation for huge organization of Internet of Things, which can be considered to support numerous existences of batteries life time. Long range is considered to build up significant space communicates (max ten kilometers in country territories) by small force utilization [1, 74]. Things to see about the innovation style is reasonable correspondence innovation used in the vitality segment for the most part in keen urban communities, for example, keen networks and building computerization frameworks, for example, savvy meters.

With the investigation through [75] targets enhancing vitality utilization through sending structure vitality the executives framework utilizing Long range protocol. Study suggests a stage in incorporating numerous frameworks, for example, cooling, lighting, and vitality observing to implement constructing vitality improvement. Creators created an AI-based brilliant control used for a business structures Heating, Ventilation, and air conditioning using Long range.

0G network is a widespread territory arrange innovation can utilize a radical-tight group. 0G networks permits gadgets for speaking by small force used for empowering Internet of Things uses [1, 78]. Aimed at the suitability of the innovation in the vitality area designed for instance, the study from [1, 79] audits the innovative improvements as well as presents 0G network as extraordinary compared to other low force contender for savvy metering for empowering constant vitality administrations for family units. What's more, the investigation in [80] look at diverse low force wide territory arrange advancements and presume 0G network is a reasonable answer for utilizing by battery operated fittings sensing devices aware in shrewd structures.

LTE-M2 is a low-power wide area network which correspondence innovation can boosts enormous quantity of Internet of Things components as well as administrations with a great information level with exceptionally small idleness. LTE-M2 is a minimal effort arrangement which shows extensive cell lifetime as well as gives upgraded inclusion. As indicated by the creators of [1, 81], because of the dormancy highlights of LTE-M2, these innovation has a prospective answer intended for perceptive vitality dissemination organizes through giving minimal effort interchanges to keen meters. Furthermore, the investigation in [1, 82] exhibits the LTE-M2 innovation for shrewd meters. Additional usage of LTE-M2 in the vitality division, study from [1, 83] presents LTE-M2 such as a likely answer meant for brilliant framework correspondences via contrasting LTE-M2 and additional correspondence advancements regarding information rate, idleness, and correspondence go.

LTE-M2 stands in 3GPP (3rd age association venture) institutionalization, which is intended to lessen the gadget multifaceted nature designed for gadget-kind correspondence [84]. LTE-M2 underpins protected correspondence, gives universal inclusion, and offers high framework limit. LTE-M2 likewise provides administrations of lesser dormancy as well as greater amount as compared to contracted group network in Internet of Things [1, 85]. Furthermore, the innovation provides vitality proficiency asset assignment used for little controlled gadgets, considering a possible answer in place of keen device [1, 86] as well as brilliant framework correspondences [1, 87].

LoRaWPAN exposed remote quality which created in the direction of building up correspondence between incredible quantity of Internet of Things gadgets as well as machineries. LoRaWPAN has prospective answer designed for shrewd meters for vitality segment [1, 88]. In light of examination in [1, 89], LoRaWPAN is a reasonable remote innovation be able to be utilized for keen household Internet of Things applications designed for smart metering also brilliant structure interchanges.

Spacecraft is one more correspondence innovation which has a broad-region inclusion also be able to bolster small information amount uses in device-to-device style [1, 90]. Spacecraft innovations are reasonable to support Internet of Things gadgets as well as equipment within distant spots. Work from [1, 91] offerings an Internet of Things-establish device-to-device spacecraft correspondence specifically material near the keen network, especially used for the broadcast as well as dispersion area. A comparable report features significance of utilizing spacecraft produced with Internet of Things interchanges in vitality area, for example, sun based and air control units [1, 92].

10.2.4   Internet of Things Information and Evaluation

Assuming as well as examining the information produced by IoT permits increasing further understanding, precise reaction to the framework, and helps settling on reasonable choices on vitality utilization of the frameworks [99].

Notwithstanding, registering IoT information presents a difficult question. Since Internet of Things information recognized as Excessive information alludes near enormous measure of organized and unstructured information, produced from different components of IoT frameworks for example, sensors, programming applications, keen or clever gadgets, and correspondence systems.

Because of the attributes of Vast information, has huge dimensions, maximum speed, as well as maximum assortment [100], it should be productively prepared to be broken down [101]. Handling the Big information is past the limit of conventional strategies, i.e., putting it away on neighborhood hard drives, registering, and dissecting them a while later. Propelled registering and explanatory techniques are expected to deal with huge information [2, 102, 103]. As given below, we clarify distributed work out also mist figuring, has broadly utilized in place of handling what's more, processing the Big information.

10.2.4.1   Distributed Evaluation

Distributed evaluation has an information preparing method that gives suggestions administrations, claims, stockpiling, what's more, figuring through the web and permits calculation of information gushed commencing Internet of Things gadgets. With distributed evaluation, gloom alludes toward "Web" as well as figuring alludes toward calculation plus preparing administrations obtainable through methodology [1, 104]. Distributed evaluation comprises equally application benefits that are gotten to by means of the Internet and the equipment frameworks, which are situated in server farms [105]. Utilizing these qualities, distributed computing empowers handling the enormous information, and gives complex calculation capacities [106]. The fundamental advantages of utilizing cloud frameworks depends on [107] (I) essentially diminishing the expense of equipment; (ii) upgrading the figuring force and capacity limit; and (iii) having multi-center structures, which facilitates the information the executives. Besides, distributed computing is a made sure about framework, which gives assets, processing force, and capacity that is required from a topographical area [108]. These highlights of distributed computing empower the large information came about because of the developing uses of IoT to be effectively examined, controlled and arranged productively [109]. What's more, distributed computing takes out the costs required for buying equipment and programming and running the calculations for handling the IoT information, coming about in extensively minimization of power required for neighborhood information calculation.

10.2.4.2   Fog Computing (Edge Computing)

In spite of the fact that distributed computing is a standout amongst other figuring standards for information handling for IoT applications. Because of the deferral and data transmission confinement of brought together assets that are utilized for information handling, progressively productive techniques are necessary. Mist processing stays circulated worldview as well as expansion of the gloom, who changes the registering as well as explanatory administrations close towards power in part of arrangement. Haze processing which is worldview allows extends the gloom by a more noteworthy scales also bolster bigger outstanding task at hand [110]. In haze registering, any gadget with processing, stockpiling, and system association capacity fills in as haze hub. The instances of these gadgets incorporate, however, are not restricted to individual PCs, modern controllers, switches, switches, and installed servers [111]. Right now worldview, haze gives IoT information preparing and capacity locally at IoT gadgets as opposed to transfer it on gloom. The upside of this methodology is that it incorporates upgraded protected administrations essential for some Internet of Things uses such as decreasing system traffic and dormancy [112]. In this manner, as opposed to the cloud figuring, mist offers preparing and registering administrations with quicker reaction with higher security. This empowers quicker dynamic and taking fitting activities.

10.3   Internet of Things within Power Region

Currently, vitality area stands profoundly reliant on continuously non-renewable energy sources, comprising about 80% of last vitality all inclusive. Unreasonable extraction and burning of petroleum products has a negative impact on the environment and human wellbeing; it also has monetary effects because of air contamination and environmental change, to give some examples. Energy productivity, i.e., devouring less vitality for conveying a similar help, and the organization of sustainable power source sources are two principle choices to lessen the negative effects of non-renewable energy source use [12, 13].

Regarding the job of Internet of Things within vitality part, as of energy abstraction, activity, what's more, upkeep (O&M) of vitality producing resources, for transmission & distribution as well as termination utilization of vitality Internet of Things be able to play significant job now decreasing vitality misfortunes as well as bringing down CO_2 emanations. An energy the executives framework in view of IoT can screen constant energy utilization and increment the degree of mindfulness about the vitality execution at any degree of the inventory network [15, 113]. This segment examines the use of IoT in energy stage organizes first. At that point, we proceed with the idea of keen urban areas, what kind of authority span used for some Internet of Things-depends on systems, for example, excellent matrices, smart structures, powerful manufacturing plants, what's more, understanding transportation. Next, we examine every one of the previously mentioned segments independently. We abridge the discoveries of this area in Tables 10.2 and 10.3.

10.3.1 Internet of Things along with Vitality Production

Programming mechanical methods as well as controlling switch also information obtaining frameworks developed well known within force part in the 1990s [1, 37]. Through checking also monitoring hardware as well as procedures, beginning times with Internet of Things began for adding near the force part through easing danger to harm for creation or on the other hand power outage. Dependability, productivity, ecological effects, and upkeep problems remain primary difficulties of ancient force units. More period with hardware into force division also unfortunate upkeep issues be able to prompt elevated level of vitality misfortunes and untrustworthiness. Resources are in some cases more than 40 years of age, pricey, and can't be supplanted without any problem. Internet of Things is able to add to diminishing approximately of such difficulties with administration with intensity units [1, 37]. Next to relating Internet of Things sensing devices, interweb-associated gadgets can recognize any disappointment in the activity or irregular reduction in energy effectiveness, disturbing the requirement for upkeep. This expands dependability and productivity of the structure, furthermore to decreasing the expense of upkeep [1, 114].

For diminishing petroleum derivative use and depending on neighborhood energy assets, numerous nations are advancing RESs. Climate reliant or variable sustainable power source (VRE) sources, for example, wind and sun-based energy, present new difficulties within vitality framework recognized as "the discontinuity challenge". Within a vitality framework by a great portion of variable renewable energy, coordinating age from vitality within request which is a major test in arrears to inconstancy through market interest bringing about confuse in various period gages. Internet of Things frameworks offer the adaptability in offsetting stage with request, who thus can decrease the difficulties of sending VRE, bringing about higher coordination portions of hygienic vitality as well as fewer Chlorhexidine gluconate discharges [1, 116]. What's more, through utilizing Internet of Things, the progressively proficient utilization through vitality be able to be accomplished at utilizing AI calculations that help decide an ideal parity of various organic market advancements [37]. For example, the utilization of man-made reasoning calculations can adjust the force yield of a warm force unit within wellsprings through internal control age, for example, collecting some little scope sunlight based PV boards [1, 117]. Table 10.2 abridges utilizations via Internet of Things from vitality division, through vitality source guideline furthermore, marketplaces.

10.3.2 Smart Metropolises

These days, the amazing pace of urbanization just as overpopulation has brought numerous worldwide concerns, for example, air and water contamination [118], vitality get to, and natural worries. By keeping in mind single principle experiments which give urban communities perfect, reasonable and dependable energy sources the ongoing improvements and advances have given a main thrust to put on practical, Internet of Things built answers used for current issues within a keen urban setting [1, 119]. Bright workshops, keen households, energy units, as well as homesteads within town be able to be associated also an information regarding the vitality utilization within various periods be able to be accumulated. On the off chance which discovered a segment, for example, local locations, expends the maximum vitality toward the evening, at that point naturally energy gave to

Table 10.2 Claims – Internet of Things for vitality region (1): rule, marketplace, and energy quantity side.

	Claim	Region	Explanation	Profits
Rule and Marketplace	Vitality establishment	Directive	Giving entry in the direction of the lattice network for several smaller customer for end to end energy skill as well as selecting the dealer easily.	Improving chain of command inside vitality source cable, bazaar control, as well as regional source; running vitality flea market as well as decreasing rates for customers; also relating responsiveness on vitality usage also productivity
	Combination of small manufacture by consumers (practical control units)	Vitality marketplace	Conglomerating weight also age as to gather of last clients to provide power, adjusting, or else save market place.	Activating little masses towards taking an interest in thoughtful market place; selection the framework through lessening burden in top occasions; get around the danger of great control advertisements by top periods; also, cultivating adaptability about framework as well as decreasing the requirement in place of adjusting resources; Proposing benefit in the direction of buyers
	Protective conservation	Upstream oil and gas industry/service firms	Error, drip, and exhaustion checking through examining of large information composed from end to end stationary as well as portable devices or else camcorder.	Decreasing hazards through distress, creation misfortune also support personal time; diminishing the expense of O&M; and forestalling mishaps also, expanding wellbeing.

(Continued)

Table 10.2 Claims – Internet of Things for vitality region (1): rule, marketplace, and energy quantity side. (*Continued*)

	Claim	Region	Explanation	Profits
Energy Source	Fault maintenance	Upstream oil and gas industry/service organizations	Recognizing disappointments and issues in vitality systems what's more, potentially fixing them basically.	Improving unwavering quality of an assistance; improving rate in fixing spillage in area warming or disappointments in power frameworks; and decreasing support time and danger of wellbeing/security.
	Energy storing and analytics	Manufacturing dealers or service companies	Breaking down market information and opportunities for enacting adaptability alternatives, for example, energy storing in the framework	Diminishing the danger of market interest imbalance; expanding benefit in energy exchange by ideal utilization of adaptable and capacity choices; and guaranteeing an ideal system for capacity resources.
	Digitalized control group	Service firms & system operative	Dissecting large information of and controlling numerous age parts by various period measures.	Cultivating safety for source; cultivating resource utilization also the executives; lessening rate for arrangement of reinforcement limit; quickening reaction towards damage of burden; also, diminishing danger for power outage.

additional sectors, for example, industrial facilities, might be limited towards adjustment the entire framework by any rate charge also danger of blockage or power outage. Within a smart city, various procedures, that is, data communication with correspondence, keen recognizable proof, area assurance, following, observing, contamination control, and personality the board can be overseen consummately by the guide of IoT innovation [120]. IoT innovations can assist with checking each item in urban. Structures, city framework, transportation, vitality systems, also advantages might be associated with sensing devices. Those associations are able to guarantee a vitality effective smart city by steady observing of information accumulated after sensing devices. Aimed at instance, through checking automobiles through Internet of Things, road illuminations know how to be organized designed for ideal utilization of vitality. Likewise, the specialists may approach the assembled data also and settle on progressively educated choices taking place to transport decisions as well as the vitality request.

10.3.3   Intelligent Lattice Network

Intelligent Grid frameworks exist current lattices conveying the best safe as well as trustworthy information and communication technology innovation to controller plus streamline vitality age, transmission & distribution frameworks, also customers. Through associating various acute measuring devices, a practicality matrix builds up a multi-way progression one of data, might be utilized on behalf of ideal the executives of the framework and effective vitality circulation [121]. The utilization of savvy framework be able to featured into various divisions as a part of the vitality framework independently, for example, vitality stage, structures, or on the other hand transportation, or they can be viewed as inside and out.

In conventional lattices, batteries were energized by connectors through power links and power inverter [1, 121] whose cells might be exciting remotely into shrewd lattice, utilizing an initial exciting innovation. What's more, in a keen matrix, the energy request example of end clients can be dissected by gathering information done with information of technology stage, aimed at instance, hour of arraigning of cell headsets or else electrical vehicles. At that point, the closest remote cell control location is able to apportion an ideal schedule opening also gadget/automobile be able to excite. One more favorable position remains utilization of Internet of Things resolve prompt improved controller what's more, checking of the battery prepared gadgets, and in this way, primary, the vitality appropriation may be balanced, also succeeding, the conveyance is a part of power towards that automobiles might be ensured. Choosing decrease unessential vitality utilization impressively. Furthermore, Internet of Things knows how to be useful in secluded along with micro-grids within certain landmasses or else associations, mostly while vitality is compulsory each and all minute using not any special case, example, within databanks. Now like frameworks, totally advantages associated with network be able to communicate through one another. Additionally, information taking place vitality request every advantage is available. That cooperation be able to guarantee the ideal administration in terms of the vitality dispersion at whatever point and wherever required. Regarding community effect of practicality lattices, as shown in Figure 10.6, within a savvy town furnished through Internet of Things-built smart frameworks, various areas of the city can be associated together [121].

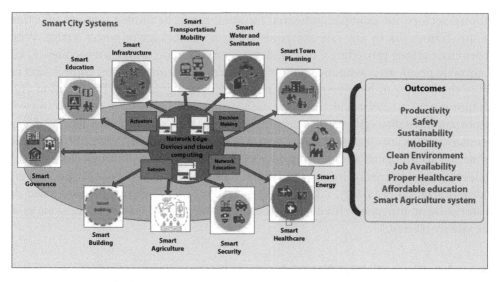

Figure 10.6 An integrated information connectivity in a smart city model.

During the collective correspondence between various areas, the shrewd lattice can caution administrators through brilliant apparatuses before any intense issue happens [113, 122]. For instance, through steady checking, it very well may be distinguished if energy request surpasses the limit of the lattice. In this manner, by securing ongoing information, various methodologies may be embraced by specialists and energy utilization might be reorganized to an alternate period after around is lesser anticipated interest. Now certain districts, shrewd (or else energetic) valuing duties have been considered at variable energy costs right now. Actual period rating duties just while vitality cost determines greater by a specific period once the utilization of vitality exists probably accepted to be maximum. From end to end the information accumulated since the segments of the are part of shrewd framework, vitality utilization also age may be splendidly streamlined as well as overseen in a long shot located systems. Decrease of transmission misfortunes in T&D organizes through dynamic voltage the board or decrease of non-specialized misfortunes utilizing a system of smart meters are different instances of relating Internet of Things [1, 37].

10.3.4   Smart Buildings Structures

The vitality utilization within urban areas might be isolated hooked on various portions; private structures (local); also business (administrations), containing plants, workplaces, also institutes, also transportation. The local vitality utilization now private segment incorporates light, hardware (apparatuses), local high temp liquid, catering, chilling, warming, air circulation, and cooling (Figure 10.7). Air conditioning energy utilization commonly represents half of energy utilization in structures [124].

In this manner, the administration of HVAC frameworks is significant in decreasing power utilization. With the headway of innovation in the business, IoT gadgets can assume a significant job to control the vitality misfortunes in HVAC frameworks. For instance, by finding some remote indoor regulators dependent on inhabitance, empty spots can be figured out.

When an empty zone is identified, a few activities are able in use to bring down vitality utilization. For example, heating, ventilation, and air conditioning frameworks are able to lessen activity

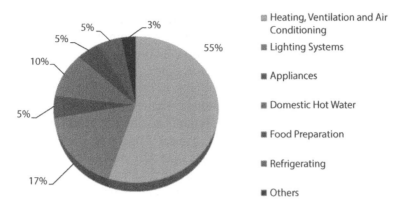

Figure 10.7 Segment of domestic energy intake.

within empty zone, who drive prompt huge decrease in vitality utilization as well as misfortunes. Internet of Things is able to likewise be applied to deal with the vitality misfortunes of illumination frameworks. Aimed at instance, from end to end relating Internet of Things-built illumination frameworks, clients initiative be cautioned while vitality utilization energies past the typical stage. Besides, via a proficient investigation which is part of the ongoing information, weight after high-pinnacle will be moved towards short-top stages. These create a noteworthy commitment towards ideal utilization as part of electric vitality [119, 125] also decreasing linked ozone depleting substance outflows. Utilizing IoT, the interest reaction will be progressively nimble and adaptable, and the observing and request side administration will become increasingly effective.

10.3.5 Powerful Usage of Vitality in Production

Internet of Things may be utilized towards structure which is completely associated also adaptable framework into business nearby decrease vitality utilization which is streamlining creation. Now in conventional manufacturing plants, amount of vitality is consumed for delivering the finished result also control the nature of the final result. Additionally, checking each single procedure requires HR to be included. Be that as it may, utilizing a dexterous and adaptable framework in smart production lines assists with perceiving disappointments simultaneously instead of remembering them by observing the items toward the finish of creation line. Consequently, an appropriate move can be made immediately to turn away inefficient creation and related waste energy. As far as checking forms during assembling, IoT, and its empowering innovation play a critical job. Door gadgets, IoT center point systems, network attendants, as well as glooms stages, that are available using savvy cell phones (example, advanced cells or else PCs) can be models of observing hardware.

Remote correspondences, for example, Wireless internet, Blue-tooth, Zig-Zag network, wireless communication protocols, or on the other hand wired interchanges, for example, network interface card know how to be utilized for interfacing entire parts of hardware [126]. In addition, to utilize Internet of Things all the extra effectively, through introducing sensing components arranged on every part of a mechanical place, segments as expend additional vitality as compared to ostensible vitality stage be able to be recognized. Therefore, each and every segment can be handily dealt with, the issues of segments can be fixed, what's more, the energy utilization of every segment can be streamlined. This famously brings about lessening the energy misfortunes in savvy plants. In an understanding plant, information handling which is significant component into entire framework, from end to end information at gloom stage (goes about as per a cerebrum) drive be broke down to support administrators settling on progressively proficient choices in time [127]. As far as observing and keeping up resources of assembling, the enormous issue in production lines exits devaluation of machineries also automated gadgets. By a fitting Internet of Things stage too instruments, best possible gadget size can be chosen to lessen mileage and the related upkeep costs. IoT-based contingent checking guarantees the mechanical gadget never arrives at its edge limit. This essentially implies the device keeps going longer and endures fewer disappointments. In addition, the disappointments which source vitality misfortune be able to foreseen toward handled. Internet of Things-built light-footed frameworks which give a keen framework to joint effort between clients, produces, and organizations. Along these lines, a particular item will be produced straightforwardly agreeing to clients' structure. Along these lines, energy expended during the way toward putting away extra parts furthermore as per the vitality squandered now distribution centers to hold onto the extra portions drive decreased altogether. Just a definite quantity of items within different sorts of self-control be produced also put away, that upgrades the executives of vitality utilization also creation proficiency [126].

10.3.6   Insightful Transport

Unique significant reasons for wind contamination with vitality misfortunes into large urban communities is abuse of reserved automobiles rather than open transport. Instead of a conventional transportation framework where every framework works autonomously, put on Internet of Things advancements into transport, alleged "smart transportation", deals a worldwide administration framework. Additionally, the constant information handling assumes a noteworthy job in rush hour gridlock the board. All the segments of the transportation framework can be associated together, and their information can be handled together. Blockage control and understanding stopping frameworks utilizing on the web maps are a few utilizations of shrewd transportation. Keen utilization of transportation empowers travelers to choose extra charge-sparing choice using smaller separation as well as the quickest course, who spares a noteworthy measure sequential and vitality [1, 120]. Residents resolve the option toward decide the appearance period also oversee the calendar all the more proficiently [125]. In this manner, time of city excursions will be abbreviated, and the vitality misfortunes will be decreased fundamentally. This can significantly lessen CO_2 outflows also extra air dirtying airs after transport [1, 119]. Table 10.3 outlines uses of Internet of Things into the vitality segment, later practicality vitality lattices at the conclusion utilization of vitality. Internet of Things-built digital representation changes a vitality framework after a one-way communication bearing, that is, since age through vitality networks towards customers, to a coordinated energy framework. Various pieces like incorporated intelligent vitality framework stay portrayed in Figure 10.8.

10.4   Difficulties - Relating Internet of Things

Other than altogether the advantages of Internet of Things in place of vitality sparing, sending Internet of Things within vitality area speaks to moves that should be tended to. This area tends to the difficulties and existing answers on behalf of relating Internet of

Table 10.3 Uses –Internet of Things within vitality area.

	Application	Sector	Description	Benefits
Communication and Supply	Smart grid-irons	Electrical lattice network organization	Policy into functioning lattice network by means of huge information as well as information and communication technologies skills such as opposite towards ancient lattice network.	Cultivating vitality proficiency as well as joining through disseminated age also burden; cultivating safety through source; and lessening requirement into reinforcement source boundary as well as expenses.
	System administration	Electrical lattice procedure & controlling	With large information by different ideas with lattice to achieve the lattice additional best possible.	Recognizing feeble focuses as well as strengthening matrix likewise also decreasing hazard through power outage.
	Combined control of rechargeable vehicle fleet (EV)	Electric grid procedure & controlling	Evaluating information of charging locations and cycling period of electric vehicle.	Cultivating more reaction related on period request at top occasions; breaking down and determining the effect of EVs on load; and recognizing regions for putting in innovative filling station also support by appropriation lattice.

(Continued)

Table 10.3 Uses –Internet of Things within vitality area. (*Continued*)

	Application	Sector	Description	Benefits
	Regulator as well as managing by automobile through lattice network	Electrical lattice network procedure & controlling	Examining capacity as well as working of Electric vehicle Such as supportive Lattice once desired.	Cultivating the adaptability included in the framework by actuating electric vehicle by providing matrix through power; Decreasing requirement used for reinforcement limit all through top periods Controller also the executives of electric vehicle armada to suggestion ideal collaboration among lattice as well as environmental studies.
	Micro-grids	Energy network	Stages such as handling a lattice self-regulating after the significant grid.	Cultivating safety of source; making compatibility also adaptability among Micro-grids plus the primary network; in addition to contribution of steady power costs aimed at the customers associated with micro-grid.
Claim Side	Regulation as well as supervision part of the Region heating system	District heating system	Examining large information regarding heat and burden within organize as well as associated customers.	Cultivating the effectiveness part of the matrix in assembly request; lessening with heat of warm liquid source as well as sparing vitality after conceivable; also distinguishing network focuses by requirement intended or deification.
	Request reaction	Domestic/ marketable & manufacturing	Significant controller that is through detaching, instable, or else flattening.	Falling request by highest period, who decreases network jamming.

(*Continued*)

Table 10.3 Uses –Internet of Things within vitality area. (*Continued*)

Application	Sector	Description	Benefits
Request reply (request side controlling)	Domestic/ marketable & manufacturing	Focal controller means Through detaching, moving, otherwise then again flattening; heap by numerous shoppers through investigating burden as well as activity of apparatuses.	Decreasing interest at top time, which itself decreases the network clog; lessening purchaser power bills; and diminishing the requirement for interest in framework reinforcement limit.
Innovative metering organization	Customer	With sensing devices as well as gadgets to Gather also examine burden with fever information at user location.	Approaching nitty determined load varieties in distinctive time scale; recognizing zones for Improving energy effectiveness (for instance excessively well-ventilated places or additional illuminations after tenants); and diminishing rate of vitality usage.
Cell-operated vitality controlling	Customer	Information examination designed for starting battery-operated ultimate at appropriate time	Deal technique for control/release of cell within various period gage; cultivating vitality proficiency, also serving the framework by top periods; also diminishing expense of vitality usage.
Intelligent structures	Customers	Central as well as isolated controller of applications and strategies.	Cultivating luxury through best mechanism of machines aa well as heating, ventilation, and air conditioning structures; decreasing physical interference, valid period with vitality; collective awareness about vitality usage with eco-friendly effect; cultivating willingness towards linking a keen network or else essential control unit; as well as enhanced mixing of spread group with storing schemes.

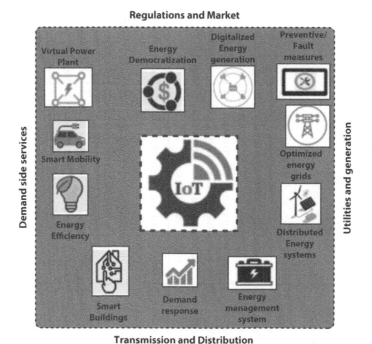

Figure 10.8 Claims of Internet of Things within incorporated intelligent vitality arrangement.

Things-built vitality frameworks. Moreover, in Table 10.4, we condense difficulties and also present arrangements of utilizing Internet of Things within vitality area.

10.4.1 Vitality Ingestion

Now vitality frameworks, the significant exertion of Internet of Things stages remain sparing vitality. Within vitality frameworks towards empower correspondence utilizing Internet of Things, a very large quantity of Internet of Things gadgets transmit information. Towards path of Internet of Things framework also convey immense measure of information produced after the Internet of Things gadgets extensive measure via vitality is required [128]. Hence, vitality utilization of Internet of Things frameworks stays such as a significant experiment. Nonetheless, different methodologies take attempted towards diminish force utilization of IoT frameworks. For instance, through site the sensing devices in the direction of rest approach also simply effort after essential. Planning effective correspondence conventions which permit circulated registering methods that empowers vitality effective correspondences has been concentrated significantly. Applying radio improvement strategies, for example, balance advancement and helpful correspondence has been considered as an answer. Additionally, vitality effective steering procedures, for example, group models and utilizing multi-way directing methods was comprehended as another arrangement [1, 129, 131].

10.4.2 Synchronization via Internet of Things through Sub-Units

The principle experiment remembers joining one of Internet of Things framework for subdivisions including vitality framework. Since subdivisions of the vitality area exist one of

Table 10.4 Experiments as well as present clarifications by use of Internet of Things within vitality region.

Task	Problem	Model Answer	Advantage
Construction proposal	Provided that a consistent endways assembly	Via varied orientation constructions	Communicating belongings also society
	Different tools	Relating open customary	Flexibility
Combination of internet of things with subdivisions	Internet of Things information controlling	Scheming mockup simulations	Actual information between procedures also subdivisions
	Combination Internet of Things through effects in structures	Molding integrated energy schemes	Decrease in cost of conservation
Regularization	Substantial arrangement of IoT devices	Significant a scheme of structures	Regularity between several Internet of Things gadgets
	Changeability between several Internet of Things gadgets	Exposed data copies also procedures	Cover several machineries
Vitality depletion	Communication as a part of great information amount	Arrangement of well-organized message rules	Equivalent vitality
	Well-organized vitality ingestion	Scattered calculating methods	Equivalent vitality
Internet of Things Safety	Extortions as well as hacking	Cryptogram patterns, scattered controller schemes	Better-quality safety
Operator isolation	Preserving customers' individual data	Requesting for operators' authorization	Allows improved management

a kind utilizing different sensor and information correspondence advancements. In this manner, arrangements are required for dealing with the information trade in the middle of subdivisions of an Internet of Things-empowered vitality framework [2, 132–134]. A methodology aimed at discovering answers for the reconciliation challenge, considering the IoT necessities of a subsystem, relates to displaying a coordinated structure in place of the vitality framework [1, 132]. Different arrangements recommend structuring co-reenactment [1] prototypes designed for vitality frameworks headed for incorporate the framework also limit bringing together defer mistake among the subdivisions [1, 135, 136].

10.4.3   Client Confidentiality

Protection alludes near one side part of single or helpful vitality purchasers towards privacy within own data once imparted to an association [1, 137, 138]. In this manner, getting to legitimate information, for example, the quantity of energy clients just as the number and kinds of apparatuses which utilize vitality become incomprehensible. In reality, these kinds of information which can be assembled utilizing IoT empowers better dynamic that can impact the energy creation, dispersion and utilization [139]. In any case, to diminish the infringement of clients' protection, it is suggested that the energy suppliers request client authorization to utilize their data [140], ensuring that the clients' data won't be imparted to different gatherings. Another arrangement would likewise be a confided in security the board framework where energy buyers have authority over their data and security is recommended [141].

10.4.4   Safety Challenges

Web of Things is one of the advances that is getting very mainstream in vitality segment everywhere throughout the world. Organizations are utilizing this innovation to their focal points and there are certainly numerous preferences to procure from it also. From shrewd inventories to keen homes and even savvy structures IoT gadgets are all over the place and vitality division is beginning to utilize these gadgets to their advantage too.

Other than the cost sparing and vitality preservation viewpoint there is another significant thing related with brilliant gadgets and IoT which is the large amount of business-basic information that is gathered from them. This information can help organizations in settling on brilliant choices and permit them to offer better types of assistance to their clients. One of the most presumed organizations all over Europe for information assortment and investigation explicitly identified with the vitality part is Electrigence. With aptitude and involvement with the applicable field, they are known for giving customer-driven information arrangements that can assist organizations with developing utilizing IoT and large information.

In any case, the entire procedure of coordinating IoT gadgets in the total vitality framework isn't a simple assignment for any organization and they face a few difficulties. This is one of the principle reasons why in spite of having various points of interest organizations at times remain reluctant in getting a full IoT-based upgrade to improve their framework.

One of the primary issues looked at by power organizations in actualizing IoT-based arrangements is the multifaceted nature of the way toward coordinating this framework over the current one. Coordinating IoT innovation on any current stage can be a major test for any organization and the entire circumstance turns out to be considerably increasingly troublesome in the vitality division because of the mind-boggling nature of the framework. For an organization lacking legitimate range of abilities, this mix turns out to be practically unthinkable which is the reason the undertaking is dropped before it even starts. In the event that electric organizations need to receive the full reward of IoT bases frameworks they ought to be happy to put resources into it first. Legitimate groups of specialists ought to be enlisted to actualize and direct the entire procedure of usage. Individuals ought to likewise be utilized to supervise the framework after its execution with the goal that the organization can get legitimate profit by these gadgets just as the information gathered from these gadgets.

Another issue that organizations face with respect to IoT gadgets in vitality arrangement is information security. There is a great deal of urgent buyer information engaged with this sort of arrangement which in inappropriate and can end up being awful for the shoppers and totally annihilate the reputation of the organization. This is a significant motivation behind why organizations should reexamine and update their information security arrangements when they move towards an IoT-based framework. Organizations should do substantial interest right now well to ensure that all the information which they gather from buyers stays safe from cybercriminals. This extra venture is something that has made a great deal of organizations reevaluate their choice with respect to IoT-based plan of action.

10.4.5   IoT Standardization and Architectural Concept

Extreme items produce enormous volumes of information. This information should be overseen, handled, moved and put away safely. Institutionalization is vital to accomplishing all around acknowledged details and conventions for genuine interoperability among gadgets and applications.

The utilization of principles:

- Guarantees interoperable and practical arrangements
- Opens up circumstances in new regions
- Permits the market to arrive at its maximum capacity

The more things are associated, the more noteworthy the security chance. Thus, security principles are likewise expected to ensure the people, organizations and governments which will utilize the IoT. IoT utilizes an assortment of advances with various measures to interface from a solitary gadget to an enormous number of gadgets. The irregularity among IoT gadgets that use various principles shapes another experiment [147]. With Internet of Things-empowered frameworks, consummate two kinds of benchmarks, containing system conventions, correspondence conventions, and information accumulation benchmarks just as administrative principles related to security and protection of information. The difficulties confronting the appropriation of gauges inside IoT incorporate the gauges for taking care of unstructured information, security and protection issues notwithstanding administrative principles for information markets [148]. A methodology for beating the test of institutionalization of IoT-based vitality framework is to characterize an arrangement of frameworks with a presence of mind of comprehension to permit all on-screen characters to similarly admittance as well as usage. One more arrangement relates to creating exposed data prototypes also conventions as a part of benchmarks through participating gatherings. It will bring about principles which are uninhibitedly and openly accessible [149].

IoT-empowered frameworks are made out of assortment of advances with expanding amount of practicality connected gadgets also sensing devices. Internet of Things stands relied near empower interchange by whenever, anyplace for any related administrations, by and large, in an autonomic and specially appointed manner. This implies Internet of Things frameworks dependent on the use reasons for existing planned via perplexing, regionalized, and portable attributes [149]. Considering the qualities and necessities of an Internet of Things claim, a basic design can't exist a special answer used for these applications. In this manner, aimed at Internet of Things frameworks, various reference models are required which are open also adhere to measures. These models likewise ought to constrain clients towards utilization have stable as well as start and move towards finish Internet of Things interchanges [149, 150].

10.5 Upcoming Developments

Internet of Things is everywhere. Working connected at the hip with advancements like blockchain and AI, it is making a huge difference, from the manner in which we request food supplies, to the manner in which we keep up machines and gear. The utilizations of IoT cuts over all fields and ventures. From utility administration and transportation to instruction and horticulture, helping organizations to convey more an incentive to customers, decrease their uses and eventually increment their overall revenue, along these lines, it is reasonable that practically all ground breaking firms currently have IoT procedures to develop their business. Notwithstanding, for people who are new to this, and working in areas of the economy that are not usually identified with innovation, it could all be difficult to grasp. Along these lines, throughout the following few articles, I will be sharing about how IoT is changing assorted enterprises, one industry after the other. This will include use cases, current industry patterns and future applications with the point of giving helpful knowledge to all trying to send IoT based arrangements.

We will commence this arrangement by analyzing the uses of IoT in the Energy business. We will look at how IoT is being utilized or can be utilized to change the energy segment from vitality age to transmission, dispersion, and utilization.

In this session we are presenting block chain technology, AI technology, and Green IOT technology that can help to solve some problems.

10.5.1 IoT and Block Chain

Block chain invention might provide straightforward groundwork towards dual devices to legitimately move little of property, e.g., currencies or else data among respectively added within a made sure about also trusty period-stepped with permission tie hand clasp. Toward authorize communication skills, Internet of Things devices resolve usage brilliant agreements argument model the understanding among the dualistic meetings. These elements authorize the self-governing functioning of keen devices lacking the necessity aimed at unified power. In case you, by then loosen up this common trade to human to human or human to things/platforms, you end up with a totally circular trustworthy automated structure.

Blockchain enables the IoT gadgets to upgrade security and get straightforwardness IoT environments. As indicated by IDC, 20% of all IoT arrangements will empower blockchain-based arrangements by 2019. Blockchain offers an adaptable and decentralized condition to IoT gadgets, stages, and applications. Banks and Financial foundations like ING, Deutsche Bank, and HSBC are doing PoC to approve the blockchain innovation. Aside from money-related establishments, a wide scope of organizations have wanted to encounter the capability of the blockchain. Then again, the Internet of Things (IoT) opens up endless open doors for organizations to run brilliant activities. Each gadget around us is presently furnished with sensors, sending information to the cloud. In this way, joining these two advances can make the frameworks effective.

Energy division leaders [18] and service organizations [78] have attested that blockchains might offer answers for difficulties in the vitality business. Some vitality agencies [3, 18] statements about block chain advances can possibly increase productivity of present vitality performs as well as procedures, be able to quicken advancement through Internet of Things stages also computerized uses also be able to give development in individual to individual vitality exchanging also decentralized age. Furthermore, they report that blockchain innovations can possibly fundamentally improve current acts of vitality undertakings and service organizations by improving inside procedures, client administrations and expenses [3, 18]. Vitality frameworks remain experiencing a modification revolution activated via headway of disseminated vitality assets data with correspondence advancements. Some of the principle experiments increasing decentralization as well as digitalization of vitality framework, who needs the thought, investigation also reception of novel ideal models and appropriated innovations. Because of their inborn environment block chains can give a promising answer for controlling, oversee progressively decentralized complex vitality frameworks and micro-grids [15, 79, 80]. Coordinating little scope renewables, disseminated age, adaptability administrations and buyer cooperation in the vitality advertise is a requesting task. A few creators [79] contend that block chains could give imaginative exchanging stages everywhere enthusiast with shoppers be able to exchange conversely the vitality additional or else adaptable interest continuously in individual premise. Dynamic purchaser cooperation can be made sure about and recorded into permanent, straightforward and carefully designed savvy contracts. Empowering such mechanized exchanging stages could be an effective method for conveying value signs and data on vitality expenses to purchasers [80], at the same time furnishing them with motivators for request reaction and keen administration of their vitality needs. Block chains can empower neighborhood vitality and customer arranged commercial centers or micro-grids that intend to help nearby power age and utilization [29]. One of the significant advantages from this methodology is diminishing transmission misfortunes and conceding costly system redesigns. Then again, vitality is as yet conveyed from side to side to bodily lattice, request with source necessity to painstakingly exist overseen then well-ordered to agree to genuine specialized imperatives and force framework solidness. As indicated by an as of late distributed article via electric industry [3, 43], the corporal trade included in power takes hence future hindered bigger selection of block chains into vitality segment, instead of utilizations in the money division. Block chains can safely record possession and causes of the vitality devoured or provided. Thus, block chain arrangements could be used for brilliant charging courses of action and sharing of assets, for example network stockpiling or micro-grids, yet in addition for utilizations of information stockpiling in keen matrices and network safety [3, 81, 82]. Significant test works of renewable energy sources keep on expanding stays

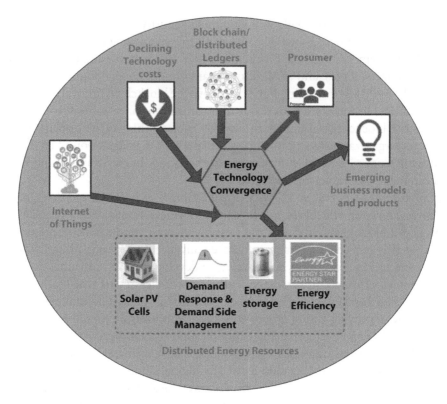

Figure 10.9 Innovation in energy sector with block chain and IOT.

keeping up the safety include in source and improving system strength. Through encouraging also quickening Internet of Things uses also empowering increasingly effective adaptability marketplaces, block chains can improve arrange versatility as well as safety of source [3, 79]. The article through Examination Organization of the Final budget [3, 16] contends like block chains might guarantee interactivity into practicality framework also Internet of Things claims presently open and straightforward arrangements. As indicated by Deloitte [20], vitality showcase activities could turn out to be progressively straightforward and proficient. Thus, this could improve rivalry and encourage customer versatility and exchanging of vitality providers. Whenever cost investment funds openings are acknowledged, we could use the innovation to enhance fuel neediness and energy moderateness issues. Figure 10.9 presents a block diagram including innovation in energy sector with block chain and IOT.

By ideals of focal points offered, block chains might give arrangements over the vitality power: that might diminish charges through enhancing vitality forms, increase vitality safety regarding cybersecurity, yet now addition go about by way of a supportive innovation which may increase safety of source, and lastly advance manageability by encouraging inexhaustible age and low-carbon arrangements.

10.5.2 Artificial Intelligence and IoT

The sustainable power source division is a developing financial power and a viable system towards improving natural maintainability. Man-made reasoning is being incorporated across significant segments of this industry, expanding the limit of information investigation.

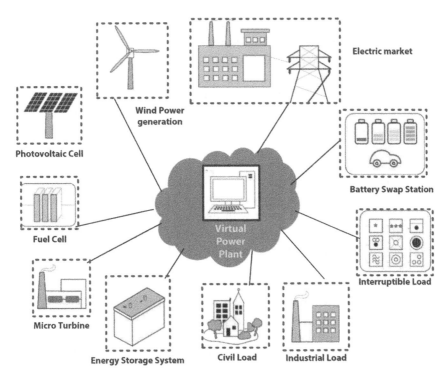

Figure 10.10 Virtual power plant with artificial intelligence and IOT.

The variable idea of climate presents innate difficulties which may make providers depend on conventional vitality sources to satisfy customer needs. Subsequently, AI-driven vitality estimating stages may hold guarantee for furnishing vitality providers with the information required to react to changes that may adversely influence activities and to design as needs be.

The Internet of Things, or IoT, has become sweeping. It's in telephones, PCs, vehicles, fridges, carporats, windows, lighting installations, traffic lights—anyplace a gadget can be fitted with Wi-Fi which can be remotely controlled, IoT has decent footings. Appropriately, the prevalence of information has extended, giving knowledge. Some portion of sustainable power source proficiency will include turning gadgets on and off when they are or aren't required. Take streetlights. There are times when lights will be required—and times when they won't. Utilizing IoT and AI mechanization to decide such limits can help ration vitality, permitting inexhaustible sources to have more noteworthy adequacy. Artificial intelligence can likewise be utilized to consequently remind individuals relating to specific exercises that could conceivably monitor vitality. In the event that a light is left on in a room where no one is, an AI gadget could check an IoT movement sensor, decide the light isn't required and naturally turn it off. This will cut the service bill and preserve vitality. Utilizing such AI with neighborhood utilities encourages a person or business to locate the most practical Texas power plans for homes or organizations.

Figure 10.10 shows a virtual power plant with artificial intelligence and IOT.

10.5.3   Green IoT

The splendid eventual destiny of green energy and Internet of Things revolves around our future condition for getting more beneficial as well as green, high-quality service, communally and naturally feasible as well as financially so. These days, the most energizing territories center around greening things, for example, green correspondence and systems administration, green structure and executions, green IoT administrations and applications, vitality sparing techniques, incorporated RFIDs and sensor systems, portability and system the board, the participation of homogeneous and heterogeneous systems, smart articles, and green confinement. The following examination fields have been explored to create ideal and effective answers related to green energy with Internet of Things:

- A requirement for ultraviolet rays to supplant huge quantity of Internet of Things gadgets particularly, within an agribusiness, circulation and checking, who resolve to assist with decreasing force utilization and contamination. Ultraviolet rays play a challenging role in innovation that will prompt green energy with Internet of Things by minimal effort, also, great proficiency.
- Communication information after the sensing devices towards the portable gloom progressively valuable. Sensing devices-gloom is incorporating remote sensing devices system also portable gloom. Which is actual warm and guaranteed innovation for green energy with Internet of Things. The interpersonal organization as an assistance might explore aimed at vitality productivity as a part of framework, administration, wireless sensor network as well as gloom the executives.
- Machine to machine correspondence assumes a basic job toward diminished vitality use, dangerous outflows. Keen machines must be more brilliant to empower robotized frameworks. Machine computerization defer must be limited on the off chance that of traffic and making important and quick move.
- Configuration Green IoT might be acquainted from with points of view which are accomplishing amazing execution and high-quality service. Searching appropriate methods for upgrading quality service factors (i.e., Data transfer capacity, deferral, and increasing output) determination give successfully also productively to green energy with Internet of Things.
- However, working on the way to green energy with Internet of Things, requirement for less vitality, searching especially for novel assets, limiting Internet of Things adverse effect taking place with soundness of humanoid also upsetting the earth. At that point green IoT can contribute fundamentally to manageable practicality furthermore, green condition.
- In request to accomplish vitality adjusting for supporting green correspondence between IoT gadgets, the radio recurrence vitality collect ought to be considered into thought.
- Further investigation is expected towards building up structure of Internet of Things gadgets that assist with lessening CO2 emanation and the vitality utilization. The most basic undertaking for shrewd and green ecological life is sparing vitality and diminishing the CO2 emanation. Figure 10.11 shows the future trends in green IoT (G-IOT).

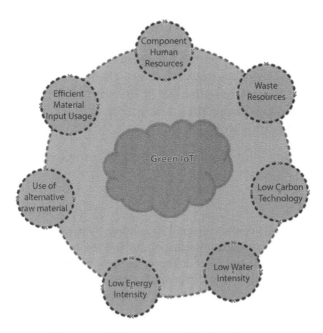

Figure 10.11 Green energy and Internet of Things as a crucial technology.

10.6   Conclusion

Organizations in the matter of sustainable power source have been encountering generous worldwide development in the course of the most recent few years. Nonetheless, with colossal scaling comes the test of continuing benefits and profitability. Dealing with these continually extending matrices expects organizations to pay special mind to ways and strategies to streamline their abilities across remote areas. One of the manners in which organizations can drive effectiveness is by grasping the universe of IoT. By actualizing keen machines and associated contraptions, organizations can utilize cutting-edge sensors to accumulate huge measures of constant vitality information and transmit it to the force lattice – for cutting-edge stockpiling and examination. IoT sensors can empower ongoing observation of intensity networks while giving executives the chance to assemble information-driven streamlining techniques.

They can likewise give better straightforwardness in the manner the energy is being consumed. That permits individuals to comprehend their vitality utilization propensities and modify them as needs be to advance use. IoT has improved the utilization of renewables radically. Energy utilities are currently utilizing the renewables to give predictable power stream to its residents. The Internet of Things has just raised the reception of sun-powered and wind vitality. Its applications are to be seen for geothermal, biogas, and hydroelectric force plants. According to a study, the worldwide geothermal asset base is considerably bigger than that of coal, gas, uranium, and oil consolidated. Unmistakably, renewables are the future. Their acknowledgment will, step by step, certainly satisfy our developing power necessities.

IoT has entered the energy business, making changes and giving certain points of interest. It is giving advantages to the vitality supplier just as the vitality shopper, the new advancements, transmission, and utilization improvements are adding to the more note-worthy benefit of saving energy. Notwithstanding these advantages, IoT still needs to con-front a few difficulties in the energy business as a result of the obsolete existing frameworks and availability issues. IoT can likewise assist us with giving energy at less expense by reus-ing systems and cost-cutting techniques. Use of IoT with blockchain AI, and green IoT consolidated all together can change the entire energy industry by observing the energy stage equipment and decreasing work.

References

Journal:
1. Stearns, P.N. Conceptualizing the Industrial Revolution. J. Interdiscip. Hist. 2011, 42,442–
2. Mokyr, J. The second mechanical transformation, 1870–1914. In *Storia dell'Economia Mondiale*; Citeseer; 1998; pp. 219–245. Accessible on the web: http://citeseerx.ist.psu.edu/viewdoc/down-load?doi=10.1.1.481.2996&rep= rep1&type=pdf (accessed 16 January 2020).
3. Jensen, M. The Modern Industrial Revolution, Exit, and the Failure of Internal Control Systems. *J. Financ.* 1993, 48, 831–880. [CrossRef]
4. Kagermann, H.; Helbig, J.; Hellinger, A.; Wahlster, W. Suggestions for Implementing the Strategic Initiative Industrie 4.0: Securing the Future of German Manufacturing Industry; Final Report of the Industrie 4.0 Working Gathering; Forschungsunion: Frankfurt/Main, Germany, 2013
5. Witchalls, C.; Chambers, J. *The Internet of Things Business Index: A Quiet Revolution Gathers Pace*; The Economist Insight Unit: London, UK, 2013; pp. 58–66.
6. Bandyopadhyay, D.; Sen, J. Web of Things: Applications and Challenges in Technology and Institutionalization. *Wirel. Pers. Commun.* 2011, 58, 49–69. [CrossRef]
7. Zakeri, B.; Syri, S.; Rinne, S. Higher sustainable power source joining into the current vital-ity arrangement of Finland–Is there any most extreme cutoff? *Vitality* 2015, 92, 244–259. [CrossRef]
8. Connolly, D.; Lund, H.; Mathiesen, B. Keen Energy Europe: The specialized and monetary effect of one potential 100% sustainable power source situation for the European Union. Reestablish. Continue. *Vitality Rev.* 2016, 60, 1634–1653. [CrossRef]
9. Grubler, A.; Wilson, C.; Bento, N.; Boza-Kiss, B.; Krey, V.; McCollum, D.L.; Rao, N.D.; Riahi, K.; Rogelj, J.; De Stercke, S.; et al. A low vitality request situation for meeting the 1.5 C target and reasonable improvement objectives without negative discharge advances. *Nat. Vitality* 2018, 3, 515–527.
10. UN. *Unique Edition: Progress towards the Sustainable Development Goals*; UN: New York, NY, USA, 2019.
11. Tan, Y.S.; Ng, Y.T.; Low, J.S.C. Web of-things empowered ongoing checking of vitality profi-ciency on fabricating shop floors. *Procedia CIRP* 2017, 61, 376–381. [CrossRef]
12. Bhattacharyya, S.C. *Vitality Economics: Concepts, Issues, Markets and Governance*; Springer: Berlin/Heidelberg, Germany, 2011.
13. Tamilselvan, K.; Thangaraj, P. Units—An epic insightful vitality productive and dynamic recur-rence scalings for multi-center inserted models in an IoT domain. *Microprocess. Microsyst.* 2020, 72, 102907. [CrossRef]
14. Zhou, K.; Yang, S.; Shao, Z. Vitality Internet: The business point of view. *Appl. Vitality* 2016, 178, 212–222. [CrossRef]
15. Da Xu, L.; He, W.; Li, S. Web of Things in Industries: A Survey. *IEEE Trans. Ind. Advise.* 2014, 10, 2233–2243.

16. Talari, S.; Shafie-Khah, M.; Siano, P.; Loia, V.; Tommasetti, A.; Catalão, J. A survey of shrewd urban communities dependent on the web of things idea. *Energies* 2017, 10, 421. [CrossRef]

17. Ibarra-Esquer, J.; González-Navarro, F.; Flores-Rios, B.; Burtseva, L.; Astorga-Vargas, M. Following the advancement of the web of things idea across various application spaces. *Sensors* 2017, 17, 1379. [CrossRef]

18. Swan, M. Sensor lunacy! the web of things, wearable processing, target measurements, and the evaluated self 2.0. *J. Sens. Actuator Netw.* 2012, 1, 217–253. [CrossRef]

19. Gupta, A.; Jha, R.K. An overview of 5G arrange: Architecture and rising advances. *IEEE Access* 2015, 3, 1206–1232. [CrossRef]

20. Stojkoska, B.L.R.; Trivodaliev, K.V. A survey of Internet of Things for keen home: Challenges and arrangements. *J. Clean. Push.* 2017, 140, 1454–1464. [CrossRef]

21. Hui, H.; Ding, Y.; Shi, Q.; Li, F.; Song, Y.; Yan, J. 5G organize based Internet of Things for request reaction in brilliant lattice: An overview on application potential. *Appl. Vitality* 2020, 257, 113972. [CrossRef]

22. Petros, anu, D.M.; Cărut, as, u, G.; Cărut, as, u, N.L.; Pîrjan, A. A Review of the Recent Developments in Integrating AI Models with Sensor Devices in the Smart Buildings Sector with the end goal of Attaining Improved Sensing, Energy Efficiency, and Optimal Building Management. *Energies* 2019, 12, 4745. [CrossRef]

23. Luo, X.G.; Zhang, H.B.; Zhang, Z.L.; Yu, Y.; Li, K. A New Framework of Intelligent Public Transportation Framework Based on the Internet of Things. *IEEE Access* 2019, 7, 55290–55304. [CrossRef]

24. Khatua, P.K.; Ramachandaramurthy, V.K.; Kasinathan, P.; Yong, J.Y.; Pasupuleti, J.; Rajagopalan, A. Application and Assessment of Internet of Things toward the Sustainability of Energy Systems: Challenges what's more, Issues. Support. Urban areas Soc. 2019, 101957. [CrossRef]

25. Haseeb, K.; Almogren, An.; Islam, N.; Ud Din, I.; Jan, Z. An Energy-Efficient and Secure Routing Protocol for Interruption Avoidance in IoT-Based WSN. *Energies* 2019, 12, 4174. [CrossRef]

26. Zouinkhi, An.; Ayadi, H.; Val, T.; Boussaid, B.; Abdelkrim, M.N. Auto-the board of vitality in IoT systems. *Int. J. Commun. Syst.* 2019, 33, e4168. [CrossRef]

27. Höller, J.; Tsiatsis, V.; Mulligan, C.; Avesand, S.; Karnouskos, S.; Boyle, D. *From Machine-to-Machine to the Web of Things: Introduction to a New Age of Intelligence*; Elsevier: Amsterdam, The Netherlands, 2014.

28. Atzori, L.; Iera, A.; Morabito, G. The Internet of Things: A study. *Comput. Netw.* 2010, 54, 2787–2805.[CrossRef]

29. Hui, T.K.; Sherratt, R.S.; Sánchez, D.D. Significant prerequisites for building Smart Homes in Smart Cities based on Internet of Things advancements. *Future Gener. Comput. Syst.* 2017, 76, 358–369. [CrossRef]

30. Evans, D. *The Internet of Things: How the Next Evolution of the Internet is Changing Everything*. CISCO White Pap. 2011, 1, 1–11.

31. Motlagh, N.H.; Bagaa, M.; Taleb, T. Vitality and Delay Aware Task Assignment Mechanism for UAV-Based IoT Platform. *IEEE Internet Things J.* 2019, 6, 6523–6536. [CrossRef]

32. Ramamurthy, A.; Jain, P. *The Internet of Things in the Power Sector: Opportunities in Asia and the Pacific*; Asian Development Bank: Mandalu Yonge, Philippines, 2017.

33. Jia, M.; Komeily, A.;Wang, Y.; Srinivasan, R.S. Receiving Internet of Things for the improvement of savvy structures: An audit of empowering advancements and applications. *Autom. Constr.* 2019, 101, 111–126. [CrossRef]

34. Li, S.; Da Xu, L.; Zhao, S. 5G Internet of Things: A study. *J. Ind. Inf. Integr.* 2018, 10,1–9. [CrossRef]

35. Watson Internet of Things. Safely Connect with Watson IoT Platform. 2019. Accessible on the web: https://www.ibm.com/web of-things/arrangements/iot-stage/watson-iot-stage (accessed 15 October 2019).

36. Kelly, S.D.T.; Suryadevara, N.K.; Mukhopadhyay, S.C. Towards the Implementation of IoT for Environmental Condition Monitoring in Homes. *IEEE Sens. J.* 2013, 13, 3846–3853. [CrossRef]

37. Newark Element. Keen Sensor Technology for the IoT. 2018. Accessible on the web: https://www.techbriefs. com/segment/content/article/tb/highlights/articles/33212 (accessed 25 December 2019).

38. Rault, T.; Bouabdallah, A.; Challal, Y. Vitality proficiency in remote sensor arranges: A top-down review. *Comput. Netw.* 2014, 67, 104–122. [CrossRef]

39. Di Francia, G. The advancement of sensor applications in the divisions of vitality and condition in Italy,1976–2015. *Sensors* 2017, 17, 793. [CrossRef]

40. ITFirms Co. 8 Types of Sensors that Coalesce Perfectly with an IoT App. 2018. Accessible on the web: https://www. itfirms.co/8-sorts of-sensors-that-mix impeccably with-an-iot-applica-tion/(accessed 27 September 2019).

41. Morris, A.S.; Langari, R. Level Measurement. In *Measurement and Instrumentation*, second ed.; Morris, A.S., Langari, R., Eds.; Academic Press: Boston, MA, USA, 2016; Chapter 17, pp. 531–545.

42. Pérez-Lombard, L.; Ortiz, J.; Pout, C. A survey on structures vitality utilization data. *Vitality Build.* 2008, 40, 394–398. [CrossRef]

43 Moram, M. Illuminating Lives with Energy Efficient Lighting. 2012. Accessible on the web: http://aglobalvillage. organization/diary/issue7/squander/lightinguplives/(accessed 27 December 2019).

44. Riyanto, I.; Margatama, L.; Hakim, H.; Hindarto, D. Movement Sensor Application on Building Lighting Establishment for Energy Saving and Carbon Reduction Joint Crediting Mechanism. *Appl. Syst. Innov.* 2018, 1, 23. [CrossRef]

45. Kim,W.; Mechitov, K.; Choi, J.; Ham, S. On track following paired closeness sensors. In *Proceedings of the IPSN 2005—Fourth International Symposium on Information Processing in Sensor Networks, Los Angeles, CA, USA, 25–27 April 2005*; pp. 301–308.

46. Pepperl+Fuchs. Sensors forWind Energy Applications. 2019. Accessible on the web: https://www.pepperl-fuchs. com/worldwide/en/15351.htm (accessed 27 December 2019).

47. Kececi, E.F. Actuators. In *Mechatronic Components*; Kececi, E.F., Ed.; Butterworth-Heinemann: Oxford, UK, 2019; Chapter 11, pp. 145–154.

48. Nesbitt, B. *Handbook of Valves and Actuators: Valves Manual International*; Elsevier: Amsterdam, The Netherlands, 2011.

49. Beam, R. Valves and Actuators. *Force Eng.* 2014, 118, 4862.

50. Blanco, J.; García, A.; Morenas, J. Plan and Implementation of a Wireless Sensor and Actuator Network to Bolster the Intelligent Control of Efficient Energy Usage. *Sensors* 2018, 18, 1892. [CrossRef] [PubMed]

51. Martínez-Cruz.; Eugenio, C. Assembling minimal effort wifi-based electric vitality meter. In *Proceedings of the 2014 IEEE Central America and Panama Convention (CONCAPAN), Panama City, Panama, 12–14 November 2014*; pp. 1–6.

52. Rodriguez-Diaz, E.; Vasquez, J.C.; Guerrero, J.M. Canny DC Homes in Future Sustainable Energy Frameworks: When proficiency and knowledge cooperate. *IEEE Consum. Electron. Mag.* 2016, 5, 74–80. [CrossRef]

53. Karthika, A.; Valli, K.R.; Srinidhi, R.; Vasanth, K. Robotization Of Energy Meter And Building A Network Utilizing Iot. In *Proceedings of the 2019 fifth International Conference on Advanced Computing Communication Frameworks (ICACCS), Coimbatore, India, 15–16 March 2019*; pp. 339–341.

54. Lee, Y.; Hsiao, W.; Huang, C.; Chou, S.T. An incorporated cloud-based savvy home administration framework with network chain of command. *IEEE Trans. Consum. Electron.* 2016, 62, 1–9. [CrossRef]
55. Kabalci, Y.; Kabalci, E.; Padmanaban, S.; Holm-Nielsen, J.B.; Blaabjerg, F. Web of Things applications as vitality web in *Smart Grids and Smart Environments*. Gadgets 2019, 8, 972. [CrossRef]
56. Jain, S.; Pradish, M.; Paventhan, A.; Saravanan, M.; Das, A. Savvy Energy Metering Using LPWAN IoT Innovation. In *ISGW 2017: Compendium of Technical Papers*; Springer: Berlin/Heidelberg, Germany, 2018; pp. 19–28.
57. Collotta, M.; Pau, G. A Novel Energy Management Approach for Smart Homes Using Bluetooth Low Energy. *IEEE J. Sel. Regions Commun.* 2015, 33, 2988–2996. [CrossRef]
58. Collotta, M.; Pau, G. An answer dependent on bluetooth low vitality for shrewd home vitality the board. *Energies* 2015, 8, 11916–11938. [CrossRef]
59. Craig, W.C. *Zigbee: Wireless Control that Simply Works*; ZigBee Alliance: Davis, CA, USA, 2004.
60. Froiz-Míguez, I.; Fernández-Caramés, T.; Fraga-Lamas, P.; Castedo, L. Structure, usage and commonsense assessment of an IoT home mechanization framework for haze processing applications dependent on MQTT and ZigBee-WiFi sensor hubs. *Sensors* 2018, 18, 2660. [CrossRef]
61. Erol-Kantarci, M.; Mouftah, H.T. Remote Sensor Networks for Cost-Efficient Residential Energy The board in the Smart Grid. *IEEE Trans. Shrewd Grid* 2011, 2, 314–325. [CrossRef]
62. Han, D.; Lim, J. Brilliant home vitality the board framework utilizing IEEE 802.15.4 and zigbee. IEEE Trans. *Consum. Electron.* 2010, 56, 1403–1410. [CrossRef]
63. Batista, N.; Melício, R.; Matias, J.; Catalão, J. Photovoltaic and wind vitality frameworks checking and building/home vitality the board utilizing ZigBee gadgets inside a shrewd network. *Vitality* 2013, 49, 306–315. [CrossRef]
64. Augustin, A.; Yi, J.; Clausen, T.; Townsley, W. An investigation of LoRa: Long range and low force systems for the web of things. *Sensors* 2016, 16, 1466.
65. Mataloto, B.; Ferreira, J.C.; Cruz, N. LoBEMS—IoT for Building and Energy Management Systems. *Hardware* 2019, 8, 763. [CrossRef]
66. Javed, A.; Larijani, H.; Wixted, A. Improving Energy Consumption of a Commercial Building with IoT and AI. *IT Prof.* 2018, 20, 30–38. [CrossRef]
67. Ferreira, J.C.; Afonso, J.A.; Monteiro, V.; Afonso, J.L. An Energy Management Platform for Public Buildings. *Hardware* 2018, 7, 294. [CrossRef]
68. Gomez, C.; Veras, J.C.; Vidal, R.; Casals, L.; Paradells, J. A Sigfox vitality utilization model. *Sensors* 2019, 19, 681. [CrossRef]
69. Pitì, A.; Verticale, G.; Rottondi, C.; Capone, A.; Lo Schiavo, L. The job of brilliant meters in empowering constant vitality administrations for family units: The Italian case. *Energies* 2017, 10, 199. [CrossRef]
70. Nair, V.; Litjens, R.; Zhang, H. Improvement of NB-IoT organization for shrewd vitality conveyance systems. *Eurasip J. Wirel. Commun. Netw.* 2019, 2019, 186. [CrossRef]
71. Li, Y.; Cheng, X.; Cao, Y.; Wang, D.; Yang, L. Shrewd Choice for the Smart Grid: Narrowband Internet of Things (NB-IoT). *IEEE Internet Things J.* 2018, 5, 1505–1515. [CrossRef]
72. Shariatmadari, H.; Ratasuk, R.; Iraji, S.; Laya, A.; Taleb, T.; Jäntti, R.; Ghosh, A. Machine-type correspondences: Current status and future points of view toward 5G frameworks. *IEEE Commun. Mag.* 2015, 53, 10–17. [CrossRef]
73. Deshpande, K.V.; Rajesh, A. Examination on imcp based grouping in lte-m correspondence for savvy metering applications. *Eng. Sci. Technol. Int. J.* 2017, 20, 944–955. [CrossRef]
74. Emmanuel, M.; Rayudu, R. Correspondence advances for savvy network applications: An overview. *J. Netw. Comput. Appl.* 2016, 74, 133–148. [CrossRef]
75. Webb, W. Weightless: The innovation to at long last understand the M2M vision. *Int. J. Interdiscip. Telecommun. Netw. (IJITN)* 2012, 4, 30–37. [CrossRef]

76. Sethi, P.; Sarangi, S.R. Web of things: Architectures, conventions, and applications. *J. Electr. Comput. Eng.* 2017, 2017. [CrossRef]
77. Wei, J.; Han, J.; Cao, S. Satellite IoT Edge Intelligent Computing: A Research on Architecture. *Hardware* 2019, 8, 1247. [CrossRef]
78. Sohraby, K.; Minoli, D.; Occhiogrosso, B.; Wang, W. A survey of remote and satellite-based m2m/iot benefits on the side of keen lattices. Crowd. *Systems Appl.* 2018, 23, 881–895. [CrossRef]
79. De Sanctis, M.; Cianca, E.; Araniti, G.; Bisio, I.; Prasad, R. Satellite Communications Supporting Internet of Remote Things. *IEEE Internet Things J.* 2016, 3, 113–123. [CrossRef]
80. GSMA. Security Features of LTE-M and NB-IoT Networks; Technical Report; GSMA: London, UK, 2019.
81. Sigfox. Make Things Come Alive in a Secure Way; Technical Report; Sigfox: Labège, France, 2017.
82. Sanchez-Iborra, R.; Cano, M.D. Cutting edge in LP-WAN answers for mechanical IoT administrations. *Sensors* 2016, 16, 708. [CrossRef]
83. Stojmenovic, I. Machine-to-Machine Communications With In-Network Data Aggregation, Processing, also, Actuation for Large-Scale Cyber-Physical Systems. *IEEE Internet Things J.* 2014, 1, 122–128. [CrossRef]
84. Chen, H.; Chiang, R.H.; Story, V.C. Business insight and examination: From large information to enormous effect. MIS Q.
85. Intel IT Center. *Huge Data Analytics: Intel's IT Manager Survey on How Organizations Are Using Big Data; Specialized Report*; Intel IT Center: Santa Clara, CA, USA, 2012.
86. Stergiou, C.; Psannis, K.E.; Kim, B.G.; Gupta, B. Secure combination of IoT and Cloud Computing. *Future Gener. Comput. Syst.* 2018, 78, 964–975. [CrossRef]
87. Josep, A.D.; Katz, R.; Konwinski, A.; Gunho, L.; Patterson, D.; Rabkin, A. A perspective on distributed computing. *Commun. ACM* 2010, 53. [CrossRef]
88. Hamdaqa, M.; Tahvildari, L. Distributed computing Uncovered: A Research Landscape; *Advances in Computers;* Elsevier: Amsterdam, The Netherlands, 2012; Volume 86, pp. 41–85.
89. Mahmud, R.; Kotagiri, R.; Buyya, R. Mist processing: A scientific classification, review and future bearings. In *Internet of Everything*; Springer: Berlin/Heidelberg, Germany, 2018; pp. 103–130.
90. Verma, M.; Bhardwaj, N.; Yadav, A.K. Ongoing proficient planning calculation for load adjusting in haze registering condition. *Int. J. Comput. Sci. Inf. Technol.* 2016, 8, 1–10. [CrossRef]
91. Atlam, H.F.; Walters, R.J.; Wills, G.B. Mist figuring and the web of things: A survey. *Large Data Cogn. Comput.* 2018, 2, 10. [CrossRef]
92. Bhardwaj, A. Utilizing the Internet of Things and Analytics for Smart Energy Management; TATA Consultancy Administrations: Mumbai, India, 2015.
93. Sigfox, Inc. Utilities and Energy. 2019. Accessible on the web: https://www.sigfox.com/en/utilities-vitality/ (accessed 27 September 2019).
94. Immelt, J.R. The Future of Electricity Is Digital; Technical Report; General Electric: Boston, MA, USA, 2015.
95. Al-Ali, A. Web of things job in the sustainable power source assets. *Vitality Procedia* 2016, 100, 34–38. [CrossRef]
96. Ejaz, W.; Naeem, M.; Shahid, An.; Anpalagan, A.; Jo, M. Effective vitality the executives for the web of things in shrewd urban areas. *IEEE Commun. Mag.* 2017, 55, 84–91. [CrossRef]
97. Mohanty, S.P. All that you needed to think about shrewd urban areas: The Internet of things is the spine. *IEEE Consum. Electron. Mag.* 2016, 5, 60–70. [CrossRef]
98. Hossain, M.; Madlool, N.; Rahim, N.; Selvaraj, J.; Pandey, A.; Khan, A.F. Job of shrewd network in sustainable vitality: A review. *Restore. Support. Vitality Rev.* 2016, 60, 1168–1184. [CrossRef]

99. Kaur, N.; Sood, S.K. A vitality effective design for the Internet of Things (IoT). *IEEE Syst. J.* 2015, 11, 796–805. [CrossRef]

100. Shaikh, F.K.; Zeadally, S.; Exposito, E. Empowering advances for green web of things. *IEEE Syst. J.* 2015, 11, 983–994. [CrossRef]

101. Lin, Y.; Chou, Z.; Yu, C.; Jan, R. Ideal and Maximized Configurable Power Saving Protocols for Crown BasedWireless Sensor Networks. *IEEE Trans. Horde. Comput.* 2015, 14, 2544–2559. [CrossRef]

102. Anastasi, G.; Conti, M.; Di Francesco, M.; Passarella, A. Vitality protection in remote sensor systems: A review. *Impromptu Netw.* 2009, 7, 537–568. [CrossRef]

103. Shakerighadi, B.; Anvari-Moghaddam, A.; Vasquez, J.C.; Guerrero, J.M. Web of Things for Modern Vitality Systems: State-of-the-Art, Challenges, and Open Issues. *Energies* 2018, 11, 1252. [CrossRef]

104. Anjana, K.; Shaji, R. A survey on the highlights and innovations for vitality productivity of keen framework. *Int. J. Vitality Res.* 2018, 42, 936–952. [CrossRef]

105. Boroojeni, K.; Amini, M.H.; Nejadpak, A.; Dragičević, T.; Iyengar, S.S.; Blaabjerg, F. A Novel Cloud-Based Stage for Implementation of Oblivious Power Routing for Clusters of Microgrids. *IEEE Access* 2017, 5, 607–619. [CrossRef]

106. Kounev, V.; Tipper, D.; Levesque, M.; Grainger, B.M.; Mcdermott, T.; Reed, G.F. A microgrid co-reenactment structure. In *Proceedings of the 2015 Workshop on Modeling and Simulation of Cyber-Physical Energy Frameworks (MSCPES), Seattle, WA, USA, 13 April 2015*; pp. 1–6.

107. Porambage, P.; Ylianttila, M.; Schmitt, C.; Kumar, P.; Gurtov, A.; Vasilakos, A.V. The mission for security in the web of things. *IEEE Cloud Comput.* 2016, 3, 36–45. [CrossRef]

108. Chow, R. The Last Mile for IoT Privacy. IEEE Secur. Priv. 2017, 15, 73–76. [CrossRef]

109. Jayaraman, P.P.; Yang, X.; Yavari, A.; Georgakopoulos, D.; Yi, X. Security protecting Internet of Things: From security systems to an outline design and proficient execution. *Future Gener. Comput. Syst.* 2017, 76, 540–549. [CrossRef]

110. Roman, R.; Najera, P.; Lopez, J. Making sure about the web of things. *PC* 2011, 44, 51–58. [CrossRef]

111. Li, Z.; Shahidehpour, M.; Aminifar, F. Cybersecurity in dispersed force frameworks. *Proc. IEEE* 2017, 105, 1367–1388. [CrossRef]

112. Tune, T.; Li, R.; Mei, B.; Yu, J.; Xing, X.; Cheng, X. A security saving correspondence convention for IoT applications in savvy homes. *IEEE Internet Things J.* 2017, 4, 1844–1852. [CrossRef]

113. Meddeb, A. Web of things measures: Who stands apart from the group? *IEEE Commun. Mag.* 2016, 54, 40–47. [CrossRef]

114. Banafa, A. IoT Standardization and Implementation Challenges. 2016. Accessible on the web: https://iot.ieee.org/ bulletin/july-2016/iot-institutionalization and-execution challenges.html (accessed 10 May 2019).

115. Chen, S.; Xu, H.; Liu, D.; Hu, B.; Wang, H. A Vision of IoT: Applications, Challenges, and Opportunitie With China Perspective. *IEEE Internet Things J.* 2014, 1, 349–359. [CrossRef]

116. Al-Qaseemi, S.A.; Almulhim, H.A.; Almulhim, M.F.; Chaudhry, S.R. IoT architecture challenges and issues Lack of standardization. In *Proceedings of the 2016 Future Technologies Conference (FTC), San Francisco, CA, USA, 6–7 December 2016*; pp. 731–738.

117. Kshetri, N. Can Blockchain Strengthen the Internet of Things? *IT Prof.* 2017, 19, 68–72. [CrossRef]

118. Alladi, T.; Chamola, V.; Rodrigues, J.J.; Kozlov, S.A. Blockchain in Smart Grids: A Review on Different Us Cases. *Sensors 2019*, 19, 4862. [CrossRef]

119. Christidis, K.; Devetsikiotis, M. Blockchains and Smart Contracts for the Internet of Things. *IEEE Access* 2016, 4, 2292–2303. [CrossRef]

120. Hawlitschek, F.; Notheisen, B.; Teubner, T. The limits of trust-free systems: A literature review on blockchain technology and trust in the sharing economy. *Electron. Commer. Res. Appl.* 2018, 29, 50–63. [CrossRef]
121. Zhu, C.; Leung, V.C.M.; Shu, L.; Ngai, E.C. Green Internet of Things for Smart World. *IEEE Access* 2015,3, 2151–2162. [CrossRef]
121. Nguyen, D.; Dow, C.; Hwang, S. An Efficient Traffic Congestion Monitoring System on Internet of Vehicles. *Wirel. Commun. Mob. Comput. 2018*, 2018. [CrossRef]
122. Namboodiri, V.; Gao, L. Energy-Aware Tag Anticollision Protocols for RFID Systems. *IEEE Trans. Mob. Comput.* 2010, 9, 44–59. [CrossRef]
123. Li, T.; Wu, S.S.; Chen, S.; Yang, M.C.K. Generalized Energy-Efficient Algorithms for the RFID Estimation Problem. *IEEE/ACM Trans. Netw.* 2012, 20, 1978–1990. [CrossRef]
124. Xu, X.; Gu, L.;Wang, J.; Xing, G.; Cheung, S. Read More with Less: An Adaptive Approach to Energy-Efficient RFID Systems. *IEEE J. Sel. Areas Commun.* 2011, 29, 1684–1697. [CrossRef]
125. Klair, D.K.; Chin, K.; Raad, R. A Survey and Tutorial of RFID Anti-Collision Protocols. *IEEE Commun. Surv. Tutor.* 2010, 12, 400–421. [CrossRef]
126. Lee, C.; Kim, D.; Kim, J. An Energy Efficient Active RFID Protocol to Avoid Overhearing Problem. *IEEE Sens. J.* 2014, 14, 15–24. [CrossRef]

Conference:

1. Datta, S.K.; Bonnet, C. MEC and IoT Based Automatic Agent Reconfiguration in Industry 4.0. In *Proceedings of the 2018 IEEE International Conference on Advanced Networks and Telecommunications Systems (ANTS), Indore, India, 16–19 December 2018*; pp. 1–5.
2. Shrouf, F.; Ordieres, J.; Miragliotta, G. Shrewd production lines in Industry 4.0: A survey of the idea and of vitality the board drew nearer underway dependent on the Internet of Things worldview. In *Proceedings of the 2014 IEEE International Conference on Industrial Engineering and Engineering Management (IEEM), Selangor Darul Ehsan, Malaysia, 9–12 December 2014*; pp. 697–701.
3. Global Energy Agency (IEA). Worldwide Energy and CO2 Status Report. 2019. Accessible on the web: https://www. iea.org/geco/(accessed 27 September 2019).
4. Intergovernmental Panel for Climate Change (IPCC). Worldwide Warning of 1.5 C: Summary for Policymakers. 2018. Accessible on the web: https://www.ipcc.ch/sr15/section/spm/(accessed 27 September 2019).
5. Motlagh, N.H.; Khajavi, S.H.; Jaribion, A.; Holmstrom, J. An IoT-based mechanization framework for more established homes: An utilization case for lighting framework. In *Proceedings of the 2018 IEEE eleventh Conference on Service-Oriented Registering and Applications (SOCA), Paris, France, 19–22 November 2018*; pp. 1–6.
6. Karunarathne, G.R.; Kulawansa, K.T.; Firdhous, M.M. Remote Communication Technologies in Internet of Things: A Critical Evaluation. In *Proceedings of the 2018 International Conference on Intelligent and Imaginative Computing Applications (ICONIC), Plaine Magnien, Mauritius, 6–7 December 2018*; pp. 1–5.
7. Lee, T.; Jeon, S.; Kang, D.; Park, L.W.; Park, S. Structure and execution of keen HVAC framework in light of IoT and Big information stage. In *Proceedings of the 2017 IEEE International Conference on Consumer Hardware (ICCE), Las Vegas, NV, USA, 8–10 January 2017*; pp. 398–399.
8. Lee, J.; Su, Y.; Shen, C. A Comparative Study of Wireless Protocols: Bluetooth, UWB, ZigBee, and Wi-Fi. In *Proceedings of the IECON 2007—33rd Annual Conference of the IEEE Industrial Electronics Society, Taipei, Taiwan, 5–8 November 2007*; pp. 46–51.
9. Choi, M.; Park,W.; Lee, I. Savvy office vitality the executives framework utilizing bluetooth low vitality based reference points also, a portable application. In *Proceedings of the 2015 IEEE*

International Conference on Consumer Electronics (ICCE), Las Vegas, NV, USA, 9–12 January 2015; pp. 501–502.

10. Han, J.; Choi, C.; Park, W.; Lee, I.; Kim, S. Brilliant home vitality the board framework including sustainable vitality dependent on ZigBee and PLC. In *Proceedings of the 2014 IEEE International Conference on Consumer Hardware (ICCE), Las Vegas, NV, USA, 4–6 January 2014*; pp. 544–545.

11. Mekki, K.; Bajic, E.; Chaxel, F.; Meyer, F. Outline of Cellular LPWAN Technologies for IoT Deployment: Sigfox, LoRaWAN, and NB-IoT. In *Proceedings of the 2018 IEEE International Conference on Pervasive Registering and Communications Workshops (PerCom Workshops), Athens, Greece, 19–23 March 2018*; pp. 197–202.

12. Pennacchioni, M.; Di Benedette, M.; Pecorella, T.; Carlini, C.; Obino, P. NB-IoT framework sending for savvy metering: Evaluation of inclusion and limit exhibitions. In *Proceedings of the 2017 AEIT International Yearly Conference, Cagliari, Italy, 20–22 September 2017*; pp. 1–6.

13. Lauridsen, M.; Kovacs, I.Z.; Mogensen, P.; Sorensen, M.; Holst, S. Inclusion and Capacity Analysis of LTE-M and NB-IoT in a Rural Area. In *Proceedings of the 2016 IEEE 84th Vehicular Technology Conference (VTC-Fall), Montreal, QC, Canada, 18–21 September 2016*; pp. 1–5.

14. Siekkinen, M.; Hiienkari, M.; Nurminen, J.K.; Nieminen, J. How low vitality is bluetooth low vitality? near estimations with zigbee/802.15. 4. In *Proceedings of the 2012 IEEE Wireless Communications furthermore, Networking Conference workshops (WCNCW), Paris, France, 1 April 2012*; pp. 232–237.

15. Lee, J.S.; Dong, M.F.; Sun, Y.H. A primer investigation of low force remote advancements: ZigBee and Bluetooth low vitality. In *Proceedings of the 2015 IEEE tenth Conference on Industrial Electronics and Applications (ICIEA), Auckland, New Zealand, 15–17 June 2015*; pp. 135–139.

16. Fraire, J.A.; Céspedes, S.; Accettura, N. Direct-To-Satellite IoT-A Survey of the State of the Art and Future Research Perspectives. In *Proceedings of the 2019 International Conference on Ad-Hoc Networks and Remote, Luxembourg, 1–3 October 2019*; pp. 241–258.

17. Jaribion, A.; Khajavi, S.H.; Hossein Motlagh, N.; Holmström, J. [WiP] A Novel Method for Big Data Analytics also, Summarization Based on Fuzzy Similarity Measure. In *Proceedings of the 2018 IEEE eleventh Conference on Administration Oriented Computing and Applications (SOCA), Paris, France, 19–22 November 2018*; pp. 221–226. 100. Chen, M.; Mao, S.; Liu, Y. Huge Data: A Survey. Crowd. Netw. Appl. 2014, 19, 171–209. [CrossRef]

18. Ji, C.; Li, Y.; Qiu, W.; Awada, U.; Li, K. Huge Data Processing in Cloud Computing Environments. In *Proceedings of the 2012 twelfth International Symposium on Pervasive Systems, Algorithms and Networks, San Marcos, TX, USA, 13–15 December 2012*; pp. 17–23.

19. Encourage, I.; Zhao, Y.; Raicu, I.; Lu, S. Distributed computing and Grid Computing 360-Degree Compared. In *Proceedings of the 2008 Grid Computing Environments Workshop, Austin, TX, USA, 16 November 2008*; pp. 1–10.

20. Khan, Z.; Anjum, A.; Kiani, S.L. Cloud Based Big Data Analytics for Smart Future Cities. In *Proceedings of the 2013 IEEE/ACM sixth International Conference on Utility and Cloud Computing, Dresden, Germany, 9–12 December 2013*; pp. 381–386.

21. Karnouskos, S. The helpful web of things empowered keen network. In *Proceedings of the fourteenth IEEE Worldwide Symposium on Consumer Electronics (ISCE2010), Braunschweig, Germany, 7–10 June 2010*; pp. 7–10.

22. Lagerspetz, E.; Motlagh, N.H.; Zaidan, M.A.; Fung, P.L.; Mineraud, J.; Varjonen, S.; Siekkinen, M.; Nurmi, P.; Matsumi, Y.; Tarkoma, S.; et al. MegaSense: Feasibility of Low-Cost Sensors for Pollution Hot-spot Recognition. In *Proceedings of the 2019 IEEE seventeenth International Conference on Industrial Informatics (INDIN), Helsinki-Espoo, Finland, 23–25 July 2019*.

23. Karnouskos, S.; Colombo, A.W.; Lastra, J.L.M.; Popescu, C. Towards the vitality productive future manufacturing plant. In *Proceedings of the 2009 seventh IEEE International Conference on Industrial Informatics, Cardiff, UK, 23–26 June 2009*; pp. 367–371.

24. M. Avci, M.E.; Asfour, S. Private HVAC load control methodology continuously power evaluating condition. In *Proceedings of the 2012 IEEE Conference on Energytech, Cleveland, OH, USA, 29–31 May 2012*; pp. 1–6.

25. Arasteh, H.; Hosseinnezhad, V.; Loia, V.; Tommasetti, A.; Troisi, O.; Shafie-khah, M.; Siano, P. IoT-based keen urban areas: A review. In *Proceedings of the 2016 IEEE sixteenth International Conference on Environment and Electrical Engineering (EEEIC), Florence, Italy, 7–10 June 2016*; pp. 1–6.

26. Lee, C.; Zhang, S. Advancement of an Industrial Internet of Things Suite for Smart Factory towards Re-industrialization in Hong Kong. In *Proceedings of the sixth International Workshop of Advanced Assembling and Automation, Manchester, UK, 10–11 November 2016*.

27. Reinfurt, L.; Falkenthal, M.; Breitenbücher, U.; Leymann, F. Applying IoT Patterns to Smart Factory Systems. In *Proceedings of the 2017 Advanced Summer School on Service Oriented Computing (Summer SOC), Hersonissos, Greece, 25–30 June 2017*

28. Wong, T.Y.; Shum, C.; Lau, W.H.; Chung, S.; Tsang, K.F.; Tse, C. Demonstrating and co-recreation of IEC61850-based microgrid insurance. In *Proceedings of the 2016 IEEE International Conference on Smart Network Communications (SmartGridComm), Sydney, Australia, 6–9 November 2016*; pp. 582–587.

29. Fhom, H.S.; Kuntze, N.; Rudolph, C.; Cupelli, M.; Liu, J.; Monti, A. A client driven security chief for future vitality frameworks. In *Proceedings of the 2010 International Conference on Power System Technology, Hangzhou, China, 24–28 October 2010*; pp. 1–7.

30. Dorri, A.; Kanhere, S.S.; Jurdak, R.; Gauravaram, P. Blockchain for IoT security and protection: The contextual analysis of a savvy home. In *Proceedings of the 2017 IEEE International Conference on Pervasive Computing and Interchanges Workshops (PerComWorkshops), Kona, HI, USA, 13–17 March 2017*; pp. 618–623.

31. Poyner, I.; Sherratt, R.S. Protection and security of shopper IoT gadgets for the unavoidable checking of defenseless individuals. In *Proceedings of the Living in the Internet of Things: Cybersecurity of the IoT—2018, London, UK, 28–29 March 2018*; pp. 1–5.

32. Roman, R.; Lopez, J. Security in the conveyed web of things. In *Proceedings of the 2012 International Gathering on Trusted Systems, London, UK, 17–18 December 2012*; pp. 65–66.

33. Dorri, A.; Kanhere, S.S.; Jurdak, R. Towards an optimized blockchain for IoT. In *Proceedings of the Second International Conference on Internet-of-Things Design and Implementation, Pittsburgh, PA, USA 18–21 April 2017*; pp. 173–178.

34. Huh, S.; Cho, S.; Kim, S. Managing IoT devices using blockchain platform. In *Proceedings of the 2017 19th International Conference on Advanced Communication Technology (ICACT), Bongpyeong, Korea,19–22 February 2017*; pp. 464–467

35. Korpela, K.; Hallikas, J.; Dahlberg, T. Digital Supply Chain Transformation toward Blockchain Integration In *Proceedings of the 50th Hawaii International Conference on Ssystem Sciences, Waikoloa, HI, USA, 4–7 January 2017*.

36. Conoscenti, M.; Vetro, A.; De Martin, J.C. Blockchain for the Internet of Things: A systematic literature review. In *Proceedings of the 2016 IEEE/ACS 13th International Conference of Computer Systems and Applications (AICCSA), Agadir, Morocco, 29 November–2 December 2016*; pp. 1–6.

37. Boudguiga, A.; Bouzerna, N.; Granboulan, L.; Olivereau, A.; Quesnel, F.; Roger, A.; Sirdey, R. Towards better availability and accountability for iot updates by means of a blockchain. In *Proceedings of the 2017 IEEE European Symposium on Security and Privacy Workshops (EuroS&PW), Paris, France, 26–28 April 2017*; pp. 50–58.

38. Samaniego, M.; Deters, R. Blockchain as a Service for IoT. In *Proceedings of the 2016 IEEE International Conference on Internet of Things (iThings) and IEEE Green Computing and Communications (GreenCom) and IEEE Cyber, Physical and Social Computing (CPSCom) and IEEE Smart Data (SmartData), Chengdu, China, 15–18 December 2016*; pp. 433–436.
39. Abedin, S.F.; Alam, M.G.R.; Haw, R.; Hong, C.S. A system model for energy efficient green-IoT network In *Proceedings of the 2015 International Conference on Information Networking (ICOIN), Siem Reap, Cambodia, 12–14 January 2015*; pp. 177–182.

11

Efficient Renewable Energy Systems

Prabhansu[1]* and Nayan Kumar[2]

[1]Mechanical Engineering Department, S. V. National Institute of Technology Surat, Gujarat, India
[2]Electrical Engineering Department, Muzaffarpur Institute of Technology, Muzaffarpur, Bihar, India

Abstract

Sustainable growth is very important today as it integrates the economic, social and environmental dimensions of life. In order to enhance this development, renewable energy systems can be hybridized and integrated with various energy storage devices to make renewable systems more reliable. The hydrogen fuel cell helps in reducing the storage cost in an energy sector. The focus is on integration of photovoltaic cell, wind energy and other forms of renewable energy. At the same time microgrid systems should have more reliability, less transmission losses and improved power system efficiency. Multigeneration is another emerging concept which involves several renewables functioning together in synchrony with one another and can provide heating, cooling, fresh water and electricity. With the advancement in technology, new, improved and efficient renewable energy systems are coming into the picture. One such technology is PV membrane systems for ensuring clean water at community level in remote areas.

Keywords: Efficient renewable systems, sustainability, multigeneration, hybrid systems, government initiatives

Introduction

The prevailing power generation technology has abruptly created a sense of insecurity across the globe due to emissions from GHG, heat release, depletion in the layer of ozone, noise pollution, change in climate, demand for power, gradual loss in non-conventional source of energy and ups and downs in its rate. From a global perspective, the demand for energy has increased exponentially and is continuing to increase at even higher rates than the rate of growth of the human population. Distributed energy resources (DER) created a better option for industries and households as well as for the economy. DER advancements include the diesel generator, micro-turbine, bio-energy advances, power device, little hydel power, etc., savvy lattice highlights energy storage stockpiling framework [1]. The sustainable power source innovations use normal assets that are normally renewing to create vitality for different applications. The majority of the inexhaustible distributed energy sources

---

*Corresponding author: prabhansu.nitp@gmail.com

Suman Lata Tripathi, Dushyant Kumar Singh, Sanjeevikumar Padmanaban, and P. Raja (eds.) Design and Development of Efficient Energy Systems, (199–214) © 2021 Scrivener Publishing LLC

actually contain less activity and upkeep investments and in general are not known much [2]. Distributed energy sources advances should be looked upon as vitality assets considering all around acknowledged by the utilization of adjustment of load, top abridgement, request reaction, top burden the board, and vitality productivity continuously power frameworks. Furthermore, they can be utilized in the arranging procedure to improve the dependability of the force framework by guaranteeing that heaps won't surpass flexibly during the framework top. Also, DERs can offer auxiliary types of assistance, for example, voltage backing and control of recurrence at lower working expenses and making effectiveness better as compared to conventional force frameworks. Additionally, little hydel power consists of reasonable vitality origin which tends to work proficiently [3]. This source of power contains monetary highlights, for example, no fuel costs; arrangement of reinforcement during power interferences, decrease of the general expense of electric vitality, and no GHG outflows, yet its activity is restricted, attributable to non-accessibility of water during the dry season [4]. Thus, small-scale hydel power operates at lower limit of factor and also with the constraints of water. Be that as it may, hydropower frameworks can be immediately brought on the web and increase and down without any problem. The same can be utilized as a manual for putting vigorously in the new innovation and methods to contemplate the impacts of DERs entrance in the force frameworks. It additionally reveals more insight into the strategies that can be utilized to expand the limit and productivity of DERs, just as to diminish expenses or dangers that are related with their applications in the force framework.

11.1   Renewable-Based Available Technologies

Inexhaustible DER advancements consider the method on the basis of availability in the neighborhood sustainable power source assets [5]. Accessibility of nearby sustainable power source assets is a significant criterion in order to choose the locally available important locales for inexhaustible distributed energy resources advancements dependent mainly on particulars of original equipment manufacturers. Sustainable distributed energy resources can be visualized as seen naturally well disposed advances due to non-emission of greenhouse gases throughout the activities. Inexhaustible distributed energy resources should be associated with network and work through an independent framework to serve private, modern, and business concerns. Also, the inexhaustible distributed energy resources shall

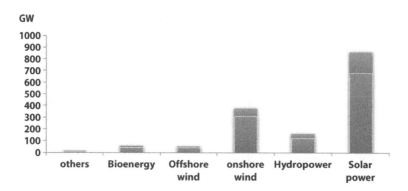

Figure 11.1   Electricity generated through different renewable energy source in 2018 [9].

lessen individual's quantity staying presently with no power globally. Ongoing studies completed by the World Energy Council tried to anticipate that force to be reckoned with yield from inexhaustible DERs will multiply from 23% in 2010 to roughly 34% in 2030 [6, 7]. Measurable data indicates that 24.5% of the total vitality used all-inclusive originates from sustainable DERs. In addition, DERs are anticipated to contribute 47.7% of the worldwide force flexibly by 2040 [8]. Figure 11.1 depicts a nice improvement in utilization as well as generation of renewable sources of energy in 2018.

11.1.1   Wind Power

Wind is a very important renewable source of energy but due to its extremely inconsistent nature, the power produced through turbines of wind is very irregular in nature. Varieties consisting of units of distributed energy resources should be associated with its framework. Another option is to work self-governing through an independent framework [10]. Wind power is bound to provide somewhere in the range of 16.7% and 18.8% of the worldwide electric force by 2030 [11]. Likewise, the ozone-depleting substance emanations are required to be diminished by more than 3 billion tons by 2030 with the utilization of the breeze framework [11].

11.1.1.1   Modeling of the Wind Turbine Generator (WTG)

The yield intensity of the breeze framework is an element of the cleared territory of the rotor, the proficiency of the breeze turbine, qualities of the breeze framework and aero-turbine execution [12]. Thus, the irregular variation occurring in the speed of wind, having stature influences the assessment assets of the turbine [13]. Thusly, a prototype can be prepared in order to evaluate the actual wind turbine framework. Force produced due to wind turbine generator relies upon the speed of wind towards the center point stature. The yield intensity of wind turbine generator is determined through change in deliberate breeze speed got on the location in order to relate the esteems at center point tallness, introduced the equation below (11.1). The existence of the speed of wind at the location of center tallness is evaluated as under [14, 15]:

$$v = v_r \left(\frac{H_{hub}}{H_r} \right)^{\alpha} \tag{11.1}$$

Where, v is the wind speed at the hub height (H_{hub}), v_r denotes the speed of wind at the chosen height H_r and α defines the surface friction coefficient of the leveled land. The values of it may vary in the range of 0.14-0.25 [16, 17]. The relationship to get a rough idea about the output power of the wind turbine generator is as under [18]:

$$P_w = \frac{1}{2} \rho A v^3 C_p \eta_g \eta_b \tag{11.2}$$

In the above-mentioned formula, ρ denotes the density of atmospheric air; v expresses the speed of wind, η_g denotes the efficiency of the generator, η_b gets the value of efficiency of gear or bearing, A here means the swept area of the rotor and C_p denotes the performance coefficient.

11.1.1.2   Categorization of Wind Turbine

Wind turbine comprises two categories. One is Horizontal Axis Wind Turbines (HAWT) and the other is Vertical Axis Wind Turbines (VAWT). These generally have different usefulness depending upon the needs. HAWT are the most used turbines and consist of generator, rotor, end to support the rotor and tail. Different sections of the HAWT mounts on the pinnacle, as the blades require fast moving air. The VAWT is structured in such a way, that it shouldn't be pointed into the course of the breeze; thus, it doesn't require the breeze detecting and direction instruments. The breeze turbines that have vertical tomahawks are beginning to turn out to be increasingly well known as a route for producing confined power, especially in context of latest developments. The activity of the HAWT and VAWT is dependent upon the accessibility and force of the wind asset. It does not end here. The generation process of electricity starts typically at 4 m/s and increases quickly to 12 m/s but thereafter it remains constant up to 25 m/s. A further increase in the speed may lead to the damage of mechanical components, hence at this speed it is made to shut down. A small change in the speed of wind may lead to huge variations in the output of power. The best option is to attach as many turbines as one can in order to get smooth output as compared to large fluctuations in the case of a single turbine [19].

11.1.2   Solar Power

The sun is the ultimate source of energy and has been exploited by human beings since time immemorial. In modern times, several solar-based technologies such as solar thermal, concentrated collectors and PV cells are contributing a major share in the overall utilization of renewable energy. There is a gradual lowering of the overall cost of the Photovoltaic systems for installing on the top of the household roof, resulting in creating a very good alternative for the generation of electrical energy [19].

11.1.2.1   PV System

The PV framework contains various boards that are associated in arrangement or corresponding to produce the necessary force requested taking into account the voltage and current appraisals determined by their particular makers [20]. The PV framework is a potential option in contrast to the ordinary force framework in light of the ecological well-disposed nature of the sun-based assets [21]. The designs of the PV framework rely upon the example of the use, operational necessities, segment topology and the heap prerequisites. The photovoltaic framework quickly develops distributed energy resources for energy since time immemorial to a portion of the open worries over the tasks of customary creating units. It has a few focal points innovations. Quick increment to the photovoltaic framework limit on the planet has been because of the high intensity of the framework compared to different sustainable advances [22–25]. The use of the PV framework in the micro-grid framework is all around acknowledged for its role as force, capable of lowering reliance on traditional producing areas. Forces gracefully get improved as the change due to low-cost raw petroleum doesn't influence the activity of a micro-grid framework that is incorporated with various PV frameworks. The monetary advantages of the PV framework can be utilized to settle the ideal activity of the customary force framework to over haul. Obtained measurable information introduced from renewable worldwide report demonstrated that the introduced limit of the PV framework toward the end of 2017 was roughly 402GW globally, and it has been anticipated to increase to about 872GW by 2030 [7, 26].

11.1.2.2   *Network-Linked Photovoltaic Grid-Connected PV Set-Up*

Matrix-associated photovoltaic frameworks have been planned through the utilization and helping buyers work related to different DERs and the utility lattice depends on certain advantages. The matrix-associated PV frameworks are comprised of the twin way flexibly the heaps legitimately associated with the AC transport framework and sends the overabundance capacity to the network at whatever point the force yield of the PV framework is more than the force required by the purchasers. The inverse happens at whatever point the force request is more than the yield of the PV framework. Some well being highlights are brought into the matrix-associated PV frameworks to keep the framework from taking care of the network at whatever point the utility lattice is down because of issues or under support [27]. Photovoltaic framework creates power asset that is straightforwardly associated with a nearby dissemination framework or associated with a host office inside the neighborhood circulation framework [28]. The mechanical progressions, environmental change approaches, and expanding buyers' heaps have expanded the possibility of the PV framework in the matrix associated and independent force framework. The PV framework presents the chances to upgrade in general framework ventures and give a scope of lattice administrations. The advantages got from the arrangement of a dependable force gracefully and investigate chances to fuse the PV framework into power markets are various.

11.1.3   Tidal Energy

As compared to wind and solar power, systems based on tidal energy are lagging behind in terms of their share in renewable energy although tidal energy has several advantages compared to wind power, as it can easily be predicted due to gravitational pull between sun and moon. The movement of oceans produced due to the above-mentioned phenomena creates a scope for harnessing its energy. A barrage is made to work on the motion of waves of the ocean in order to produce energy. With the fall and rise in the level of tides, ocean waves are allowed to flow through the channels of the turbines, the rotation of which produce power. It has got very few parts and it is very easy to operate. There is another essential part of the lagoon which plays an important role, i.e., embankment. The important role of this component is to incorporate wateright leak operation so that either the water inside should not leave or water should not be allowed to enter the lagoon. The turbines are installed to extract the key potential energy due to differences in water on two different sides of the lagoon. Another key feature of the lagoon is the sluices that allow a large quantity of water to enter or exit within a very short span of time [19].

11.1.4   Battery Storage System

The discontinuous nature of the nearby sustainable power source assets combined with the need to have a continuous force consistent with insignificant fuel and discharge costs have required the consolidation of battery framework into an independent or on the other hand network-associated power framework. The battery framework is utilized in the mix vigorously with inexhaustible distributed energy resources in order to diminish impacts arising due to random nature of nearby sustainable power source assets in a micro-grid framework [29]. This will decrease the impacts of intensity change and improve the unwavering quality of intensity gracefully. The choice of suitable battery stockpiling innovations depends on the predominant presentation of one battery stockpiling innovation on the other. The framework of the existing battery is for parameters like the price, encompassing rise in degrees, natural effects and condition of charge, obligation cycle, voltages impacts, adaptability, and pace of charging, vitality thickness, and pace of releasing. The recorded components are utilized for deciding the span of life and the good decision for battery framework. Its framework should be arranged for few classes considering the reaction times, limits, capacities, advancements, and type of vitality put away in the framework [30].

11.1.5   Solid Oxide Energy Units for Enhancing Power Life

SOFCs are progressively utilized as circulated power age innovations because of their high proficiency and multi-fuel capacity.

11.1.5.1   *Common Utility of SOFC*

The Japanese have increased the installation of family units of SOFC to 10% [31]. A few examinations (i.e., [32]) researched the warm and electricity conduct of solid oxide fuel cell [38] completed investigations and showed the fact that expanding the working degree of solid oxide fuel cell in between 650-750 °C, its electrical efficiency can be expanded. Dependable force and warmth flexibly is a necessity for business and open locales, for example, places of business, large lodgings, schools, and shopping centers. These locales give incredible chances to SOFCs to be utilized for conveying an age of warmth and power. In addition, dispatchable SOFCs empower administrators to give lattice backing to a neighborhood utility or a free framework administrator, which will assist with keeping away from speculations into fortifying power systems and new age limits. Utilizations in principles of solid oxide fuel cell for ventures incorporate reinforcement energy producing plant. SOFCs can give power to impetus and administration of naval force ships, flexible vitality to the makeshift camp of an uncovered base, and go about in aviation-based armed forces applications. For armed force and naval utilizations, solid oxide fuel cell incorporate assistant force and impetus of heavily clad trucks, versatile station of force and army correspondence centers, submerged marines, etc. Since SOFCs are quiet, dependable, strong, and uninterruptible they are a perfect alternative for vitality in military applications. Besides the great warmth dismissal capacity makes it feasible for a SOFC impetus framework to get good power and also become appropriate to get actively used. [33] embraced an actual existence cycle appraisal way to deal with assessing the exhibition of solid oxide fuel cell creates a type of helper frameworks of business trips. Demonstration was done about the creation of fuel stages significantly affecting the existence cycle execution of SOFCs. From the existence cycle perspective, bio-methanol was recognized as a domain amicable fuel for SOFCs.

11.1.5.2   Integrated Solid Oxide Energy Components and Sustainable Power Life

The fundamental thought of a half breed, sustainable, SOFC power-age framework is to utilize the overflow power from sustainable power sources, for example, sunlight-based and wind turbine to deliver H2. This combustible gas can be easily stored and used when required. Power age procedure by means of solid fuel cell warmth may be utilized for the achievement of gracefully warm request region warming framework. It ought to be noticed the electrical productivity demonstrates lesser warmth capacity of the solid oxide fuel cell. The association was concerned about the mode of force framework; half breed framework can be partitioned into two classes, specifically lattice associated and independent. For the most part in the lattice associated activity of solid oxide fuel cell gets resolved for amplification of the benefit for framework to consider power costs. In this way SOFCs are basically utilized for producing power during top hours when power costs are unexpectedly higher. Accessibility of the H_2 stockpiling guarantees can produce power to fill the hole between power request and sustainable age. Hydrogen stockpiling is significant so as to boost the adaptability of a crossover vitality framework. H_2 stockpiling fuel cell consists of adaptable vitality stockpiling answers networks. [34] evaluated presentation (full circle effectiveness) of a vitality stockpiling. Power is created due to changing over primarily made out blend containing H_2O and carbon dioxide. Procedure of electrolysis is used where, methane produced likewise gets delivered because of legitimate working circumstances, happens strongly indicated about a pile of full circle proficiency accomplished works at 700°C. Straight to the point M. Frank *et al.* [35] structured and did a trial on a ReSOC framework as vitality stockpiling that can be up scaled to offer adaptable types of assistance to control matrices. In energy unit, effectiveness provides full circle proficiency of as high as 51%. [36] Investigated presentation in terms of a coordinated solid oxide fuel cell packed vitality of air stockpiling framework in order to provide negligible-emanation power top interest. [37] showed half breed vitality framework including a SOFC, sunlight-based boards, and stream changing power. Utilization left with bio-energy gets solid oxide fuel cell a situation well-disposed choice for power age. A cross breed SOFC and smaller scale energized dissected [38] appropriated age power and warmth. [39] examined utilization for different rural deposits framework. [40] contemplated force and warmth left alone co-firing framework comprising bio-fuels-took care of solid oxide fuel cell. Sun oriented warm framework delivered nearby processing gathered slime. Warm force recuperated utilized piece warm burden, sun oriented warm assistant heater providing remainder warmth. Right now, notwithstanding, there is noteworthy enthusiasm for investigating the collaborations between vitality organizes through coupling segments, for example, capacity to-gas [41], power devices, and warm vitality stockpiling. With increase in number of non-conventional energy and also for greater flexibility in its utilization, there is concern across the globe for its proper and efficient utilization. A couple of models are given here to show the developing requirement for adaptability in different vitality frameworks.

11.2 Adaptability Frameworks

Vitality stockpiling frameworks are productive choices to adjust power flexibly and request within the sight of variable inexhaustible age. Vitality stockpiling devices assimilate surplus power produced by sustainable-request infuse power framework interest. Different vitality stockpiling advances and frameworks are right now a work in progress. An immense amount of subsidizing is spent annually on innovative work of vitality stockpiling advances. Siphoned packed stockpiling frameworks. These frameworks, one of a kind quality as far as cost, limit potential, stockpiling time, effectiveness depend upon the user. Framework example are electrolytes, stockpiling, and also a power module go about vitality stockpiling utilizing abundance power changing over at that point put away utilized an energy component create power interest. H_2 capacity framework lessens inexhaustible force shortening. Hydrogen delivered by sustainable power source can be utilized in a strong oxide energy component works joined warmth force framework. Accordingly the inexhaustible power that would be in any case diminished is utilized to decrease ozone-depleting substance outflows in the force and warmth areas. By utilizing advances, for example, layer creation, conceivable to give quick reaction auxiliary administrations to control frameworks. Hydrogen delivered likewise infused petroleum frameworks shape-enhanced flammable choice gives critical stockpiling limit in nations and districts that have created gaseous petrol framework. In those areas, hydrogen can be utilized to give occasional capacity to sustainable power source.

11.2.1 Distributed Energy Resources (DER)

Distributed energy resources contain little scope consolidate different varieties for age, stockpiling advancements and vitality observing and control offices to give a potential option in contrast to progress of the traditional force framework [42]. The introduced close to area used associated with lattice work independent frameworks work freely network. Distributed energy resources age and capacity advancements ordered dependent limit with respect to private, business, and mechanical force and warmth arrangements. Also, the DER innovations are empowered by the arrangement creators to boost their advantages, for example, creation of power, warming, and cooling. Attributable to this, a few benchmarks, advertise components, and administrative structures have been acquainted by government offices with adequately outfit the advantages of the DERs. These systems are started to ensure the security of intensity flexibly consistently. Distributed energy resources advancements broadly give power, heat, answers various clients over significant specialized, monetary ecological advantages force framework versatility and productivity. DERs can likewise improve lattice adjusting and reasonable augmentation of the matrix to detached networks. Different parts of significance of DER in the force framework are as per the following: intensity gracefully, reduction in dependability on intensity framework lessen identified with blackouts, reduction in greenhouse gas emission, introduce extra creating, hazard gracefully chance, subordinate help now and again, improve vitality effectiveness and nearby monetary turn of events.

(i) Utility of DER
Abrupt expanded force requests combined lack force flexibly, issues, urged look for wellsprings intensity gracefully based specialized, financial, and ecological advantages [43].

The acknowledgment of DERs is focused on the lower working expenses and being simple and quicker to introduce when contrasted and the non-renewable energy source based creating units. DER advances can be utilized for different applications dependent on business status, financial aspects, accessibility, and natural contemplations. These elements are utilized to choose the suitable DER innovations to give quick answers for various force issues.

(ii) Stand-alone

An independent force framework -lattice framework regions attached network inferable from monetary and specialized imperatives [22]. Independent framework free matrix work viably related to nonrenewable and sustainable DERs, just as electric stockpiling frameworks. The utilization of the independent framework in the rustic zones is more financially savvy than stretching out the transmission lines to such areas. Moreover, the independent framework is likewise used by people who live near the utility lattice and wish to obtain independence from the utilities to demonstrate their duty to manageability of sustainable power source. The independent frameworks are commonly intended to join different DER advances to create a solid force, lessen diminish burden related interferences. Methodologies incorporate utilization of decrease estimation power satisfy purchaser needs framework. Utilization independent activity relies upon some foremost factors, for example, outflows, expenses and expense.

(iii) Shaving of peaks

Advancements used to create force in order to buy exorbitant. In corporate top interest force request extremely can't satisfy force need attributable constrained force age limit. Utilized pinnacle decrease top interest as opposed to expose a few clients to baseless force blackouts. Intended gracefully control pinnacle this manner giving various monetary advantages shoppers reason for using top build age capacity system simultaneously to decrease monetary impact of burden profoundly factor. Thus, gives snappy reaction to control request, ideal answer pinnacle use advancements pinnacle arrangement restricts.

(iv) Power as backup

Utilized force arrangement conditions force gracefully isn't solid attributable to an enormous number event of intensity blackouts span reestablish flexibly. Utilization framework give ideal answer for fulfill the heap need when the force gracefully is interfered. Likewise, inferable from certain advantages, for example, a dependable activity and diminished operational personal time, they can flexibly some basic burdens during the force blackouts pending when force administration reestablished [43]. Ideal choice because of insecure force flexibly from the utilities relies upon how every now and again the fire long function every force framework mix an assortment reserve numerous advantages, extraordinary compared to other force arrangements dependent on working expenses and force blackouts decrease.

(v) Power in difficult times

Additionally intended crisis arrangements matrix network associated frameworks. DERs for crisis power arrangements include the full scope of empowering advancements, for example, sustainable and nonrenewable DERs, vitality stockpiling frameworks, and clever control innovation. DERs' capacity arrangements likewise guarantee the force flexibly manageability and cost-adequacy in a broad extent of uses. DERs are utilized for crisis power arrangements in an assortment of settings, for example, private, business, mechanical, server farms, correspondence offices, and present day security observing focuses. The benefits crisis incorporate snappy beginning, fast assaulting term intensity interferences, interference framework backing constant activity different areas of the economy. In any case, the working constrained inferable from emanations contaminations.

(vi) Load shedding

Distributed energy resources are used force framework worldwide vitality and natural goals dependent solid, moderate, vitality stage enhance vitality frameworks over different pathways, for example, electrical, warm, fills, water, correspondence, and physical scales. Burden shortening structured conceivably diminish force request vitality utilization pinnacle use various decreases blockage network, regular pinnacle entirety intensity, request heap habitats more prominent force created [23]. It diminishes clog framework emergency related occasion. Specific situation, numerous shoppers urged introduce forestall expense related reduction. The quantity introduced better limits to be utilized by the buyers to fulfill necessary needs. One more task is to diminish financial effect heap abridgement shoppers.

(vii) Combination of both heat as well as power

Joined warmth force innovation included, miniaturized scale turbine, energy component creation force warmth arrangements. Planned makers recoup squandered warm vitality from the regular creating units for private, modern, civil, and business warming advances squander warmth used innovation because of usage productivity and monetary possibilities [44]. It is intended to catch the warmth that would somehow have been squandered to give significant warm vitality to mechanical and residential applications. It will in general be arranged offices warm vitality all the while. Figure 11.2 shows the sugar bio-energy transferred to the grid in Brazil in between 2010 and 2018.

(viii) Demand Response

Request reaction decreases the measure of intensity of clients' reaction upon heightening inspiration installments and is deliberately intended to cut usage being vitality specific [46]. Utilization advancements an interest reaction arrangement depends on the decrease of intensity gracefully from the dissemination organizes administrators with the nearby infusion of intensity at the heap communities. The gracefully from the utilities is decreased

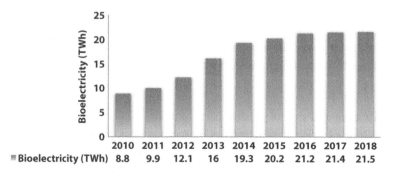

Figure 11.2 Sugar based bio-energy produced and transferred to the grid [45].

and the general framework steadiness is kept up (if not improved) as the save flexibly limit is expanded. In certain circumstances, utilized increase, yet advantages constrained fiscal remuneration destinations bear decrease superfluous burdens as mentioned.

11.2.2 New Age Grid Connection

Shrewd matrix characterized systems consolidates various producing, savvy lattice highlights, stacks, productively pass on sufficient limit, builds network proficiency, maintainability, availability, self-recuperating, wellbeing, and dependability [43]. Brilliant network progression tends goal improving presentation force frameworks dependent joint efforts among clients. Fast interest establishments conventional force framework PC helped framework utilized age, dispersion, utilization [22]. Attributable quick development worldwide force request, change of the costs of petroleum products and the decrease in DERs costs throughout the most recent couple of years, the open doors for DER advances in the brilliant network associated power framework appear to be expanding. A savvy vitality framework can coordinate and upgrade so as bring down, decrease ozone harming substance (GHG) emanations, and improve the effectiveness of intensity frameworks. The mix of different DER advancements can likewise be utilized to multiply the estimations of the shrewd network.

(i) Advantages of Distributed energy resources in terms of smart grid
Advantages savvy framework summed up [44]:

- Keen network permits infiltration insignificant expense improving dependability intensity flexibly.
- Distributed energy resource advancements assume job expense vitality investment funds, achieved by improving the vitality proficiency and lessening the pinnacles request.
- The use of DER advances in the savvy network decreases the working expenses.
- The use of savvy framework innovation gives various power advantages to customers by effectively using the force framework parts.
- The usage of shrewd lattice highlights can securely satisfy buyer power requests at natural expenses.

(ii) How to connect Distributed energy resources to grids
Shrewd framework permits various shoppers to control their machines with various DERs dependent on the accessibility of nearby sustainable power source assets. The overabundance power created by every buyer can be taken care of into the network. The framework is arranged in a manner that at whatever point nearby sustainable assets is inaccessible; the force request of the buyers is met from the utility matrix. In any case, the utilities face various issues so as to interface little DERs to the brilliant framework, in light of the unwavering quality, security, permit levy certain nations.

(iii) Metering through net
Keen utilized quantify contrast power created shoppers network. Shows charge customers dependent vitality month to month premise [46]. Stage furnished use permits purchasers

gracefully overabundance produced network vitality usage. Numerous nations' private business clients are dependent particular necessities. Permits solitary bidirectional shrewd used vitality customers' framework abundance vitality shopper's criticism matrix.

(iv) Expenditure involved

Levies technique intended quicken interests advances permitting vitality created purchaser made up vitality criticism framework. Taxes, so as quantify surge power for every client freely. Primary vitality network, subsequent over abundance vitality produced by every shopper that is taken care of go into the utility lattice. This empowers power utilization and power age to be valued independently.

11.3   Conclusion

The 21st Conference of Parties held in Paris in 2015 called for limiting the maximum increase in the average temperature of the globe below 2°C. Beside this, sustainable growth is very important in today's scenario as it integrates economic, social and environmental dimensions of life. In order to enhance this development, harnessing of renewable energy is an essential task for every country. In this regard, comparison based on frequency stability, power quality, voltage stability, voltage ride through and power regulations was investigated by one of the review papers. It was also found that in 2018 26% of total produced global power was made by renewable energy systems. The impact on the environment while generating electricity is minimal. For stable and continuous operation of the power system, it is important to ensure certain standards, requirements and rules. The smart grids based on efficient renewable energy system is the need of the hour at both municipal as well as district level. In another study, it was shown that partnership-based collaborations should be encouraged from private, community and government communities. In one paper, an analysis was performed on different storage technologies for hybrid renewable energy systems consisting of hydrokinetic, diesel generator and photovoltaic.

Generally unique vitality frameworks of power, gas, area warming/cooling, and hydrogen had moderately hardly any associations and were structured and worked autonomously of one another. Associations occur through vitality transformation between various vitality bearers and its stockpiling to offer types of assistance and guarantee that each is overseen ideally. From the specialized perspective the joining of multi-vector vitality frameworks expands the challenges of overseeing and working complex vitality frameworks. So as to dissect the communications and interdependencies among various vitality frameworks at various spatial and worldly scales, improved demonstrating devices are required to contemplate the effect of falling disappointments influencing the unwavering quality of vitality supplies. In addition, more programming devices (arranging, reproduction, and operational control) are expected to measure the presentation of the incorporated vitality frameworks under various situations. Furthermore, appraisal philosophies and assessment rules are required to evaluate the techno-financial execution of the coordinated vitality frameworks. In view of the assessment models, standard test systems should be intended to help the applicable investigations and approve the created models.

References

1. Zobaa, A. F., Bansal, R. C., Manana, M. eds. (2011). *Power Quality: Monitoring, Analysis and Enhancement*, InTech.
2. Adefarati, T., Bansal, R. C. (2017). Reliability and economic assessment of a microgrid power system with the integration of renewable energy resources, *Appl. Energy*, 206, 911-933.
3. Bhatti, T., Bansal, R. C., Kothari, D. P. (2004). *Small Hydro Power Systems*, Dhanpat Rai & Co., New Delhi.
4. Doolla, S., Bhatti, T., Bansal, R. (2011). Load frequency control of an isolated small hydro power plant using multi-pipe scheme, *Electr. Power Compon. Syst.* 39(1), 46-63.
5. Arulampalam, A., Mithulananthan, N., Bansal, R. C., and Saha, T. (2010). Micro-grid control of PV-wind-diesel hybrid system with islanded and grid connected operations, *IEEE InternationalConference on Sustainable Energy Technologies (ICSET)*, pp. 1-5.
6. Salvatore, J. (2013). *World Energy Perspective: Cost of Energy Technologies*, World Energy Council, London, UK.
7. Renewables (2018) global status report, Available online: http://www.ren21.net/wp-content/uploads/2018/06/17-8652_GSR2018_FullReport_web_final_.pdf.
8. Demirbas, A. (2009). Global renewable energy projections, *Energy Sources B*, 4(2), 212-224.
9. Al-Shetwi, A. Q., Hannan, M. A., Jern, K. P., Mansur, M., & Mahlia, T. M. I. (2019). Grid-connected renewable energy sources: Review of the recent integration requirements and control methods. *Journal of Cleaner Production*, 119831.
10. Gidwani, L., Tiwari, H., Bansal, R. (2013). Improving power quality of wind energy conversion system with unconventional power electronic interface, *Int. J. Electr. Power Energy Syst.* 44(1), 445-453.
11. Global Wind Energy Council (GWEC), Available online: http://www.gwec.net/globalfigures/graph.
12. Chong, W., Naghavi, M., Poh, S., Mahlia, T., Pan, K. (2011). Techno-economic analysis of a wind–solar hybrid renewable energy system with rainwater collection feature for urban high-rise application, *Appl. Energy*, 88(11), 4067-4077.
13. Kong, S., Bansal, R., Dong, Z. (2012). Comparative small-signal stability analyses of PMSG-, DFIG and SCIG-based wind farms, *Int. J. Ambient Energy*, 33(2), 87-97.
14. Patel, M. R. (2005). *Wind and Solar Power Systems: Design, Analysis, and Operation*, CRC Press.
15. Belfkira, R., Zhang, L., Barakat, G. (2011). Optimal sizing study of hybrid wind/PV/diesel power generation unit, *Sol. Energy*, 85(1), 100-110.
16. Del Granado, P. C., Pang, Z., Wallace, S. W. (2016). Synergy of smart grids and hybrid distributed generation on the value of energy storage, *Appl. Energy*, 170, 476-488.
17. Rocchetta, R., Li, Y., Zio, E. (2015). Risk assessment and risk-cost optimization of distributed powergeneration systems considering extreme weather conditions, *Reliab. Eng. Syst. Saf*, 136, 47-61.
18. Ashok, S. (2007). Optimised model for community-based hybrid energy system, *Renew. Energy*, 32 (7), 1155-1164.
19. Qadrdan, M., Xu, X., Haghi, E., & Williams, C. (2020). Renewable power generation. In *Design and Operation of Solid Oxide Fuel Cells*, 297-310. doi:10.1016/b978-0-12-815253-9.00010-0.
20. Adefarati, T., Bansal, R.C. (2017). Reliability assessment of distribution system with the integration of renewable distributed generation, *Appl. Energy*, 185, 158-171.
21. Tazvinga, H., Thopil, M., Numbi, P.B., Adefarati, T. (2017). Distributed renewable energy technologies, in: *Handbook of Distributed Generation*, Springer, pp. 3-67.
22. Adefarati, T., Bansal, R. C. (2016). Integration of renewable distributed generators into the distribution system: a review, *IET Renew. Power Gener.* 10(7), 873-884.

23. Ahmad, M. (2017). *Operation and Control of Renewable Energy Systems*, John Wiley & Sons.

24. Ma, L. (2016). Multi-party energy management for smart building cluster with PV systems using automatic demand response, *Energ. Buildings*, 121, 11-21.

25. Tazvinga, H., Hove, T. (2010). *Photovoltaic/Diesel/Battery Hybrid Power Supply System*, VDM Publishers,.

26. Taylor, M., Daniel, K., Ilas, A., So, E.Y. (2015). *Renewable Power Generation Costs in 2014*, International Renewable Energy Agency, Masdar City, Abu Dhabi.

27. Florida solar energy center creating energy independence, Available online: http://www.fsec.ucf.edu/en/consumer/solar_electricity/basics/types_of_pv.htm.

28. Bansal, R. C. and Bhatti, T. (2008). *Small Signal Analysis of Isolated Hybrid Power Systems: Reactive Power and Frequency Control Analysis*. Alpha Science.

29. Battke, B., Schmidt, T. S. (2015). Cost-efficient demand-pull policies for multi-purpose technologies– The case of stationary electricity storage, *Appl. Energy*, 155, 334-348.

30. Evans, A., Strezov, V., Evans, T. J. (2012). Assessment of utility energy storage options for increased renewable energy penetration, *Renew. Sustain. Energy Rev.* 16(6), 4141-4147.

31. Government of Japan, https://www.gov-online.go.jp/eng/publicity/book/hlj/html/201706/201706_10_en .html.

32. Ullah, K. R., Akikur, R. K., Ping, H. W., Saidur, R., Hajimolana, S. A., Hussain, M. A. (2015). An experimental investigation on a single tubular SOFC for renewable energy based cogeneration system, *Energy Convers. Manage.* 94, 139-149.

33. Strazza, C., Del Borghi, A., Costamagna, P., Traverso, A., Santin, M. (2010). Comparative LCA of methanol-fuelled SOFCs as auxiliary power systems on-board ships, *Appl. Energy*, 87, 1670-1678.

34. Perna, A., Minutillo, M., Cicconardi, S. P., Jannelli, E., Scarfogliero, S. (2016). Performance assessment of electric energy storage (EES) systems based on reversible solid oxide cell, in: *71st Conference of the Italian Thermal Machines Engineering Association*, ATI2016, 14_16, Turin, Italy.

35. Frank, M., Deja, R., Peters, R., Blum, L., Stolten, D. (2018). Bypassing renewable variability with a reversible solid oxide cell plant, *Appl. Energy*, 217, 101-112.

36. Nease, J., Monteiro, N., Adams, T. A. (2016). Application of a two-level rolling horizon optimization scheme to a solid-oxide fuel cell and compressed air energy storage plant for the optimal supply of zero-emissions peaking power, *Comput. Chem. Eng.* 94, 235-249.

37. Sadeghi, S. (2018). Study using the flow battery in combination with solar panels and solidoxide fuel cell for power generation, *Sol. Energy*, 170, 732-740.

38. Perna, A., Minutillo, M., Jannelli, E., Cigolotti, V., Nam, S. W., Yoon, K. J. (2018). Performance assessment of a hybrid SOFC/MGT cogeneration power plant fed by syngas from a biomass down-draft gasifier, *Appl. Energy*, 227, 80-91.

39. Zabaniotou, A. (2014). Agro-residues implication in decentralized CHP production through a thermochemical conversion system with SOFC, *Sustain. Energy Technol. Assess.* 6, 34-50.

40. Mehr, A. S., Gandiglio, M., Mosayeb Nezhad, M., Lanzini, A., Mahmoudi, S. M. S., Yari, M. (2017). Solar-assisted integrated biogas solid oxide fuel cell (SOFC) installation in wastewater treatment plant: energy and economic analysis, *Appl. Energy*, 191, 620-638.

41. Maroufmashat, A., Fowler, M. (2017). Transition of future energy system infrastructure; through power-to-gas pathways, *Energies*, 10(8), 1089.

42. Adefarati, T., Bansal, R. C., Justo, J. J. (2017). Techno-economic analysis of a PV–wind–battery–diesel standalone power system in a remote area, *J. Eng.* (13), 740-744.

43. Adefarati, T., Bansal, R.C., Justo, J. J. (2017). Reliability and economic evaluation of a microgrid power system, *Energy Procedia*, 142, 43-48.

44. FEMP (2002) US Department of Energy, Using distributed energy resources-a how-to guide for federal energy managers, *Cogener. Compet. Power J.* 17(4), 37-68.

45. Lima, M. A., Mendes, L. F. R., Mothé, G. A., Linhares, F. G., de Castro, M. P. P., da Silva, M. G., Sthel, M. S. (2020). Renewable energy in reducing greenhouse gas emissions: reaching the goals of the Paris agreement in Brazil, *Environmental Development*, 33, 100504.

46. Zhu, J. (2015). *Optimization of Power System Operation*, John Wiley & Sons.

12

Efficient Renewable Energy Systems

Dr. Arvind Dhingra

Faculty, Electrical Engineering Department, Guru Nanak Dev Engineering College, Ludhiana, India

Abstract

In the trying times of today, especially the developing countries are facing challenges to meet their growing energy needs. With environmental norms becoming stricter, the only way out which seems viable is use of renewable energy. However, although renewable energy systems have been used for quite some time now, their efficiency remains a big question in regard to their proper utilization. The efficiency levels of 15-30% of renewable resources energy systems do not compare favourably with their non-renewable counterparts. Efforts are being made by researchers all over the globe to increase the energy efficiency for these systems. This chapter presents the journey of renewable energy systems and highlights the efforts being made the world over to increase their efficiency.

Keywords: Renewable energy, wind, solar, ocean, biomass, geothermal

12.1 Introduction

Energy has been the main driver for mankind's progress. Since the invention of wheel and fire, energy has been in demand for all chores mankind does for a living. Until very recently the whole world was highly dependent on fossil fuels. Fossil fuel is non-renewable fuel and takes a number of years to form. Also the burning of this fuel leads to environmental pollution. This calls for an innovative approach for meeting energy requirements. Non-conventional or renewable energy resources fit the bill and hence offer a probable solution.

12.1.1 World Energy Scenario

World energy consumption is the sum total of energy produced and consumed from all sources of energy. While considering energy consumption another term that requires some explanation is the "total primary energy supply." Here primary energy implies that energy which is found naturally and is not subject to any human processing. Primary energy could be renewable or non-renewable. Total primary energy supply is the differential of sum of energy production minus the storage changes which may happen. This factor does not include the conversion efficiency. This exclusion leads to wrong figures in regard to the

Email: arvinddhingra@gmail.com

Suman Lata Tripathi, Dushyant Kumar Singh, Sanjeevikumar Padmanaban, and P. Raja (eds.) Design and Development of Efficient Energy Systems, (215–228) © 2021 Scrivener Publishing LLC

Table 12.1 The primary energy supply & consumption.

Year	Primary energy supply (TPES)	Final energy consumption	Electricity generation
1973	71,013 (Mtoe 6,106)	54,335 (Mtoe 4,672)	6,129
1990	102,569	–	11,821
2000	117,687	–	15,395
2010	147,899 (Mtoe 12,717)	100,914 (Mtoe 8,677)	21,431
2011	152,504 (Mtoe 13,113)	103,716 (Mtoe 8,918)	22,126
2012	155,505 (Mtoe 13,371)	104,426 (Mtoe 8,979)	22,668
2013	157,482 (Mtoe 13,541)	108,171 (Mtoe 9,301)	23,322
2014	155,481 (Mtoe 13,369)	109,613 (Mtoe 9,425)	23,816
2015	158,715 (Mtoe 13,647)	109,136 (Mtoe 9,384)	
2017	162,494 (Mtoe 13,972)	113,009 (Mtoe 9,717)	25,606

poor energy conversion ratios for sources such as Solar or wind. A lot of energy gets wasted during the conversion process. The Table 12.1 cites some figures of primary energy supply, final energy consumption and electricity generation through the years starting from the early 1970s to 2017. It can be seen from this table that consumption patterns have shown a steady rise over recent years.

If we look at the world energy production Figure 12.1, especially electrical energy, it can be seen that most of the electrical energy, around 38%, is being produced using coal,

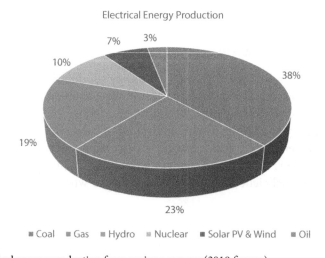

Electrical Energy Production

■ Coal   ■ Gas   ■ Hydro   ■ Nuclear   ■ Solar PV & Wind   ■ Oil

Figure 12.1 Electrical energy production from various sources (2018 figures).

followed by gas (23%), hydro (19%), nuclear (10%), solar PV & wind (7%) and oil (3%). This is depicted in the pie diagram below.

12.2   Sources of Energy: Classification

The sources of energy can be classified as:

1. Primary and Secondary
2. Conventional and Non-conventional
3. Renewable and Non renewable
4. Commercial and non-commercial sources

Primary sources of energy are those which are found in nature. For example: coal, lignite.

Secondary sources of energy are those in which energy is derived using primary sources. For example: oil.

Conventional sources are the sources which have been known to mankind for a long duration of time and their usage has been in vogue. For example: wood, coal.

Non-conventional sources of energy are those whose usage for energy production has recently been discovered. For example: solar, wind.

Renewable energy sources are the ones which are not depleted with passage of time or usage. For example: hydro power.

Non-renewable energy sources are those which get exhausted with the passage of time or usage. For example: coal.

Commercial sources of energy are those for which we need to pay for their usage. For example: coal.

Non-commercial sources of energy are those in which the only cost involved is in harnessing the energy. For example: solar.

12.3   Renewable Energy Systems

As discussed above, renewable energy systems are those which do not get exhausted when they are used. In fact nature replenishes them. Renewable energy sources are as listed below:

- Solar
- Wind
- Geothermal
- Biomass
- Ocean
- Hydrogen

All these sources can also be categorised as Non-conventional energy sources since their usage for energy harness has just begun.

12.3.1   Solar Energy

The energy derived from the sun is called Solar energy. The radiations of the sun have immense energy in them. The question is, how can this immense energy be harnessed? There are two methods of extracting the sun's energy. They are:

a) Solar Photovoltaic
b) Solar Thermal

We shall be discussing both these technologies in detail in subsequent sections.

12.3.2   Wind

The energy from wind pressure is another useful source of energy. With a basic wind speed, we can run wind turbines to harness this energy. As of today, India stands at fourth position in the world for extracting power from wind.

12.3.3   Geothermal

The earth's crust has an enormous amount of energy stored in it. This energy comes out in various forms such as hot molten lava, hot springs. The technology for harnessing this energy are discussed in subsequent sections.

12.3.4   Biomass

All the living plant kingdom is an immense source of energy. All living beings carry energy. The energy from biomass can be extracted using various means which are discussed further.

12.3.5   Ocean

The waves of the ocean have a lot of energy. Some authors take the ocean energy as a form of solar energy only.

12.3.6   Hydrogen

Hydrogen as a form of energy has been exploited very recently. It is a source of immense energy with the only limitation being the technology for controlling the energy produced.
Let us now discuss these sources and the techniques to harness power from them.

12.4   Solar Energy

The sun is a storehouse of power. At any point of time, a very large number of reactions are happening in the sun's crust. Each reaction releases a lot of energy. Travelling through the atmosphere, this energy reaches the earth. The sun emits electromagnetic radiations. A large chunk of the radiations emitted from the sun (approximately 99%) are in visible, ultra-violet and infra-red spectrum wavelengths. The sunlight we see is the electromagnetic radiation from the sun. This wavelength waves contain lot of heat energy which can be harnessed. As per the World Meteorological Organization, the direct radiation, or irradiance, as it is called, received from the sun is around 120 W/m2. The time taken by sunlight to reach the earth is 8.3 minutes. The irradiance from the sun shows seasonal and latitudinal variations. It becomes a challenge for engineers and scientists to develop devices to effectively trap the immense energy from the sun and convert it into useful purpose.

There are various technologies available for harnessing the sun's energy. They are:

a) Photovoltaic
b) Concentrating power technology
c) Water heating or solar thermal
d) Passive heating or daylight heating
e) Process heat

- Photovoltaic: This is the technology which is used to convert the energy received from the sun to electrical energy. Solar photovoltaic cells are made for achieving this. The solar cells or the PV cells are made of semi-conductor material like silicon and these materials convert the sun's energy to electricity. Semi-conductor materials require less energy to make their valence electrons free. These free electrons, when they move in a particular fashion, produce current. The photovoltaic cells are assembled in the form of panels which are usually flat in shape. These panels are mounted on structures in such a way that sunlight falls directly on them for a major part of the day. Single solar cells are also used in watches, calculators, etc.
- Concentrating Power Technology: The concentrating power technology works on the principle of concentrating the sun's rays at a single point to raise the temperature of the point. Special types of mirrors are used in this arrangement. Here only the heat content of the sun is used and light energy does not play any role. There are three types of solar concentrators which are prevalent in the market:
    i)   Parabolic Trough Type Collectors: In this type of collector, several U-shaped mirrors which have long lengths and are usually rectangular in shape are used. The angle of these mirrors are so adjusted as to enable the reflected waves from the mirrors to meet at a single point. Here a pipe carrying oil or fluid is kept. The heat energy boils the oil or fluid and converts it to steam which is then used to run a generator. This is shown in Figure 12.2 below:
    ii) Dish/engine system: In this type of arrangement shown in Figure 12.3, a dish made of mirrors is made. The angles are so adjusted to ensure that the reflected waves meet at a single point, concentrating the sun's heat. The single concentrating point has an engine placed. Due to the concentrated heat falling on the engine, it gets heated up and this can be used to run a turbine.
    iii) Tower Power System: In this type of arrangement shown in Figure 12.4, a large number of mirrors are placed in field such that their

Figure 12.2 Parabolic trough arrangement.

Figure 12.3 Dish type collectors.

Figure 12.4 Tower type power system.

combined reflected energy falls on the top of a tower. The receiver is placed at the top of this tower. The receiver has molten salt which gets heated up due to concentrated heat and gets converted to steam which is then used to run the turbine.

- Water heating or Solar Thermal: This technology of harnessing power from the sun is one of the most efficient technologies. But the arrangement shown in Figure 12.5 required is too elaborate and costly. This is used for house heating and water heating. To harness energy using this technology, glass tubes

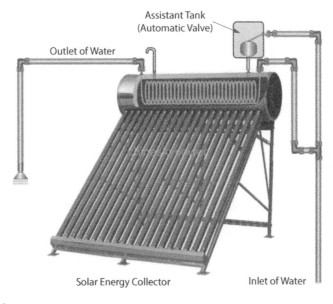

Figure 12.5 Water heating.

are used. These tubes are coloured black and are housed in flat plate collectors which have photo sensitive material. The collectors have a glass cover and the pipes are placed inside it. The sunlight, when it falls on the tubes after passing through the glass, heats up the water flowing inside the pipes. This is then circulated to extract the heat for building. This heat is also used to heat water as in geysers. The heated water may also be stored in insulated tanks to be used for some purpose later on.

- Passive Heating or daylight heating: Passive heating (Figure 12.6) makes use of the building design to extract the sun's heat. We are aware that south-facing buildings receive more sunlight than any other building orientation. This effect is used in passive heating. Most of the windows are kept facing south in order to utilize the sun's heat to the maximum. The floors and walls are also made of materials which absorb heat. This arrangement does not have any active component involved and as such the name is passive heating.
- Process Heating: This technology is used to heat or cool a building using the sun's energy (Figure 12.7). This technology is useful in heating large industrial buildings. For use of this technology, a specific building design is required. Also, the material used for construction needs to be specific.

The basic component used in all the above technologies for harnessing the sun's energy is the solar cell. The manufacture of a solar cell is a costly process and as such the cost of harnessing solar energy is high. Continued research has been able to bring down the cost of solar cells and subsequently solar panels. But still more research is required to increase the efficiency of the solar cell and also decrease its cost further.

Figure 12.6 Building using passive heating.

Figure 12.7 Use of process heat for buildings.

12.5 Wind Energy

Wind energy is also treated as a form of solar energy. The logic in doing so is that winds are produced and circulated due to heating of earth's atmosphere because of sunlight. The earth's surface is uneven and also the earth rotates around the sun. In addition to this, owing to latitudinal differences, the earth's atmosphere not heated uniformly all along. All these are the causes of wind flow.

In order to harness the energy from wind, wind turbines are used Figure12.8. These wind turbines have blades resembling the propeller blades. The blades are mounted on the shaft. In cases where the blades are oriented in a vertical circular fashion, the wind turbine is called as vertical turbine. When the turbine blades are oriented in a circle parallel to surface of earth, it is called as horizontal turbine. As stated earlier, due to uneven winds, wind power can be harnessed at a few locations only. The minimum wind speed required for proper harnessing of wind energy is 5 nautical miles per hour. Another disadvantage of wind energy is its intermittent nature, i.e., we do not get constant supply output. The wind turbines require a large human-free and obstruction-free area for installation.

The principle of operation of wind turbines is simple. The turbine blades are rotated by the pressure of wind on aero dynamically designed blades of the turbine. This makes the shaft of the rotor on which the blades are mounted to rotate, which runs the turbine and produces the electricity. Here the kinetic energy of air is being converted to the pressure energy which drives the turbine blades. The factors that influence the power output from wind turbines include the wind speed, area swept by blades and density of air. The relation of power with these factors is depicted in the equation below:

$$P = \frac{1}{2}\rho A V^{-3}$$

Where P is power in watts or kilowatts
ρ is density of air
A is area being swept by turbine blades
V is velocity of air.

As can be seen from above relation, the wind speed has a considerable impact on the output. A small increase in wind speed can help increase the power enormously. Density of air also affects the production of power. The more is the air density, the more is the power produced. Air density itself is a function of temperature and altitude. The swept area is the area being swept by the turbine blades while moving. But there are physical limitations to increasing the size of blades beyond a certain reasonable limit.

There are a number of factors which need to be taken care of while locating the wind turbines. These include:

Selection of site: Site should be so selected as to be away from population. The area should be free of any obstructions and should be easily accessible for maintenance purposes. Also, it should be such that power produced can be extracted easily.

Wind speeds: Reasonable amount of wind speed should be available at all times. The wind speed is the major factor to decide for location of wind turbines. Anemometers are used to gauge the wind speeds.

Other factors: Factors such as air being dense but free from corrosive materials, temperature prevailing at site, etc., are also considered while deciding the location of wind power plants.

Most of the wind turbines use induction generators owing to the intermittent nature of the energy being produced. In order to keep the outflow of energy from wind turbines maintained at a level, doubly fed induction generators (DFIG) are being used these days. This arrangement ensures nearly constant power output for the duration of the working of wind turbines. These generators have efficiencies in the range of 80-90%.

Figure 12.8 Wind turbines.

With the passage of time, the capacity of wind turbines has increased. Starting in the mid-1980s when the turbine capacity was about 0.05MW, wind energy generation has reached levels of 2mW in onshore and 3-5MW in offshore conditions. The wind turbines which are available commercially have ratings of the range of 8MW.

12.6   Geothermal Energy

Geothermal energy is the energy beneath the earth's crust. It is the energy stored in rocks, magma and fluids inside the earth's crust. The amount of energy is enormous. The first usage of geothermal energy was reported in Italy in 1904. Thereafter constant efforts have been made to harness the power from the geothermal resource. As of 2018, the energy harnessed from geothermal route stood at 13.3GW.

In order to harness the energy from earth's crust, deep wells are dug into underground reservoirs from where the access is made to steam and hot water inside the earth's crust. The steam is extracted to run turbines to produce electricity. Three types of geothermal power plants are known as: Dry steam type, flash and binary. Out of these, the dry steam type is the oldest form of the technology known. In this type of a plant the dry steam is used directly to run a turbine and produce electricity. In flash-type geothermal plants, high pressure hot water gets converted to low pressure cool water which then runs the turbine. In binary type, as the name suggests, two liquids are involved. The hot water from earth's crust is passed through another liquid, sometimes referred to as secondary liquid, which is heated and gets converted to vapour. This vapour is then used to run the turbine.

The use of geothermal energy has been seen in over 20 countries around the world including India. India has a geothermal power plant operational in Kashmir (example as shown in Figure 12.9). The United States of America is the largest producer of geothermal energy.

Figure 12.9 Geothermal plant in Iceland.

Geothermal energy is also found entrapped in hot water springs which are found naturally at many places in the world. Molten magma coming out of volcanoes is also a source of geothermal energy. The disadvantage associated with geothermal energy is the difficulty in handling very high temperatures of steam and lava. Another disadvantage is the sulphur content associated with steam from earth's crust.

The advantages of geothermal energy are that it is a carbon free and sustainable form of energy. The amount of carbon monoxide as released during harnessing of geothermal energy is 1/6th of a natural gas plant producing energy. Geothermal energy finds application in home heating. Earth has an estimated potential of 2TW.

Geothermal plants have reported high efficiencies in the range of 80% or higher.

12.7 Biomass

Biomass is one of the oldest sources of energy known to mankind. It goes back to the days when humans lived in caves, and wood (biomass source) was used to produce heat and light energy. All living things on this earth constitute biomass. Biomass energy is the energy derived from organic matter. Certain crops are particularly grown as energy-producing crops, for example, jatropha, etc. The energy from biomass can be harnessed in two ways:

i)   By burning biomass to produce heat, which heats up the water/fluids to convert them into gaseous form which is then used to run turbines.
ii)   By making brickets: The biomass is dried and processed to make brickets. These are then burnt to get energy.

In addition to plant matter, biomass energy is also found in sewage. The algae in sewage have potential to produce energy.

Diesel and petrol are also forms of biomass as they are produced due to slowed decomposition of plant matter buried deep under the earth's crust.

12.7.1 Forms of Biomass

The following are known forms of biomass:

Wood and agricultural-based products: These include logs, wood chips, sawdust, corn cobs, wheat and rice husk, etc.

Biofuels: These are fuels derived from plants especially grown for this purpose. These include plants like jatropha. Biofuels include bio diesels and bio ethanol.

Solid Waste: The solid waste as produced in our homes or from industries is an immense source of power. 1 ton of solid biomass waste has energy comparable to 500 tons of coal-based energy.

Biogas: Biogas is a rich source of energy. It is produced by composting of cow dung. The cow dung is put into a pit and slurry is made with some water. The mixture is left to ferment for 14-21 days. Biogas which is rich in Methane is produced, and this can directly be combusting as fuel.

The biomass-based plants have efficiencies ranging from 60 to 80%.

12.8   Ocean Power

Tidal power or ocean power is also one clean source of power. Tides are produced due to the gravitational pull of sun and moon and the pull of earth's gravitation. The kinetic energy from tides is used to drive turbines to produce electricity. Tidal power is costly to produce. Sihwa Lake Tidal Power Station in South Korea, with an installed capacity of 254MW, is the largest tidal power plant. One major advantage of tidal energy is that it is predictable. This helps to design efficient plants. Also, the life span of tidal plants is more than other plants like solar or wind.

12.9   Hydrogen

Hydrogen is an immense source of power. Both the splitting of hydrogen and joining of hydrogen atoms are a source of unparalleled energy. The fission and fusion reactions as they are called are sources of power. The difficulty in harnessing power from hydrogen is that reaction control is difficult. Also, hydrogen is corrosive. But with advancement of technology, hydrogen is being used for harnessing power as in a hydrogen fuel cell. The conversion efficiency of hydrogen systems is high. Hydrogen is a perennial source of clean energy.

12.10   Hydro Power

Power when produced using water is called hydro power. Dams are constructed on rivers to store water which when released through pen stock or tunnels hits the turbine blades. The turbines produce electrical power which can be used. Mini- and micro-hydel plants are also prevalent. These are basically small-size plants. Hydro power plants have high initial costs but low operating costs. They have long lives and are a clean source of power.

12.11   Conclusion

It is seen that a number of renewable sources of energy are available for harnessing energy. Most of these sources are underexploited to date due to the large cost involved in the conversion process. Some of these resources have been harnessed for a long time now, for example, hydro, biomass.

There is a need to develop techniques to harness these abundantly available resources at reasonable cost so that the future energy needs of mankind are fulfilled without polluting the environment.

References

https://www.science.org.au/curious/technology-future/concentrating-solar-thermal
https://steemit.com/solar/@woleybabz/a-tower-that-gives-power
http://buildesign.co.ke/solar-water-heating-systems-for-homes/

13

Agriculture-IoT-Based Sprinkler System for Water and Fertilizer Conservation and Management

Dilip Kumar* and Ujala Choudhury

Dept. of Electronics and Communication Engineering, Sant Longowal Institute of Engineering and Technology, Deemed to be University, Govt. of India, Sangrur, India

Abstract

In India, improper irrigation practices stand as major key concern in agricultural sector. The flooding is one of the Traditional irrigation techniques that cause over-irrigation and water logging condition for the crop. A rough estimate shows that flooding results nearly 60% of total water wastage and comparably poor crop yield. Therefore, it is necessary to focus on the type of irrigation technique that can conserve water and enhance the crop productivity. In this chapter, Internet of Things (IoT) based sprinkler irrigation system is discussed that schedules the irrigation time and duration for Wheat (i.e., Triticum, aestivum) crop based on both Wheat's critical growth stages and the content of the moisture in the soil. The desired proportion of soluble Nitrogen, Phosphorus, and Potassium (NPK) from a storage tank can also be applied through sprinklers along with irrigation water as and when required by the crop. The developed system is embedded with sensors that continuously monitor soil moisture, temperature and humidity. Real Time Clock (RTC) tracks the time and date of irrigation schedule and Water flow sensor measures the volume of water used in each irrigation. Subsequently, these monitored parameter values are stored in the cloud via Internet helps the agriculture researchers and scientists to remotely analyze these parameters. In addition, they can also remotely control the actuators and retract the system at the time of adversity. Moreover, this IoT system saves their time and frequent visits to the remote locations for collecting experimental data.

Keywords: Cloud, internet of things (IoT), moisture, wheat, sensors, sprinkler

13.1 Introduction

Agriculture is the largest livelihood provider in India and this sector has to feed more than a billion people by 2020. On the one hand, we have to meet a rapid increase in demand for food and on the other hand, we have to conserve available natural resources. In conventional practices, farmers and agricultural researchers would visit the field for manual collection of data regarding the soil moisture content, its PH and nutrition levels, the canopy temperature, ambient humidity, measurement of volume of water used for irrigation, and

---

*Corresponding author: dilip.k78@gmail.com

Suman Lata Tripathi, Dushyant Kumar Singh, Sanjeevikumar Padmanaban, and P. Raja (eds.) Design and Development of Efficient Energy Systems, (229–244) © 2021 Scrivener Publishing LLC

so on. These practices become tedious and consume energy. In contrast to the above convention, Internet of Things (IoT) technologies provide best solutions that ease the task of monitoring and analysis while at the same time open up a wide range of prospect for making better future decisions. An IoT-based system monitors the crop field with the help of sensors and automates the irrigation system. The farmers can monitor the field conditions from anywhere.

According to a survey in 2016, only 20% of companies are anticipating commercial IoT solutions by 2020 while the rest are still in the innovation stage. However, IoT solutions in the agricultural sector have always remained at the top of the management agenda of these companies for a country like India. As per the market research, the global Smart Irrigation market is expected to reach USD1,504.6 million by 2022, at a CAGR of 17.2% between 2016 and 2022. These investments on IoT-based smart farming target precise exploitation of available resources for better production and huge economic returns to the farmers.

Water is one of the major requirements for the crop but unfortunately, its availability has been dcreasing at an alarming rate. As evident from Tables 13.1 and 13.2, this sector remains the most vulnerable to water crisis conditions. Moreover, farmers fail to utilize the available water in optimum quantity because of unawareness. Farmers use Flood irrigation (furrow irrigation) techniques to irrigate almost every crop, which cause huge wastage of water. In this system, the amount of water which is flooded from one end of the field is not pre-quantified and mostly depends on the farmer's rough vision of land wetness. This practice frequently causes over-irrigation due to limited control and decision factors governing the watering systems and results in leaching, drainage, degradation of ground water level and deep percolation addition to saline groundwater [2]. In this traditional method, irrigating the crop even if the crop does not demand water increases water wastage by 60%. The use of this type of irrigation should be avoided in order to protect groundwater from organic contamination and reduce water wastage [3].

However, it is observed that controlling the inflow rate of the irrigation systems has a good impact on the agricultural performances. Such water supply systems are called micro-irrigation systems. They are Drip irrigation systems and Sprinkler irrigation systems. These systems increase the irrigation efficiency to an average of 70% as compared to 30% in flooding along with a tremendous rise in distribution efficiency of water up to 75% [4].

Table 13.1 Water requirement of India for different sectors accessed by NCIWRD, 1999 - Projected up to 2025.

Sectors	1997-98	2010		2025	
		Low	High	Low	High
Agriculture	524	543	557	561	611
Domestic	30	42	43	55	62
Industries	30	37	37	67	67
Power	9	18	19	31	33

NCIWRD: National Commission on Integrated Water Resource Development.

Table 13.2 Per capita annual water availability of India [1].

Year	Population (million)	Average annual availability per capita (m³/year)
2001	1029 (2001 census)	1816
2011	1210 (2011 census)	1545
2025	1364 (projected)	1340
2050	1640 (projected)	1140

In [5], the authors observe nearly the same improvement in the "water use efficiency" and "water productivity" which had a direct effect on water economy and food economy.

Drip irrigation system is the most efficient system but it has proved to be very expensive when it is designed for irrigating closely spaced crops such as rice, wheat, cotton and sunflower. In such a case, sprinkler systems can be beneficial [6, 7]. It also addresses the water clogging problem faced in drip irrigation.

A sprinkler irrigation technique ensures effective management of water resources when used for irrigation of major cereal crops under water scarcity condition. It can be controlled by its flow rates and the duration for which it should perform irrigation. In references [8–10], the authors have studied that scheduling the irrigation on the basis of factors such as soil moisture, climatic conditions such as temperature and humidity and specific growth stage of the crop has an inevitable effect on the crop yield and productivity. Hence, in order to practically implement precision irrigation, decision-supporting tools such as monitoring along with a control system has to be developed. Manual methods are cumbersome as they often require Researchers and farmers to constantly visit the site for manual measurement, while real-time measurements of these parameters using sensors gives them the benefit of remotely monitoring this information in the form of texts sent to their mobile devices over a cellular network [11, 12]. A wireless sensor network is developed to collect environment data and send control command to turn on/off irrigation system. A greenhouse smart management system is developed using Wireless Sensor Network (WSN) to improve the crop yields along with application of the agricultural resources at the right time and place [13, 14]. However, the range of these networks over which the data is fetched, monitored and assessed is limited.

The advent of IoT technology has revolutionized the world of ICT and has made the long-range connectivity of things a reality. IoT technology in agriculture is characterized by a network of sensors deployed in the fields for collecting information based on which the farmer obtains the optimum level of efficiency, precision irrigation and fertigation for saving the environment and water consumption. Information collected by sensors can be retrieved and shared from any place via internet.

The rise of multimedia, social media and the IoT has exponentially increased the volume of information that is being shared. The cloud is actively used to handle a large amount of data. It exploits the data to identify and analyse behavioral patterns in the associated data to best construct tactics and operations to minimize uncertainty [15, 16]. To effectively monitor the status of monitoring objects, it ensures rapid data transfer and reliable storage, and also equips the system with tools for processing and analyzing data metrics [17].

In this chapter, an IoT-based Sprinkler irrigation system is developed that can schedule the irrigation time and duration for the Wheat crop which is cultivated on sandy loamy soil. The Phenology of wheat is extensively studied to identify the critical growth stages based on which probable irrigation dates for the crop are projected. Moreover, soil type and its moisture availability, optimum canopy temperature and humidity required at each stage are major considerations based on which duration of each irrigation is determined. This system comprises soil moisture sensor, temperature and humidity sensor to sense physical variation, a microcontroller unit for data processing, an in-built gateway module to send the data, a display unit, RTC and water flow sensor for timekeeping. After getting a complete knowledge about when and how much to irrigate the crop, each sensor module is programmed to resolve any interruption generated based on the decision variables mentioned above. The information from the sensors is further uploaded to the cloud for storage and sharing with remotely located Research labs and the farmer via internet. Node Red is an application in the cloud for designing graphical user interface (GUI) for monitoring the statistic of real-time data collected over a period of time.

13.1.1   Novelty of the Work

- IoT cloud platform is used to store, share and analyze the sensor data retrieved over a period of time. Cloud helps us to gain a deep insight about the trend that the data follows and initiate any appropriate action, if required.
- This prototype acknowledges the importance of scheduling irrigation for the wheat crop under different considerations like its growth phase, soil moisture and climatic conditions.
- It completely hands over the control of the system to the Research laboratories and the farmers so that they can take immediate decisions and alter the system functionality under adverse conditions.
- Soluble fertilizers can be distributed in appropriate proportion using a Sprinkler system without any human intervention. This ensures precision in use of fertilizers and enhances safety to human health.

13.1.2   Benefit to Society

- It promises huge revenue returns to the farmer and the economy. With minimal investment and precise use of available resources, higher yield per hector and dry matter are obtained.
- Cloud includes many data management and programming tools that can structure the huge volume of datasets into meaningful knowledge, assisting the Researchers in better decision making.
- Remotely monitoring the real-time scenario in the field relaxes the Researchers and farmers from the duty of visiting the field at regular intervals, thereby saving energy, time and reducing panic conditions.

- High priority is given to human safety from fertilizers and animals as most of the activity in the field is free from human efforts.

This chapter is organized as follows: in the next section, we outline the development of the proposed model. In section 13.3 a detailed description of the crop, hardware and software of the system is given, in section 13.4 different layers of system architecture are discussed, in section 13.5 calibration of sensor is formulated and testing of system is presented, Section 13.6 presents the layout of the sprinkler system, and section 13.7 discusses testing. In section 13.8 the results are discussed, and section 13.9 is the conclusion.

13.2 Development of the Proposed System

The developed embedded system serves as a special purpose computer system which is programmed to perform Sprinkler Irrigation. This system will meet the objectives of proper scheduling of irrigation of Wheat crop under the consideration of various parameter values that are measured using the sensors mentioned below. The measured value is continuously compared with the threshold values that are predefined and specific for a specific growth stage of Wheat.

It comprises components viz., YL-69 resistive type soil moisture sensor, DHT22 as temperature and humidity sensor, Raspberry pi Model B, Arduino Uno, LCD display, relay to control water pumped to the Sprinkler as given in Figure 13.1.

13.3 System Description

The description of the prototype is a step-by-step report on the design flow of the proposed model. Basically, it is broadly categorized into three modules:

- Study of the crop under experiment.
- Hardware of the system.
- Software of the system.

13.3.1 Study of the Crop Under Experiment

Wheat is one of the major crops being cultivated in the country. It is grown over 13% of the total cropped area in India. It is a Rabi crop which is sown in the beginning of winter and harvested in the beginning of summer. Well-drained loam and sandy loam soils are suitable for cultivation of this crop. Soil moisture availability, climatic variability are seen to have greatly affected the response of Wheat's growth [10]. These factors also act as a driving force in scheduling the irrigation of the crop. Remotely sensed canopy temperature and their implications in scheduling irrigations for Wheat crops is studied to find the range of favorable temperature to be maintained for optimum yield and saving of irrigation water over the plots that are frequently irrigated at critical growth stages [9].

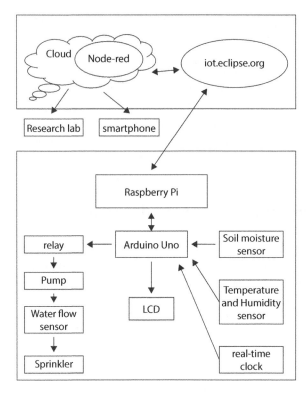

Figure 13.1 Block diagram of the proposed system.

Temperatures (Temp) that lie outside this range can have severe consequences on the crop, significantly reducing yields, dry matter and can cause production to cease. Wheat is quite sensitive to water stress condition which has marked negative effect on Relative Growth Rate in wheat [18]. A maximum of 45% water deficit condition must be allowed between two consecutive irrigation periods to get a better water use efficiency and to avoid anomaly in production rate [19].

Critical growth stages of Wheat include Crown Root Initiation stage (C), Tillering stage (T), Jointing stage (J), flowering (F), milking stage (M), dough stage (D) which onsets on certain days after sowing (DAS) as shown in Figure 13.2. An experiment to evaluate the effect of irrigation on grain yield of wheat was conducted in which five different irrigation treatments were followed at critical growth stages. Results showed that irrigation at five major stages (C+T+L+M+D) increased the number of tiller production, Leaf area index, dry matter and grain yield [20].

Chemical fertilizers has a pivotal role in improving crop production. Most of the time the soil is deficient in the appropriate amount of nitrogen (N), phosphorus (P) and potassium (K) concentration required for increased crop yields. Consequently, the demand for use of NPK fertilizers has increased many fold since their introduction in the late 1950s [21]. However, the use of these fertilizers must ensure balance in proportion for their efficient utilization. The method and time of application are also important and influence optimum use efficiency. In [22], the authors note that application of NPK to wheat can be done all at

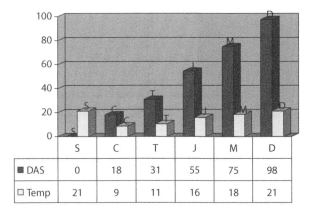

	S	C	T	J	M	D
■ DAS	0	18	31	55	75	98
□ Temp	21	9	11	16	18	21

Figure 13.2 DAS versus critical growth stages and optimum temperature (°C) required for Wheat.

once at the time of sowing, but that improved results are obtained if half of the N and all of the P and K are applied at sowing and another half of N is applied at the first irrigation. The NPK in standard proportion of 120+60+60 kg NPK ha^{-1} respectively is recommended. This system sprinkles 60+60+60 kg NPK ha^{-1} quantity of NPK at the time of sowing followed by only 60 kg N ha^{-1} at the first irrigation.

13.3.2   Hardware of the System

A low-cost, resistive type soil moisture analog sensor module YL-69 is used to continuously measure the moisture content of the soil. A composite digital sensor DHT22 reads the ambient temperature ranging from -40°C to 80 with ±0.5°C accuracy and humidity ranging from 0-100% with ± 2-5% accuracy. Real-time clock module DS1307 is used for tracking the date and timing of each irrigation. All the sensors are interfaced with an AVR RISC-based microcontroller ATMEGA 328 for processing of raw data. A 16x2 LCD is connected for displaying the sensor data, pump running conditions and date and time of irrigations. An electromechanical relay switch is used to turn on/off a submersible AC pump that lifts water from a reservoir whenever a control signal is generated from Arduino Uno GPIOs. YF-S201 Hall effect water flow sensor is connected across the pipes to measure the flow rate of water. Raspberry pi 3 Model B is serially interfaced with Arduino. It is a single-board computer with extended memory of 1 GB and inbuilt Wi-Fi. This feature of raspberry pi helps in wireless transmission of data on to the cloud.

13.3.3   Software of the System

ATMEGA 328 is programmed using an open-source software i.e., Arduino Integrated Development Environment. This compiler is coded in C++ programming language. Serial monitor of Arduino console displays the data from sensors. Raspberry pi is programmed in python language. Programming includes functions to serially fetch data from Arduino and publish to the cloud via broker. The working operation of developed system is illustrated in Figure 13.3.

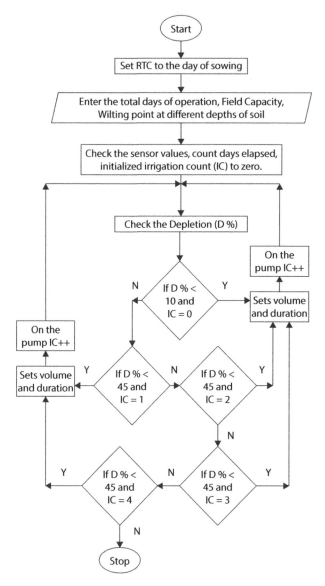

Figure 13.3 Flow chart.

13.4 Layers of the System Architecture

The entire model can be divided into different layers for proper understanding.

13.4.1 Application Layer

It is a user interface layer which includes dashboard and applications on devices such as desktops, cell phones of farmers to monitor real-time soil moisture, temperature, humidity according to which a decision can be made to control the pump. It connects the open-source broker with the help of Message queue telemetry transport MQTT client application.

Data transfer can be made even more secure with the help of any developed broker instead of open source.

13.4.2 Cloud Layer

It is the layer where the information is stored, processed, classified and formatted. Some powerful database management tools aggregate the data set and perform certain analytics on them so that a future decision can be wisely taken. IBM Bluemix cloud service is used to avail these features. A programming tool Node Red on the cloud widen the scope to publish and subscribe the data on any device connected to internet from anywhere. It uses advanced dashboard setting to display the real-time data at the front end.

13.4.3 Network Layer

This layer includes communication technology like Wi-Fi and protocols that set up rules to govern transmission among two or more entities of this system. It assigns a frame for communication with proper encapsulation and error detection. Transmission control protocol/Internet Protocol TCP/IP guides the data packets transferred between the webpage in cloud to the Raspberry pi. MQTT is a lightweight communication protocol through which raspberry pi can publish-subscribe real-time data to the desktop at research labs; farmers phone via an open-source broker i.e., iot.eclipse.org.

13.4.4 Physical Layer

This layer consists of all the physical devices and modules which collect information like IoT sensors which measure various parameters like temperature, humidity, soil moisture, water flow rate, microcontrollers which process the raw data, actuators, display unit.

13.5 Calibration

Volumetric Water Content, VWC of soil is measured as the ratio of volume of water to volume of dry soil. It is mathematically expressed in percentage as,

$$\text{VWC}(\%) = \frac{\beta_W}{\beta_D} * 100 \tag{13.1}$$

where β_W is volume of water and β_D is volume of dry soil.

A low-cost soil moisture sensor YL-69 is calibrated to read the VWC at three different depths of soil: 0-15 cm, 15-30 cm, 30-45 cm as plant root zone mostly lie in these ranges. Calibration involves mapping of sensor output voltage obtained in wet soil to the VWC of the soil at that point.

Firstly, in order to calculate moisture content of the soil, volumetric method is followed. It is a direct method of moisture measurement in which a known volume of water is added to a known volume of dry soil. Soil is ensured to be dry after heating it in an oven for 24 hours at around 105°C. The percentage of VWC is evaluated using Eq. (13.1). Six different experiments are carried out in which each time a defined quantity of distilled water is added to soil. Distilled water doesn't alter the salinity of soil which might affect the moisture value. The water is allowed to get absorbed in the soil until it confirms uniformity [22, 23]. The sensor installed in the soil shows different voltage levels and the corresponding raw analog output on serial monitor at each trial. These values are recorded as shown in Table 13.3. The data set of each calibration experiment is fed into Microsoft Excel spreadsheet to obtain best fit curves, trend line equations and regression as shown in Figures 13.4(a) and 13.4(b). The Figure 4(b) infers that moisture reading is almost linear up to 20% VWC and it exhibits non-linearity beyond it while the overall regression stays at 95.90%. The sensor reads a maximum of 4.82V which is only 5% of moisture in complete dry state. After calibrating the sensor, we headed on to measure moisture level at different depths of root zone. Although root zone extends far deeper in the soil, it is observed that water extraction by plant is maximum within 0 to 45 cm soil layer. Field Capacity (FC) and Permanent Wilting Point (WP) of the soil at different depths are measured in 2-3 days post-irrigation until the water has distributed uniformly in the field as shown in Table 13.4. The FC, WP is measured followed by evaluation of Maximum allowable depletion (MAD) of available soil

Table 13.3 Calibrated data Of Yl-69.

Dry soil volume (ml)	Wet soil volume (ml)	Volume of water added (ml)	Sensor raw output	Sensor output voltage (V)	VWC in %
580	580	0	1021	4.82	5
580	630	50	772	3.69	8.62
580	730	150	276	1.32	25.86
580	830	250	211	1.01	43.10
580	880	300	192	.92	51.72
580	930	350	180	.89	60.34
580	1160	580	0	0	100

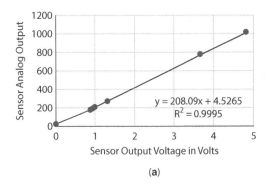

(a)

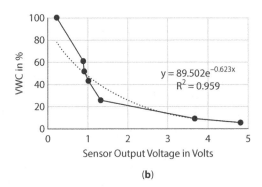

(b)

Figure 13.4 Plots between (a) Sensor output voltage and sensor analog voltage (b) Sensor output voltage and VWC.

Table 13.4 FC and WP at different depths of soil.

Depth of root zone (cm)	FC_i	Field capacity (%)	Wilting point (%)
0-15	FC_1	31	5
15-30	FC_2	25	5
30-45	FC_3	18	5

water (ASW= FC-WP) and the volume of water (V_d) that must be applied to replenish the depleted water from soil [19] by using mathematical equations,

$$Depletion(\%) = 100 * \frac{1}{n} \sum_{1}^{n} \frac{FC_i - \alpha_i}{FC_i - WP} \tag{13.2}$$

where n is the number division of effective depth of root, FC_i and α_i is the field capacity and soil moisture at ith depth of soil respectively in Eq. (13.2).

$$V_d = \frac{MAD(FC - WP)R_Z A}{100} \tag{13.3}$$

where R_Z is the effecting rooting depth, A is the area of the site under experiment in Eq. (13.3). These Eq. (13.2) and Eq. (13.3) form a foundation of scheduling the irrigation timing and the volume of water to be applied on each irrigation.

13.6   Layout of the Sprinkler System

An area of 25x25 square meter Wheat crop is taken for field testing of the system. Water from the tube well reservoir is pumped into PVC mainline pipes of 1 inch to reach the sprinkler head via lateral pipes of 1/2 inch with a working pressure rating of 3.0 kg/cm². An Impact Sprinkler of nozzle size 3.5mm and trajectory of 25° is used for uniform distribution over a radius of 11.9 m as shown in Figure 13.5. The design details of Irrigation system is given in Table 13.5.

13.7   Testing

For testing purpose, the system is set up in the laboratory that is comprised of microcontrollers embedded with three soil moisture sensors installed at three different depths of soil, temperature and humidity sensors at various locations to read the climate variation, RTC, a relay to control an AC submersible pump connected to sprinkler via water flow sensor as shown in Figure 13.6. Firstly, RTC is initialized with the current time and date to mark the

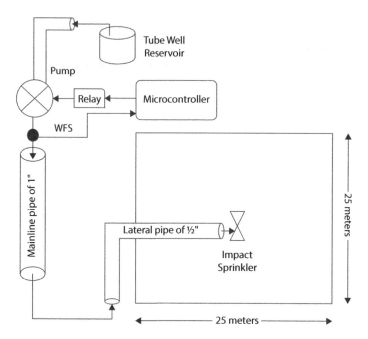

Figure 13.5 Layout of the sprinkler system.

Table 13.5 Design details and irrigation data.

Parameters	Units
Crop	Wheat, maize, barley
Irrigation area	625 m²
Water source	Tube well reservoir
Crop spacing	7-15 cm
Type of Sprinkler	Impact Sprinkler
Nozzle size	3.5 mm
Trajectory	25°
Irrigation Intervals	Depends on depletion %
Discharge rate	12.6 liters/min
Required pressure at head	3.0 kg/cm²
Range of sprinkling	11.9 m

beginning of the testing process. This enables a counter to count the number of days and time elapsed since start of this system.

The system is so programmed that the first irrigation is done by the system when the moisture content falls below 10% at CRI stage, which arrives in approximately 18 DAS.

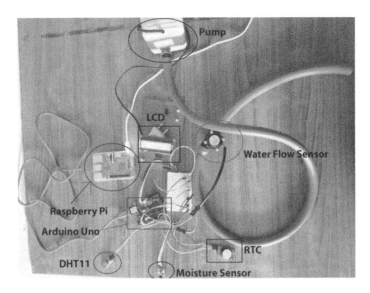

Figure 13.6 Testing system for lab and field.

This particular condition is met to avoid growth of weeds. Subsequent irrigations are scheduled when MAD falls below 45% as evaluated by Eq. (13.2). In such case, Arduino send a controlling signal to turn on the relay. Relay turns on the pump until the predefined volume determined by Eq. (13.3) is delivered to the field.

Every activity such as sensing, actuating is monitored on a real-time basis using the cloud. Raspberry pi is programmed to serially fetch all sensor data and upload those on IBM Bluemix cloud. The cloud provides a huge database for management of information of soil, climate, irrigation schedules and volume of water collected over longer periods. The benefit of remotely monitoring and controlling the system is given to the Researchers, scientists and farmers by using Node-Red and smartphone App. Dashboard is created on Node-Red to visualize real-time variation in the parameters as shown in Figure 13.7(a) and 13.7(b).

13.8   Results and Discussion

Back-end monitoring and analysis of the system under testing is first done on the serial monitor of Arduino IDE. Sensor readings and the status of irrigation are systematically produced on the laptop screen. This information is then sequentially sent to the cloud via broker to be stored. A powerful application in the cloud, i.e., Node-Red is used to retrieve the data published on to the broker. It deploys various palettes and nodes to receive the incoming information. The data so received are in the form of strings and hence, need splitting operation in order to map each payload to its corresponding graphical interfaces. It is very simple to design the dashboard in this platform. Front-end monitoring and analysis of the system is done by real-time data being displayed on the dashboard as shown in Figure 13.7 (a). Nevertheless, this application is loaded with features to design our own control panel on web page as shown in Figure 13.7(b). The Researchers and farmers can download the web page and MQTT Dashboard App on their portable devices such as laptop, desktop and cell phones to immediately view these data and control pump in cases of emergency.

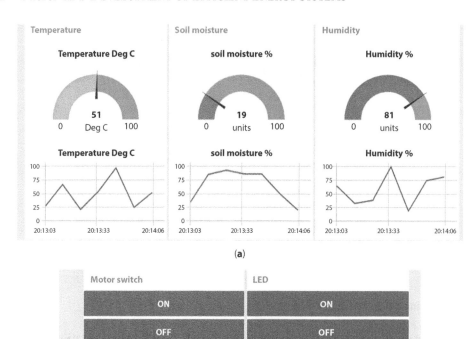

Figure 13.7 Snapshot of (a) Gauges and charts on cloud showing real-time data. (b) Control panel designed on Node-Red.

13.9   Conclusion

This chapter presents a developed programmable system which improves the water saving by 55% and decreases the wastage of fertilizer by 25%. The system determines the optimal time for irrigating the wheat and also customizes the sprinkling of fertilizers based on the concerned crop. It can be reprogrammed for other crops such as maize and barley, taking their growth phase, water depletion percentage, fertilizer requirements and plant water intake into consideration. A moisture sensor YL-69 is calibrated and Lab tested. The curve fit value indicates high degree of linearity i.e., 95.90% with R^2 value. It also successfully implements IoT and cloud computing to smartly manage, store and study the parameters historic as well as real-time data to establish a futuristic approach in farming-related decision making.

References

1. Cronin, A. A., Prakash, A., Priya, S., & Coates, S. (2014). Water in India: situation and prospects. *Water Policy*, 16(3), 425-441.
2. Pereira, L. S., Oweis, T., & Zairi, A. (2002). Irrigation management under water scarcity. *Agricultural Water Management*, 57(3), 175-206.

3. Fait, G., Balderacchi, M., Ferrari, F., Ungaro, F., Capri, E., & Trevisan, M. (2010). A field study of the impact of different irrigation practices on herbicide leaching. *European Journal of Agronomy*, 32(4), 280-287.

4. Pitts, D., Peterson, K., Gilbert, G., & Fastenau, R. (1996). Field assessment of irrigation system performance. *Applied Engineering in Agriculture*, 12(3), 307-313.

5. Pereira, L. S., Cordery, I., & Iacovides, I. (2012). Improved indicators of water use performance and productivity for sustainable water conservation and saving. *Agricultural Water Management*, 108, 39-51.

6. Kukal, S. S., Jat, M. L., & Sidhu, H. S. (2014). Improving water productivity of wheat-based cropping systems in South Asia for sustained productivity. In *Advances in Agronomy*, 127, 157-258. Academic Press.

7. *AgriFarming* (2018) [Online]. Available: http://www.agrifarming.in/drip-irrigation-vs-sprinkler

8. Zipoli, G. (1989, June). Remote sensing for scheduling irrigation: review of thermal infrared approach. In *Symposium on Scheduling of Irrigation for Vegetable Crops under Field Condition* 278, 281-288.

9. Porter, J. R., & Gawith, M. (1999). Temperatures and the growth and development of wheat: a review. *European Journal of Agronomy*, 10(1), 23-36.

10. Kansara, K., Zaveri, V., Shah, S., Delwadkar, S., & Jani, K. (2015). Sensor based automated irrigation system with IOT: A technical review. *International Journal of Computer Science and Information Technologies*, 6(6), 5331-5333.

11. Nagothu, S. K. (2016, February). Weather based smart watering system using soil sensor and GSM. In *2016 World Conference on Futuristic Trends in Research and Innovation for Social Welfare (Startup Conclave)* (pp. 1-3). IEEE.

12. Jagtap, P. S., & Hatkar, A. P. (2016, August). Smart monitoring and controlling of wind farms based on WSN. In *2016 1st India International Conference on Information Processing (IICIP)* (pp. 1-5). IEEE.

13. Hamouda, Y. E. (2017, October). Smart irrigation decision support based on fuzzy logic using wireless sensor network. In *2017 International Conference on Promising Electronic Technologies (ICPET)* (pp. 109-113). IEEE.

14. Aazam, M., Khan, I., Alsaffar, A. A., & Huh, E. N. (2014, January). Cloud of Things: Integrating Internet of Things and cloud computing and the issues involved. In *Proceedings of 2014 11th International Bhurban Conference on Applied Sciences & Technology (IBCAST) Islamabad, Pakistan, 14th-18th January, 2014* (pp. 414-419). IEEE.

15. Gupta, R., Gupta, H., & Mohania, M. (2012, December). Cloud computing and big data analytics: What is new from databases perspective?. In *International Conference on Big Data Analytics* (pp. 42-61). Springer, Berlin, Heidelberg.

16. Rovnyagin, M. M., Odintsev, V. V., Fedin, D. Y., & Kuzmin, A. V. (2018). Cloud computing architecture for high-volume monitoring processing. In *2018 IEEE Conference of Russian Young Researchers in Electrical and Electronic Engineering (EIConRus)* (pp. 361-365). IEEE.

17. Turner, N. C., & Begg, J. E. (1981). Plant-water relations and adaptation to stress. *Plant and Soil*, 58(1-3), 97-131.

18. Panda, R. K., Behera, S. K., & Kashyap, P. S. (2004). Effective management of irrigation water for maize under stressed conditions. *Agricultural Water Management*, 66(3), 181-203.

19. Sharma, D. K., Kumar, A., & Singh, K. N. (1990). Effect of irrigation scheduling on growth, yield and evapotranspiration of wheat in sodic soils. *Agricultural Water Management*, 18(3), 267-276.

20. Mohammadi, K. (2012). Phosphorus solubilizing bacteria: occurrence, mechanisms and their role in crop production. *Resour Environ*, 2(1), 80-85.

21. Khan, Mahar Sujawal, and Muhammad Iqbal Makhdum. "Optimum time of NP application to wheat under irrigated conditions." *Pakistan Journal of Agricultural Research* 9, Vol. no. 1 pp. 6-10, 1988.

22. Khan, M. S., & Makhdum, M. I. (1988). Optimum time of NP application to wheat under irrigated conditions. *Pakistan Journal of Agricultural Research*, 9(1), 6-10.

23. Hedley, C. B., & Yule, I. J. (2009). A method for spatial prediction of daily soil water status for precise irrigation scheduling. *Agricultural Water Management*, 96(12), 1737-1745.

A Behaviour-Based Authentication to Internet of Things Using Machine Learning

Mohit Goyal[1]* and Durgesh Srivastava[2]

[1]Research Scholar, Dept. of CSE, BRCM CET, Bahal, Bhiwani, India
[2]Associate Professor, Department of CSE, UIE, Chandigarh University, India

Abstract

This chapter discusses new security challenges in the Internet of Things (IoT) using machine learning algorithm. The IoT, a system of interrelated computing devices, and its quick development and distribution is becoming essential for internet users and smart device users. Nowadays, IoT is a descriptive term in which all things must be connected to the network. It has been assumed that the usage of IoT is not constrained to just hardware and software, but also includes the various things and even people that have unique identification which has the ability to exchange information over a network. IoT will be important in the near future because it will provide opportunities for new services and new inventions, and all these new services and things will be linked to one another and furthermore ready to speak with one another. This concept leads to new authentication security challenges, which is a key aspect of this chapter. IoT is in great demand due to the necessity of standardization and proper structure which explain how this technology will be implemented and how all these devices will exchange information with one another from the point of view of security. So, researchers put more focus on how to provide a secure solution for authentication.

Generally in behavior-based authentication, all IoT users used pin, and password, but the main difficulty in these types of authentication techniques are the unwillingness of users to memorize the combination of various alphabets and numbers and symbols, which can easily be forgotten. The biometric behavioral-based authentication has three main modules: 1) data capture 2) Feature extraction 3) classifier. Now, the researcher will concentrate on extracting the behavior-related features for users and also will apply the same for authenticating to the user. The aim is to determine the classifier technique that mainly will use a machine learning algorithm for providing the behavior-based biometric authentication which is based on human behavior. It will be noted here that different machine learning algorithms (for example, KNN, SVM and so forth) can be efficiently used to authenticate the user by using biometric authentication (such as Signature, gaits, etc). The present work would show the utilization of machine learning algorithms to confirm the identity of user or analyze its relative execution. In view of their result, we will then discuss the appropriateness of several algorithms. Finally, we will briefly discuss the reasonableness of machine learning algorithm to security as verification for coming work.

Keywords: Internet of Things (IoT), machine learning, authentication, biometric

*Corresponding author: mohitims84@gmail.com

Suman Lata Tripathi, Dushyant Kumar Singh, Sanjeevikumar Padmanaban, and P. Raja (eds.) Design and Development of Efficient Energy Systems, (245–264) © 2021 Scrivener Publishing LLC

14.1 Introduction

Internet of Things (IoT) is an enlargement of the Internet to the physical world where all objects collect information and interact with their environments without or with few human interventions. An internal threat is another important problem in the field of IoT security due to human interaction that has been present for quite some time. The war between cybercriminals and data security experts has increased considerably in the recent past. New and convoluted techniques for assault are being evolved by criminals at a perilous rate by exploiting the complicated behavior of the present systems. Computer emergency response teams have reported a growing number of new types of vulnerabilities in recent years. Nonetheless, proactive methods for accomplishing security have existed for quite a while; these methodologies are purposed to stop and identify such assaults. Assault has been a long-standing issue in the field of security for internet-enabled devices and has recently received extensive consideration. So these days, providing security to an internet-enabled device has become a daunting task. At this stage, authentication is used as a main tool for providing security in IoT. An authentication procedure checks the identification of a user, process, or device, and after verification permits only valid users to utilize the resources and services in an authoritative manner, and rejects the unidentified user. These days, user authentication is a main matter and so is a challenge that has become more crucial than before.

In an IoT network, various authentication models can be used like smart card and password and biometric-based authentication. It deals with identification of individual humans based on their behavior and biological characteristics. Biometric authentication as security considers two aspects of human body characteristics: distinctiveness and permanence. Some of the most popular physiological and behavioral symptoms that are used in IoT biometric security are fingerprint, face, iris, hand, gaits, and DNA (deoxyribonucleic acid). Behavior-based authentication is used as a main biometric authentication tool for providing security to IoT devices and their data. Machine Learning has made extremely encouraging progress in software engineering in recent decades up to the present and has gained accomplishments in taking care of data classification issues. It principally manages making logical programs that consequently lead to better understanding. The learning experience is given as data and genuine learning is obtained with the assistance of algorithms.

In this chapter, some significant machine learning algorithms and techniques that provide behavior-based biometric authentication to IoT devices are described in further detail. After that, further sections of the chapter also look at a few essentials of IoT and describe the aspects of security by presenting a few fundamentals of machine learning algorithm.

14.2 Basics of Internet of Things (IoT)

This chapter presents thoughts from the domain of Internet of Things and machine learning algorithm which may be utilized to address a portion of difficult issues encountered in the protection space for the client. The term "Internet of Things" was introduced by Kevin Ashton in a 1999 presentation at Proctor & Gamble. Internet of Things referred to a new aspect of the internet in which things began to interact with each other. Generally, the convergence of wireless technologies, micro-electro mechanical systems, micro-services and the internet is included in the term IoT. The convergence has helped to fill the gap between operational technology and information technology, enabling unstructured machine-produced data to be analyzed for future predictions [1, 2]. In the early 1980s, we saw the first internet-enabled appliance, a Coke vending machine at Carnegie Mellon University. Using the web, programmers understood the status of the machine, whether there would be a cold drink available or not.

IoT can be seen as a primal concept for generating solutions for coming problems. IoT can be defined as "a proposed advancement of the Internet where objects have organized availability, permitting them to send and get information". The issue with IoT isn't conveying sensors all over but the formation of frameworks that can misuse the entirety of the accessible information. "Sensors and actuators installed in physical object are connected via with wired and remote systems" [2].

Defining the term IoT can be to some degree troublesome in light of the fact that it has numerous definitions depending upon who is characterizing the term. The fundamental idea of IoT is to associate things together, in this way empowering these "things" to speak with one another and empowering individuals to speak with them [3]. The most indispensable part to accomplishing IoT is communication, in light of the fact that in order to interconnect various gadgets they should be capable of exchanging information. All the different properties, for example, sensing, being able to catch data, store, and data processing are unnecessary, except if your gadget explicitly requires one of these properties. Be that as it may, the capacity to exchange information is essential when marking a gadget as an IoT gadget. How this is performed is relatively less significant, because the actual physical and connection layer interaction medium inside IoT can be realized from various perspectives.

Table 14.1 shows different characteristics of IoT. In this, the connectivity enabled the Internet of Things by bringing together daily things. It is important because each object contributes to best performance of IoT. By connecting things with applications smartly, new options are created in the market for IoT. In IoT, the elementary task is to gather data from the surrounding environment, but in those surroundings, changes occur frequently.

Table 14.1 Internet of Things' characteristics.

Characteristics	Description
Connectivity	Everything can be related with the overall data and communication system in a world.
Security	In IoT, security can be implemented at various places, such that, at various device, or network and also on transmitted data.
Diversify	It is considered as one of the unique feature of IoT. IoT equipments are worked on various hardware and network, but can communicate with each other and utilize the services of each other.
Dynamic nature	The changes occur very frequently in connected devices. So adoption of changes is crucial task.
At Large level	In IoT, the networks of connected devices are spread at very large scale, much more than devices. To store the data that comes from these devices and their operated result is very important.

Thereafter, the situations of connected devices also change very frequently. The number of connected devices can differ dynamically. So, working in dynamic nature is not an easy task. To support the heterogeneity is the greatest challenge as there are a variety of protocols being used. Interaction with various gadgets through different systems will be challenging from the security and technical points of view, as protocol may vary contingent upon whether the devices are imparting any information through some interface (wide area cellular or Wi-Fi, radio, Ethernet, etc., are examples of interface). So, security and privacy protection are some of the main relevant requirements for the IoT. Multiple security threats will be created when everything is connected. So at that time providing confidentiality, integrity, availability, and authenticity will become a challenging task.

Various security challenges and threats have an impact on an IoT device. So, it will be a huge error to neglect security concerns. It is crucial to secure all the devices which are situated at various ends at network and also to network itself or transmitted data. A secure IoT network can be fruitful to accomplish desired functions effectively. In IoT, security is a general need for all users, because a sensor may have personal information. Now at this stage, Privacy implementation has also become crucial or mandatory [3].

14.2.1 The IoT Reference Model

IoT architecture is partitioned mainly into three layers: Application Layer, Network Layer and Perception Layer. One more layer, support layer, can also be included in IoT architecture, since a support layer consist of a cloud computing [2, 16]. The most common IoT architecture is displayed in Figure 14.1.

The application layer is situated at the top in IoT architecture among all layers. The main function of this layer is to fill the spaces in between user and applications. It can be utilized in various sectors such as disaster management, health sector, and ecological atmosphere to these applications with the help of automatic solution. It provides the customized solution to user as per its special type needs. The network layer is considered as the brain of IoT architecture, since all main operations are actually executed by this. It provides help to all other layers, whenever required. It is also responsible for establishing security to all, so that data can be communicated securely among all layers. It gathers data and information and delivers the collected data to the server and also connects the perception layer from the server. On the basis of all these functions, this layer is to be considered the most developed layer as compared to the others [3].

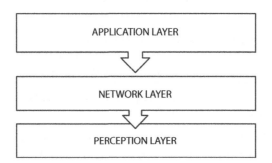

Figure 14.1 Obaidat *et al.* Reference architecture for IoT [16].

Table 14.2 Various security solutions at layers in IoT architecture.

Application layer	Secrecy, security audit and antivirus, data secrecy and integrity
Network layer	Integrity protection and signaling, data confidentiality
Perception layer	Data confidentiality, data integrity protection, and device integrity validation, device access control

The perception layer is the bottommost layer of IoT architecture. Its main functions are to collect required and useful data from various sources like things, and the environment, and convert them into digital form. The main aim is communication and unique-address identification in between short distance techniques. It is also known as recognition layer. As compared to direct conversation, indirect conversation needs an entry gate through which the information is transferred by the network. As a measure against unethical and illegal accesses in IoT, various steps are taken for providing authentication and authorization [4]. However, other security solutions are essential as per their personal capabilities for all IoT layers in addition to authentication and authorization. These are given below in Table 14.2.

14.2.2 Working of IoT

To see how IoT functions, we will discuss its components. Also, we will clarify how IoT works by examining some real-time models. The whole IoT process starts with the equipment themselves, like smartphones, smart watches, electronic instrumentss like TV, washing machine, which support interactions with the IOT platform. Just as internet has altered the way we work and talk with each other, by connecting us through the World Wide Web (WWW), the IoT takes the network to the next level by associating different devices consistently to the web. This can encourage human-to-machine dialogue and furthermore promote machine-to-machine communication. This has implications in many areas of life, including business applications in the area of driveless vehicles, industry line robotization, clinical, human administration, retail, home modernisation. Here, four fundamental components of IoT system will be identified to explain how IoT works.

14.2.2.1 Device

The main task of a sensor is to collect required data from the environment and transmit it to the upcoming layer. Different IoT components shown in figure shown in Figure 14.2.

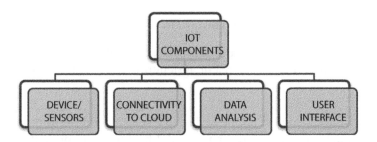

Figure 14.2 Components of IoT [10].

An IoT device may have more than one sensor and they can be grouped for the purpose of effectively sensing. Various sensors may be used in an IoT device. Some are listed below:

- Light intensity detectors
- Temperature sensors and thermostats
- Proximity detection
- RFID tags.

Accelerometer, Gyroscope sensors, are types of sensors which are used in many sensor-enabled devices like smartphones and smart wearables.

14.2.2.2   Connectivity to Cloud

For connecting the data from one layer to another layer (cloud), the sensor transfers data to the cloud through an efficient way. When data is transmitted from one phase to another, security provision is essential for transmitted data. The cloud is basically a set of server which is connected to internet always. Satellite networks, cellular networks, Wi-Fi, Bluetooth, wide-area networks, low-power wide-area network, and lots of additional ones are the mediums of communication through which the sensor can be associated with the cloud.

14.2.2.3   Data Analysis

A conversion to analog data from multiple smart-enabled devices and sensors into important form which may be used in further detailed analysis or interpretation. This process is called data processing. When gathered data is received by the cloud various algorithm are used here for analysis and processing on data. In this chapter various machine learning algorithms will be used for accurate analysis.

14.2.2.4   User Interface

The main responsibility in any system is to provide the information to the user. The work of user interface is to monitor or control the available data. User interaction might be very essential in one situation, such as what will happen if the temperature is too high or an intruder is in your home? Then to handle these situations, the user plays a role. As an interface, the user will use that device that is compatible with all wireless standards [3, 4].

14.2.3   Utilization of Internet of Things (IoT)

The term "IoT" is being utilized in various aspects; for example, human body, household appliance, transportation, industrial area or agriculture. Details of how they all utilize IoT are given below:

- In human body context, empowering IoT sensing and network, for example, tracking activity, physical and mental health condition and alternative important information, can not only monitor the user's current lifestyle, but also effect improvement by alerting the user to unhealthy actions.

- Concerning the house, home automation is one little utility of IoT which can handle all equipment installed in the house, such as lighting, air conditioning; due to this, energy saving is becoming the main advantage. Another small use is to keep plants alive by automatic watering system in home. Now, use of IoT is changing very rapidly to its newest roles, such as home security systems and cameras, smart speaker and other home appliances [3].

- In the transportation context, vehicle parking (smart parking), road safety, automatic toll collection, speed control, etc., are various examples where IoT can be used daily. IoT-enabled vehicles provide help in reduction of traffic accidents, by giving an alert to the driver at various critical moments, by giving training to machine by using machine learning algorithm.

- The main objectives of IoT implementation in industry is controlling business resources, reducing expenses and maintaining quality and consistency in operational procedure so that assets and money can increase. An IoT device collect the data by using various connected equipments and locations and people and then analyses the data. It helps in the control and operation of various operational machines and industrial systems and helps in keeping a record of various assets by updating automatically and giving information about these whenever required.

- In context of agriculture, there are various uses of IoT in farming, such as gathering data about temperature, rain, air speed, and pest control, soil information and better seeds. Obtaining these data improves the quality of soil, minimizes the risks as much as possible and reduces waste. By implementing all these, the effort maintain crops can be minimized [4].

As soon as the uses of IoT increased, security become a serious matter in terms of privacy. Consequently, many steps will be taken in favor of safety.

14.3 Authentication in IoT

Before discussing behavior-based authentication, we will explain the concept of authentication. An authentication is the process of recognizing users and devices in a network and gives permission to access to authorized persons and valid devices. It is the verification of claimed user identity. It is mainly used to set up a user identity and assure that the users are who they say they are [5, 6].

14.3.1 Methods of Authentication

Uniqueness of security measures is the main essential factor for the authentication process. Generally, these are classified into the following categories: authentication based on knowledge, authentication based on possession, authentication based on biometric [5, 7]. Figure 14.3 depicts the hierarchy of user authentication methods.

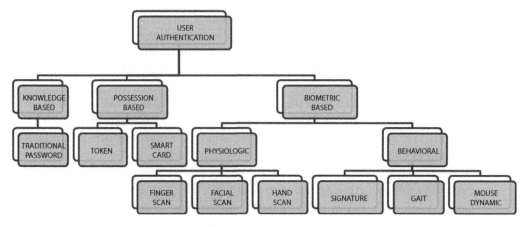

Figure 14.3 Vongsingthong *et al.* hierarchy of user authentication method [6].

14.3.1.1   *Authentication Based on Knowledge*

Authentication based on knowledge is generally used to provide the security to the systems. Anything that a person can remember and then write, say, and do, perform, or otherwise recall whenever required. All these tasks fall into this category. The two popular instances are the password or pin. The pin or password is generally inputted at the start of any work which gives permission only to those who have the right way to access the system [7, 8].

A traditional password does not require any specialized personal ability; they are straightforward to use, and also straightforward to recollect. Brute force attacks, password guessing, and key-loggers are various problems concerning passwords, which is why the use of password alone is now not enough. Whenever a password is maliciously obtained, the perpetrator can easily start exploiting a victim's account. This is a main demerit of passwords [5, 7].

14.3.1.2   *Authentication Based on Possession*

The usage of a conventional password has already been assumed as unsecure and non-convenient from a security point of view. Authentication based on possession method was used to eliminate the ability of an attacker to guess the password and also is forecast to increase the scale of protection. Smart card and Quick Response (QR) code, token, etc., are various example of those methods which utilized mainly those items the user possessed personally. A hardware token is an object and device which may be utilized at the authentication procedure. They are present in many forms like in smartphones or an easy-access device such as key fobs [5, 11]. The mixture of PIN and smart card has been proposed as a smart card reader (NFC-enabled smartphones) approach. The temporary PIN is established as a permanent PIN, which may decrease the chance of attack because makes the attacker unable to identify the main PIN [12].

To authenticate the user, QR code identification approach was applied. At the time of identification step, the user does an urge from the server, in exchange; the server will obtain the information for the user. An advantage of given methodology is that it is more advanced than the certificate system [12, 13]. To abolish the danger of inference-based passwords from knowledge-based methodology, possession-based methodology is demonstrated. At the time of the authentication process, the presence of a token is mandatory; the presence of token can also become a disadvantage, because the token can be lost or stolen, so an assailant could benefit and make an apparently authentic access. Due to this, possession-based methodology has been assumed as insecure to authenticate the user. Figure 14.4 brief outline of possession-based methods.

14.3.1.3 *Authentication Based on Biometric*

The utilization of individual attributes is a good arrangement as its corresponds to knowledge-based authentication and possession-based authentication [5, 9]. Second, authentication based on biometric methodology cannot be forgotten or omitted, unlike physical-token, QR code, and PIN [14]. A biometric method is mainly a pattern recognition methodology that identifies an individual depending on a characteristic factor obtained by a particular physiological or behavioral feature that the individual either has or displays. This type of authentication methodology is capable of recognizing the user as it is based on some unique physiological or behavioral features.

14.3.1.3.1 Authentication Based on Physical Biometric

Finger scan, iris check, retina scan, hand scan, and facial scan are various different techniques of physical biometrics methodology, which was introduced or evolved by utilizing measurement from the human parts [15, 16]. Many times it has been proved that the most accurate result may be gained through utilizing the physiological biometric-based methodology. Table 14.3 displays the essence of physiological biometric-based methodology to authenticate the user. Fingerprint has demonstrated the excellent performance among all, so it's become a very renowned option in biometric-based techniques. The utilization of a

Table 14.3 Brief outline of possession-based method.

Main mechanism	Method	Merits	Demerits
PIN & Smart card	Smart card reader (smartphones with NFC)	An attacker's chance becomes less to find the permanent pin by using temporary pin	Using of public computer system may be dangerous from security point of view for input and output operations
Acoustic token / Magnetic token	Static magnetic fields and sound waves	Chances of theft in personal information are very few	A single loose factor and element in efficiency can be cause of problem for the users
Quick Response (QR) code	User authentication by recognizing QR code	• Easy to access • Less cost • No need to memorize	

fingerprint is very easy and is best for getting accurate resulta in authentication; that is the main advantage of using fingerprint. Presently, the fingerprint scanner is mainly utilized more by all users. The main disadvantage of finger scan is that the finger cannot be identified properly through the scanner at once due to frequently being used in various hobbies of the user such as typing, and kitchen work in case of women, etc, [17, 18]. So in view of these points, this chapter does not much prefer the physical biometric authentication.

14.3.1.3.2 Authentication Based on Behavioral Biometric

The behavioral biometrics is another type of biometric-based technique, where the user's verification depends on their various style such as automatic signature, the method of user's step of walking (known as gaits), or mouse dynamics [19, 20].

Commonly, a magnetometer is used to find the direction of movement, whereas gyroscopic sensor and accelerometer is used to find gait recognition. K-NN algorithm (K-nearest neighbor) is used as a classifier approach to verify the various functions [22]. Like other biometric-based authentication, the gaits also have the same capacity. However, fixed distances have to be walked by the user for the verification before procedure of verification will occur [33, 34].

Keystroke dynamics is among self-driven ways to validate the identity of the user based on the modus and rhythm of typing on the keyboard [23]. The verification of identity of user depends on the typing style on the keyboard. For the evolution and implementation of any system, Support vector machine (SVM) and Random forest are two techniques which are commonly used in keystroke dynamics [23]. Support vector machine (SVM) classifier

Table 14.4 Brief outline of physical biometric-based method.

Mechanism	Method	Merits	De-merits
Finger scan	Edge-based method	Use is easy	Result can vary due to camera quality
		No one can access device, if theft	Not good in performance
Finger scan	Area segmentation on Image preprocessing	Use is easy	The higher templates that save in enrollment database, the execution time for the verification increases
Facial scan	Fast semi-3D face vertical pose recovery	Security were strong with attaching password with Face scan	Required more energy utilization
	Chaos theory is main base of Fragile watermarking	Authentication process is done in less time due to high speed	Less secure as compared to rest of methods
Iris scan	Daubechies wavelet transform	Enhance the assumption of performance	Utilized more time and energy

[24], sometimes fuzzy modeling approach can be used in offline signature verification. Table 14.4 displays the essence of behavioral biometric-based methodology.

14.4 User Authentication Based on Behavioral-Biometric

This section focuses on the search for great methods of behavioral-based biometric user authentication using machine learning approach. For getting effective results and increasing the performance of the system, implementation of behavioral-based biometric authentication is a good solution. Due to this, an excellent classifier technique is developing to resolve the exactness issues associated with behavioral-based biometric user authentication. That is why the machine learning concept will be discussed here. Table 14.5 gives a brief outline of behavioral biometric-based method.

Table 14.5 Brief outline of behavioral biometric-based method.

Mechanism	Method	Merits	De-merits
Gaits	KNN used as linear regression	Working with always same capability	Users have to keep same type of behavior during time of operating of device which is best ever in all condition
	Nearest neighbor classifier	Does not require more user interaction explicitly during the identification process	Need of timely comparison measurement of Accelerator
Keystroke dynamic	Support vector machine	Performances are good as compared to other biometrics factor such as fingerprint identification, etc.	Variation in typing even within same day
		Easy for implementation and cost is too cheap	Does not consider the importance of time
	Random forest	Cost is low as compared to others	Not adequate for a more -security Condition
		Can be change at situation of compromise	
Signature	Fuzzy	Good technique for automatic signature checking	
	Support vector machine		Predetermined number of data tests to be utilized for learning

14.4.1 Machine Learning

Machine learning is an automated method for studies of algorithm, which describe algorithm implementation including its structure and various functions. Instead of rigidly following fixed program instructions, these algorithms work to build this type of model which is basically made to work on estimate-based data and its implementation is also based on random inputs. This model extracts the summary from present data using a mathematical and statistical framework and by using these inferences making a forecast for the unknown data. Supervised, unsupervised, semi-supervised, and reinforcement learning algorithms are the main classifications of the ML algorithms. To find fixed patterns in sensor data more attention is essential in machine learning. For accomplishing this task, discussion in this section is towards two types of machine learning which are named supervised and unsupervised learning. These classifications and determination of machine learning procedure rely upon the idea of presence of data [26].

14.4.1.1 Supervised Machine Learning

Supervised learning is demonstrated when special targets are described to reach from a somewhat fixed set of inputs. For this kind of learning, the data is first labeled followed by learning with labeled data (having inputs and wanted results). For classification of the data more accurately, supervised machine learning can be used and it is likewise utilized when the sort of data and desired outcome or labels is already known [26]. It attempts to recognize naturally rules from accessible datasets, and also tries to describe different classes, and lastly anticipates the having a concerned of components (articles, people, and rules) to a given class.

Supervised learning methods have two instances: first, Regression, and second, classification, where regression functions with regular outcomes and classification functions with discrete results. Support Vector Regression (SVR), linear regression, and polynomial regression are examples of different regression techniques and are generally used [24]. Classification algorithms have a few general examples, such as, K-nearest neighbor, logistic regression, and Support Vector Machine [25]. A neural network is an example of such algorithms which may be used for both classification and regression but these types of algorithms can be more.

14.4.1.2 Unsupervised Machine Learning

Unsupervised learning methods are utilized to train the system, when results are not well-described and also the system has to search the structure in the raw data. Unsupervised learning incorporates clustering which group's things dependent on founded equally standard as K-means clustering. The level of exactness of prescient analytics depends upon how well different Machine learning procedures have used past data to make models and, how well it is prepared to anticipate the coming qualities. In predictive modeling, different machine learning algorithms are utilized such as SVR, neural networks, and Naive Bayes, etc. [24]. Outsider data are those which will not have the option to include into group effectively. Clustering algorithm is sub-classified into two algorithms: hierarchical based and flat/partitioning-based clustering [26].

In this chapter, we are considering a focus on behavioral-based biometric measurement (gait). So firstly, the gait-based data is collected and then analyzed. These data are sufficiently informative to recognize a targeted individual or not. For storing and extracting the gait-based data in a database, the machine learning algorithm is used. Now, various types of machine learning algorithm explanation are mandatory.

14.4.2   Machine Learning Algorithms

Different machine learning algorithms are described below. Figure 14.4 demonstrate the varied machine learning approach and models.

14.4.2.1   RIPPER

The one well-known example among all rule-based learning algorithms is RIPPER. It is a rule-based learner that makes a collection of rules that cognize the classes while decreasing the number of mistakes. The mistake is described by the quantity of training examples misclassified by the rules [26].

14.4.2.2   Multilayer Perceptron

An MLP produces an output set with the help of an input set, so it is called feedforward artificial neural network. An MLP is characterized by various layers of input nodes related as directed graph in between input and output layer. "Vanilla" neural network is an informal term for a Multilayer perceptron, specially that time they have one hidden layer. Generally, MLP have three layers of nodes: an input layer, a hidden layer and an output layer. One or more Linear Threshold Unit (LTU) is also known as hidden layer. In MLP excluding of input layer, every node as a neuron utilizes a nonlinear activation function. All layers are tightly interconnected to other layers, except the output layer [27].

14.4.2.3   Decision Tree

Decision tree is one of the most renowned machine learning algorithms. This is an example of supervised learning algorithm and is used for classification problems. In this algorithm,

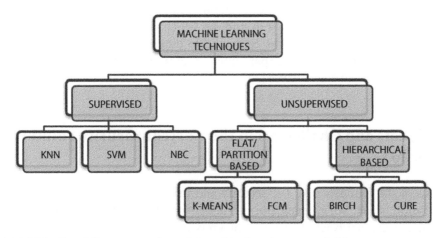

Figure 14.4 Mahadi *et al.* Demonstrate the varied machine learning approach [5].

the data set is divided into two or more small homogenous sets based on important attributes and independent variables. Categorical and continuous dependent variables are variables in which this algorithm works well by classifying [28].

14.4.2.4   Random Forest

It is an example of supervised learning algorithm. According to its name first of all, it has to create a forest any way and also make it random. The result of algorithm directly depends on the number of trees in the forest, if the trees are more then got result will be as correct. The process for finding main node or dividing the feature node will implement at random basis. This shows the main difference between Random Forest algorithm and the decision tree algorithm [29].

14.4.2.5   Instance-Based Learning

Instance-based learning is a family of various learning algorithms. Sometimes, it is also known as memory-based learning. It is an extension of nearest-neighbor (K-NN) algorithm. It builds hypotheses with the help of training instances itself, so it is called instance-based learning, instance-based learners. It may keep a new instance or throw a previous instance far [22, 30].

14.4.2.6   Bootstrap Aggregating

Bagging is another popular name of Bootstrap aggregating. It is basically a group of meta-algorithms to achieve more durability and accuracy of machine learning algorithms used in statistical classification and regression. Generally, it is applied to decision tree methods; it can also be used with any type of method. The main functions are reduction in variance and providing the help in avoiding over fitting [31].

14.4.2.7   Naïve Bayes

These algorithms are a group of classification algorithm and its implementation depends on Bayes Theorem or probability theory. It is not one algorithm but a collection of multiple algorithms, in where each algorithm works on one common rule. The data given for training should have a range. So, it is tried to find out which range of data is submitted. Naive Bayes classifiers are mainly applied as compared to other algorithm in machine learning since this is easy in implementation. Spam filters, analysis on textual data or medical diagnosis, are the main use of Naïve Bayes [32].

14.5   Threats and Challenges in the Current Security Solution for IoT

An analysis of the foundation of the security and privacy issues is crucial for successful implementation of IoT. So, it's mandatory to understand whether or not the IoT's security and challenges such as privacy are modern or a mixture of the heritage from the recent processing [16]. Symmetry and asymmetry security theme in IoT and the IT devices is the main center. The major elements in discussion of symmetry and asymmetry comprise software and hardware and its application. The basic primal equality is between the security problems in old IT domain and the IoT, according to this classification. Although, the pre-assumption of IoT is that the resource-constraints inhibit adjustment of pre-achievable refined security solutions in IoT networks. Now, Machine learning will provide authentication, which based on new patterns is one solution of IoT's protection and privacy problems. For example, IoT devices may require a new type of upgraded other machine learning algorithms to adapt to protection and privacy because of computational limitations. Despite that, quantity of devices in IoT faces different difficulties for the protection components [26].

A major factor identified in IoT security is use of knowledge-based authentication; for example, a weak password can lead to security violation. Although the password can be changed frequently, that is not sufficient from the security point of view. So instead of using knowledge-based, the focus is on behavior-based authentication. Moreover, it will likewise diminish consumer trust and along with debasing the importance of these solutions [21]. So now, an all-inclusive protection and secrecy approach towards IoT will have selections with present protection actions along with improvements in terms of new, sharp, solid, transformative, and adaptable instruments to address new security challenges.

14.6   Proposed Methodology

An individual's style of walking is known as gait; each human being has a unique pattern of walking (gait) and they also have efficiency to demonstrate it on the basis of their gait-based biometric behavior. To capture the gait data various sensors are used, such as movable or non-movable sensors. To understand the complicated gait motion of human beings, statistical features are calculated. The process of recognition and verification of a particular individual's walking style is called gait identification.

After this, machine learning models are schooled to identify an individual using these characteristics. Velocity, linear distance between two consecutive placements of the same foot, linear distance between the placements of both feet, number of step as per time unit, and foot's direction during the step, etc., are many vital criteria which are used to explain a gait pattern. Commonly, gait-based biometric is utilized for medical and healthcare applications, but nowadays it is also used for IoT-based biometric experiments. For examining gait-related activity, the following operations are mandatory to implement. They are displayed in Figure 14.5.

14.6.1   Collection of Gait Dataset

The methods for obtaining the original gait data rely upon how to identify the gait. One camera, numerous cameras, proficient motion captures model (for example VICON) and camera with deep sensor (for example Kinect) are generally all used to obtain gait data.

14.6.2   Gait Data Preprocessing

The ways for pre-processing are unique, relating to the terms of getting gait, for example, in single camera-based methodologies, the preprocessing is typically the background modification, which is used to get the body outline of strolling individuals.

Figure 14.5 Various gait operations in proposed method.

14.6.3   Reduction in Data Size

Since a person's walk is a type of recurring sign, a unique gait pattern can involve many gait cycles (series of walks). By this, gait data can decrease since one complete gait pattern has all gait features.

14.6.4   Gaits Feature

Gait identification methodologies have to include many gait features and they affect the performance of gait recognition. Gait features may be classified into two features: handcrafted and machine-learned features. The handcrafted people are comfortable for generalization of various data sets, but the machine-learned people generally felt better with special data set.

14.6.5   Classification

Gait classification, for example: gait recognition, is to utilize the classifiers on the gait features. The classifiersare classified into various algorithms (KNN,SVM) that convert the input data to specific range, which has made enough progress in face recognition, hand writing recognition, speech recognition etc.

In continuation of description of methodology, as discussed earlier, various machine learning algorithms are selected to implement behavioral-based biometric authentication on HugaDB's data by using WEKA framework. The WEKA framework was used to execute the selected machine learning algorithms. Without bothering about the mathematics or the programming, it gives a graphical user interface to investigating and exercises with different machine learning calculations on datasets. So for the implementation of machine learning related task, WEKA is a very suitable platform. HugaDB is an open-source database for human gait analysis. It also consists of continuous recordings of combined activities, such as walking, running, taking stairs up and down, sitting down, and so on. Here, data were gathered from various sensor-enabled devices, which consist of many movable sensors that are attached to the person either directly or indirectly. In addition, many other sensors can also be used with the human body for measuring muscle activity.

14.7 Conclusion and Future Work

This chapter does a study of various machine learning methods in the area of a behavioral biometric authentication. At first here, present fundamentals of IoT were discussed, and also the warnings about and solutions towards security as per today's environment. By considering these security factors, details of various authentication methods also were given above. After that, the section on user authentication based on behavioral-biometric gave details of different types of machine learning algorithm. Finally, this chapter obtained important information expected for increasing the positive effect concerning the resultant behavioral-biometric authentication by implementing the gait's activities with the help of various machine learning algorithms.

In this chapter, all analysis has proposed on HugaDB (human gait analysis data base). Here, data were gathered from various sensor networks which see only the human body motion (such as feet, speed, etc). The future work intends to make a superior framework by utilizing own dataset to accomplish higher exactness and will improve the speed of usage by implementing on different devices. This study can be very useful in real life to identify the suspect one and unaware people in near future.

References

1. Patel, K.K., & Patel, M. S. (2016). Internet of Things- IoT: Definition,Characteristics, Architecture, Enabling Technologies, Application & Future Challenges. In *International Journal of Engineering Science and Computing*. (pp. 6122-6131).
2. Noor, B.M.M & Hassan, H.W. (2019). Current research on Internet of Things (IoT) security: A survey. *Computer Networks*, vol. 148 (pp. 283-294).
   Suoa, H., Wan, J., Zoua, C., & Liua, J. (2012). Security in the Internet of Things: A Review. In *International Conference on Computer Science and Electronics Engineering*. (pp. 648-651).
4. Subbarao, G. (2019). Security Solution for the IOT Devices. In *Global Journal of Computer Science and Technology: A Hardware & Computation*. (pp. 8-14).
5. Mahadi, A.N., Mohamad, A.M., Mohamad, I.A., Mokhairi, M., Kadir, A.F.M., & Mamat, M. (2018). A Survey of Machine Learning Techniques for Behavioral-Based Biometric User Authentication. In *Recent Advances in Cryptography and Network Security*, IntechOpen. (pp. 42-59).
6. Vongsingthong, S., & Boonkrong, S. (2015). A survey on smartphone authentication. In *Walailak Journal of Science and Technology*. (pp. 1-19).
7. Sahu, S.B., & Singh, A. (2014). Survey on various techniques of user authentication and graphical password. In *International Journal of Computer Trends and Technology (IJCTT)*. (pp. 98-102).
8. Bhanushali, A., Mange B., Vyas H., Bhanushali H., & Bhogle P. (2015). Comparison of graphical password authentication techniques. In *International Journal of Computer Applications*. (pp. 11-14).
9. Saifan, R., Salem A., Zaidan, D., & Swidan, A. (2016). A survey of behavioral authentication using keystroke dynamics: Touch screens and mobile devices. *Journal of Social sciences*. (pp. 29-41).

10. Gupta, N. (2018, June 18). Four Components of IoT. [https://medium.com/@nvngpt888]. Accessed at 27 March 2020.

11. Bojinov, H., & Boneh, D. (2011). Mobile Token-based authentication on a budget. In *Proceedings of the 12th Workshop on Mobile Computing Systems and Applications* – HotMobile. (pp. 14-19).

12. Ghogare, S.D., Jadhav, S.P., Chadha, A.R., & Patil, H.C. (2012). Location based authentication:A new approach towards providing security. In *International Journal of Scientific and Research Publication*. (pp. 1-5).

13. Bianchi, A., Oakley, I., & Kwon, D.S. (2011). Using mobile device screens for authentication. In *Proceedings of the 23rd Australian Computer-Human Interaction Conference*. (pp. 50-53).

14. Lakshmi, P.V., & Susan, S.V. (2010). Biometric authentication using ElGamal cryptosystem and DNA sequence. In *International Journal of Engineering Science and Technology*. (pp. 1993-1996).

15. Prabhakar, S., Pankanti, S., & Jain, A.K. (2003). Biometric recognition: Security and privacy concerns." In *IEEE Security & Privacy Magazine*. (pp. 33-42).

16. Obaidat, M.S., Rana, S.P., Maitra, T., Giri, D., & Dutta, S. (2018). Biometric Security and Internet of Things (IoT). In *Biometric-Based Physical and Cybersecurity Systems*, Chapter 19, Springer International Publishing. (pp. 477-509).

17. Stein, C., Nickel, C., & Busch, C. (2012). Fingerphoto recognition with smartphone cameras. In *Proceedings of the International Conference of the Biometrics Special Interst Group*. (pp. 1-12).

18. Gupta, P., Wee, T.K., Ramasubbu, N., Lo, D., Gao, D., & Balan, R.K. (2012). Creating memorable fingerprints of mobile users. In *IEEE International Conference on Pervasive Computing and Communications Workshops, PERCOM Workshop*. (pp. 479-482).

19. Somnath, D., & Samanta, D. (2010). Improved feature processing for iris biometric authentication system. In *International Journal of Computer Systems Science and Engineering* (IJCSSE). (pp. 500-507).

20. Babich, A. (2012). Biometric authentication. Types of Biometric Identifiers. In HAAGA – HELIA University, Bachelor's Thesis Degree Programme. (pp. 1-56).

21. Buriro, A., Crispo, B., Delfrari, F., & Wrona, K. (2016). A novel behavioral biometrics for smartphone user authentication Hold & Sign. In *IEEE Conference on Mobile Security Technologies*. (pp. 1-11).

22. Nickel, C., Wirtl, T., & Busch, C. (2012). Authentication of Smartphone users based on the way they walk using k-NN algorithm. In *IEEE International Conference on Intelligent Information Hiding and Multimedia Signal Processing (IIH-MSP)*. (pp. 16-20).

23. Shen P, Jin A, Tee C, & Song T. (2010). Expert systems with applications keystroke dynamics in password authentication enhancement. *Elsevier Journal*. (pp. 8618-8627).

24. Justino, E.J.R., Bortolozzi, F., & Sabourin, R. (2005). A comparison of SVM and HMM classifiers in the off-line signature verification. In: *Pattern Recognition Letters*. (pp. 1-9).

25. Srivastava, K.D., Patnaik, S.K., & Bhambhu, L. (2010) Data Classification: A Rough-SVM Approach. In *Contemporary Engineering Sciences*. (pp. 77-86).

26. Hussain, F., Hussain, R., Hassan, A.S., & Hossain, E. (2019). Machine Learning in IoT Security: Current Solutions and Future Challenges. Article In arXiv.org. (pp. 1-24).

27. Marius, P. Balas, B.E, Popescu, L.& Mastorakis E.N. (2009). Multilayer perceptron and neural networks. In *WSEAS Transactions on Circuits and Systems*. (pp. 579-588).

28. Patel, R.B., & Rana, K.K. (2014). A Survey on Decision Tree Algorithm For Classification. In *International Journal of Engineering Development and Research*. (pp. 1-5).

29. Biau, G. (2012). Analysis of a Random Forests Model. In *Journal of Machine Learning Research*, (pp. 1063-1095).

30. Aha, W.D., Kibler, D., & Albert, K.M. (1991). Instance-Based Learning Algorithms. In *Machine Learning*, Kluwer Academic Publishers, Boston. (pp. 37-66).

31. Machova, K., Puszta, M., Barcák, F. & Bednár, P. (2006). A comparison of the bagging and the boosting methods using the decision trees classifiers. *Journal in ComSIS*. (pp. 58-72).
32. Kaviani, P. & Dhotre. S. (2017) Short Survey on Naive Bayes Algorithm. *International Journal of Advance Engineering and Research Development*. (pp. 607-611).
33. Grawemeyer, B., & Cox, R. (2005). Developing a Bayes-net based student model for an External Representation Selection Tutor. In *International Conference on Artificial Intelligence in Education*. (pp. 1-4).
34. Kececi, A., Yildirak, A., Ozyazici, K., Ayluctarhan, G., Agbulut, O., & Zincir, I. (2020). Implementation of machine learning algorithms for gait recognition. In *International Journal Engineering Science & Technology*. (pp. 1-7).

A Fuzzy Goal Programming Model for Quality Monitoring of Fruits during Shipment Overseas

Pushan Kr. Dutta*, Somsubhra Gupta, Simran Kumari and Akshay Vinayak

*Amity University Kolkata, Major Arterial Road (South-East), Action Area II,
Newtown, Kolkata, West Bengal, India*

Abstract

The Internet of Things (IoT) extended to IoE (Internet of Everything) aims at connecting and correlating various objects with the help of internet. The rapid development in the field of IoT has made its place in the agricultural domain as well. The motivation behind this work is to apply knowledge in the Food Preservation Sector in which quality monitoring of foods and food products are essential. The concern is restricted to fruits quality monitoring when transported overseas. A system has been proposed to analyse the ambient conditions of fruits shipped to different countries overseas. When fruits are imported or exported, due to prolonged storage and anonymous reasons, deterioration in the quality of fruits in terms of taste and freshness occurs. Due to the diminishing quality, several other crates or containers are influenced and it becomes unhygienic for consumption. To avoid such circumstances, monitoring of fruits shipment overseas has been proposed in this work. In the model formulation of the problem, system components, software components are explicitly defined. In doing so, monitoring of essential parameters and performance indicators such as humidity, temperature, vibration, oxygen, carbon dioxide, and ethylene has been taken into consideration. In the working/solution process, an illustrative fuzzily defined mathematical framework for optimizing food quality has also been provided. Emphasis was given not only to ensure fruit safety but also to avoid foodborne diseases.

Keywords: IoT, fruit monitoring, temperature-humidity, GPS, shipment overseas, wireless connection

15.1 Introduction

Quality of fruits during shipment is hugely impacted by the surroundings at the time of storage; we can control the quality of fruits once they are harvested. Therefore, it becomes necessary to maintain a proper ecosystem [1]. Quality is one of the complex parameters of many more attributes that are constantly tested by the consumer. Fruits quality is perishable due to varied reasons (variation in temperature while storing, bad weather conditions, humid containers, the ripening of some pre-plugged fruits, vibrations occurring due to high tides

---

Corresponding author: pkdutta@kol.amity.edu

Suman Lata Tripathi, Dushyant Kumar Singh, Sanjeevikumar Padmanaban, and P. Raja (eds.) Design and Development of Efficient Energy Systems, (265–284) © 2021 Scrivener Publishing LLC

and low tides) which need to be controlled or looked upon. Effective observation of these environmental conditions can help us maintain the quality of fruits and hence save us from acute loss. This project follows a modern approach towards IoT-based systems and is helpful for tracking various kinds of sensor data [2] and providing us with the apparent output required [3, 4] for purposes of analysis and study.

15.2   Proposed System

15.2.1   Problem Statement

A system is required for a food and beverage chain. The food and beverage chain is responsible for importing and exporting fruits from their firm to another outlet present in various other countries, due to which they need to send their fruit items via a shipment and some other mode of transport. In day-to-day technique, the fruits items that are shipped to different countries follow the same old authentic ways. The processes include shipment with the help of crates, reefers, containers. These crates sometimes get damaged, and sometimes fruits inside them get spoilt. To maintain the system, we need to implement or check some necessary factors to control the loss of products (in this case fruits) shipped. The factors that we are checking are temperature, humidity, oxygen level, carbon dioxide level, ethylene level, and vibration [5]. The proposed system will run to check these factors and give an update to the base station situated on land by the company authorities [6, 7]. And henceforth necessary actions will be taken accordingly to make sure the shipped fruits inside the reefers are in edible condition.

15.2.2   Overview

In this project, we have designed and executed the prototype of the system where NODEMCU ESP8266 the microcontroller with built-in Wi-Fi facilities is working as a sensor root node and other sensors connected to it are working as a sensor node, for fruit storage containers and the central base station are connected to the cloud where MySQL open-source database server supports data storage facilities [8–10]. The sensor values are collected and stored in the cloud and then sent to the base station that is connected with the help of IP addresses.

The project is developed as a wireless system of monitoring, using wireless protocols, and is capable of integrating with the base station, gateway and the internet. With the help of data received at the base station, we can keep an eye on the fruit containers such that we can protect them from the conditions that arise at the line of sight.

The above Figure 15.1 illustrates the scenario of the proposed system as to how the system will be running. At the first place, all the necessary sensors will be installed inside the reefer. These sensors will be integrated with the microcontroller. The microcontroller will then be responsible for serial communicating with the data logger which will display the data readings, then with the help of IEEE802.11 (Wi-Fi) [11–13] connection is established with the server. All the data that are fetched get stored in the cloud or database. Finally, any applicant who wants to read the data or control the system can check their Personal Digital Assistants (PDA).

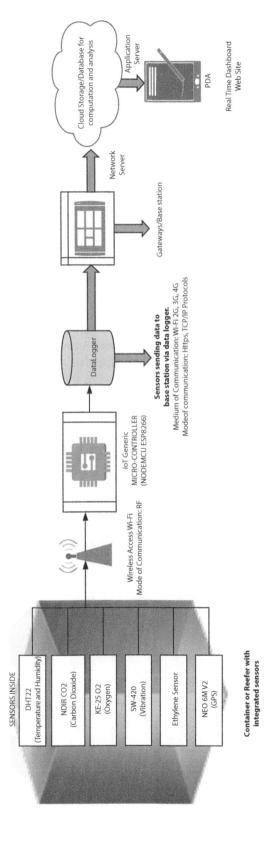

Figure 15.1 Block diagram.

15.2.3   System Components

A. *Hardware Components:*

    a) NODEMCU ESP8266 (Microcontroller, Figure 15.2) - We have used NODECU ESP8266 as our project microcontroller to integrate all the sensors that have been used. It is a well-known microcontroller for Arduino projects because of its embedded Wi-Fi [14] services to establish a wireless connection between server and client, more flash memory, bigger Ram, and a dual-core processor which makes this microcontroller a compact and precise one to be used in our project.

B. *Sensors*

    a) DHT 22 (Figure 15.3) - The sensor is capable of determining the <u>temperature and humidity</u> of the surrounding atmosphere with its nodes. The sensor consists of capacitive nodes of humidity and a thermistor for temperature readings with the help of which we have determined the ecosystem inside the containers. This sensor intern will help us regulate the humidity and temperature inside the reefer or the vessel in which fruits will be transported.

    b) NEO 6M V2 - This sensor is also known as <u>GPS (Global Positioning Systems) module</u>. This device consists of a chip that receives and transmits the GPS signal from the satellite that revolves around the earth and accordingly assists the user in drawing the longitude and latitude, such that one can track the position or area where this device is active. We have

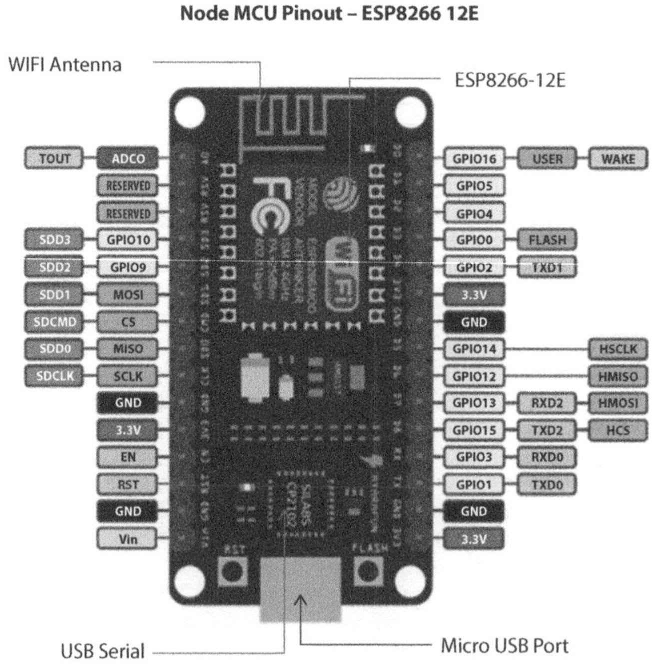

Figure 15.2 NODEMCU ESP8266 Pinouts.

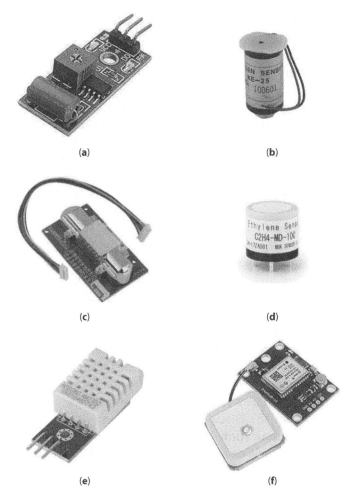

Figure 15.3 (a) SW-420 Vibration Sensor, (b) KE-25 Oxygen Sensor, (c) NDIR Carbon Dioxide Sensor, (d) Ethylene Sensor, (e) DHT 22 Temperature and Humidity Sensor, (f) NEO 6M V2 GPS Module.

used this sensor to track the shipment of the fruit container so that we can easily find the location of the ship.

c) **SW-420** - The <u>vibration sensor</u> makes us aware of the reefers rapid two and fro movement due to which the quality of the transported fruits may be negatively impacted. The more the vibration the more the damage caused to the fruits and hence the more the loss. This sensor is used to check the wholesome packaging of the cargo such that we are capable of reducing the damage caused to the fruits.

d) **KE-25** - <u>Oxygen sensor</u>, effective in sensing the presence of oxygen inside the reefer such that the fruits transported remain fresh during their journey. With the help of this sensor, the user can regulate the presence of oxygen and avoid deterioration of the quality of fruits.

e) **NDIR** - <u>Carbon Dioxide Sensor</u> is a similar type of sensor as the oxygen sensor; this sensor is proficient in sensing the carbon dioxide content inside the reefer. During long-term storage, due to adverse weather conditions fruits tend to ripe, and ripening fruits release some gases, including carbon dioxide. Carbon dioxide helps in quick respiration of fruits, therefore controlling Co_2 emission helps maintain the condition of fruits for a long period of time.

f) **Ethylene Sensor** - This sensor conceives the presence of ethylene gas. The ethylene gas is invaluable due to its ability to initiate the process of ripening of fruits, vegetable flowers, etc. Ethylene gas is also harmful to fruits and other food products because it increases the aging process and decreases the product quality. We are using this sensor to regulate the amount of ethylene excreted from the fruits to keep them fresh for a longer period of time.

C. *Software Components:*

a) **Arduino Software** - To get started with NODEMCU microcontroller we need an IDE (Integrated Development Environment) to process the running state of the sensor. This software is open source and can work on Mac, Windows, and Linux. The environment of the system is basically scripted in java which makes it platform-independent [15-17]. This software is independent of any Arduino board. The basic programming language, which can be called the Arduino language, is embedded C++ or C. An IDE normally consists of a source code editor, build automation tools, and a debugger. Most modern IDEs have intelligent code completion.

b) **MySQL Database** - Storing sensors extracted data to MySQL database and retrieving that data to the dashboard so that operations can be performed on them [18]. Discussed later in this report.

c) **Wireless Communication** - Establishment of remote connection with the server taking the help of TCP/IP and HTTP/HTTPS protocol. Discussed later in this report.

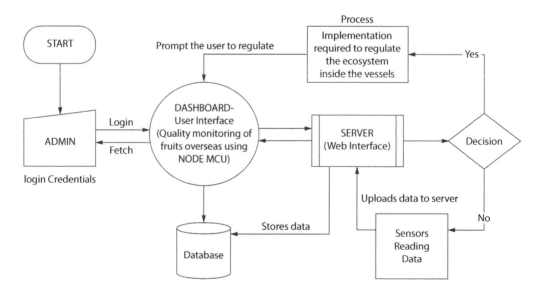

Figure 15.4 System structure.

15.3 Work Process

15.3.1 System Hardware

Independent systems have different designs and are based on different functionalities. In this project, the design includes a single microcontroller, various types of sensors, internet connectivity for the prototype, and a laptop (Figure 15.4). Apart from the server, the entire unit will be placed inside the vessel or the container with the fruits which will not only track the shipment but also create a healthy environment for shipment.

In the current working process, the microcontroller is configured with some of the sensors, namely NEO 6M V2 the GPS Module, DHT22, and SW-420 sensor [20] to get the location (here longitude and latitude) of the vessel shipment, its temperature, humidity, and vibration. The system generates an output which is then sent to the remote server with the help of wireless connection, TCP/IP, and HTTPS protocol. The server is connected to the cloud (Database) and the data is stored in the cloud itself [21]. This output is also reflected in the dashboard that fetches the data from the database and helps the user to keep an eye on the quality of fruits that are being shipped. By regulating the physical environment inside the reefer to the desired condition the user ensures fruit safety and hence establishes quality shipment overseas [18].

15.3.2 Connections and Circuitry

a) **NODEMCU ESP8266:** To operate the microcontroller power source needed is 3.3V- 4.7V, which is given through USB port via laptop or with the help of batteries.

b) **DHT 22 (Temperature and Humidity):** Data pin of sensor is connected to the microcontroller with the digital output pin D5.

c) **SW-420 (Vibration):** Data pin of sensor is connected to the microcontroller with the analog output pin A0.

d) **NEO 6M V2 (GPS Module):** It requires Rx and Tx for receiving and transmission of signals and is connected to Rx and Tx of the microcontroller.

e) **KE-25 (Oxygen Sensor):** Data pin of sensor is connected to the microcontroller with the analog output pin A0.

Sampling Rate: To upload the code it requires a sampling rate of 9600-15200 bps [22].

15.4 Optimization Framework

In a real-world decision-making situation, problems with uncertainty, imprecision, partial truth inexactness are addressed fuzzily. Fuzzy Goal Programming (FGP) concept employed here is a standard optimization model used to enhance performance of the components. Now, fuzzy goals are expressed in the following Section 15.4.1.

15.4.1 Fuzzy Goal Description

Though monitoring system parameters are deterministically defined, their performance level is bound to include uncertainty depending on the fruits preservation mechanism or situation. Hence these crisply defined arguments are put in an optimal pattern.

Mainly five performance goals are taken into consideration. Those are, System components viz. microcontroller and sensor, and three software components: software, database and communication.

Let l_k be the imprecise aspiration level of the k-th objective $G_k(X)$, (k = 1,2,...., K). The fuzzy goals may appear in any of the form:

$$G_k(X) \gtrsim l_k \qquad \text{and} \qquad G_k(X) \lesssim b_k,$$

With vector of decision variables X in which $\gtrsim$ and $\lesssim$ indicates fuzzily greater than and fuzzily less than as specified by Zimmermann [23].

Now, in this fruit preservations context, the fuzzy goals, taking into considerations the humidity, temperature, vibration, oxygen, carbon dioxide, and ethylene, are characterized by their respective membership functions.

15.4.2   Characterizing Fuzzy Membership Function

Let the lower- and upper-tolerance ranges be respectively denoted by $r_{\ell k}$ and r_{uk}, for goal achievement at desired aspiration level l_k of the k-th fuzzy goal. Then $\mu_k(X)$, the membership function for the fuzzy goal $G_k(X)$ can be characterized as mentioned below [24]:

$\mu_k(X)$ takes the following form for the restriction of the type $\gtrsim$

$$\mu_k(X) = \begin{cases} 1 & \text{if } G_k(x) \geq l_k, \\ \dfrac{G_k(x)-(l_k-r_{\ell k})}{r_{\ell k}} & \text{if } b_k - r_{\ell k} \leq G_k(x) < l_k, \\ 0 & \text{if } G_k(x) < l_k - r_{\ell k}, \end{cases} \tag{15.1}$$

where $(l_k - r_{\ell k})$ represents the fuzzy goal's lower-tolerance limit for achievement.

$\mu_k(X)$ takes the following form for $\lesssim$ type of restriction:

$$\mu_k(X) = \begin{cases} 1 & \text{if } G_k(x) \geq l_k, \\ \dfrac{(l_k+r_{uk})-G_k(X)}{r_{uk}} & \text{if } l_k < G_k(x) \leq l_k + r_{uk}, \\ 0 & \text{if } F_k(x) > l_k + r_{uk}, \end{cases} \tag{15.2}$$

where $(l_k + r_{uk})$ represents the fuzzy goal's upper-tolerance limit for achievement.

15.4.3   Construction of FGP Model

Following is the pre-emptive priority structure based FGP model of the problem:

Find X so as to

$$\text{Minimize } F = [P_1(d^-), P_2(d^-), ..., P_i(d^-), ..., P_I(d^-)]$$

and satisfy

$$\frac{G_k(x) - (l_k - r_{\ell k})}{r_{\ell k}} + d_k^- - d_k^+ = 1$$

$$\frac{(l_k + r_{uk}) - G_k(x)}{r_{uk}} + d_k^- - d_k^+ = 1$$

$$d_k^-, d_k^+ \geq 0, \quad k = 1, 2, ..., K, \tag{15.3}$$

In which d_k^-, d_k^+ represents the under- and over-deviational variables of the k-th goal and Z represents the vector of I priority achievement function. $P_i(d^-)$ is a linear function of the weighted under-deviational variables where $P_i(d^-)$ is of the form

$$P_i(d^-) = \sum_{k=1}^{K} w_{ik}^- d_{ik}^-; w_{ik}^-.d_{ik}^- \geq 0, \quad (k = 1, 2, ..., K; i \leq K),$$

where d_{ik}^- represent d_k^- at the i-th priority level, w_{ik}^- is the numerical weight associated with d_{ik}^- i.e. the weight of importance, of the k-th goal relative to other which are grouped at the i-th priority level , for achieving the aspired level.
The w_{ik}^- values are determined as [13]:

$$w_{ik}^- = \begin{cases} \dfrac{1}{(r_{\ell k})_i}, & \text{for the defined } \mu_k(x) \text{ in (1)} \\[3mm] \dfrac{1}{(r_{uk})_i}, & \text{for the defined } \mu_k(x) \text{ in (2)} \end{cases} \tag{15.4}$$

In which, $r_{\ell k}$ and r_{uk} are used to present, at the i-th priority level.

15.4.4   Definition of Variables and Parameters

Decision variables:

(i)   Independent variable
    x_{ij} = performance count of the Microcontroller during the time period i for the packaged fruit indexed j.

(ii) Dependent variable

Sn$_{ij}$ = Performance count i-th sensor for the packaged fruit indexed j.

St$_{ij}$ = Performance count of the monitoring Software with total monitoring vertical i for the packaged fruit indexed j. j.

DB$_{ij}$ = Concurrency controlled entry in the i-th database for the packaged fruit indexed j.

Fuzzy environmental performance indicators:

H   = Estimated average measure of Humidity during preservation period.

T   = Estimated mean temperature during fruit preservation period.

TM$_j$ = Estimated deviational measure at session I from mean temperature during fruit preservation period.

Vb = The measure of perturbation/vibration that the packaged fruits are subjected to.

OX$_i$ = The mean measure of Oxygen supply rate at session i.

C$_i$ = The mean measure of Carbon supply rate at session i.

Eth$_i$ = The mean measure of Ethyline supply rate at session i.

Crisp coefficients:

C$_{ij}$ = Estimated session-wsie cost for deployment of fruit preservation system during session i for the packaged fruit indexed j.

Now, for the defined variables and parameters, the algebraic structure of the fuzzy goals are described in the following Section 15.2.5.

15.4.5   Fuzzy Goal Description

1. Manpower requirement goal:
   Deployment of manpower to deploy during different sessions of the preservation period is a necessary requirement and corresponding fuzzy goal expression appears as

$$\sum_{i=1}^{m}\sum_{j=1}^{n} X_{ij} \cdot \underset{\sim}{\leq} R \tag{15.5}$$

(i) Fruit package-wise allocation
Depending on sustaining normalcy, a minimum number of attainment values for all resource parameters across the sessions are needed.

The goal expression takes the form

$$\sum_{j=i}^{n} X_{ij} \underset{\sim}{>} R_i, \qquad i = 1, 2, ..., m \tag{15.6}$$

15.5   Creation of Database and Website

15.5.1   Hosting PHP Application and Creation of MySQL Database

The goal here is to create a database along with the website for the project such that sensors data can be stored and analyzed as per requirements. For this, we need to have the domain name of this project and hosting account which will allow the user to store sensor readings from the microcontroller, i.e., NODEMCU ESP8266 so that one can visualize the readings from anywhere in the world by accessing the server name and domain address [25–27].

15.5.2   Creation of API (Application Programming Interfaces) Key

An API is a tool that makes a website's data digestible for a computer. Through it, a computer can view and edit data, just like a person can, by loading pages with sensors data and submitting forms and many other things. When systems link up through an API, we say they are integrated. One side the server that serves the API, and the other side the client that consumes the API and can manipulate it.

Here API key value is generated from the GoDaddy developers page and then used to link both the PHP code and ESP8266 code as well so that the data can be transferred from NODEMCU to the website.

15.5.2.1   *$api_key_value = "3mM44UaC2DjFcV_63GZ14aWJcRDNmYBMsxceu";*

Here API key value is generated from Google's cloud platform for using maps services such as

src=https://maps.googleapis.com/maps/api/js?key=AIzaSyAk4BBCmeZuWv0oV_uTjF9wBeW9YocUbOc&callback=myMap

15.5.2.2   *Preparing Mysql Database*

Creation of database, username, password and SQL table.

```
$dbname = "Data_Final1";
$username = "projectIIT";
$password = "projectIIT@123";
```

15.5.2.3   *Structured Query Language (SQL)*

Structured Query Language is a standard Database language which is used in this project to create, maintain and retrieve the relational databases.

Creating a SQL table
After creating database and User account info, with the help of cPanel and "PhpMyAdmin" creation of a database table is done for the project. To create the table following code snipped is required.

CREATE TABLE SensorData (

id INT (10) UNSIGNED AUTO_INCREMENT PRIMARY KEY,
value1 VARCHAR (10),
value2 VARCHAR (10),
value3 VARCHAR (10),
value4 VARCHAR (10),
value5 VARCHAR (10),
value6 VARCHAR (10),
reading_time TIMESTAMP DEFAULT CURRENT_TIMESTAMP ON UPDATE
CURRENT_TIMESTAMP

Value insertion into the database

$sql = "INSERT INTO SensorData (id, value1, value2, value3, value4, value5, value6)
VALUES (" . id. "', " . $value1 . "', " . $value2 . "', " . $value3 . "', " . $value4 . "', " . $value5
. "', " . $value6 . "')";

Displaying the data on the website:

$sql = "SELECT id, value1, value2, value3, value4, value5, value6, reading_time FROM
SensorData ORDER BY ID DESC LIMIT 1";

15.5.2.4   Use of HTTP (Hypertext Transfer Protocol) in Posting Request

The Hypertext Transfer Protocol (HTTP) is designed to enable communications between clients and servers. HTTP works as a request-response protocol between a client and a server. Here, when the client submits the HTTP request to the server, the server returns the response to the client. This response contains the data displayed from the sensors which are the requested content. This is how it works.

POST is used to send data to a server to create/update a resource.

Function in PHP for taking the input:

$value1 = test_input($_POST["value1"]);

Preparing HTTP POST request data (The code snippet is from Arduino IDE)

String httpRequestData = "api_key=" + apiKeyValue + "&value1=" + String(dht.
readTemperature())

+ "&value2=" + String(dht.readHumidity()) +"&value3=" + String(gps.location.lat(),8)
+"&value4=" + String(gps.location.lng(),8)+ "&value5=" + String(analogRead(Vib))+
"&value6=" + String(oxy,4)+ "";   Serial.println(httpRequestData);

<u>Sending HTTP POST request</u>

Int httpResponseCode = http.POST(httpRequestData);

15.5.2.5   Adding a Dynamic Map to the Website

Here the data values from the GPS sensor is retrieved by the website and is displayed on the map dynamically. This is updated in a certain time interval and the variation helps in tracking the exact location of the ship. The below code receives the latitude and longitude from the sensor:

center:new google.maps.LatLng('. $row_value3 . ', '. $row_value4 .'),

15.5.2.6   Adding Dynamic Graph to the Website

The website is linked with another page that displays the graphs of the sensor data for the whole day. Here we are displaying the graph of temperature, humidity, vibration, and oxygen data values. Below is the code snippet for the creation of graphs.

```
// function for creation of graphs.

function createTemperatureGraph(){
  const temperature = document.getElementById('temperature').getContext('2d');
  temperaturemyChart = new Chart(temperature, {
   type: 'line',
  data:{
 labels: [],
      datasets:[
        {
          label: "Temperature (Celsius)",
          data: [],
          backgroundColor: "transparent",
          borderColor: "orange"
        }
     ]
    },
    options: {
      scales: {
            yAxes: [{
            ticks: {
           beginAtZero: false
          }
        }]
      }
    }
  });
}
```

15.5.2.7   Adding the Download Option of the Data Set

With the display of graphs, there is another option of downloading the data set for the whole day. The data set is available in .txt and JSON format. Below is the code snippet for creation of download option.

```
// function for creation of download option.

function generate () {
link_div.style.display = 'none'
button.innerHTML = 'Generating... please wait...'
button.removeEventListener('click', generate)

 fetch ("http://emsig.co.in/Data_Final111/data.php", {
    headers: {
       'Content-Type': 'application/json',
    },
  })
  .then (data => data.json())
  .then (data => {
   const all_data = "text/json;charset=utf-8," + encodeURIComponent(JSON.stringify(data))
   setDataForDownload(all_data)
  })
}
button.addEventListener('click', generate)
```

15.6   Libraries Used and Code Snipped

Libraries are a collection of code that makes it easy for us to connect to a sensor, actuator, display, module, etc. There are hundreds of additional libraries available on the Internet for different sensors. To use the additional libraries, we will need to install them from the library manager which is available in the sketch dialog box [28].

Libraries Used:

    a) **include <DHT.h>:** This sensor is used for obtaining the temperature and humidity readings. The library helps in activating the sensors circuitry such that the sensor is able to transmit data.

    b) **#include<TinyGPS++.h> and #include<SoftwareSerial.h>:** The GPS Module requires two sets of the library for operation. The Tiny GPS library is used to draw the coordinates (longitude and latitude) of the module from where it is operated. On the other hand, Software Serial is used for creating a serial communication with the microcontroller so that the modules can deliver the outcome.

c) **#include <ESP8266WiFi.h>:** To run the module on internet connectivity we require either GSM or Wi-Fi connectivity, for this server and client connection need to be established. This library helps in establishing the connection between the server and the client.

d) **#include<ESP8266HTTPClient.h>:** This library is similar to the above library; it identifies the client and helps in connection establishment.

Code Snippet:

a) **Connecting to the internet and server**
   const char* ssid   = "Akki"; /* Wi-Fi Credentials
   const char* password = "aezakmi1"; (User Id, Password)*/
   const char* serverName = "http://emsig.co.in/Data_Final111/post-esp-data.
      php"; // server name
    String apiKeyValue = "3mM44UaC2DjFcV_63GZ14aWJcRDNmYBMsx-
      ceu"; /* API value to connect to the specific server and client */

b) **Connecting to the client**
   WiFi.begin(ssid, password);
   // checking for ssid and password for connectivity
   Serial.println("Connecting…");
   while(WiFi.status() != WL_CONNECTED)

Figure 15.5 shows a prototype of the problem with blinking LED and Figure 15.6 gives the details of LED blinking with the second type sensor.

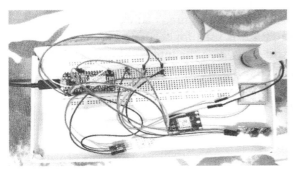
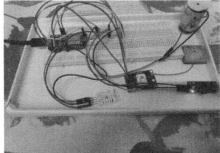

Figure 15.5 Working prototype of the problem with blinking LED.

Figure 15.6 LED blinking with the second type sensor.

c) Fetching data from sensors

```
if(WiFi.status()== WL_CONNECTED){ HTTPClient http;  // client con-
    nected http.begin(serverName); // server begin
    // Specify content-type header
http.addHeader("Content-Type", "application/x-www-form-urlencoded");
    // Preparing HTTP POST request data
String httpRequestData = "api_key=" + apiKeyValue + "&value1=" +
    String(dht.readTemperature()) + "&value2=" + String(dht.readHu-
    midity()) + "&value3=" + String(gps.location.lat(),8) + "&value4=" +
    String(gps.location.lng(),8) + "&value5=" + String(analogRead(Vib)) +
    "&value6=" + String(oxy)+ "";
Serial.print("httpRequestData: ");
Serial.println(httpRequestData);
    // printing/sending data to database
```

Figure 15.7 presents the measurement of the temperature and humidity modules in four different cases. Figure 15.8 shows the module output associated with the data for temperature and humidity.

15.7   Mode of Communication

a) **Radio Frequency**: It is the oscillation rate of an alternating electric current or voltage or of a magnetic, electric or electromagnetic field or mechanical system in the frequency range from around twenty thousand times per second to around three hundred billion times per second.

b) **HTTP/HTTPS:** Hypertext Transfer Protocol Secure is an extension of the Hypertext Transfer Protocol (HTTP). It is used for secure communication over a computer network and is widely used on the Internet. In HTTPS, the communication protocol is encrypted using Transport Layer Security (TLS), or, formerly, its predecessor, Secure Sockets Layer (SSL). The protocol is therefore also often referred to as HTTP over TLS or HTTP over SSL.

c) **TCP/IP:** or the Transmission Control Protocol/Internet Protocol, is a suite of communication protocols used to interconnect network devices on the internet. TCP/IP can also be used as a communications protocol in a private network (an intranet or an extranet).

15.8   Conclusion

The proposed system is designed for monitoring the quality of the fruits that are transported overseas. Which on result maintains the artificial ecosystem inside the vessel to preserve the quality of the fruits for a longer period of time to avoid loss and maintenance of hygiene [30, 31]. This project incorporates the cloud and IoT technology with the use of different sensors and their connectivity and also establishes the inference to the user by creating the user-friendly environment which in result will show the effective utilization of current computer-aided engineering and technology. The proposed model is just a prototype and

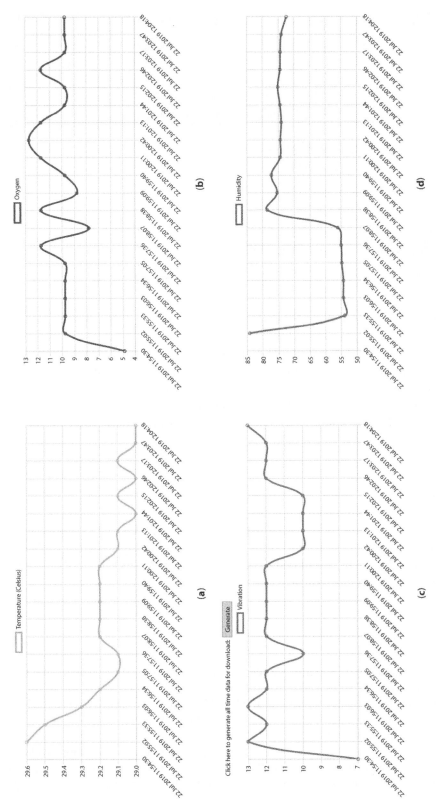

Figure 15.7 (a–d) Measurement of the Temperature and Humidity in four different cases.

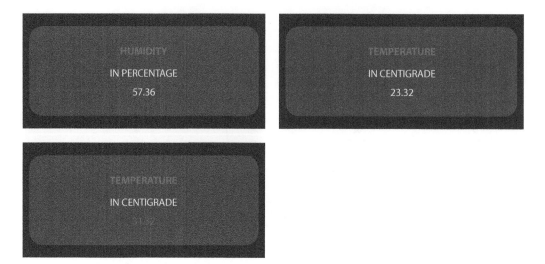

Figure 15.8 Module output associated with the data for temperature and humidity (a,b).

cannot serve its purpose at the line of sight. Establishment of Wi-fi is nearly negligible at the line of sight or maybe costlier [29].

Use of industrial sensors instead of small prototyped sensors to deal with the real-life scenario will help in the integrity of the project. Use of satellite communication, another mode of wireless communication instead of Wi-Fi will initiate handsome connectivity and provide robustness to the medium. Use of heavy-duty microcontrollers (Industrial Microcontroller) such as LoRa Node and LoRa WAN can increase the efficiency of the project.

Abbreviations

IoT (Internet of Things), SQL (Structured Query Language), PDA (Personal Digital Assistants), Wi-Fi (Wireless Fidelity), GPS (Global Positioning Systems), NDIR (Non-Dispersive Infra-Red), IDE (Integrated Development Environment), TCP/IP (Transmission Control Protocol/ Internet Protocol)

References

1. J. Rodrguez-Bermejo, P. Barreiro, J. Robla, and L. Ruiz-Garca, "Thermal study of a transport container," *Journal of Food Engineering*, vol. 80, no. 2, pp. 517-527, 2007.
2. L. Ruiz-Garcia, L. Lunadei, P. Barreiro, and I. Robla, "A review of wireless sensor technologies and applications in agriculture and food industry: state of the art and current trends," *Sensors*, vol. 9, no. 6, pp. 4728-4750, 2009.
3. N. Heidmann, S. Janssen, W. Lang, and S. Paul, "Implementation and verification of a low-power uhf / lf wireless sensor network as part of the intelligent container," *Procedia Engineering*, vol. 47, no. 0, pp. 68-71, 2012, 26th European Conference on Solid-State Transducers, fEUROSENSORg 2012.

4. Hasegawa, Yuki, Anita Lloyd Spetz, and Donatella Puglisi. "Ethylene gas sensor for evaluating postharvest ripening of fruit." In *2017 IEEE 6th Global Conference on Consumer Electronics (GCCE)*, pp. 1-4. IEEE, 2017.

5. O'Neal, D. Patrick, M. Adam Meledeo, Justin R. Davis, Bennett L. Ibey, V. Alexander Gant, Michael V. Pishko, and Gerard L. Coté. "Oxygen sensor based on the fluorescence quenching of a ruthenium complex immobilized in a biocompatible poly (ethylene glycol) hydrogel." *IEEE Sensors Journal* 4, no. 6 (2004): 728-734.

6. Sundgren, H., F. Winquist, and I. Lundstrom. "Artificial neural networks and statistical pattern recognition improve MOSFET gas sensor array calibration." In *TRANSDUCERS'91: 1991 International Conference on Solid-State Sensors and Actuators. Digest of Technical Papers*, pp. 574-577. IEEE, 1991.

7. P. A. Shinde, Y. B. Mane, "Advanced vehicle monitoring and tracking system based on Raspberry Pi", Intelligent Systems and Control (ISCO) 2015 IEEE 9th International Conference on, pp. 1-6, 2015.[online] Available: http://simcom.ee/modules/gsm-gprs-gnss/sim808/.

8. S. M. Mamduh et al., "Odour and Hazardous Gas Monitoring System for Swiftlet Farming using Wireless Sensor Network (WSN)", Chemical Engineering Transactions, vol. 30, pp. 331-336, 2012.

9. A. R. Ibrahim, N. H. N. Ibrahim, A. N. Harun, M. R. M. Kassim, S. E. Kamaruddin and G. Witjaksono, "Bird Counting and Climate Monitoring using LoRaWAN in Swiftlet Farming for IR4.0 Applications," 2018 2nd International Conference on Smart Sensors and Application (ICSSA), Kuching, 2018, pp. 33-37.doi: 10.1109/ICSSA.2018.8535955.

10. Zhibo Pang, Jun Chen, David Sarmiento Mendoza, Zhi Zhang, Jie Gao, Qiang Chen, Lirong Zheng, "Mobile and wide area deployable sensor system for networked services", *Sensors 2009 IEEE*, pp. 1396-1399, 2009.

11. Eirini Karapistoli, Ioanna Mampentzidou, Anastasios A. Economides, "Environmental Monitoring Based on the Wireless Sensor Networking Technology", *International Journal of Agricultural and Environmental Information Systems*, vol. 5, pp. 1, 2014.

12. Sakai, Y., Y. Sadaoka, M. Matsuguchi, and K. Hirayama. "Water resistive humidity sensor composed of interpenetrating polymer networks of hydrophilic and hydrophilic and hydrophobic methacrylate." In *TRANSDUCERS'91: 1991 International Conference on Solid-State Sensors and Actuators. Digest of Technical Papers*, pp. 562-565. IEEE, 1991.

13. Hammond, J. M., R. M. Lec, X. J. Zhang, D. G. Libby, and L. A. Prager. "An acoustic automotive engine oil quality sensor." In *Proceedings of International Frequency Control Symposium*, pp. 72-80. IEEE, 1997.

14. Eom, Jimi, Woobin Lee, and Yong-Hoon Kim. "Textile-based wearable sensors using metal-nanowire embedded conductive fibers." In *2016 IEEE SENSORS*, pp. 1-3. IEEE, 2016.

15. Zaidi, Nayyer Abbas, M. Waseem Tahir, Michael Vellekoop, and Walter Lang. "Using Allan variance to determine the resolution of ethylene gas chromatographic system." In *2017 IEEE SENSORS*, pp. 1-3. IEEE.

16. Hallur, Veena, Bhagyashree Atharga, Amruta Hosur, Bhagyashree Binjawadagi, and K. Bhat. "Design and development of a portable instrument for the detection of artificial ripening of banana fruit." In *International Conference on Circuits, Communication, Control and Computing*, pp. 139-140. IEEE, 2014.

17. Formisano, Fabrizio, Ettore Massera, Saverio De Vito, Antonio Buonanno, Girolamo Di Francia, and Paola Delli Veneri. "RFID tag for vegetable ripening evaluation using an auxiliary smart gas sensor." In *SENSORS, 2014 IEEE*, pp. 2026-2029. IEEE, 2014.

18. García-Salinas, Carolina, Perla A. Ramos-Parra, and Rocío I. Díaz de la Garza. "Ethylene treatment induces changes in folate profiles in climacteric fruit during postharvest ripening." *Postharvest Biology and Technology* 118 (2016): 43-50.

19. Maduwanthi, S. D. T., and R. A. U. J. Marapana. "Induced ripening agents and their effect on fruit quality of banana." *International Journal of Food Science* 2019 (2019).

20. Esser, Birgit, Jan M. Schnorr, and Timothy M. Swager. "Selective detection of ethylene gas using carbon nanotube-based devices: utility in determination of fruit ripeness." *Angewandte Chemie International Edition* 51, no. 23 (2012): 5752-5756.

21. P. Corke, T. Wark, R. Jurdak, W. Hu, P. Valencia, and D. Moore, "Environmental wireless sensor networks, *Proc. IEEE*, vol. 98, no. 11, pp. 1903-1917, Nov. 2010.

22. H. J. Zimmermann, "Fuzzy Programming and Linear Programming with Several Objective Functions", *Fuzzy Sets and Systems*, 1, 1978, pp. 45 – 55.

23. B. B. Pal, B. N. Moitra, U. Maulik, "A Goal Programming Procedure for Fuzzy Multiobjective Linear Fractional Programming Problem", *Fuzzy Sets and Systems*, 139, pp. 395 – 405, 2003.

24. B.B. Pal, S. Sen and B.N. Moitra, "Using Dinkelback Approach for Solving Multiobjective Linear Fractional Programming Problems", *Proceedings of 2nd National Conference on Recent Trends in Information System, J.U., Kolkata, W.B., India*, pp. 149-152, 2008.

25. Zaidi, Nayyer Abbas, M. W. Tahir, P. P. Vinayaka, F. Lucklum, M. Vellekoop, and W. Lang. "Detection of ethylene using gas chromatographic system." *Procedia Engineering* 168 (2016): 380-383.

26. Steffens, C., E. Franceschi, F. C. Corazza, P. S. P. Herrmann Jr, and J. Vladimir Oliveira. "Gas sensors development using supercritical fluid technology to detect the ripeness of bananas." *Journal of Food Engineering* 101, no. 4 (2010): 365-369.

27. Bastuck, Manuel, Donatella Puglisi, J. Huotari, T. Sauerwald, J. Lappalainen, A. Lloyd Spetz, Mike Andersson, and A. Schütze. "Exploring the selectivity of WO3 with iridium catalyst in an ethanol/naphthalene mixture using multivariate statistics." *Thin Solid Films* 618 (2016): 263-270.

28. Puglisi, Donatella, Jens Eriksson, Christian Bur, Andreas Schuetze, Anita Lloyd Spetz, and Mike Andersson. "Catalytic metal-gate field effect transistors based on SiC for indoor air quality control." In *Journal of Sensors and Sensor Systems*, vol. 4, pp. 1-8. Copernicus, 2015.

29. Bur C., Bastuck M., Puglisi D., Schütze A., Lloyd-Spetz A., Andersson M., "Discrimination and Quantification of Volatile Organic Compounds in the ppb-Range with Gas Sensitive SiC-FETs Using Multivariate Statistics," *Sensors and Actuators B*, 2015, Vol. 214, pp. 225-233

30. Puglisi D., Eriksson J., Andersson M., Huotari J., Bastuck M., Bur C., Lappalainen J., Andreas S., Lloyd-Spetz A., "Exploring the Gas Sensing Performance of Catalytic Metal/Metal Oxide 4H-SiC Field Effect Transistors", *Materials Science Forum*, 2016, Vol. 858, pp. 997-1000.

16

Internet of Things – Definition, Architecture, Applications, Requirements and Key Research Challenges

Dushyant Kumar Singh, Himani Jerath and P. Raja*

Lovely Professional University, Phagwara, Punjab, India

Abstract

Today internet is easily accessible to most of the population of the world. And with the increase in accessibility of the internet and advancement in the technology, a new form of technology has emerged i.e., Internet of Things (IoT). It is one of the trending and promising research topics with infinite research opportunities. IoT has been able to develop a new form of communication i.e., machine to machine communication apart from already existing communication, i.e., human to machine and human to human. IoT is penetrating deep in different application areas like consumer electronics, health care, industrial automation, smart homes, public administration, mobile health care, smart grids, intelligent energy management, traffic management and many others. But as with the other technologies, besides presenting numerous opportunities, IoT also comes with its own design challenges and security issues. This review chapter gives an overview of the various requirements for IoT system and architecture, highlights different research challenges in IoT and security issues connected with IoT.

Keywords: Internet of Things (IoT), IoT architecture, IoT design, IoT security

16.1 Introduction

IoT is a trending field these days and comes along with different standardization, design, architecture and security challenges. In the decade from 2010 to 2020 much research was conducted in the field of IoT but very few publications were found addressing and highlighting the challenges of IoT. Figure 16.1 below gives the publication data searched with keyboard "IoT" and "IoT Challenges".

The current chapter on IoT highlights the various definitions, proposed architecture, application, implementation requirement for IoT systems in section 16.2. Looking into the various heterogeneous application fields, it is always challenging to design a common solution for the IoT applications, which leads to various design challenges and security issues

---

Corresponding author: raja.21019@lpu.co.in

Suman Lata Tripathi, Dushyant Kumar Singh, Sanjeevikumar Padmanaban, and P. Raja (eds.) Design and Development of Efficient Energy Systems, (285–296) © 2021 Scrivener Publishing LLC

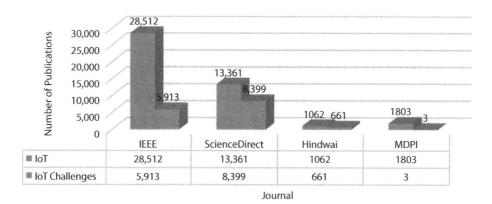

Figure 16.1 Publication data for IoT and its challenges.

associated with IoT which are presented in section 6 under Key Research Challenges in Internet of Things (IoT).

16.2   Defining the Term Internet of Things (IoT)

The main concept behind the IoT device is to exchange the valuable information between uniquely identifiable real-world devices equipped with leading technology like Wireless Sensor Network (WSN) and Radio-Frequency Identification (RFID) which is to be processed for decision making. With the IoT the communication process has been revolutionized. The generic form of communication is either human to human or human to machine but IoT has given rise to machine to machine (M2M) communication, giving a great future to internet [1].

IoT is an interconnected network of things that are used on a daily basis. It can also be treated as a self-configurable network. It allows day-to-day objects, embedded with electronic circuits, to be sensed and controlled remotely through a network. Connecting a number of objects to internet creates a dynamic global network with the ability of self-configuration [2].

In [3] and [4] IoT has been viewed in three paradigms – internet oriented (middleware), things oriented (sensors), and semantic oriented (knowledge). The IoT covers the various aspect of extending the internet into the physical world with the deployment of various distributed devices having embedded identification. IoT gives the concept of linking the digital entities with the physical on through suitable information and communication technology, thus giving a whole new area of applications.

In [3] various definitions of IoT have been given. As per one definition by RFID group,

"The worldwide network of interconnected objects uniquely addressable based on standard communication protocols."

European Research Cluster has defined IoT as follows:

'Things' are active participants in business, information and social processes where they are enabled to interact and communicate among themselves and with the environment by exchanging data and information sensed about the environment, while reacting autonomously to the real/physical world events and influencing it by running processes that trigger actions and create services with or without direct human intervention.

Yet another definition of IoT is given by Forrester Research:

Uses information and communications technologies to make the critical infrastructure components and services of a city's administration, education, healthcare, public safety, real estate, transportation and utilities more aware, interactive and efficient.

The definition of IoT given by the authors in [3] is not restricted to any standard protocol and will allow long-lasting development and deployment of IoT applications with state-of-the-art protocols. The IoT definition according to authors in [3] is

Interconnection of sensing and actuating devices providing the ability to share information across platforms through a unified framework, developing a common operating picture for enabling innovative applications. This is achieved by seamless ubiquitous sensing, data analytics and information representation with Cloud computing as the unifying framework.

16.3   IoT Architecture

The paper [1] has given the projected penetration of IoT by 2020 as given by the Cisco. The paper has discussed six-layer architecture of IoT, namely Coding layer, Perception layer, Network layer, Middleware layer, Application layer and Business layer as shown in Figure 16.2.

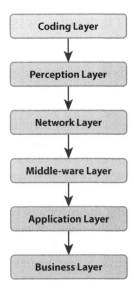

Figure 16.2 IoT Architecture [1].

The coding layer is responsible for assigning a unique ID to each device through which the device of interest is identified. The coding layer basically gives the address to each device on the IoT network. The second layer in the IoT architecture presented is the perception layer, which give the physical meaning to each and every object in the IoT network. It consists of sensors like temperature, humidity acceleration, etc. The function of the perception layer is to gather information about the object, like its temperature and humidity, and pass the gathered information to the network layer. Before passing the information to the network layer, the perception layer converts the information into digital signals. The network layer passes all the digital information received from the perception layer to the middleware layer of IoT architecture information using any of the transmission mediums like Wi-Fi, Bluetooth, Zigbee, etc. The middleware layer is basically the cloud which processes the information so received from the network layer. The application layer is helpful in developing the IoT on a large scale and includes applications like smart homes, industry, smart planet, smart transportation. The business layer of IoT architecture is responsible for managing the application, services and research related to the IoT [1].

After discussing the IoT architecture, paper [1] discussed the history of IoT. The first application of IoT was developed in 1982 as a modified coke machine, which was connected to internet for the purpose of reporting about drinks contained and their temperature. Thereafter, in 1991, a ubiquitous computing concept to IoT was given by Mark Weiser. In 1999, Bill Joy discussed Device to Device communication and Kevin Ashton coined the term Internet of Things in the same year.

IoT integrates the physical devices with cyber physical infrastructure by embedding the electronics into the everyday objects and making them "smart". In this context IoT may refer to i) a global network connecting the smart objects through extended internet technologies, ii) a set of technologies needed to support such vision, and iii) opening new opportunities in the market and business with the different applications and services exploiting such technologies. Three pillars of IoT, based on the ability of smart objects, are identification – a device should be identifiable; communication – a device should be able to communicate; and ability to interact – a device should be able to interact with other devices or with an end user or with other entities in a network. If IoT is viewed at the components level, IoT is based on the notion of "smart object" or "things" [4]. Smart object is defined in [4] is as follows:

- An object with physical embodiment and features such as shape, size, etc.
- An object having communication capabilities to get discovered, identified and be able to receive messages and respond to incoming messages.
- An object having a unique identifier for identification.
- An object with a minimum of one name and address. The name of the object is a human readable description of the object and address is the machine-readable string used to communicate or send messages to the device.
- An object with some computing capabilities. The processing capabilities can be as simple as just matching the incoming message string with the given footprint to the capability of the object of performing complex calculation like network discovery and management, image processing, etc.
- An object able to sense physical parameters like temperature, humidity, height above sea level, radiation level, etc. An object may also possess the facility to actuate or trigger actions depending on the sensed parameters.

16.4   Applications of Internet of Things (IoT)

In [4] the author has identified six major application areas where IoT can provide competitive solutions for current problems.

1. **Smart home** or smart building equipped with IoT technology helps in reducing the resource consumption and also helps to improve the satisfaction level of the people living in it. In a smart building application, sensors are required to sense the consumption of resources and other parameters to monitor the user's needs. This needs high standardization for the interoperability of various subsystems.

2. **Smart cities** are a cyber physical ecosystem deploying advanced communicating services to improve the quality of life of the citizens and optimize the usage of the city's physical resources. Smart parking system, automated parking advice system, monitoring of car traffic, flow of vehicles, detection of polluting level and accident scene analysis are some of the prominent applications where an important role is being played by the IoT.

3. In **Environmental monitoring,** IoT's real-time processing along with the capability to communicate with a large number of devices provides an excellent platform for monitoring of the environmental conditions that endanger human life. Due to its capability of sensing in a distributed and self-managing network, sensing the physical natural phenomena like temperature, wind, rain, etc., and effortlessly integrating such heterogenous data makes IoT suitable to be applied to environmental monitoring applications.

4. **Health care** is yet another application area where IoT can play a major role. Enhancing the monitoring of patient parameters like body temperature, blood pressure, breathing activities and wearables with sensors such as accelerometer and gyroscope monitoring patient activities are some of the areas where health care can benefit from IoT. By interconnecting such heterogenous sensors the comprehensive monitoring of a patient's condition is possible and may be helpful in addressing any deterioration in the condition of the patient.

5. **Smart business** is another application where RFID is already being used for inventory management. RFIDs are attached to the items for e-monitoring and RFID readers are placed throughout the monitoring facility. Real-time monitoring of product availability, stock maintenance and control over the production process, product quality, and detection of self-life deterioration of product are some of the tasks performed by an IoT system in Smart Business.

6. **Security and Surveillance** are considered to be an important application and challenge of IoT. Keeping a check on the behavioral monitoring through various sensors, personal identification using biometrics and early warning systems are a few aspects that are being provided as cheaper and less invasive solutions. On the basis of the data generated, the various IoT applications are given in Figure 16.3 [3].

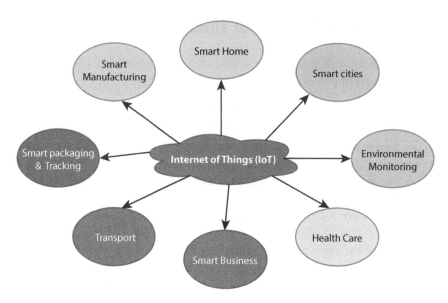

Figure 16.3 Application areas of Internet of Things (IoT) [3].

The components of IoT which make it ubicomp (ubiquitous computing) are: 1) Hardware consisting of sensors, communication technology, actuator and to be added on also consists of microcontroller or microprocessor-based processing boards, 2) Middleware comprises cloud service for storage and computing, and 3) Presentation, the easy to understand and visualize user interface accessible from any platform. The IoT elements identified in [3] which make up the above three components in IoT are Radio Frequency Identification (RFID), Wireless Sensor Networks (WSN) – WSN hardware, WSN communication stack, WSN middleware, secure data aggregation, Addressing schemes, Data storage and analytics and Visualization.

The IoT in the near future will make it possible for everyday objects to be equipped with microcontrollers; transceivers for communication and required protocol enabling them to communicate with each other and also with the users. This will make the internet more immersive and pervasive. The heterogeneous application fields of IoT, such as applications areas like consumer electronics, health care, industrial automation, smart homes, public administration, mobile health care, smart grids, and intelligent energy management, make it a daunting challenge to identify a solution capable of satisfying the requirements of all possible applications. This sometimes leads to propagation of different or sometimes incompatible solutions of practical implementation of IoT systems [5].

16.5 Requirement for Internet of Things (IoT) Implementation

The basic and key feature of IoT is embedding of computing and communication features into everyday objects. An IoT system should fulfill the following requirements:

1. **Scalability:** In 2013 there were about 9 billion interconnected devices and by 2020 this figure is expected to rise to 24 billion devices [3]. It is a perception

that every device has its own virtual representation and with that many devices are interconnected through IoT infrastructure; scalability is desired in IoT architecture for future new IoT applications [6].

2. **Interoperability:** IoT consists of the heterogeneous application areas, and IoT objects may communicate from various service networks. Therefore, in order to empower the IoT devices to communicate from various networks too, all types of IoT application, interoperability is desired [6].

3. **Identification:** In IoT each object needs to be identified specifically. The object may be identified as an individual or as a member of any class, like a pen is a member of a wide class of pens which is not specific and is taken in a generalized manner. This may be achieved by means of RFID tags or any suitable method, but identification of object is desired [2].

4. **Sensing/Actuation:** Sensing and actuation is desired to interface the IoT device with the real-time world around. A device can be interfaced with physical environment passively, performing sensing, or actively, performing action [2].

5. **Resource Control and Management:** The various devices participating in IoT application must be remotely operating as this will help in controlling the device remotely when operator is not present at site. This constraint of resource redundancy may affect the IoT application and it is necessary to balance the load for proper resource utilization [6].

6. **Energy Efficiency:** Lifetime is the most important aspect for smart objects; moreover, the energy consumption of networks is also increasing day by day with the increase in data rate and hence it is desirable for such devices to be more based on green technology; they should be energy efficient [6, 7].

7. **Quality of Service (QoS):** Quality of Service is also an important requirement of IoT architecture. QoS is nonfunctional facility factor which can be obtained by organizing the service provided and retrieval. For instance, Real Time Systems impose requirements of high precedence for a particular performance and it is desired that only compulsory information be retrieved in response to the addressed request [6].

8. **Security:** Security is the most important aspect for IoT objects, which may suffer physical damage and data loss as information is transferred and processed in a hostile environment [6, 7].

16.6 Key Research Challenges in Internet of Things (IoT)

The future of the IoT faces many challenges and needs deliberation by experts to address these challenges. Some of the key research challenges in IoT are listed below:

16.6.1 Computing, Communication and Identification

IoT is envisioned as the development of the technique to transform devices to smart devices and making them capable for communication, computing and identification. The process in which computation is distributed evenly in order to reduce communication overhead is known as in-network processing or computing [4]. The existence of interconnected links between the objects in IoT needs research consideration with existing tools, methods [8]. There are many possible solutions proposed like RF front end activation pattern, i.e., sleep period, integrating energy harvesting from several sources for sensors like solar, piezocrystals and others [4]. IoT is a very heterogeneous network with a variety of devices from various application areas. This complicates the process of communication amounts the IoT nodes resulting in fraudulent, delayed communication [9, 10]. IoT also suffers from the challenge of identity management, which requires the unique identity for all the physical devices. The current technology deployed is short-range RF identifiers. As the IoT includes a very large number of nodes which are expected to increase in the future, further research is needed in the identification for IoT nodes to operate in a dynamic heterogeneous network [4, 8, 7]. The IPv4 protocol uses only a 4-byte address so new addressing policies are needed in which IPv6 may be a strong contender [8]. Consequently there is need of an IoT architecture that can support low-power, low-cost and yet fully functional networks and devices and is compatible with well-established communication technologies and standards, addressing the huge number of the devices connected to a system [4, 8].

16.6.2 Network Technology

The IoT consists of connecting the devices from various networks in which user happens to be human, machines. WSN is the dominant network technology in IoT [5, 8]. With the increasing number of connected devices in the system infrastructure, it is going to face many challenges like providing service to the different types of IoT-connected devices. Thus, there is a requirement of scaling up the IoT architecture in order to handle the large number of devices [15]. Interoperability of IoT devices amongst the various service providers is also important. The technical challenges in interoperability are standards, protocols, and semantics; the challenges are to ensure that every node in IoT architecture is trustworthy for processing and handling the data. The pragmatic challenges are to design a strategy for realization of ability in an IoT system to observe the intention of participating elements [15]. Protocol forms the backbone for a data tunnel between IoT node and the outer world. Many energy-efficient MAC protocols are proposed like TDMA (collision free), FDMA (collision free with additional circuitry), TCP/IP, Ipv4 and IPv6 for node addressing but none of them are suitable as more "things" available in IoT [5]. Research focus is needed on exploitation of networks for IoT, scalability of network infrastructure, interoperability of networks, identifying the new protocols to handle the network traffic with more devices added, adaptability to heterogeneous networks environment [5, 8, 15].

16.6.3 Greening of Internet of Things (IoT)

The network nodes in IoT need or are expected to be independent, battery operated, and life span is most important in smart objects participating in IoT application. Energy consumption increases with the computational capabilities and high rate transmission of data. In near future IoT will lead to significant increase in energy consumption, thus there will emerge the need and research for energy-efficient sensing and green energy to make the network devices more energy efficient [5, 13, 15].

16.6.4   Security

In IoT security of the embedded devices along with the data is the major issue and challenge. As for embedded system, security is not at all new but as more and more devices are connected, potential threats to security scales up [14]. In IoT, as all the devices are connected to each other, IoT architecture is complex because of the heterogeneity in IoT applications which provide attackers with a platform to invade the system [10, 15]. IoT architecture suffers from numerous device- or network-based security issues like object safety and security, data confidentiality, unauthorized access, network security and security due to diversity in the IoT applications [1, 5, 6, 8, 9, 11–13].

16.6.5   Diversity

IoT is a heterogeneous network and almost every application nowadays intends to use an IoT network. As a result, the market is being flooded with IoT devices with fewer safety checks, and it has been observed that more than 90% of the devices suffer from firmware security vulnerability. The challenge is that it is difficult to design a common security system for such diverse IoT devices [9].

16.6.6   Object Safety and Security

IoT objects may spread over a large geographical area in which they can be easily accessed by attackers. So they need to be protected against physical damage and logical attack by malicious entities [12, 13].

16.6.7   Data Confidentiality and Unauthorized Access

Data confidentiality and unauthorized access represent the fundamental security issues in IoT architecture. It includes defining the access control and object authentication process. Data confidentiality seems more relevant in the business context, as data confidentiality may be important to protect competitiveness and market values [1].

16.6.8   Architecture

Also, in IoT devices sensors provide the data for processing, and it is required to have proper encryption technique for data transmitted to maintain data integrity. The threat associated with this may be more logically represented in Figure 16.4 below [9].

Many access controls have been proposed to ensure authentication. Widely used is Role Based Access System (RBAS) [1]. The main advantage of RBAS is that the access rights can be changed based on the role assigned to the user. RFID is the main authorization technology and with more and more devices being integrated in the IoT, RFID lacks proper authentication mechanism [6, 13].

16.6.9   Network and Routing Information Security

In IoT data from a large number of sensors travels over the diverse network through wired or wireless links using various routing protocols like TCP/IP. The network should be able

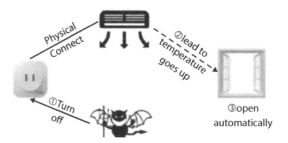

Figure 16.4 Block diagram showing an IoT system.

to handle the data and provide security against external interference or monitoring [6]. Routing information attacks mainly focus on routing protocols of IoT, which may lead to extended source path and end-to-end delay in transmission. This leads to requirement of secure network protocols to establish a secure link among IoT devices and provide quality services [13].

In the last few years IoT has emerged as a hot research and application area. The concept behind the (IoT is to embed the intelligence to the objects so that they can communicate autonomously and can exchange information. IoT transitions human-to-human communication to human-to-machine and machine-to-machine communication. This paper presents the major requirements for the implementation of an IoT system and finally addresses the various research and implementation challenges faced by IoT technology. Deployment of IoT solutions could be hard and will bring more serious security problems and other challenges. This creates a new era of research in which the focus of researchers will be to solve the issues presented by IoT. The major challenges being presented by IoT is scalability as more and more devices are being added at a very fast rate. The next most prominent research fields in IoT are communication range, data storage and power management. In addition to challenges presented, IoT will be significantly benefitting people, professionals and economies in the near future.

References

1. Farooq, M.U.; Waseem, M.; Mazhar, S.; Khairi, A.; and Kamal, T,; A Review on Internet of Things (IoT). International Journal of Computer Applications 2015, 113, 1:1-7.
2. Monika. and Sharma, R.; Research paper on Internet of things. International Journal in Multidisciplinary and Academic Research 2017, 6, 3:1-7.
3. Gubbi, J.; Buyya, R.; Marusic, S. and Palaniswami, M.; Internet of Things (IoT): A vision, architectural elements, and future directions. Future Generation Computer Systems 2013, 29: 1645-1660.
4. Miorandi, D.; Sicari, S.; Pellegrini, F.D. and Chlamtac, I.; Internet of things: vision, application and research challenges. Adhoc Networks 2012,10:1497-1516.
5. Zanella, A.; and Vangelista, L.; Internet of Things for Smart Cities. IEEE Internet of Things Journal 2014, 1:22-32.
6. Burhanuddin, M.A.; Mohammed, A.; Ismail, R. and Basiron, H; Internet of Things Architecture: Current Challenges and Future Direction of Research. International Journal of Applied Engineering Research 2017, 12,21:11055-11061.

7. Kahan, R.; Khan, S.U.; Zaheer, R. and Khan, S.; Future Internet: The Internet of Things Architecture, Possible Applications and Key Challenges. In: 10th International Conference on Frontiers of Information Technology, Islamabad: IEEE Xplore 2012, 257-260.

8. Ray, P.P.; A survey on Internet of Things architectures. Journal of King Saud University – Computer and Information Sciences 2018, 30:291-319.

9. Khalid, A.; Internet of Thing Architecture and Research Agenda. International Journal of Computer Science and Mobile Computing 2016, 5, 3:351-356.

10. Jindal, F.; Jamar, R. and Churi, P.; Future and Challenges of Internet of Things. International Journal of Computer Science & Information Technology 2018, 0, 2:13-25.

11. Lin, J.; Yu, W.; Zhang, N.; Yang, X.; Zhang, H. and Zaho, W.; A Survey on Internet of Things: Architecture, Enabling Technologies, Security and Privacy, and Applications. IEEE Internet of Things Journal 2017, 4, 5:1-17.

12. Zhou, W.; Zhang, Y.; and Liu, P.; The Effect of IoT New Features on Security and Privacy: New Threats, Existing Solutions, and Challenges Yet to Be Solved. IEEE Internet of Things Journal 2018, 6,2:1606-1616.

13. Suo, H.; Wan, J.; Zou, C. and Liu, J.; Security in the Internet of Things: A Review.In: International Conference on Computer Science and Electronics Engineering, Hangzhou: IEEE Xplore 2012, 3:648-651.

14. Babar, S.; Stango, A.; Prasad, N.; Sen, J. and Prasad, R.; Proposed Embedded Security Framework for Internet of Things (IoT). In: 2nd International Conference on Wireless Communication, Vehicular-Technology, Information Theory and Aerospace and Electronics System Technology (Wireless VITAE), Chennai: IEEE Xplore 2011.

15. Ukil, A.; Sen, J. and Koilakonda,S.; Embedded Security for Internet of Things. In: 2nd National Conference on Emerging Trends and Applications in Computer Science, Shillong: IEEE Xplore 2011.

17

FinFET Technology for Low-Power Applications

Bindu Madhavi*, Suman Lata Tripathi and Bhagwan Shree Ram

School of Electronics and Electrical Engineering, Lovely Professional University, Punjab, India

Abstract

In this chapter, advanced FinFET Technology is reviewed over conventional type MOSFET to evaluate the parameters like performance, power optimization in VLSI circuits using predictive technology computer-aided design (TCAD) Simulator. FinFET technology using TCAD simulator is to evaluate prefabrication transistor performance. TCAD simulation is an essential tool for the identification of variable sources and to predict their control in the development of technology and power optimization. It also plays a vital role in developing accurate statistical compact models for SRAM design, characterization, circuit simulation and verification. A two-stage compact model strategy will be used to understand the interplay between the process and statistical variability. In this article, the parameters like short channel effect, quantum tunneling effect and hot electron effect are explained. The short channel will reduce the voltage variations that are obtained while processing. The Quantum mechanism will reduce the power consumption in a very effective way. Hot electron effect will accelerate the electrons while processing. Hence by using the FinFET strategy this effect will reduce the voltage variations, power consumption. FinFET is also explored for different low-power CMOS-based digital circuit and memory applications.

Keywords: FinFET, TCAD, variability, dtco, short channel effect, quantum tunnelling, hot electron effect

17.1 Introduction

Increasing complexity with several applications per IC chip leads VLSI designer to rework for IC area, execution, cost and reliability; power considerations that were generally of just optional significance a few decades ago but as of late power is being given a practically identical load to region and speed. Low cost, high-performance devices are used in the IC technology and this will change from micron devices to submicron devices [1]. The ICs are needed to be optimized for speed and power consumption that are conflicting in nature, i.e., higher speed prompts higher power scattering and the other way around. Convenient and handheld devices request fast calculation and complex usefulness with low power utilization [2]. For these applications, normal power utilization is a vital structure imperative to be considered. The power is beginning to Confine the speed of VLSI processors.

---

*Corresponding author: bindumadhavi.t@gmail.com

Suman Lata Tripathi, Dushyant Kumar Singh, Sanjeevikumar Padmanaban, and P. Raja (eds.) Design and Development of Efficient Energy Systems, (297–306) © 2021 Scrivener Publishing LLC

Low leakage current and high current drive capability of FinFET show its suitability for the low power consumption, high switching speed and improved power delay product compared to conventional CMOS [3].

The requirement for low power Consumption is expanding as parts are getting to be battery-worked, smaller and require greater usefulness and highlights. Designers experience a few emphases to streamline control to accomplish their capacity spending plans. In spite of the fact that power is to be enhanced at all dimensions of deliberations, improvements in early structure stages have much effect in lessening power. As a result of the shrinking of the devices, transistor leakage power has expanded exponentially. As the component measure ends up smaller, shorter direct lengths will result in an increment in the subthreshold current. In light of scaling, subthreshold voltage additionally results in increment in subthreshold current since transistors can't be killed totally. It is vital to pick the circuit topology that would yield wanted execution for a given power spending plan. The proposed FinFET-based circuit reduces the leakage current which ultimately results in energy consumption reduction [4].

Numerous procedures utilized for improvement of intensity are the asynchronous logic and adiabatic logic. These two advances have been joined to make an Asynchronous, Adiabatic Logic philosophy, called Asynchrobatic Logic. The fundamental low-control structure systems incorporate clock gating for lessening dynamic power, or multiple voltage thresholds (multi-Vt) to diminish dynamic power. At the circuit level, low-power technique can be utilized for general computerized frameworks. There are various conventional strategies on low-power configuration, including Power Island, Clock Gating, Transistor Resizing, and Operating in sub-edge routine, MTCMOS, VTCMOS, and various leakage power reduction techniques, for example, utilizing Sleep Transistor, Forward/Reverse Body Biasing. The studies show that FinFET is immune to short channel effects (SCEs) and has better high frequency operations [5].

FinFETs having various structure alternatives and better authority over channel give low force designs and higher noise resistance. A fin field-effect transistor (FinFET) is a multi-gate device; it is type of MOSFET (metal-oxide-semiconductor field-effect transistor) that built on a substrate where the gate is placed on two, three, or four sides of the channel, forming a double gate structure. Compared to the more usual planar technology, FinFET transistor technology has many more significant advantages in Integrated Circuits design. It has been observed that the number of transistors on a given area of silicon doubles every two years. FinFETs can be designed as 2D and 3D structures that rise above the substrate and 3D structures just resemble as a fin. FinFET uses lower threshold voltages and also results in better performance with lower power dissipation. Figure 17.1 shows the structure of vertical channel FinFET.

Customary CMOS Technology is seriously influenced by the short channel impacts when it goes past 45nm. Therefore gate FinFET innovation [6] has been presented to overcome requirements of the ordinary mass CMOS scaling by changing the structure of the device, to such an extent that MOSFET gate length can be scaled further with thick oxide. Hence, the scaling should be possible in the FinFET Technology past the constraint of traditional mass CMOS. The design of FinFET diminishes the transistor spillage with a superior command over the channel. CMOS simple circuits, since the inventory voltage has downsized, a portion of the transistors work in the close to limit system, and this locale accordingly should be precisely spoken to by the LUT approach being utilized.

The arrangement obstruction of the fins and the lower portability in a channel along the fin sidewalls corrupts the most extreme drive current. FinFET is centered around the

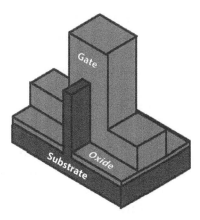

Figure 17.1 Basic Structure of FinFET.

fluctuation of mindful minimal model extraction and age innovation supporting structure innovation co-improvement (DTCO) [3]. DTCO has gotten obligatory in trend-setting innovation hubs [5, 6]. Different Oscillations are using in the stages of inverter addition and it provides the same range of frequency. Propagation delay increases the addition of more inverting stages in the circuit. The number of stages is related to the delay of Propagation which adds the oscillation frequency. When a stage of inverting goes beyond nine it is not practically acceptable to the addition. It increases the disappearance of the power circuit. The most important measurable factor is power in the designing of VLSI.

Based on CMOS produces signals of less frequency when the numbers of delay cells are added. Hence it ingests less energy. When hundreds of an inverting stage is added and it gives very low oscillating frequency then it is easy to design and invent. Frequency variation range is several in voltage controlled oscillator from megahertz to gigahertz. A voltage-controlled oscillator is used to achieve a small frequency range oscillation. It overcomes some problems like manufacturing complexity, power of high consumption and noise of large phases. A good voltage controlled oscillator design more ideal characteristics and satisfy the noise of the minimum phase, consumption of lower power, high gain factor and frequency linearity high.

In the design block voltage controlled oscillator is most important in the frequency of radio wireless communication system. It converts the voltage of input into the frequency of output. Voltage controlled frequency are of two types; one is an oscillator of Waveform and the other is an oscillator of resonant. Voltage-controlled oscillators are having control to hold the range. Voltage-controlled oscillator provides circuitry clock for design. It adjusts the phase-locked loop frequency filter. It is similar to those frequencies of oscillation reverse osmosis that's controlled by the current with the help of an inverter. The design proposed is mainly used to design the phase-locked loop. Much reverse osmosis has wafers which act like line structures of test scribed. The measuring effects are used for manufacturing the process of variation during wafer testing.

17.2   Exiting Multiple-Gate MOSFET Architectures

Today versatile and registering markets keep on improving at a fast rate conveying more execution in smaller structure factors with higher force efficiencies. As per Moore's law, the number of transistors in a region should therefore rise consistently. To accomplish this, transistors ought to get smaller to oblige therefore the number per unit territory. While downsizing the device channel length, the short channel impacts are raised. Based on the technology of scaling FinFET will solve the problems which are related to the effects of the channel. This is done when the scaling process is continued. More FinFET can be implemented on the same area of the chip due to low leakage power consumption. Hence from this it can be observed that FinFET technology progress will be maintained in a particular manner. Figure 17.2 (a), (b) shows a conventional ultra-thin body MOSFET and double-gate MOSFET.

The structure of DG is rotated by maintaining the gate leakage current in lowest form. By using the standard lithography technique all the gate electrodes in the transistor will be self-aligned. Figure 17.3 (a), (b), (c) shows a comparison of planner double gate with vertical Fin shaped double-gate (DG-FinFET) and triple-gate (TG-FinFET) structures [8, 10]. When the device is in OFF-state the channel will conduct low leakage current in through the body in this planar substrate. In FinFETs the length of the gate is equal to the thickness of the channel. In the 1980s, a quarter century ago, multi-gate MOSFET has introduced. From this multi-gate transistor operation it can be observed that this will improve the switching properties of bias effect [9]. In the same way this transistor will deplete the silicon body fully based on the effect of bias.

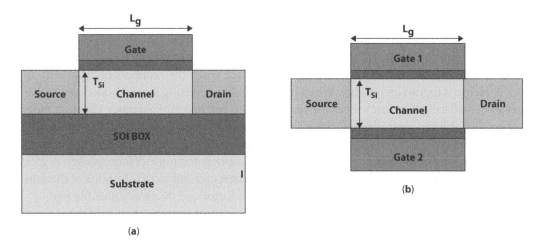

Figure 17.2 (a) Ultra-thin body (b) Dual gate.

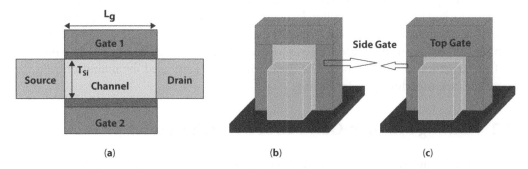

Figure 17.3 (a) Planar double-gate FET (b) 90° rotation DG-MOSFET (c) 90° rotation TG-MOSFET.

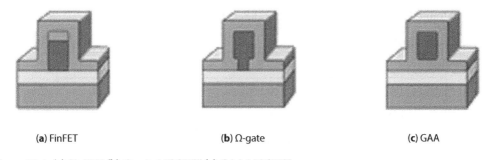

(a) FinFET   **(b)** Ω-gate   **(c)** GAA

Figure 17.4 (a) FinFET (b) Ω-gate MOSFET (c) GAA MOSFET.

Hence a decade later FinFET is introduced by using SOI substrate. By using the devices of silicon nano wires, the horizontal gate-all-around (GAA) transistor will be created and enabled. The drive current of the transistor will be increased when the nano wires are stacked on the top of the transistor. Figure 17.4 presents the structural comparison of FinFET with Ω-gate MOSFET and GAA MOSFET.

The chip designers have to concentrate mainly on power consumption, speed, silicon area and delay. CMOS is the most widely used technology for integrated circuit design. To implement any digital circuit, both n-MOSFET and p-MOSFETs are required. The reliability of another aspect needs to be considered for any Chip design. It was observed that FinFET with SOI layer shows a self-heating effect because of the presence of an insulating layer between the channel and planner bulk region. So, the self-heating effect that is also known as negative temperature bias was overcome through bulk FinFET structures with bottom spacers [11]. The bulk FinFET structure was also explored for low-power and high-speed operations.

17.3   FinFET Design and Analysis

There is a silicon fin in the structure of FinFET device. This silicon fin is placed on either side of the substrate of the silicon insulator. There are generally two gates in this device that are independently operated. Different configurations are available in the FinFET and it is shown in Figure 17.5. This characteristic will vary VGS in the device of n-type FinFET. Hence compared to double-gate mode in FinFET device swing degradation and drain induced barrier are less in single-gate mode. Table 7.1 presents the ON and OFF state current of independent gate FinFET (IG-FinFET) [7] for different values of back-gate bias voltages.

The effective electrical width of the device is based on fin height. The variation in fin height directly transfers to width variation in the device. All fin-based devices will affect

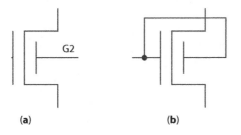

(a)   **(b)**

Figure 17.5 (a) IG-FinFET (b) Shorted Gates.

Table 17.1 Current I_{ON} and I_{OFF} for different back-gate voltages.

Back gate voltages	I_{on} (A)	I_{off} (A)
$V_{G2} = V_{G1}$	3×10^{-3}	1.02×10^{-7}
$V_{G2} = -0.4V$	5.41×10^{-4}	4.64×10^{-10}
$V_{G2} = -0.2V$	7.52×10^{-4}	4.2×10^{-9}
$V_{G2} = 0V$	1.05×10^{-3}	9.2×10^{-8}
$V_{G2} = 0.2V$	1.31×10^{-3}	5×10^{-6}

with the same percentage of error in device width. Fins need to be very tall in size to match or exceed the effective width of the FinFET device (Figure 17.6). If the selected fin width is below the level of controllable capabilities of optical lithography, then it results in poor fin width control. Also, the line edge roughness (LER) of the process leads to considerable variability in local fin width (LWR).

Threshold voltage reduces with increased fin-thickness. At shorter channel lengths, the surface potential depends not only on capacitive coupling between the gate and the channel region but also on the capacitance of source/fin and drain/fin junction. As the fin-thickness increases, the width of the source/fin and drain/fin depletion region increases, which decreases the source/fin and drain/fin junction capacitances. As a result the gate to surface potential coupling increases and hence the threshold voltage decreases with the increased film thickness.

The effect of threshold voltage reduces with the increase in the thickness of the fin. The surface potential depends not only on capacitive coupling between the gate, the channel region but also on the capacitance of source and drain junction at the shorter channel lengths. Whenever there is an increase in the fin-thickness, then there increases the width of the source and drain/depletion region, with which it decreases capacitances at the source and drain junction. Thus, it results in an increase in the gate to surface potential coupling and hence it increases the film thickness with the decrease in the voltage. At low supply voltages, the I_{ON}/I_{OFF} ratio is higher for FinFET when compared with Bulk CMOS and at the same time at high supply voltages, the I_{ON}/I_{OFF} ratio is higher for bulk CMOS that FinFET. Thus the bulk CMOS has a lower I_{OFF} when compared with the FinFET and the FinFET has

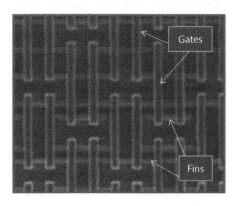

Figure 17.6 Fin width variability.

a higher I_{ON} compared to bulk CMOS. TCAD tool is needed to perform device optimization and support device and process integration engineers. Below 20nm technology node, the Fin-shaped Field Effect Transistor or Tri-gate transistor requires extensive use of 3D TCAD simulations and random variability in transistor performance is determined using the noise like impedance field method via 3-D device TCAD simulations.

For instance, a 14nm FinFET structure appears in Figure 17.7. It shows a pattern in the entryway opposition which is not quite the same as the regular planar gadgets. As the blade number increments from 2 to 8, the entryway obstruction of the FinFET diminishes. The inborn addition (gm/gds) of 14nm FinFET is 3.8 occasions higher than that of 28nm and expends 37% less DC power than 28nm RF FET at the most extreme fT. In 3-D structure, 14nm FinFET has a beneficial format with territory adequacy (- 47%), contrasted with 28nm planar gadget for the door width.

Short-channel effects (SCE) can be mostly ascribed to the drain induced barrier lowering (DIBL) impact which causes a decrease in the edge voltage as the channel length diminishes. Be that as it may, in an SOI gadget SCE is additionally impacted by thin-film thickness, dainty film doping thickness, substrate biasing and covered oxide thickness.

Short channel effects arise due to the parasitic electric fields from the source and drain region which ultimately affects the drain current. In a MOSFET, it is expected that the gate has the ultimate control over the channel, thereby controlling the drain current. In the case of short channel devices, where the channel length is in the order of the source and drain regions, the gate doesn't get complete control of the channel and hence "short channel effects" arise. In the case of FinFET, the gate is present all around the channel like a fin (hence the name), giving the gate complete control over the channel. Table 17.2 shows a comparison among bulk MOSFET with FinFET in terms of performance parameters.

A quantum tunneling effect consists of both n source and p drain. In the design of FinFET the band to band tunneling effect puts a new scaling factor. This is used as a mechanism for the operation of this FiFET design. The electron-hole pair generated by the quantum to quantum tunnel effect will overlap the region of the gate and drain and contribute the high channel doping.

In the hot electron effect based on FinFET, hot electrons are an integral part of the operation conditions. There is no way to prevent the generation of hot electrons since they are always present in normal operation. The hot electrons effect arises mainly due to the high

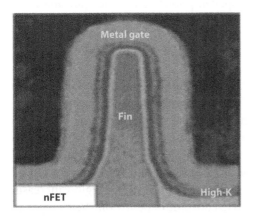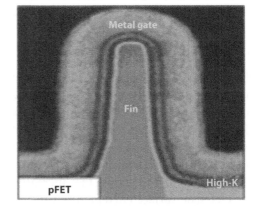

Figure 17.7 14nm FinFET Structure.

Table 17.2 Comparison of MOSFET and FinFET.

Name of parameter	Bulk mosfet	FinFET
Short Channel Effect	Here gate has the ultimate control over the channel	The gate is present all around the channel
Quantum Tunnelling	Power consumption is more Channel doping is low	Power consumption is less and Channel doping is high
Hot Electron Effect	Electrons won't get accelerated in this channel	Electrons are an integral part of the operating conditions

electric field stress inside the channel region with a shrinking device size. This may induce degradation of the gate oxide.

17.4 Low-Power Applications

The FinFET has emerged as a promising candidate to replace conventional MOSFET in CMOS-based digital circuit design for low-power applications. Several digital applications can be implemented with nFinFET and pFinFET replacing conventional MOSFETs. TCAD also helps in software-based design and analysis of CMOS-based implementation using advanced FET like FinFET.

17.4.1 FinFET-Based Digital Circuit Design

The FinFET can replace conventional n-MOSFET and p-MOSFET in CMOS VLSI circuit design. Several applications related to combinations and sequential circuit can be easily implemented with it for low-power and high-speed operations.

17.4.2 FinFET-Based Memory Design

Smart portable devices need bulk memories with SRAM and DRAM cell that consume less power to enhance battery lifetime [12–14]. The design of SRAM cell with 7nm technology node made is feasible for a smart device like laptop, cell phones and other portables and wearables. Figure 17.8 presents the FinFET-based design of SRAM and DRAM cells.

17.4.3 FinFET-Based Biosensors

FinFET can be used for biomedical applications by incorporation of nano-gap cavity region under the side gate just like existing DGMSFET-based biosensors [15]. The cavity region introduced is dielectrically modulated through the changes in presence of bio-species and shows a considerable change in electrical parameters of the device. These changes can be observed and measured to detect the presence of biomolecule. A GaAs FinFET [16] based biosensor was proposed with cavity region between gate and source drain region (Figure 17.9). It was shown that increase in dielectric constant of cavity region increases the ON-state surface current. The value of dielectric constant depends on the changes in bio-species present in cavity region.

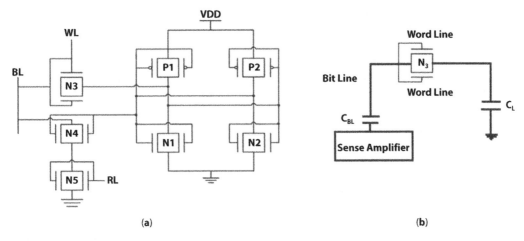

Figure 17.8 (a) 7T SRAM cell with FinFET (b) 1T DRAM cell with FinFET.

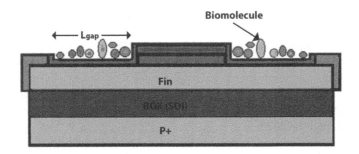

Figure 17.9 Side view of FinFET as biosensing cavity region.

17.5   Conclusion

From the literature survey, a comparison of performance characteristics of FinFET over the conventional planar device has been observed. The short channel will reduce the voltage variations that are obtained while processing. The Quantum mechanism will reduce power consumption in a very effective way. A hot electron effect will accelerate the electrons while processing. The predictive simulation tool TCAD with DTCO (Design Technology Co-optimization) process having limitations in terms of channel length and capacitive effect. Thus, it can overcome by reducing the length of the channel like 14nm (example) which increases the performance of the circuit. It clearly shows that FinFET-based logical circuits are promising substitutes compared to conventional Bulk CMOS.

References

1. Mukku P.K., Naidu S., Mokara D., Pydi Reddy P., Sunil Kumar K. (2020) Recent Trends and Challenges on Low-Power FinFET Devices. In: Satapathy S., Bhateja V., Mohanty J.,

Udgata S. (eds) *Smart Intelligent Computing and Applications. Smart Innovation, Systems and Technologies*, vol 160. Springer, Singapore.

2. J. Zhang, G. Niu, W. Cai and K. Imura, "Comparison of PMOS and NMOS in a 14-nm RF FinFET technology: RF Characteristics and Compact Modeling," 2020 IEEE 20th Topical Meeting on Silicon Monolithic Integrated Circuits in RF Systems (SiRF), *San Antonio, TX, USA*, 2020, pp. 47-49.

3. B. G. Kumar, S. V. Gaded and P. Srividya, "Power and Delay Optimization of FinFET based Adiabatic Logic SRAM Cell," 2019 4th International Conference on Recent Trends on Electronics, Information, Communication & Technology (RTEICT), Bangalore, India, 2019, pp. 617-621.

4. Senthil Kumar V.M., Ravindrakumar S. (2019) Design of an Area-Efficient FinFET-Based Approximate Multiplier in 32-nm Technology for Low-Power Application. In: Wang J., Reddy G., Prasad V., Reddy V. (eds) *Soft Computing and Signal Processing. Advances in Intelligent Systems and Computing*, vol 898. Springer, Singapore.

5. S. M. Sharma, S. Dasgupta and M. V. Kartikeyan, "FinFETs for RF Applications: A Literature review," *2018 Conference on Emerging Devices and Smart Systems (ICEDSS), Tiruchengode, 2018*, pp. 280-287.

6. R. S. Pal, S. Sharma and S. Dasgupta, "Recent trend of FinFET devices and its challenges: A review," 2017 Conference on Emerging Devices and Smart Systems (ICEDSS), Tiruchengode, 2017, pp. 150-154.

7. G. Pei and E. C. C. Kan, "Independently driven DG MOSFETs for mixed-signal circuits: Part I–Quasi-static and nonquasi-static channel coupling," *IEEE Trans. Electron Devices*, vol. 51, no. 12, pp. 2086-2093.

8. Namrata Mendiratta, Suman Lata Tripathi, "A Review on Performance Comparison of Advanced MOSFET Structures below 45nm Technology node," *Journal of Semiconductors*, IOP science, vol. 41, pp.1-10, 2020.

9. Shekhar Verma, Suman Lata Tripathi, Mohinder Bassi "Performance Analysis of FinFET device Using Qualitative Approach for Low-Power applications" *Devices for Integrated Circuit (DevIC)*, pp. 84-88, 23-24 March, 2019, Kalyani, India.

10. S L Tripathi, Ramanuj Mishra, R A Mishra, "Characteristic comparison of connected DG FINFET, TG FINFET and Independent Gate FINFET on 32 nm technology" *IEEE ICPCES*, pp.1-7, December, 2012

11. S L Tripathi, Ramanuj Mishra, V Narendra, R A Mishra, "High performance Bulk FinFET with Bottom Spacer," *IEEE CONECCT*, pp.1-5, 2013.

12. Nachappa S.M., Jeevitha A.S., Vasundara Patel K.S., "Comparative Analysis of Digital Circuits Using 16 nm FinFET and HKMG PTM Models" FICC, *Advances in Intelligent Systems and Computing*, vol 886. Springer, 2019.

13. T. Santosh Kumar, Suman Lata Tripathi, "Implementation of CMOS SRAM Cells in 7, 8, 10 and 12-Transistor Topologies and their Performance Comparison," *International Journal of Engineering and Advanced Technology (Scopus)*, Vol. 8 (2S2), pp. 227-229, January 2019.

14. Suman Lata Triapthi, "Low Power High Performance Tunnel FET: Analysis for IOT applica-tions," in *Handbook of Research on the Internet of Things Applications in Robotics and Automation*. IGI Global, ISBN: 9781522595748, pp. 47-57, 2019.

15. Namrata Mendiratta, Suman Lata Tripathi, Sanjeevikumar Padmanaban and Eklas Hossain, "Design and Analysis of Heavily Doped n+ Pocket Asymmetrical Junction-Less Double Gate MOSFET for Biomedical Applications" *Applied Sciences*, MDPI, vol. 10, pp. 2499, 2020.

16. Anuj Chhabraa, Ajay Kumarb, Rishu Chaujara, "Sub-20 nm GaAs junctionless FinFET for bio-sensing application," *Vacuum*, vol. 160, pp. 467–471, 2019.

18

An Enhanced Power Quality Single-Source Large Step-Up Switched-Capacitor Based Multi-Level Inverter Configuration with Natural Voltage Balancing of Capacitors

Mahdi Karimi[1], Paria Kargar[1], Kazem Varesi[1]* and Sanjeevikumar Padmanaban[2]

[1]Power Electronics Research Lab. (PERL), Faculty of Electrical Engineering, Sahand University of Technology, Tabriz, Iran
[2]Department of Energy Technology, Aalborg University, Esbjerg, Denmark

Abstract

This chapter proposes a single-source high step-up switched-capacitor based 19-level inverter topology with enhanced power quality that can be extended by addition of switched-capacitor units. The extended topology can produce larger gain and voltage steps. The reduced DC source, increased gain per devices, increased steps per devices, self-voltage balancing of capacitor, capability of supplying low/medium power factor loads, low THD (high quality) of generated output voltage waveform and downsized output filter are important merits of suggested topology. The normalized voltage stress on level generation part is equal or less than 33%, which is another important advantage. The relatively high voltage stress on H-bridge switches ($=V_{o,max}$) is main shortcoming of suggested topology. The proper operation of suggested topology has been confirmed by simulation results.

Keywords: Multi-level inverter, power quality, step-up, switched-capacitor, voltage stress

18.1 Introduction

Over the last decade, due to the increasing demand for high power quality, Multi-Level Inverters (MLIs) have attracted particular attention [1]. The high power quality and low Total Harmonic Distortion (THD) are prerequisite requirements in industrial applications such as: Hybrid Electric Vehicles (HEVs), Flexible Alternating Current Transmission System (FACTS) devices, reactive power compensators, AC motor drives, renewable energy systems and Microgrids [2–5]. The MLIs can suitably be applied in medium or high voltage/power applications [6]. These converters produce a high-quality stair-case output voltage with minimum THD [7]. The THD of generated output voltage in MLIs can be further reduced by proper switching techniques, like Selective Harmonic Elimination (SHE). Simple structure,

---

*Corresponding author: k.varesi@sut.ac.ir

Suman Lata Tripathi, Dushyant Kumar Singh, Sanjeevikumar Padmanaban, and P. Raja (eds.) *Design and Development of Efficient Energy Systems*, (307–338) © 2021 Scrivener Publishing LLC

easy control, low Electro-Magnetic Interference (EMI), low voltage stress on semiconductors and eliminated or reduced-size output filter are other important advantages of MLIs [8, 9]. The MLIs employ single or several DC sources as inputs to produce stair-case AC output voltage [10]. In Microgrids, the input DC sources of MLIs can be provided by solar cells (PVs), Fuel Cells (FCs), wind turbines or batteries [11–13]. The MLIs can effectively be utilized in grid-tied or off-grid applications. Figure 18.1 describes the role of MLIs in a typical Microgrid. Usually, a step-up DC-DC converter is required for lifting low output voltage of PVs, FCs or batteries. But in the case of high-gain inverters, the DC-DC converters can be removed.

In recently published articles, various topologies and control strategies have been presented for multi-level converters. The MLI structures can be classified into three general types: 1) Diode Clamp Multi-Level Inverters (DCMLIs) 2) Flying Capacitor based Multi-Level Inverters (FCMLIs), and 3) Cascaded Multi-Level Inverters (CMLIs) [14, 15]. The voltage balancing of capacitors is the main challenge in DCMLIs and FCMLIs [16]. Also, the large number of diodes and capacitors required in DCMLIs and FCMLIs is another drawback. Although CMLIs utilize less diodes and capacitors, they usually require many DC voltage sources, leading to increased cost, weight and size of converter, whereas FCMLI and DCMLI use only single DC source [17, 18]. In recent years, many new topologies have been suggested to address the limitations of classical converters, which attempt to reduce the number of devices (sources, switches, gate-driver circuits, diodes and capacitors) [19]. The switched-capacitor based MLIs are well known for their reduced source count. These converters can be categorized as: 1) step-down [20], 2) step-up or high-gain [21, 22] 3) unity-gain [23, 24]. In the former, the maximum output voltage is larger than the sum of DC sources, but in the latter, the $V_{o,max}$ is the same as the sum of input DC sources. Three new single DC source 9-level switched-capacitor based multi-level inverters have been suggested in [25–27]. Self-voltage balancing of capacitors, boosting capability and generating negative voltage level without H-bridge are significant advantages. However, high ratio of the number of semiconductors per number of levels is the main disadvantage of these topologies. In [28], a unity-gain T-type based multi-level inverter based on switched-capacitor cells has

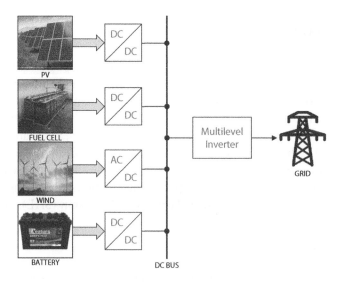

Figure 18.1 The role of multi-level inverters in a typical Microgrid.

been described which benefits from Natural voltage balancing of capacitor with simple control strategy, inherent generating negative voltage levels. In the other side, the high number of DC voltage sources which leads to high cost, weight and size of the converter is the main drawback. A new K-type single-source switched-capacitor cell-based multi-level inverter has been suggested in [29]. High step-up capability, modularity and self-voltage balancing of capacitors are the main benefits. High per unit total voltage stress is the important disadvantage of this structure. A P-type single-source switched-capacitor module for asymmetric multilevel inverters has been suggested in [30]. Natural voltage balancing of capacitors, boosting capability and producing negative voltage levels without additional circuit are the main advantages. However, High per unit total voltage stress is the significant shortcoming. A new single-source switched-capacitor multi-level inverter with gain of 2 has been suggested in [31]. Inherit generating negative voltages levels and natural voltage balancing of capacitors are its merits. High ratio of the number of semiconductors per number of levels is the important drawback. A new T-type modular single-source MLI based on switched-capacitor cells has been presented in [32]. High boosting capability and generating negative voltage levels without H-bridge are the significant benefits. However, a high number of capacitors and IGBTs which leads to high cost and size of the converter is the main disadvantage. Two novel 9-level switched-capacitor based inverters have been suggested in [33, 34] where, inherent producing negative voltages levels and step-up capability are the main merits. On the other hand, the high ratio of the number of semiconductors per number of levels is the important shortcoming of these structures. In [35], a new step-up single-source switched-capacitor based multi-level inverter has been presented. Natural voltage balancing of capacitor and low per unit total voltage stress are the main advantages. High ratio of the number of semiconductors per number of output voltage levels is the important disadvantage. A new 7-level inverter based on switched-capacitor cell has been suggested in [36]. High boosting factor is the main benefit. However, producing negative voltage levels with H-bridge which leads to high voltage stress on H-bridge switches is the significant drawback. A 5-level single-source switched-capacitor based module for multi-level inverters has been suggested in [37]. Inherent generating negative voltage levels and boosting capability are the main merits. A high number of semiconductors is the main disadvantage. A generalized H-bridge based switched-capacitor multi-level inverter has been presented in [38]. Step-up capability and charging capacitors at different values are its advantages. However, a high number of DC sources is required to achieve a higher number of output voltage levels and using H-bridge for generating negative voltage levels are the major disadvantages.

In this chapter, a new switched-capacitor based 19-level inverter has been suggested, which benefits from reduced switches per levels, large boosting factor and natural voltage balancing of capacitors without any additional control circuitry. The relatively high voltage stress on switches of H-bridge is considered as the major drawback of suggested topology.

18.2 Suggested Topology

18.2.1 Circuit Configuration

The suggested configuration (shown in Figure 18.2) is composed of 1) level generation unit, and 2) polarity generation unit. The switched-capacitor structure realizes the level generation

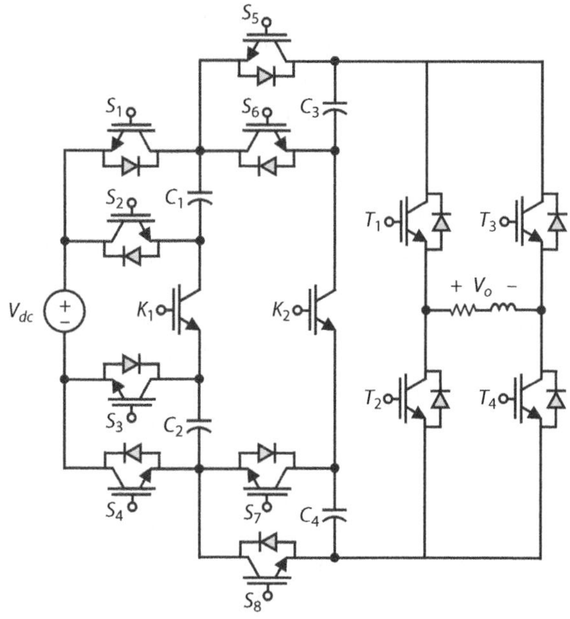

Figure 18.2 Suggested 19-level inverter topology.

unit, where the polarity generation unit is provided by an H-bridge. The suggested structure produces 19 voltage levels using single DC source, 4 capacitors $(C_1\text{-}C_4)$ and 14 unidirectional switches $(S_1\text{-}S_8, K_1, K_2 \& T_1\text{-}T_4)$. Since each unidirectional switch requires a driver circuit, the number of switches and gate-driver circuits are the same. The $S_1\text{-}S_8$ and $T_1\text{-}T_4$ switches are composed of an IGBT and an antiparallel-diode. The K_1 and K_2 switches have no antiparallel diode. Thus:

$$N_{Step} = 19, N_{DC} = 1, N_{Capacitor} = 4, N_{Switch} = N_{IGBT} = N_{Driver} = 14, N_{Diode} = 12 \quad (18.1)$$

To avoid short circuiting of capacitor, the $(S_1, S_2), (S_3, S_4), (S_5, S_6), (S_7, S_8)$ switches should not be turned on simultaneously. Also, to prevent short circuiting of input DC source, the switch sets of $(S_2\text{-}S_3, K_1), (S_1\text{-}S_6, S_4\text{-}S_7, K_2), (S_1, S_4, S_5, S_8, T_1\text{-}T_2)$ and $(S_1, S_4, S_5, S_8, T_3\text{-}T_4)$ should be switched in a complementary manner.

18.2.2   Generation of Output Voltage Steps

The switching scheme and charge/discharge status of capacitors during generation of each output voltage levels have been shown in Table 18.1. Note that "1" and "0" represent the ON and OFF states of switches, respectively. Also, "▲", "▼" and "-" are the symbols showing respectively the charging, discharging or not-used states of capacitors. As seen from Table 18.1, the $(S_1, S_2), (S_3, S_4), (S_5, S_6), (S_7, S_8), (T_1, T_2)$ and (T_3, T_4) switches are switched in a complementary manner.

Based on the switching pattern shown in Table 18.1, the voltage of C_1, C_2, C_3 and C_4 capacitors are regulated to $V_{dc}, V_{dc}, 3V_{dc}$ and $3V_{dc}$, respectively. Thus: $V_{C1} = V_{C2} = V_{dc}$ and $V_{C3} = V_{C4} = 3V_{dc}$. Accordingly, the maximum achievable output voltage is equal to summation of input DC

Table 18.1 Switching states, output voltage and capacitors mode of suggested topology.

S_1	S_2	S_3	S_4	S_5	S_6	S_7	S_8	K_1	K_2	T_1	T_2	T_3	T_4	C_1	C_2	C_3	C_4	V_o
0	1	1	0	0	1	1	0	0	0	1	0	0	1	▶	▶	▶	▶	$9V_{dc}$
1	0	1	0	0	1	1	0	1	0	1	0	0	1	◀	▶	▶	▶	$8V_{dc}$
0	1	0	1	0	1	1	0	1	0	1	0	0	1	▶	◀	▶	▶	
1	0	0	1	0	1	1	0	0	0	1	0	0	1	–	–	▶	▶	$7V_{dc}$
0	1	1	0	1	0	1	0	0	1	1	0	0	1	▶	▶	◀	▶	$6V_{dc}$
0	1	1	0	0	1	0	1	0	1	1	0	0	1	▶	▶	▶	◀	
1	0	1	0	0	1	0	1	1	0	1	0	0	1	◀	▶	▶	–	$5V_{dc}$
0	1	1	0	0	1	0	1	1	0	1	0	0	1	▶	◀	▶	–	
1	0	0	1	0	1	0	1	0	0	1	0	0	1	–	–	▶	–	$4V_{dc}$
0	1	0	0	1	0	0	1	0	0	1	0	0	1	▶	▶	–	–	$3V_{dc}$
1	0	1	0	1	0	0	1	1	0	1	0	0	1	◀	▶	–	–	$2V_{dc}$
0	1	1	0	1	0	0	1	0	0	1	0	0	1	▶	◀	–	–	
1	0	0	1	1	0	0	0	0	0	1	0	1	0	–	–	–	–	V_{dc}
1	1	1	1	0	0	0	0	1	0	1	0	1	0	◀	–	–	–	0^+
0	1	1	0	1	0	1	0	0	1	0	1	0	1	–	◀	◀	–	0^-
0	1	1	0	0	1	0	1	0	1	0	1	0	1	–	–	–	◀	

(Continued)

Table 18.1 Switching states, output voltage and capacitors mode of suggested topology. (*Continued*)

S_1	S_2	S_3	S_4	S_5	S_6	S_7	S_8	K_1	K_2	T_1	T_2	T_3	T_4	C_1	C_2	C_3	C_4	V_o
1	0	0	1	1	0	0	1	0	0	0	1	1	0	-	-	-	-	$-V_{dc}$
1	0	1	0	1	0	0	1	1	0	0	1	1	0	◀	▶	-	-	$-2V_{dc}$
0	1	0	1	1	0	0	1	1	0	0	1	1	0	▶	◀	-	-	$-3V_{dc}$
0	1	1	0	1	0	0	1	0	0	0	1	1	0	▶	▶	-	-	
1	0	0	1	1	0	1	0	0	0	0	1	1	0	-	-	-	▶	$-4V_{dc}$
1	0	1	0	0	1	0	1	1	0	0	1	1	0	◀	▶	▶	-	$-5V_{dc}$
0	1	0	1	0	1	0	1	1	0	0	1	1	0	▶	◀	▶	-	
0	1	1	0	1	0	1	0	0	1	0	1	1	0	▶	▶	◀	▶	$-6V_{dc}$
0	1	1	0	0	1	0	1	0	1	0	1	1	0	▶	▶	▶	◀	
1	0	1	0	0	1	1	0	0	0	0	1	1	0	-	-	▶	▶	$-7V_{dc}$
1	0	0	1	0	1	1	0	1	0	0	1	1	0	◀	▶	▶	▶	$-8V_{dc}$
0	1	1	0	0	1	1	0	1	0	0	1	1	0	▶	◀	▶	▶	
0	1	0	1	0	1	1	0	0	0	0	1	1	0	▶	▶	▶	▶	$-9V_{dc}$

source and voltage of C_1 to C_4 capacitors, $V_{o,max}=V_{dc}+V_{C1}+V_{C2}+V_{C3}+V_{C4}=9V_{dc}$. For better understanding, the equivalent circuits of suggested topology during different switching states have been shown in Figures 18.3–18.12. The on-state semiconductors as well as the components on flow path have been shown in blue. Also, the regulated voltage of capacitors in each state have been shown in green boxes next to each capacitor. The complete description of each state is presented in the following.

Producing $V_o = \pm 9V_{dc}$ (Figure 18.3): Sine $V_{C1}=V_{C2}=V_{dc}$ and $V_{C3}=V_{C4}=3V_{dc}$, the level generation unit produces the $9V_{dc}$ by cascaded connection of input source and C_1-C_4 capacitors through S_2, S_3, S_6 and S_7 switches. The polarity of output voltage is decided by H-bridge. The positive polarity is produced by turning the T_1 and T_4 switches on. The negative polarity is also reached by conducting the T_2 and T_3 switches.

Producing $V_o = \pm 8V_{dc}$ (Figure 18.4): There are two different switching states (modes) for generating $8V_{dc}$ in level generation unit.

1) *First mode*: In this state the S_1, S_3, S_6, S_7 and K_1 switches are ON. So, the $8V_{dc}$ is generated by cascaded connection of input DC source and C_2, C_3 and C_4 capacitors. Simultaneously, the C_1 is charged by input DC source to V_{dc} through S_1 and S_3 switches ($V_{C1}=V_{dc}$). In his state, the C_2, C_3 and C_4 capacitors are discharged.

2) *Second mode*: The $8V_{dc}$ can also be generated at level generation unit by series connection of input DC source and C_1, C_3 and C_4 capacitors, through S_6, S_7 and K_1 switches. At the same time, the voltage of C_2 is charged to V_{dc} by input DC source, through S_2, S_4 switches ($V_{C2}=V_{dc}$). In his state, the C_1, C_3 and C_4 capacitors are discharged.

The positive load voltage polarity can be produced by turning the (T_1, T_4) switches on. The negative polarity is also generated by (T_2, T_3) switches.

Producing $V_o = \pm 7V_{dc}$ (Figure 18.5): In this state, the S_1, S_4, S_6 and S_7 switches are turned on. Accordingly, the $7V_{dc}$ is produced at the output port of level generation unit by series

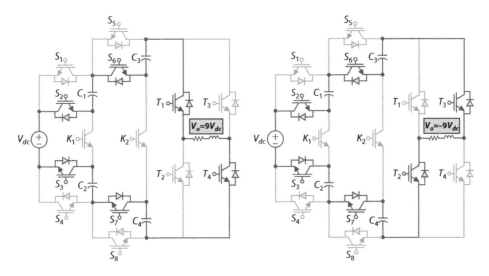

Figure 18.3 Operational modes for producing $\pm 9V_{dc}$ output voltage steps.

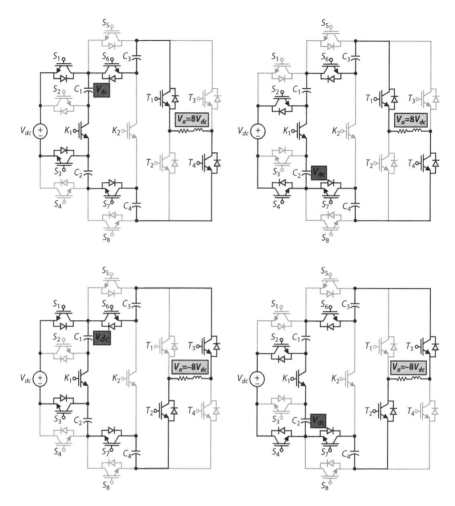

Figure 18.4 Operational modes for producing $\pm 8V_{dc}$ output voltage steps.

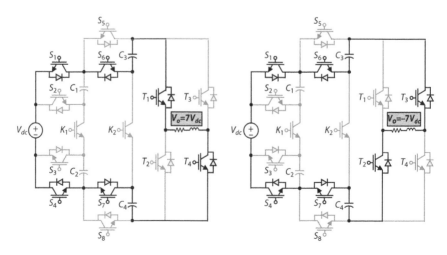

Figure 18.5 Operational modes for producing $\pm 7V_{dc}$ output voltage steps.

connection of input DC source, C_3 and C_4 capacitors. Consequently, the C_3 and C_4 capacitors are discharged. Also, the C_1 and C_2 capacitors are not utilized.

The positive and negative polarities are produced on the load respectively by turning on the (T_1, T_4) and (T_2, T_3) switch pairs.

Producing $V_o = \pm 6V_{dc}$ (Figure 18.6): The C_3 and C_4 capacitors ($V_{C3}=V_{C4}=3V_{dc}$) are cascaded by turning the K_1 switch on. As the result, the $6V_{dc}$ is produced at output port of level generation unit. Two different scenarios can be considered for charging of C_3 and C_4 capacitors.

1) *First scenario*: If the S_2, S_3, S_5 and S_7 switches conduct, the C_3 will be paralleled with series connection of input DC source, C_1 and C_2 capacitors. Therefore, the C_3 will be charged to $V_{C3}=V_{dc}+V_{C1}+V_{C2}=3V_{dc}$.
2) *Second scenario*: By turning the S_2, S_3, S_6 and S_8 switches on, the cascaded connection of input DC source, C_1 and C_2 is paralleled with C_4 capacitor. So, the C_4 is charged to $V_{C4}=V_{dc}+V_{C1}+V_{C2}=3V_{dc}$.

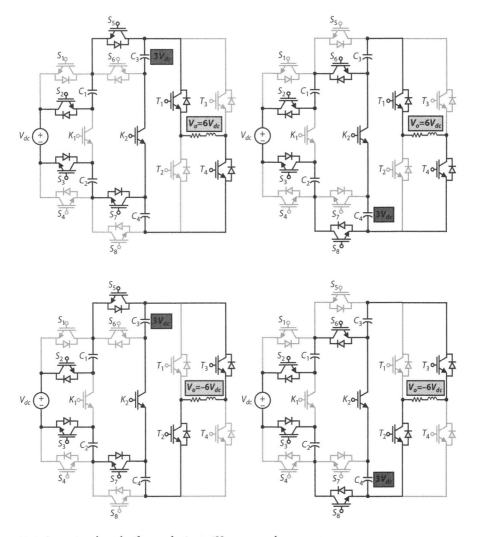

Figure 18.6 Operational modes for producing $\pm 6V_{dc}$ output voltage steps.

In both scenarios, the C_1 and C_2 capacitors are discharged. Also, the turning on of (T_1, T_4) or (T_2, T_3) switch pairs will lead respectively to positive and negative load voltage polarity.

Producing $V_o = \pm 5V_{dc}$ (Figure 18.7): The generation of $5V_{dc}$ in level generation unit can be accomplished by two different switching states, which are elaborated in the following.

1) *First switching state*: In this state the S_1, S_3, S_6 and S_8 switches are turned on. So, the $5V_{dc}$ is created by cascaded connection of input DC source, C_2, C_3 and C_4 capacitors at the output port of level generation unit through. In this state, the input DC source charges the C_1 to V_{dc} through S_1, S_3 and K_1 switches ($V_{C1} = V_{dc}$). Also, the C_2, C_3 and C_4 capacitors are discharged.

2) *Second switching state*: In this mode, the series connection of input DC source, C_1, C_3 and C_4 capacitors produces the $5V_{dc}$ at the output port of level generation unit. Simultaneously, the voltage of C_2 is charged to V_{dc} by input DC source, through S_2, S_4 and K_1 switches ($V_{C2} = V_{dc}$). In his state, the C_1, C_3 and C_4 capacitors are discharged.

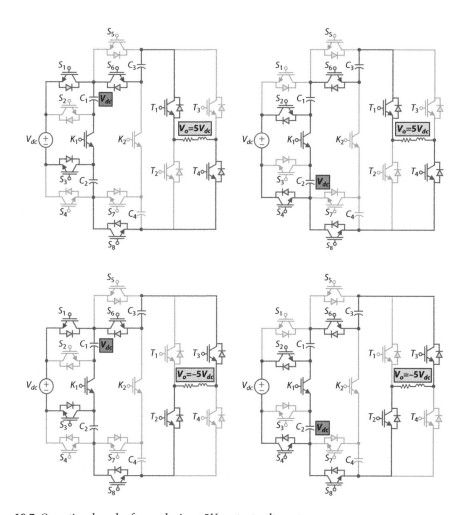

Figure 18.7 Operational modes for producing $\pm 5V_{dc}$ output voltage steps.

The positive and negative load voltage polarities can be produced respectively by turning the (T_1, T_4) or (T_2, T_3) switch pairs.

Producing $V_o = \pm 4V_{dc}$ (Figure 18.8): The level generation unit can produce $4V_{dc}$ by cascading the input DC source and C_3 (or C_4) capacitor. In this study, the $V_o = 4V_{dc}$ has been realized by series connection of input DC source and C_3 capacitor, through S_1, S_4, S_6, S_8, T_1 and T_4 switches. Also, the $V_o = -4V_{dc}$ has been realized by series connection of input DC source and C_4 capacitor, through S_1, S_4, S_5, S_7, T_2 and T_3 switches.

Producing $V_o = \pm 3V_{dc}$ (Figure 18.9): In this state, the cascaded connection of input DC source, C_1 and C_2 capacitors produces the $3V_{dc}$ at level generation unit, through S_2, S_3, S_5 and S_8 switches. The conduction of (T_1, T_4) or (T_2, T_3) switch pairs will respectively lead to positive and negative output voltage polarities.

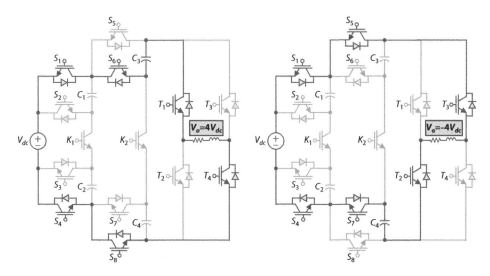

Figure 18.8 Operational modes for producing $\pm 4V_{dc}$ output voltage steps.

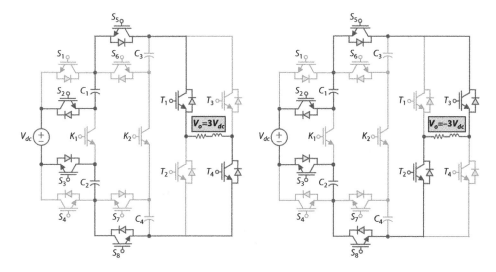

Figure 18.9 Operational modes for producing $\pm 3V_{dc}$ output voltage steps.

Producing $V_o = \pm 2V_{dc}$ **(Figure 18.10):** The $2V_{dc}$ can be produced in level generation unit through two different switching states, which are described in the following.

1) *First switching state*: In this state the S_1, S_3, S_5 and S_8 switches are turned on. So, the $2V_{dc}$ is created by cascaded connection of input DC source and C_2 capacitor. In this state, the input DC source charges the C_1 to V_{dc} through S_1, S_3 and K_1 switches ($V_{C1} = V_{dc}$). Also, the C_3 and C_4 capacitors are not utilized.

2) *Second switching state*: In this mode, the series connection of input DC source and C_1 capacitor generates the $2V_{dc}$ at level generation unit. Simultaneously, the C_2 is paralleled with input DC source and its voltage is regulated to V_{dc}, through S_2, S_4 and K_1 switches ($V_{C2} = V_{dc}$). In his state, the C_3 and C_4 are not used.

The positive and negative load voltage polarities are obtained through (T_1, T_4) or (T_2, T_3) pairs, respectively.

Producing $V_o = \pm V_{dc}$ **(Figure 18.11):** In this state, the V_{dc} can be provided by input DC source in level generation unit through S_1, S_4, S_5 and S_8 switches. To produce positive or

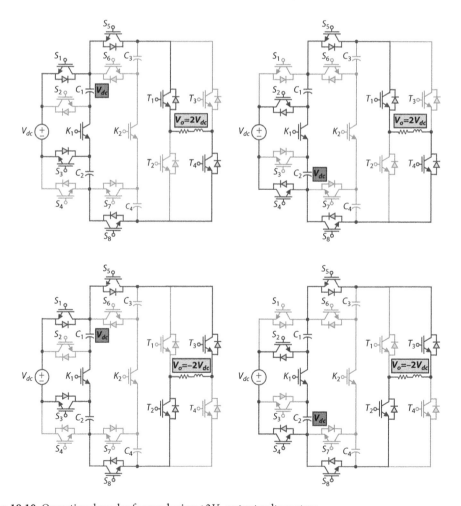

Figure 18.10 Operational modes for producing $\pm 2V_{dc}$ output voltage steps.

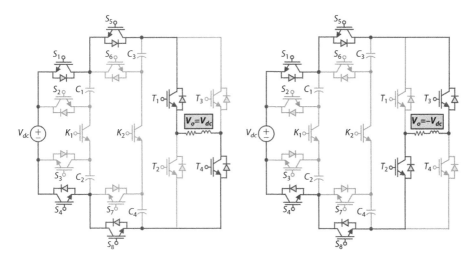

Figure 18.11 Operational modes for producing $\pm V_{dc}$ output voltage steps.

negative output voltage polarities, the (T_1, T_4) or (T_2, T_3) switch pairs should respectively be turned on.

Producing $V_o = 0$ (Figure 18.12): The zero level can be produced by conduction of (T_1, T_3) or (T_2, T_4) switch pairs. Based on charging process of C_1-C_4 capacitors, four scenarios can be assumed that are explained in the following.

1) *First scenario*: The C_1 capacitor can be charged by input DC source to V_{dc} $(V_{C1} = V_{dc})$, through S_1, S_3 and K_1 switches.
2) *Second scenario*: The C_2 capacitor can be charged by input DC source to V_{dc} $(V_{C2} = V_{dc})$, through S_2, S_4 and K_1 switches.
3) *Third scenario*: The C_3 capacitor is paralleled with series connection of input DC source, C_1 and C_2 capacitor, through S_2, S_3, S_5 and S_7 switches. Accordingly: $V_{C3} = V_{dc} + V_{C1} + V_{C2} = 3V_{dc}$.
4) *Fourth scenario*: The C_4 capacitor is paralleled with series connection of input DC source, C_1 and C_2 capacitor, through S_2, S_3, S_6 and S_8 switches. So, the C_4 is charged to $V_{C4} = V_{dc} + V_{C1} + V_{C2} = 3V_{dc}$.

According to Figures 18.4, 18.6, 18.7, 18.10, 18.12, there are two operational modes for generating $\pm 2V_{dc}$, $\pm 5V_{dc}$, $\pm 6V_{dc}$ and $\pm 8V_{dc}$ voltage steps. This is to regulate the voltage of capacitors on desired values.

As shown in Figures 18.3-18.12, the maximum output voltage of suggested topology is $V_{o,max} = V_{dc} + V_{C1} + V_{C2} + V_{C3} + V_{C4} = 9V_{dc}$. Therefore, the converter gain is up to 9 times the input voltage, as follows:

$$Gain = \frac{V_{o,max}}{V_{dc}} = \frac{V_{dc} + V_{C_1} + V_{C_2} + V_{C_3} + V_{C_4}}{V_{dc}} = \frac{9V_{dc}}{V_{dc}} = 9 \tag{18.2}$$

The considerable boosting capability of suggested topology makes it suitable for PV or FC applications. Also, the need for the step-up DC-DC converter in Figure 18.1 is eliminated.

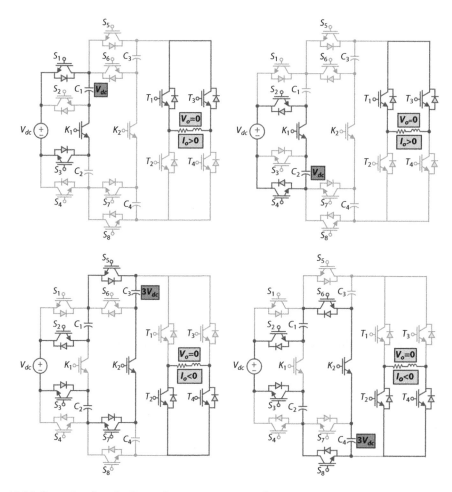

Figure 18.12 Operational modes for producing zero output voltage step.

18.2.3   Voltage Stress of Switches

The highest voltage that a semiconductor tolerates in off mode is called voltage stress. Table 18.1 shows the voltage stresses on switches of suggested structure. According to Table 18.2, the voltage stress on S_1-S_8 and K_1-K_2 switches are equal or less than 33% of $V_{o,max}$, which is very small. But the voltage stress on T_1-T_4 switches is $V_{o,max}$.

Note that the Normalized Voltage Stress (*NVS*) and Average of *NVS* (*ANVS*) are defined as:

$$NVS = \frac{VS}{V_{o,\max}}, ANVS = \frac{\Sigma NVS}{N_{Switch}} \tag{18.3}$$

18.3   Cascaded Configuration of Suggested Topology

The cascaded connection of the suggested structure has been shown in Figure 18.13. To achieve a higher number of output voltage levels as well as less total harmonic distortion at

Table 18.2 Voltage stresses on switches.

Switches	Voltage Stress (*VS*)	Normalized Voltage Stress (*NVS*)
S_1-S_4 and K_1	V_{dc}	11.11[%]
S_5-S_8 and K_2	$3V_{dc}$	33.33[%]
T_1-T_4	$9V_{dc}$	100[%]
Total Voltage Stress (*TVS*)	$56V_{dc}$	
Average Normalized Voltage Stress (*ANVS*)	44.44[%]	

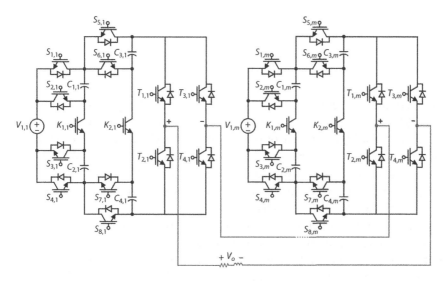

Figure 18.13 Cascaded configuration of suggested structure.

the output, the suggested cascaded model can be used. It is true that the number of levels will be higher in this case, but it should be noted that the number of required tools, including DC sources, switches, diodes and drivers, will increase, which will increase the cost, volume and dimensions of the converter.

Key parameters of cascaded version of suggested topology has been shown in Table 18.3.

18.4   Modulation Technique

In this paper, the Nearest level or fundamental Frequency modulation technique has been used to produce the output voltage levels of suggested structure [39, 40]. In fundamental Frequency modulation technique, the sinusoidal reference is compared with the constant values and the closest level to the reference wave is produced at the output of converter. This method can be used in applications with high power levels and it has a simple control strategy without complicated calculations. In this technique, switching losses are reduced

Table 18.3 Key parameters of cascaded configuration of suggested topology.

Parameter	Value
Number of steps (N_{Step})	$19m$
Number of DC voltage sources (N_{DC})	m
Number of capacitors ($N_{Capacitor}$)	$4m$
Number of IGBTs (N_{IGBT})	$14m$
Number of drivers (N_{Driver})	$14m$
Number of diodes (N_{Diode})	$12m$
Maximum output voltage ($V_{o,max}$)	$9m$
Gain	9
Total voltage stress (TVS)	$56m$

and the semiconductor elements operate at a low switching frequency. The total harmonic distortion (THD) is high but another advantage of this method is the ability to generalize the converters with a high number of output voltage levels. Usually, the amplitude of the reference wave is equal to or very close to the number of the highest level of positive voltage that can be generated. In this simulation, due to the production of 19 levels, we set the amplitude of the reference wave 8.9. A sinusoidal reference wave with a frequency of 50 Hz and a zero-angle phase has been selected.

The difference between reference waveform and nearest producible step is called "error". As shown in Figure 18.14, when error reaches its maximum value ($Error_{max} = 0.5$), the switching is performed so the next adjacent level be produced. The relationships and ON-state switches for producing each step has been shown in Table 18.4. With the help of Table IV and logic gates, fire pulses related to switches are produced. For example, the switching pulse of K_2 is produced by output of OR gate, whose inputs are 5.5<Ref<6.5, -0.5<Ref<0.5 and -6.5<Ref<-5.5. The output signal is sent to the IGBT gate by the driver circuit.

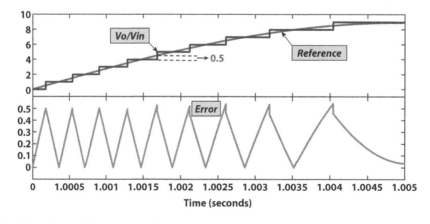

Figure 18.14 Fundamental frequency method.

Table 18.4 Look-up table for generating output voltage levels.

Relations	Switches	V_O
$8.5<Ref<9.5$	$S_2, S_3, S_6, S_7, T_1, T_4$	$9V_{dc}$
$7.5<Ref<8.5$	$S_2, S_4, S_6, S_7, K_1, T_1, T_4$	$8V_{dc}$
	$S_1, S_3, S_6, S_7, K_1, T_1, T_4$	
$6.5<Ref<7.5$	$S_1, S_4, S_6, S_7, T_1, T_4$	$7V_{dc}$
$5.5<Ref<6.5$	$S_2, S_3, S_6, S_8, K_2, T_1, T_4$	$6V_{dc}$
	$S_2, S_3, S_5, S_7, K_2, T_1, T_4$	
$4.5<Ref<5.5$	$S_1, S_3, S_6, S_8, K_1, T_1, T_4$	$5V_{dc}$
	$S_2, S_4, S_6, S_8, K_1, T_1, T_4$	
$3.5<Ref<4.5$	$S_1, S_4, S_6, S_8, T_1, T_4$	$4V_{dc}$
$2.5<Ref<3.5$	$S_2, S_3, S_5, S_8, T_1, T_4$	$3V_{dc}$
$1.5<Ref<2.5$	$S_2, S_4, S_5, S_8, K_1, T_1, T_4$	$2V_{dc}$
	$S_1, S_3, S_5, S_8, K_1, T_1, T_4$	
$0.5<Ref<1.5$	$S_1, S_4, S_5, S_8, T_1, T_4$	V_{dc}
$-0.5<Ref<0.5$	S_2, S_4, K_1, T_1, T_3	0^+
	S_1, S_3, K_1, T_1, T_3	
	$S_2, S_3, S_5, S_7, K_2, T_2, T_4$	0^-
	$S_2, S_3, S_6, S_8, K_2, T_2, T_4$	
$-1.5<Ref<-0.5$	$S_1, S_4, S_5, S_8, T_2, T_3$	$-V_{dc}$
$-2.5<Ref<-1.5$	$S_2, S_4, S_5, S_8, K_1, T_2, T_3$	$-2V_{dc}$
	$S_1, S_3, S_5, S_8, K_1, T_2, T_3$	
$-3.5<Ref<-2.5$	$S_2, S_3, S_5, S_8, T_2, T_3$	$-3V_{dc}$
$-4.5<Ref<-3.5$	$S_1, S_4, S_5, S_7, T_2, T_3$	$-4V_{dc}$
$-5.5<Ref<-4.5$	$S_2, S_4, S_6, S_8, K_1, T_2, T_3$	$-5V_{dc}$
	$S_1, S_3, S_6, S_8, K_1, T_2, T_3$	
$-6.5<Ref<-5.5$	$S_2, S_3, S_5, S_7, K_2, T_2, T_3$	$-6V_{dc}$
	$S_2, S_3, S_6, S_8, K_2, T_2, T_3$	
$-7.5<Ref<-6.5$	$S_1, S_4, S_6, S_7, T_2, T_3$	$-7V_{dc}$
$-8.5<Ref<-7.5$	$S_1, S_3, S_6, S_7, K_1, T_2, T_3$	$-8V_{dc}$
	$S_2, S_4, S_6, S_7, K_1, T_2, T_3$	
$-9.5<Ref<-8.5$	$S_2, S_3, S_6, S_7, T_2, T_3$	$-9V_{dc}$

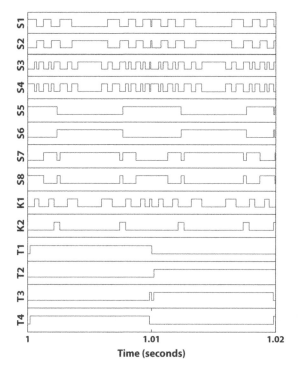

Figure 18.15 Gate pulses for switches of suggested structure.

Therefore, switching pulses are generated with the above strategy. These pulses are shown in Figure 18.15. As can be seen, a large number of switches have a low operating frequency.

18.5 Power Loss Analysis

Power losses in SCMLIs are divided into three categories: conduction losses, switching losses, and capacitors ripple losses.

18.5.1 Conduction Losses

One of the most important power losses in the SCMLIs is the conduction losses, which is caused by the parasitic resistance including ON-state resistance of the semiconductors and equivalent series resistance of capacitors (ESR) which reduces the output efficiency. Conduction losses related to power switches and power diodes are calculated according to the Equations (18.4), (18.5) [3, 41].

$$P_{cond,sw}(t) = V_{on,sw} \times i_{sw,avg} + R_{on,sw} \times i_{sw,rms}^2 \tag{18.4}$$

$$P_{cond,D}(t) = V_{on,D} \times i_{D,avg} + R_{on,D} \times i_{D,rms}^2 \tag{18.5}$$

Where, i_{rms} is the rms current of diodes and IGBTs, i_{avg} is the average current of semi-conductors, $V_{on,sw}$ is the on-state voltage across the collector and emitter, $V_{on,D}$ is the voltage drop of diode in connection state, $R_{on,sw}$ is the on-state resistance of IGBTs and $R_{on,D}$ is the resistance of the diode across conduction state.

In the process of generating voltage levels, a number of IGBTs, diodes are used, so the conduction losses of suggested SCMLI can be obtained from the equivalent circuit of each output voltage state. Therefore, the conduction losses for the production of different voltage levels are calculated as Equations (18.6)–(18.23):

$$P_{cond}(9V_{dc}) = 6V_{on,sw} \times i_{sw,avg} + 6R_{on,sw} \times i_{sw,rms}^2 \tag{18.6}$$

$$P_{cond}(-9V_{dc}) = 6V_{on,sw} \times_{sw,avg} + 6R_{on,sw} \times i_{sw,rms}^2 \tag{18.7}$$

$$P_{cond}(8V_{dc}) = 6V_{on,sw} \times i_{sw,avg} + 6R_{on,sw} \times i_{sw,rms}^2 + V_{on,D} \times i_{D,avg} + R_{on,D} \times i_{D,rms}^2 \tag{18.8}$$

$$P_{cond}(-8V_{dc}) = 6V_{on,sw} \times i_{sw,avg} + 6R_{on,sw} \times i_{sw,rms}^2 + V_{on,D} \times i_{D,avg} + R_{on,D} \times i_{D,rms}^2 \tag{18.9}$$

$$P_{cond}(7V_{dc}) = 4V_{on,sw} \times i_{sw,avg} + 4R_{on,sw} \times i_{sw,rms}^2 + 2V_{on,D} \times i_{D,avg} + 2R_{on,D} \times i_{D,rms}^2 \tag{18.10}$$

$$P_{cond}(-7V_{dc}) = 4V_{on,sw} \times i_{sw,avg} + 4R_{on,sw} \times i_{sw,rms}^2 + 2V_{on,D} \times i_{D,avg} + 2R_{on,D} \times i_{D,rms}^2 \tag{18.11}$$

$$P_{cond}(6V_{dc}) = 6V_{on,sw} \times i_{sw,avg} + 6R_{on,sw} \times i_{sw,rms}^2 + V_{on,D} \times i_{D,avg} + R_{on,D} \times i_{D,rms}^2 \tag{18.12}$$

$$P_{cond}(-6V_{dc}) = 6V_{on,sw} \times i_{sw,avg} + 6R_{on,sw} \times i_{sw,rms}^2 + V_{on,D} \times i_{D,avg} + R_{on,D} \times i_{D,rms}^2 \tag{18.13}$$

$$P_{cond}(5V_{dc}) = 5V_{on,sw} \times i_{sw,avg} + 5R_{on,sw} \times i_{sw,rms}^2 + 2V_{on,D} \times i_{D,avg} + 2R_{on,D} \times i_{D,rms}^2 \tag{18.14}$$

$$P_{cond}(-5V_{dc}) = 5V_{on,sw} \times i_{sw,avg} + 5R_{on,sw} \times i_{sw,rms}^2 + 2V_{on,D} \times i_{D,avg} + 2R_{on,D} \times i_{D,rms}^2 \tag{18.15}$$

$$P_{cond}(4V_{dc}) = 3V_{on,sw} \times i_{sw,avg} + 3R_{on,sw} \times i_{sw,rms}^2 + 3V_{on,D} \times i_{D,avg} + 3R_{on,D} \times i_{D,rms}^2 \tag{18.16}$$

$$P_{cond}(-4V_{dc}) = 3V_{on,sw} \times i_{sw,avg} + 3R_{on,sw} \times i_{sw,rms}^2 + 3V_{on,D} \times i_{D,avg} + 3R_{on,D} \times i_{D,rms}^2 \tag{18.17}$$

$$P_{cond}(3V_{dc}) = 4V_{on,sw} \times i_{sw,avg} + 4R_{on,sw} \times i_{sw,rms}^2 + 2V_{on,D} \times i_{D,avg} + 2R_{on,D} \times i_{D,rms}^2$$
(18.18)

$$P_{cond}(-3V_{dc}) = 4V_{on,sw} \times i_{sw,avg} + 4R_{on,sw} \times i_{sw,rms}^2 + 2V_{on,D} \times i_{D,avg} + 2R_{on,D} \times i_{D,rms}^2$$
(18.19)

$$P_{cond}(2V_{dc}) = 4V_{on,sw} \times i_{sw,avg} + 4R_{on,sw} \times i_{sw,rms}^2 + 3V_{on,D} \times i_{D,avg} + 3R_{on,D} \times i_{D,rms}^2 \quad (18.20)$$

$$P_{cond}(-2V_{dc}) = 4V_{on,sw} \times i_{sw,avg} + 4R_{on,sw} \times i_{sw,rms}^2 + 3V_{on,D} \times i_{D,avg} + 3R_{on,D} \times i_{D,rms}^2$$
(18.21)

$$P_{cond}(V_{dc}) = 2V_{on,sw} \times i_{sw,avg} + 2R_{on,sw} \times i_{sw,rms}^2 + 4V_{on,D} \times i_{D,avg} + 4R_{on,D} \times i_{D,rms}^2$$
(18.22)

$$P_{cond}(-V_{dc}) = 2V_{on,sw} \times i_{sw,avg} + 2R_{on,sw} \times i_{sw,rms}^2 + 4V_{on,D} \times i_{D,avg} + 4R_{on,D} \times i_{D,rms}^2$$
(18.23)

Total conduction loss is derived by sum of conduction loss of each output voltage level except zero voltage level. As a result, total conduction losses are as (18.24):

$$P_{cond,total} = P_{cond}(9V_{dc}) + \ldots + P_{cond}(2V_{dc}) + P_{cond}(V_{dc}) + P_{cond}(-9V_{dc}) + \ldots$$
$$+ P_{cond}(-2V_{dc}) + P_{cond}(-V_{dc})$$
(18.24)

18.5.2 Switching Losses

The switching loss of switch is due to the overlap of its voltage and current while its state changes. Switching losses in ON-state can be calculate by considering switching frequency and OFF-state voltage [41].

$$P_{sw,i(on)} = f_s \int_0^{t_{on}} V_{off-state,i}(t)i(t)dt$$

$$= f_s \int_0^{t_{on}} \left[-\frac{V_{off-state,i}}{t_{on}}(t - t_{on}) \right] \left[\frac{I_{on-state1,i}}{t_{on}} t \right] dt \qquad (18.25)$$

$$= \frac{1}{6} \times f_s \times V_{off-state,i} \times I_{on-state1,i} \times t_{on}$$

Also, switching losses in off-state can be calculate by considering switching frequency and off-state voltage.

$$P_{sw,i(off)} = f_s \int_0^{t_{off}} V_{off-state,i}(t)i(t)dt$$

$$= f_s \int_0^{t_{off}} \left[\frac{V_{off-state,i}}{t_{off}} t \right] \left[-\frac{I_{off-state2,i}}{t_{off}}(t-t_{off}) \right] dt \tag{18.26}$$

$$= \frac{1}{6} \times f_s \times V_{off-state,i} \times I_{on-state2,i} \times t_{off}$$

While, t_{on} is the time to turn on the switch after the initial delay and t_{off} is the time to turn off the switch after the delay in this process. $V_{off\text{-}state,i}$ is the OFF-state voltage of ith switch, $I_{on\text{-}state1,i}$ is the current of ith switch when the switch becomes completely on, and $I_{on\text{-}state2,i}$ is the current of ith switch before the turn-off of the switch. Switching frequency or f_s is obtained as Equation (18.27), (18.28):

$$f_{s,on} = N_{s,on} \times f_{ref} \tag{18.27}$$

$$f_{s,off} = N_{s,off} \times f_{ref} \tag{18.28}$$

$N_{s,on}$, $N_{s,off}$ are the number of turning ON and OFF of each switch in a cycle. Also, f_{ref} is the output voltage frequency which is same as the sinusoidal reference waveform.

Finally, switching losses is derived by Equation (18.29):

$$P_{sw,total} = \sum_{i=1}^{N_{Switch}} (P_{sw,i(on)} + P_{sw,i(off)}) \tag{18.29}$$

18.5.3 Capacitor Losses

Capacitor losses are divided into two categories: Ripple losses (P_R) and conduction losses of capacitors (P_{CC}).

Capacitors ripple losses or P_R occur due to the voltage difference between the input DC source and the capacitor during the capacitor discharging period. The capacitors ripple losses are obtained by Equation (18.30).

$$P_{Ripple} = \frac{f_{ref}}{2} \left(\sum_{i=1}^{N_{Capacitor}} C_i (\Delta V_{Ripple} \times V_C)^2 \right) \tag{18.30}$$

In Equation (18.30) C_i is the capacitance of each capacitor, ΔV_{Ripple} is allowable size of the ripple voltage of the capacitors and V_C is the magnitude of the voltage which the capacitor is charged.

The conduction losses of capacitor occur due to equivalent series resistance of capacitor (r_c). This parameter is calculated as Equation (18.31).

$$P_{CC} = \left(\frac{2\pi f_{ref}}{\pi}\right) \sum_{i=1}^{N_{Capacitor}} r_C(i_{C,i})^2 dt \qquad (18.31)$$

Finally, the capacitor's losses are calculated by relation (18.32):

$$P_{cap} = P_R + P_{CC} \qquad (18.32)$$

Finally, the converter efficiency is calculated by Equation (18.33):

$$\eta = \frac{P_{out}}{P_{in}} = \frac{P_{out}}{P_{out} + P_{Loss}} = \frac{P_{out}}{P_{out} + P_{Cond} + P_{sw} + P_{cap}} \qquad (18.33)$$

18.6   Design of Capacitors

ΔQ_C is the maximum amount of a capacitor discharged in a cycle and is obtained using Equation (18.34).

$$Q_C = \int_{t_x}^{t_y} I_{Load}\sin(2\pi f_{ref}t)dt \qquad (18.34)$$

The $[t_x, t_y]$ time interval is the discharge time of each capacitors. To get a maximum of ΔQ_C, the maximum value of the interval must be selected. According to Figure 18.16, the maximum discharge time of capacitor C_1-C_4 is $[t_8, t_9]$.

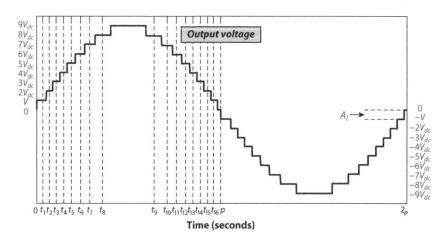

Figure 18.16 Output voltage of suggested topology.

Table 18.5 Relationships for calculating output t_1-t_{16}.

Equation	No.	Equation	No.
$t_1 = \dfrac{\sin^{-1}\left(\dfrac{A_l}{A_{ref}}\right)}{2\pi f_{ref}}$	(18.35)	$t_2 = \dfrac{\sin^{-1}\left(\dfrac{2A_l}{A_{ref}}\right)}{2\pi f_{ref}}$	(18.36)
$t_3 = \dfrac{\sin^{-1}\left(\dfrac{3A_l}{A_{ref}}\right)}{2\pi f_{ref}}$	(18.37)	$t_4 = \dfrac{\sin^{-1}\left(\dfrac{4A_l}{A_{ref}}\right)}{2\pi f_{ref}}$	(18.38)
$t_5 = \dfrac{\sin^{-1}\left(\dfrac{5A_l}{A_{ref}}\right)}{2\pi f_{ref}}$	(18.39)	$t_6 = \dfrac{\sin^{-1}\left(\dfrac{6A_l}{A_{ref}}\right)}{2\pi f_{ref}}$	(18.40)
$t_7 = \dfrac{\sin^{-1}\left(\dfrac{7A_l}{A_{ref}}\right)}{2\pi f_{ref}}$	(18.41)	$t_8 = \dfrac{\sin^{-1}\left(\dfrac{8A_l}{A_{ref}}\right)}{2\pi f_{ref}}$	(18.42)
$t_9 = \dfrac{\pi-\sin^{-1}\left(\dfrac{8A_l}{A_{ref}}\right)}{2\pi f_{ref}}$	(18.43)	$t_{10} = \dfrac{\pi-\sin^{-1}\left(\dfrac{7A_l}{A_{ref}}\right)}{2\pi f_{ref}}$	(18.44)
$t_{11} = \dfrac{\pi-\sin^{-1}\left(\dfrac{6A_l}{A_{ref}}\right)}{2\pi f_{ref}}$	(18.45)	$t_{12} = \dfrac{\pi-\sin^{-1}\left(\dfrac{5A_l}{A_{ref}}\right)}{2\pi f_{ref}}$	(18.46)
$t_{13} = \dfrac{\pi-\sin^{-1}\left(\dfrac{4A_l}{A_{ref}}\right)}{2\pi f_{ref}}$	(18.47)	$t_{14} = \dfrac{\pi-\sin^{-1}\left(\dfrac{3A_l}{A_{ref}}\right)}{2\pi f_{ref}}$	(18.48)
$t_{15} = \dfrac{\pi-\sin^{-1}\left(\dfrac{2A_l}{A_{ref}}\right)}{2\pi f_{ref}}$	(18.49)	$t_{16} = \dfrac{\pi-\sin^{-1}\left(\dfrac{A_l}{A_{ref}}\right)}{2\pi f_{ref}}$	(18.50)

For suggested structure t_1-t_{16} are calculated as relations in Table 18.5.

It must to be noted that in Equations (18.35)–(18.50), A_l, A_{ref} are about 1, 8.9 respectively. Therefore, by determining the amount of permissible ripple in each capacitor, the amount of capacitance is obtained by Equation (18.51).

$$C \geq \frac{Q_C}{V_{ripple} \times V_C} \tag{18.51}$$

18.7   Comparative Analysis

To evaluate the suggested structure, it is compared with the structures presented recently. The parameters selected for comparison are: number of output voltage steps (N_{Step}), number of sources (N_{DC}), number of capacitors ($N_{Capacitor}$), number of IGBTs (N_{IGBT}), number of diodes (N_{Diode}), number of driver circuits (N_{Driver}), total voltage stress (*TVS*), per-unit total voltage stress (*TVS$_{pu}$*), maximum output voltage ($V_{o,max}$), variety of capacitors, cost function (*CF*), Gain (*G*) and using H-bridge in structures (*HB*). It must to be noted that *CF* and *TVS$_{pu}$* are defined as Equations (18.52), (18.53).

$$CF = \left(N_{IGBT} + N_{Diode} + N_{Driver} + N_{Capacitor} + \frac{TVS}{G} \right) N_{DC} \qquad (18.52)$$

$$TVS_{pu} = \frac{TVS}{V_{o,\mathbf{max}}} \qquad (18.53)$$

As given from Table 18.6 the variety of capacitors for suggested structure is 2, which indicates the capacitors of suggested topology have different values. This indicates the flexibility of the suggested structure. It should be noted that in only 5 of the 14 structures under comparison, the variety of capacitors is 2. As shown in Figures 18.17–18.21, the presented structure has been compared with other topologies by 5 parameters. In each section, the lowest number shows the best structure from that point of view. The suggested structure and presented structures in [36] and [38] are required H-bridge to producing negative voltage levels, which leads to higher total voltage stress of converter.

As shown in Figure 18.17, the suggested structure has a smaller ratio of sources per number of levels compared to other structures. This indicates that instead of using DC sources, capacitors are used in the suggested structure to generate DC voltage. This leads to a significant reduction in the cost, volume and especially the weight of the suggested converter.

As evident from Figure 18.18, the suggested structure is ranked third among the 15 structures in terms of the number of capacitors and the number of levels. This cannot be considered a disadvantage for the suggested structure, as it is true that the presented structures in [30] and [38] have fewer capacitors but at the same time use more dc sources (2 and 3, respectively).

As given from Figure 18.19, the suggested structure and the presented structure in [38] use a smaller number of semiconductor elements compared to other structures. This leads to a reduction in losses, the cost of cooling for switches and diodes, the cost of the driver circuits related to the switches and the volume of the suggested structure.

One of the most important parameters that is always questioned in the case of multilevel converters is the total voltage stress. The suggested structure has a lower ratio of per-unit voltage stress per the number of steps compared to other structures. This is shown in Figure 18.20. The voltage stress of the switches directly affects parameters such as the cost of the switches, the conduction losses of the converters and the dimensions and cost of the equipment are used to cool the switches.

Table 18.6 Component counts of suggested structure and presented structures in [1–14].

Topology	Suggested	[25]	[26]	[27]	[28]	[29]	[30]	[31]	[32]	[33]	[34]	[35]	[36]	[37]	[38]
N_{step}	19	9	9	9	17	13	17	9	13	9	9	5	7	5	19
N_{DC}	1	1	1	1	3	1	2	1	1	1	1	1	1	1	3
$N_{Capacitor}$	4	2	2	2	5	4	2	2	6	4	2	2	2	2	2
N_{IGBT}	14	10	12	11	10	12	18	10	23	8	12	6	8	7	12
N_{Diode}	12	8	12	11	18	10	18	11	22	12	12	8	10	10	14
N_{Driver}	14	9	12	10	10	11	13	8	19	8	12	6	8	7	12
TVS	56	11	21	10	47	17	57	24	40	16	10.5	8	18	9	66
TVS_{pu}	6.22	5.5	5.25	5	5.88	5.67	7.13	6	6.67	4	5.25	4	6	4.5	7.3
G	9	2	4	2	1	1.5	2	2	6	4	2	2	3	2	3
$V_{o,max}$	9	2	4	2	8	3	8	4	6	4	2	2	3	2	9
Variety of capacitors	2	1	2	1	2	2	2	1	1	2	1	1	1	1	1
CF	50.22	34.5	43.25	39	270	48.3	159	43	76.6	36	43.25	26	34	30.5	186
HB	YES	NO	NO	NO	NO	NO	NO	NO	NO	NO	NO	NO	YES	NO	YES

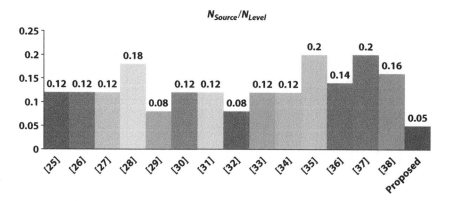

Figure 18.17 Number of sources per number of levels.

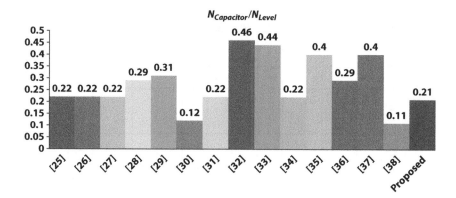

Figure 18.18 Number of capacitors per number of levels.

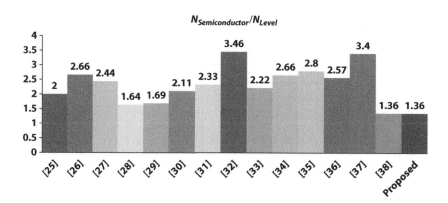

Figure 18.19 Number of semiconductors per number of levels.

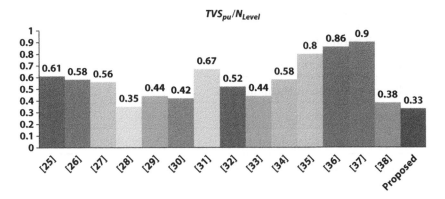

Figure 18.20 Per-unit total voltage stress per number of levels.

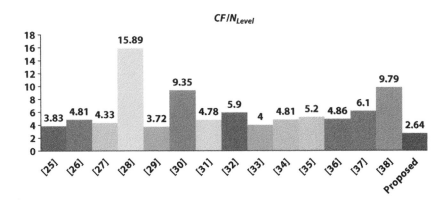

Figure 18.21 Cost function per number of levels.

So far, four comparison parameters have been studied. The parameter that contains all of the above is called the cost function. The cost function discusses the status of structures in general and is a good parameter for determining the superiority of structures over each other. As shown in Figure 18.22, the suggested structure has a lower ratio of CF per number of levels, which indicates the optimal status and superiority of the suggested structure over other structures.

18.8   Simulation Results

To certify correct performance of suggested 19-level structure, it is simulated in MATLAB/SIMULIK software. The simulation parameters are given in Table 18.7. The nearest level method is used in simulations.

The load voltage and current waveform of the suggested structure are shown in Figure 18.22. According to Figure 18.22, the suggested topology has successfully produced 19 voltage steps: $0, \pm 100[V], \pm 200[V], \cdots, \pm 900[V]$. The maximum output voltage and load current are respectively about $V_{o,max} = 900[V]$ and $I_{o,max} = 4.76[A]$. In this scenario, the measured efficiency of suggested structure is about $94.1[\%]$. The output voltage and current have a

Table 18.7 Simulation parameters.

Circuit parameters	Value
Reference waveform Frequency (f_r)	$50[Hz]$
Reference waveform Magnitude (m)	8.9
Input DC Voltage (V_{dc})	$100[V]$
Capacitances of suggested topology (C_1, C_2)	$4700[\mu F]$
Capacitances of suggested topology (C_3, C_4)	$2200[\mu F]$
Load (R-L)	$100[\Omega]$–$500[mH]$

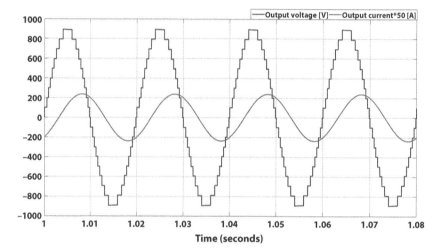

Figure 18.22 Output voltage and current waveforms.

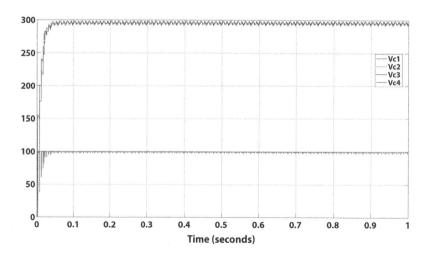

Figure 18.23 Voltage waveform of C_1-C_4 capacitors.

phase difference about 57.52 degrees, which is validated by $\Delta\varphi = tan^{-1}(L\omega/R)$. This phase difference verifies effective functionality of suggested structure on supplying R-L loads.

Figure 18.23 shows that the voltage of C_1, C_2 capacitors are regulated on 100[V]. Also, the voltage of C_3, C_4 capacitors are approximately set to 300[V]. This figure confirms the natural voltage balancing of capacitors, which leads to simple and easy control strategy.

According to Figure 18.24, which shows the FFT analysis of output voltage, the amplitude of harmonic orders are less than 1.5% of fundamental frequency order. Also, the THD

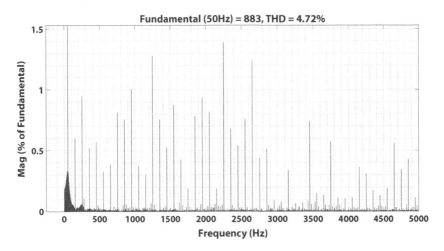

Figure 18.24 FFT analysis of suggested topology.

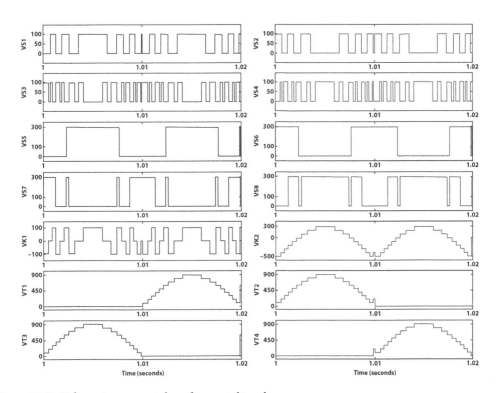

Figure 18.25 Voltage stress on switches of suggested topology.

of output voltage of suggested structure is only about 4.72%, which reduces the filter size at the output side. This reduces the total weight, cost, and volume of converter.

The stress voltage of suggested structure switches has been shown in Figure 18.25. As evident from Figure 18.25, the stress voltage of switches are about: $V_{Stress-S1} = 100[V]$, $V_{Stress-S2} = 100[V]$, $V_{Stress-S3} = 100[V]$, $V_{Stress-S4} = 100[V]$, $V_{Stress-S5} = 300[V]$, $V_{Stress-S6} = 300[V]$, $V_{Stress-S7} = 300[V]$, $V_{Stress-S8} = 300[V]$, $V_{Stress-K1} = 100[V]$, $V_{Stress-K2} = 300[V]$, $V_{Stress-T1} = 900[V]$, $V_{Stress-T2} = 900[V]$, $V_{Stress-T3} = 900[V]$, $V_{Stress-T4} = 900[V]$ which is confirmed by Table 18.2.

The current stress of all switches are approximately equal to load current and about 4.76[A].

18.9   Conclusions

This study suggested a new switched-capacitor based multi-level inverter. High step-up capability, simple control, self-voltage balancing of the capacitors, increased steps per devices, and improved power quality of load voltage are other benefits of the suggested structure. Extended model of the suggested structure has been introduced in this paper. The suggested structure is capable of supplying R-L loads. The ability to produce a high number of levels results in a decrease in THD, which decreases the size and volume of the output filter. This leads to reduction in the cost, size and weight of the suggested SCMLI. The suggested structure was compared with similar structures that have been recently presented and simulated to realize its performance in MATLAB/SIMULINK software. According to the results of the comparison and simulation section, the correct and effective performance of the suggested topology is accepted.

References

1. P. R. Bana, K. P. Panda, and G. Panda, "Power quality performance evaluation of multilevel inverter with reduced switching devices and minimum standing voltage," *IEEE Transactions on Industrial Informatics*, 2019.
2. J. Rodriguez, J.-S. Lai, and F. Z. Peng, "Multilevel inverters: a survey of topologies, controls, and applications," *IEEE Transactions on Industrial Electronics*, vol. 49, pp. 724-738, 2002.
3. T. Roy and P. K. Sadhu, "A Step-up Multilevel Inverter Topology using Novel Switched Capacitor Converters with Reduced Components," *IEEE Transactions on Industrial Electronics*, 2020.
4. K. Varesi, M. Karimi, and P. Kargar, "A New Basic Step-Up Cascaded 35-Level Topology Extendable To Higher Number of Levels," in *2019 10th International Power Electronics, Drive Systems and Technologies Conference (PEDSTC)*, 2019, pp. 291-296.
5. J.-S. Lai and F. Z. Peng, "Multilevel converters-a new breed of power converters," *IEEE Transactions on Industry Applications*, vol. 32, pp. 509-517, 1996.
6. K. Varesi, M. Karimi, and P. Kargar, "A New Cascaded 35-Level Inverter with Reduced Switch Count," in *Iranian Conference on Renewable Energy & Distributed Generation (ICREDG)*, 2019.
7. F. Esmaeili and K. Varesi, "A novel single-phase multi-level inverter topology based on bridge-type connected sources with enhanced number of levels per number of devices," *Journal of Energy Management and Technology*, vol. 4, pp. 37-47, 2020.
8. E. Babaei and S. S. Gowgani, "Hybrid multilevel inverter using switched capacitor units," *IEEE Transactions on Industrial Electronics*, vol. 61, pp. 4614-4621, 2013.

9. R. S. Alishah, S. H. Hosseini, E. Babaei, M. Sabahi, and G. B. Gharehpetian, "New high step-up multilevel converter topology with self-voltage balancing ability and its optimization analysis," *IEEE Transactions on Industrial Electronics,* vol. 64, pp. 7060-7070, 2017.

10. M. Karimi, P. Kargar, and K. Varesi, "A Novel Sub-Multilevel Cell (SMC) with Increased Ratio of Number of Levels to Number of Sources and Switches," in *Iranian Conference on Renewable Energy & Distributed Generation (ICREDG),* 2019.

11. R. Barzegarkhoo, H. M. Kojabadi, E. Zamiry, N. Vosoughi, and L. Chang, "Generalized structure for a single phase switched-capacitor multilevel inverter using a new multiple DC link producer with reduced number of switches," *IEEE Transactions on Power Electronics,* vol. 31, pp. 5604-5617, 2015.

12. M. Vijeh, M. Rezanejad, E. Samadaei, and K. Bertilsson, "A general review of multilevel inverters based on main submodules: Structural point of view," *IEEE Transactions on Power Electronics,* vol. 34, pp. 9479-9502, 2019.

13. L. G. Franquelo, J. Rodriguez, J. I. Leon, S. Kouro, R. Portillo, and M. A. Prats, "The age of multilevel converters arrives," *IEEE industrial Electronics Magazine,* vol. 2, pp. 28-39, 2008.

14. E. Babaei and S. H. Hosseini, "New cascaded multilevel inverter topology with minimum number of switches," *Energy Conversion and Management,* vol. 50, pp. 2761-2767, 2009.

15. T. Roy, P. K. Sadhu, and A. Dasgupta, "Cross-Switched Multilevel Inverter Using Novel Switched Capacitor Converters," *IEEE Transactions on Industrial Electronics,* vol. 66, pp. 8521-8532, 2019.

16. A. A. Gandomi, K. Varesi, and S. H. Hosseini, "Control strategy applied on double flying capacitor multi-cell inverter for increasing number of generated voltage levels," *IET Power Electronics,* vol. 8, pp. 887-897, 2015.

17. P. Kargar, M. Karimi, and K. Varesi, "A Novel Boost Switched-Capacitor Based MultiLevel Inverter Structure," *in 2020 11th International Power Electronics, Drive Systems and Technologies Conference (PEDSTC), Tehran, Iran, 2020: IEEE.*

18. F. Esmaeili and K. Varesi, "A Modified Single-Phase Multi-Level Inverter with Increased Number of Steps," in *Iranian Conference on Renewable Energy & Distributed Generation (ICREDG),* 2019.

19. M. Karimi, P. Kargar, and K. Varesi, "A Novel High-Gain Switched-Capacitor Based 11-Level Inverter Topology," *in 2019 The 34th International Power System Conference (PSC), Tehran, Iran, 2019: IEEE.*

20. F. Esmaeili and K. Varesi, "An Asymmetric Multi-Level Inverter Structure with Increased Steps per Devices," in *2020 11th International Power Electronics, Drive Systems and Technologies Conference (PEDSTC),* Tehran, Iran, 2020, pp. 1-5.

21. S. Deliri Khatoonabad and K. Varesi, "A Novel Dual-Input Switched-Capacitor Based 27-Level Boost Inverter Topology," in *28th Iranian Conference on Electrical Engineering (ICEE2020),* Tabriz, Iran, 2020.

22. S. Deliri Khatoonabad and K. Varesi, "An Extended High Step-Up Switched-Capacitor Based Multi-Level Inverter Topology," in *2019 International Power System Conference (PSC),* Tehran, Iran, 2019, pp. 459-464.

23. A. Taheri, A. Rasulkhani, and H.-P. Ren, "An Asymmetric Switched Capacitor Multilevel Inverter With Component Reduction," *IEEE Access,* vol. 7, pp. 127166-127176, 2019.

24. M. Karimi, P. Kargar, and K. Varesi, "Two Novel Switched-Capacitor Based Multi-Level Inverter Topologies," *in 2019 The 34th International Power System Conference (PSC), Tehran, Iran, 2019: IEEE.*

25. M. D. Siddique, S. Mekhilef, N. M. Shah, N. Sandeep, J. S. M. Ali, A. Iqbal, *et al.,* "A Single DC Source Nine-Level Switched-Capacitor Boost Inverter Topology with Reduced Switch Count," *IEEE Access,* 2019.

26. N. Sandeep, J. S. M. Ali, U. R. Yaragatti, and K. Vijayakumar, "Switched-Capacitor-Based Quadruple-Boost Nine-Level Inverter," *IEEE Transactions on Power Electronics,* vol. 34, pp. 7147-7150, 2019.

27. P. Bhatnagar, R. Agrawal, N. K. Dewangan, S. K. Jain, and K. K. Gupta, "Switched capacitors 9-level module (SC9LM) with reduced device count for multilevel DC to AC power conversion," *IET Electric Power Applications,* vol. 13, pp. 1544-1552, 2019.

28. B. Mahato, S. Majumdar, and K. C. Jana, "Single-phase Modified T-type–based multilevel inverter with reduced number of power electronic devices," *International Transactions on Electrical Energy Systems,* vol. 29, p. e12097, 2019.

29. J. Zeng, W. Lin, D. Cen, and L. Junfeng, "Novel K-Type Multilevel Inverter with Reduced Components and Self-Balance," *IEEE Journal of Emerging and Selected Topics in Power Electronics,* 2019.

30. E. Samadaei, M. Kaviani, M. Iranian, and E. Pouresmaeil, "The P-Type Module with Virtual DC Links to Increase Levels in Multilevel Inverters," *Electronics,* vol. 8, p. 1460, 2019.

31. R. Barzegarkhoo, M. Moradzadeh, E. Zamiri, H. M. Kojabadi, and F. Blaabjerg, "A new boost switched-capacitor multilevel converter with reduced circuit devices," *IEEE Transactions on Power Electronics,* vol. 33, pp. 6738-6754, 2017.

32. M. Khenar, A. Taghvaie, J. Adabi, and M. Rezanejad, "Multi-level inverter with combined T-type and cross-connected modules," *IET Power Electronics,* vol. 11, pp. 1407-1415, 2018.

33. M. Saeedian, M. E. Adabi, S. M. Hosseini, J. Adabi, and E. Pouresmaeil, "A Novel Step-Up Single Source Multilevel Inverter: Topology, Operating Principle, and Modulation," *IEEE Transactions on Power Electronics,* vol. 34, pp. 3269-3282, 2018.

34. M. Saeedian, E. Pouresmaeil, E. Samadaei, E. Manuel Godinho Rodrigues, R. Godina, and M. Marzband, "An innovative dual-boost nine-level inverter with low-voltage rating switches," *Energies,* vol. 12, p. 207, 2019.

35. M. Saeedian, S. M. Hosseini, and J. Adabi, "Step-up switched-capacitor module for cascaded MLI topologies," *IET Power Electronics,* vol. 11, pp. 1286-1296, 2018.

36. W. Peng, Q. Ni, X. Qiu, and Y. Ye, "Seven-level inverter with self-balanced switched-capacitor and its cascaded extension," *IEEE Transactions on Power Electronics,* vol. 34, pp. 11889-11896, 2019.

37. M. Saeedian, S. M. Hosseini, and J. Adabi, "A Five-Level Step-Up Module for Multilevel Inverters: Topology, Modulation Strategy, and Implementation," *IEEE Journal of Emerging and Selected Topics in Power Electronics,* vol. 6, pp. 2215-2226, 2018.

38. Y. C. Fong, S. R. Raman, Y. Ye, and K. W. E. Cheng, "Generalized Topology of a Hybrid Switched-Capacitor Multilevel Inverter for High-Frequency AC Power Distribution," *IEEE Journal of Emerging and Selected Topics in Power Electronics,* 2019.

39. P. M. Meshram and V. B. Borghate, "A simplified nearest level control (NLC) voltage balancing method for modular multilevel converter (MMC)," *IEEE Transactions on Power Electronics,* vol. 30, pp. 450-462, 2014.

40. M. Pérez, J. Rodríguez, J. Pontt, and S. Kouro, "Power distribution in hybrid multi-cell converter with nearest level modulation," in *2007 IEEE International Symposium on Industrial Electronics,* 2007, pp. 736-741.

41. A. Taghvaie, J. Adabi, and M. Rezanejad, "A self-balanced step-up multilevel inverter based on switched-capacitor structure," *IEEE Transactions on Power Electronics,* vol. 33, pp. 199-209, 2017.

Index

Also of Interest

Check out these other related titles from Scrivener Publishing

Electrical and Electronic Devices, Circuits, and Materials: Technical Challenges and Solutions, edited by Suman Lata Tripathi, Parvej Ahmad Alvi, and Umashankar Subramaniam, ISBN 9781119750369. Covering every aspect of the design and improvement needed for solid-state electronic devices and circuit and their reliability issues, this new volume also includes overall system design for all kinds of analog and digital applications and developments in power systems. *DUE IN SPRING 2021*

Green Energy: Solar Energy, Photovoltaics, and Smart Cities, edited by Suman Lata Tripathi and Sanjeevikumar Padmanaban, ISBN 9781119760764. Covering the concepts and fundamentals of green energy, this volume, written and edited by a global team of experts, also goes into the practical applications that can be utilized across multiple industries, for both the engineer and the student. *DUE IN SPRING 2021*

Microgrid Technologies, edited by C. Sharmeela, P. Sivaraman, P. Sanjeevikumar, and Jens Bo Holm-Nielsen, ISBN 9781119710790. Covering the concepts and fundamentals of microgrid technologies, this volume, written and edited by a global team of experts, also goes into the practical applications that can be utilized across multiple industries, for both the engineer and the student. *DUE IN SPRING 2021*

Progress in Solar Energy Technology and Applications, edited by Umakanta Sahoo, ISBN 9781119555605. This first volume in thenew groundbreaking series, Advances in Renewable Energy, covers the latest concepts, trends, techniques, processes, and materials insolar energy, focusing on the state-of-the-art for the field and written by a group of world-renowned experts. *NOW AVAILABLE!*

Energy Storage 2nd Edition, by Ralph Zito and Haleh Ardibili, ISBN 9781119083597. A revision of the groundbreaking study of methods for storing energy on a massive scale to be used in wind, solar, and other renewable energy systems. *NOW AVAILABLE!*

Nuclear Power: Policies, Practices, and the Future, by Darryl Siemer, ISBN 9781119657781. Written from an engineer's perspective, this is a treatise on the state of nuclear power today, its benefits, and its future, focusing on both policy and technological issues. *NOW AVAILABLE!*

Zero-Waste Engineering 2nd Edition: A New Era of Sustainable Technology Development, by M. M. Kahn and M. R. Islam, ISBN 9781119184898. This book outlines how to develop zero-waste engineering following natural pathways that are truly sustainable using methods that have been developed for sustainability, such as solar air conditioning, natural desalination, green building, chemical-free biofuel, fuel cells, scientifically renewable energy, and new mathematical and economic models. *NOW AVAILABLE!*

Sustainable Energy Pricing, by Gary Zatzman, ISBN 9780470901632. In this controversial new volume, the author explores a new science of energy pricing and how it can be done in a way that is sustainable for the world's economy and environment. *NOW AVAILABLE!*

Advanced Petroleum Reservoir Simulation, by M.R. Islam, S.H. Mousavizadegan, Shabbir Mustafiz, and Jamal H. Abou-Kassem, ISBN 9780470625811. The state of the art in petroleum reservoir simulation. *NOW AVAILABLE!*

Sustainable Resource Development, by Gary Zatzman, ISBN 9781118290392. Taking a new, fresh look at how the energy industry and we, as a planet, are developing our energy resources, this book looks at what is right and wrong about energy resource development. This book aids engineers and scientists in achieving a true sustainability in this field, both from an economic and environmental perspective. *NOW AVAILABLE!*

The *Greening of Petroleum Operations*, by M. R. Islam *et al.*, ISBN 9780470625903. The state of the art in petroleum operations, from a "green" perspective. *NOW AVAILABLE!*

Emergency Response Management for Offshore Oil Spills, by Nicholas P. Cheremisinoff, PhD, and Anton Davletshin, ISBN 9780470927120. The first book to examine the Deepwater Horizon disaster and offer processes for safety and environmental protection. *NOW AVAILABLE!*

Biogas Production, Edited by Ackmez Mudhoo, ISBN 9781118062852. This volume covers the most cutting-edge pretreatment processes being used and studied today for the production of biogas during anaerobic digestion processes using different feedstocks, in the most efficient and economical methods possible. *NOW AVAILABLE!*

Bioremediation and Sustainability: Research and Applications, Edited by Romeela Mohee and Ackmez Mudhoo, ISBN 9781118062845. Bioremediation and Sustainability is an up-to-date and comprehensive treatment of research and applications for some of the most important low-cost, "green," emerging technologies in chemical and environmental engineering. *NOW AVAILABLE!*

Green Chemistry and Environmental Remediation, Edited by Rashmi Sanghi and Vandana Singh, ISBN 9780470943083. Presents high quality research papers as well as in depth review articles on the new emerging green face of multidimensional environmental chemistry. *NOW AVAILABLE!*

Printed and bound by CPI Group (UK) Ltd, Croydon, CR0 4YY

27/10/2024

14580478-0004